Dustin Hoffman

Dustin Hoffman

Ronald Bergan

VIRGIN

To Fay, my witty and brave mother

First published in Great Britain in 1991 by
Virgin Books
338 Ladbroke Grove
London W10 5AH

Copyright © 1991 Ronald Bergan

Cataloguing in Publication Data available from the British Library

ISBN 1–85227–378–X

Typeset by Phoenix Photosetting, Chatham, Kent
Printed and bound in Great Britain by
Mackays of Chatham PLC, Chatham, Kent

CONTENTS

List of illustrations   vii
Acknowledgements   ix
1   Sir Dustin Hoffman?   1
2   The Movie Star in the Fifth Row   2
3   Nebbish Without a Cause   4
4   The King of Acne   6
5   In Pasadena   19
6   New York, New York – a Wonderful Town?   26
7   The Ugly Kid Next to the Lead   35
8   Hoffman/Burns/Terminal   43
9   Eh? Dustin Who?   47
10   My Son, the Movie Star   54
11   'Movies Aren't Made for Tuxedos'   64
12   Dustbin Hoffman   73
13   *John and Mary*; Dusty and Anne   84
14   One Little Indian   95
15   Bombs Away!   101
16   'Jesus, I Got 'Em All!'   108
17   Hoffman – Italian Style   116
18   Heat and Dustin   120
19   Lenny   127
20   Bernstein   140
21   What Makes Dustin Run?   146
22   Little Tough Guy   153
23   Who Is David Puttnam and Why Is He Saying Those Terrible Things About Me?   160
24   *Kramer vs Kramer*; Hoffman vs Hoffman   171
25   Hoffman/Hoffwoman   184
26   Death of a Shrimp   201
27   Camel Droppings   210

CONTENTS

28 'A Pain in the Ass!'   218
29 Uh, Oh!   224
30 Dustbone Meets Shakespeare   237
31 Mongrels, Mumbles and Munificence   248
32 Dusty Meets His Maker   255
   Filmography   259
   Index   265

ILLUSTRATIONS

Between pp. 86 and 87

Dustin in *Jimmy Shine*, New York, 1968
In *Danton's Death* at the Pasadena Playhouse, 1957
In *The Graduate*, 1967, with Anne Bancroft
In the final moments of *The Graduate* with Katharine Ross
In *John and Mary*, 1969, with Mia Farrow and Peter Yates
As Ratso Rizzo in *Midnight Cowboy*, 1969, with Jon Voight
Ratso
As the young Jack Crabb, with Faye Dunaway, in *Little Big Man*, 1970
The 121-year-old Jack in *Little Big Man*
In the title role of *Alfredo Alfredo*, 1971, with Stefania Sandrelli
In *Who Is Harry Kellerman and Why Is He Saying Those Terrible Things About Me?*, 1971
As Dega with Steve McQueen in *Papillon*, 1973
Dustin's first wife, Anne, as Mrs Dega
As Lenny Bruce in *Lenny*, 1974

Between pp. 150 and 151

With Ulu Grosbard on location for *Straight Time*, 1978
With Robert Redford in *All the President's Men*, 1976
In Laurence Olivier's grip in *Marathon Man*, 1976
Matching up to Vanessa Redgrave in *Agatha*, 1979
With Meryl Streep and director Robert Benton while making *Kramer vs Kramer*, 1979
In the title role of *Tootsie*, 1982, with Jessica Lange
With Kate Reid in the film of *Death of a Salesman*, 1985
In *Rain Man*, 1988, with Tom Cruise
With Matthew Broderick in *Family Business*, 1989
In conversation with the author in London, April 1989
With director Sidney Lumet, 1989
During rehearsals for the 1989 London stage production of *The Merchant of Venice*

ACKNOWLEDGEMENTS

I wish to thank the following for their invaluable assistance: Jane Alexander, Tony Beard, Paul Brooke, Stuart Burge, Peggy Ebright, Natasha Grey, Penny Haig, Sir Peter Hall, Arthur Hiller, Thelma Holt, Marthe Keller, Henry Livings, Stuart Mackay, Dr Sidney Malitz, Louis Malle, John Mortimer, Susan Naulty, June Nelsey, Dr John M. Oldham, Brian Poyser, Judi Record, Dr Frederick Ricci, Bob Ross, Volker Schlöndorff, Donahue B. Silvis, Kathleen Tynan and Peter Yates.

I'm also greatly indebted to the following books and articles for quotations and/or facts:

Books

Adventures in The Screen Trade by William Goldman (Macdonald 1984); *The Andy Warhol Diaries* (Simon and Schuster 1989); *A Biographical Dictionary of the Cinema* by David Thomson (Secker and Warburg 1979); *Broadway Anecdotes* (Bloomsbury 1989); *Enigma – David Puttnam, the Story So Far* by Andrew Yule (Mainstream 1988); *Death of a Salesman* by Arthur Miller (1949); *Dustin* by Michael Freedland (Virgin 1989); *Fast Fade* (De La Court 1989); *The Films of Dustin Hoffman* by Douglas Brode (Citadel Press 1983); *The Graduate* by Charles Webb (Constable 1964); *Making Tootsie* by Susan Dworkin (Newmarket Press 1983); *Reverse Angle: Film reviews* by John Simon (Potter 1982); *Sam Peckinpah* by Doug McKinney (Twayne 1979); *Steve McQueen* by Penina Spiegel (Collins 1986); *Uneasy Stages: Theatre reviews* by John Simon (Random House 1975); *Warren Beatty* by David Thomson (Secker and Warburg 1987).

Articles

Hollis Alpert (*Saturday Review*, 6 July 1968); Peter Biskind (*Premiere*, February 1989); Peter Biskind (*Premiere*, July 1990); David Blum (*The Sunday Times*, 16 March 1987); Tom Burke (*The New York Times*, 16 March 1969); Tim Cahill (*Rolling Stone*, 5 December 1974); Donald Chase (*International Herald Tribune*, 14 December 1988); Gerald Clarke (*Time*,

3 December 1979); Joseph Gelmis, Brian Case (*Time Out*, 25 January 1989); Germaine Greer (*Esquire*, July 1973); Pauline Kael (*The New Yorker* weekly); Gary Smith (*Rolling Stone*, 3 February 1983).

I have also quoted from *The South Bank Show* (LWT, 29 September 1989) and The Screen *Guardian* Event (NFT, 30 April 1989).

   Quotations from the poems by e. e. cummings quoted by kind permission of HarperCollins Publishers.

1

Sir Dustin Hoffman?

I was literally shit-scared on the first night.

THURSDAY, 1 JUNE 1989. It is pelting with rain. Charing Cross Road looks like a Venice canal. The first-night audience is arriving at the Phoenix Theatre for *The Merchant of Venice*, one of the most awaited West End openings for years. As Dame Peggy Ashcroft is struggling to put her umbrella down in the packed and poky entrance, a young fan asks for her autograph. 'Buzz off!' explodes Dame Peggy. In the crowded foyer, I catch glimpses of Sir Peter Hall with his wife-to-be, Nicky Frei, and Jennifer, his daughter by Leslie Caron; Paul and Linda McCartney; Sir John Mills and his wife Mary; Jeffrey and Mary Archer; Billy Connolly; Joan Collins accompanied by a very handsome, very young escort; and a crowd of rent-a-celebrities.

Meanwhile, the man they have all come to see as Shylock is nervously sitting on the loo. He has been in the lavatory so often and so long in the days before the opening that the cast have put a plaque up on the door, reading 'Dustin Hoffman Is Here', which they have all signed.

[*Act I, Scene III. Enter Bassanio with Shylock the Jew.*]
(One or two people start to clap. It is not taken up. This is not Broadway.)
Shylock: Three thousand ducats – well.
Dustin is on his way.

Two hours later:
Shylock: I pray you, give me leave to go from hence; I am not well; send the deed after me and I will sign it. (*Exit Shylock for the last time*).
Curtain. Rapturous applause. Both Shakespeare and Dustin Hoffman have survived. For the little Jewish boy from Los Angeles to have played Shakespeare in the Bard's own land and be applauded by an English audience is, to him, a greater achievement than the two Oscars he has won. Back to the loo . . . 'Dustin Hoffman Is Here.'

2

The Movie Star in the Fifth Row

Once you are in the public eye, you think you are something. But you just happen to be a commodity they want. Success can really cripple you.

EXACTLY A DECADE before *The Merchant of Venice*, I attended a matinee performance of *Sugar Babies* on Broadway starring Ann Miller and Mickey Rooney, a gloriously vulgar tribute to vaudeville by two of Hollywood's legends. I was sitting in the circle amidst a group of middle-aged 'girls' who had come into town to see a show. (I had managed to get my ticket only because one of their number could not make it at the last moment.)

Suddenly, about halfway through the first act, a buzz went along the rows, like a message over a telegraph line. Bzz, Bzz, Bzz. Each 'girl' was passing on some bit of information to the next until the news reached my ears. 'Dustin Hoffman's in the audience,' I was told in an excited whisper. 'Pass it on to Selma.' I am not in the habit of talking in the theatre, and dislike others doing so, so I kept this choice bit of information from Selma. As a result, my informant, from whom I received a powerful whiff of Brooklyn Nights, leaned across me and loudly whispered the news to the matron on my left. 'Dustin Hoffman's in the audience! Downstairs!'

Forget Ann Miller and Mickey Rooney, whom the 'girls' had paid to see. They were more interested in a small, dark, 42-year-old man sitting in the fifth row. The whole circle swayed as my companions leant over to get a good look at him. It was more exciting for them simply to see him sitting in the audience than to watch Miller and Rooney slogging their guts out on stage. The performers were only doing what was expected of them, but Dustin Hoffman sitting there in the fifth row was just like us. He was part of the audience of which we were members.

Fame, above all show-business fame, has an almost magical effect on those without it. The anonymous seem to need to be near it, read about it, and touch it. An autograph is proof that one has been in the sacred presence. Like the millions who kiss the foot of a sacred statue in the hope of increasing their holiness, millions reach out to touch the famous in the hope that fame will rub off on them. Unknown faces light up in the presence of celebrated faces familiar from magazines, newspapers, TV and, especially, film. Fame generates desirability, sexuality . . . and power. When the image is blown up to larger-than-life size, the audience is among giants. Even the smallest of men become huge figures towering over the huddled anonymous masses in the dark. For the leviathans, who were once minnows, fame is a revenge on insignificance, a defiance of mortality.

When Dorothy, the Cowardly Lion, the Tin Man, the Scarecrow and the dog Toto are ushered into the presence of the Wizard of Oz, his face appears fearsome on a large screen, and his voice is like thunder. 'The Great Oz has every intention of granting your requests,' he booms. Toto trots over to the curtain and pulls it back, revealing the 'great and powerful' Wizard as merely a frightened old man whose voice and features have been magnified to create awe among his followers. The film projector creates the same effect, magnifying actors and actresses, and enveloping them in an aura of inaccessibility. When they are seen 'in the flesh' – in the street, in restaurants, in the fifth row of theatres – they seem like deities who have deigned to descend to earth for a short while, taking on human dimensions in order to mingle with us mortals. And, during their sojourn, the gods might choose someone from among us, a Leda or an Alkmene; and the goddesses might find a Paris or an Adonis to have a little fun with before returning to Olympus . . . or Beverly Hills.

My neighbours at *Sugar Babies* were busily demonstrating that – had anyone doubted it – the star mystique has not diminished since the studio publicity machines stopped creating calculated images in the fifties. 'There's Dustin Hoffman down there,' said Selma, pointing towards the orchestra stalls. 'Look!' she insisted. Not wishing to be snooty, and knowing that I would have to sit with her and her friends for another hour or so, I leaned forward and saw the back of Hoffman's head. As backs of heads go, it was not unpleasant, nor was it one of the best I had ever seen, but it was undoubtedly one of the most famous.

The owner of the head had been in movies since 1967. There was now a new generation of actors in place as the eighties dawned – John Travolta, Sylvester Stallone and Richard Gere – but *Kramer vs Kramer* had just been released, and Dustin Hoffman was once again, after a slight falling off, the white hottest star in Hollywood. Exactly a decade later there would be Tom Cruise, Matthew Broderick and Rob Lowe, all of them younger than Dustin was when he started in films. But he would continue to be a force into the nineties. How and why has this seemingly unlikely candidate for movie stardom achieved exactly that for over two decades? The following pages are, I hope, a kind of answer.

3

Nebbish Without a Cause

I could have been a great actor today, if I'd never gone into the movies.

IN THE GOLDEN Age of Hollywood, when studios were feudal states, their most illustrious citizens were made into glamorous figures living on another more elevated plane. They were wealthier, more beautiful, more elegant, more dangerous, more heroic, more saintly, more noble and more wicked than ordinary folk. They lived in splendour, untouched by the realities of life outside.

Gradually, in the fifties, a growing number of independent producers, including actors John Wayne, Frank Sinatra, Gregory Peck, Robert Mitchum, Kirk Douglas and Burt Lancaster, broke the stranglehold of the major studios. At the same time, the most dramatic change came in screen acting. The new style derived from a group of stage actors and directors who had formed the Actors Studio in New York in 1948. It was there that the acting technique known as 'The Method' was advanced, influenced by the teachings of the Russian stage director Konstantin Stanislavsky. He stressed a more instinctive approach to acting, enabling the performers to arrive at their interpretation of a role through seeking equivalent emotions in their own experiences. The actor who more than any other typified the Method School was Marlon Brando. Others such as Rod Steiger, Eli Wallach, Montgomery Clift, Joanne Woodward, Anthony Perkins, Karl Malden, Paul Newman and James Dean benefited from his example. It did, however, become the most caricatured of acting styles with its mumbling delivery, shrugging of shoulders, fidgeting and scratching. Along with this style went a deliberately anti-glamorised image. Humphrey Bogart commented, 'I came out here with one suit and everybody said I looked like a bum. Twenty years later, Marlon Brando comes out with only a sweat shirt and the town drools over him. That shows how much Hollywood has progressed.' Joan Crawford, a remnant of past glamour, claimed, 'I don't believe you want to go to the theatre and see someone you can see next door.'

Yet it was precisely because the growing youth audience could imagine the new stars living next door that they seemed particularly attractive. Stars were no longer considered 'Them'; they were 'Us'. With youth

4

culture beginning to infiltrate the movies in the fifties, it was possible for the first time for young people to identify with certain stars. Brando projected an anti-conformist image, and Dean was the personification of adolescent rebellion and despair.

In 1955, a spotty, runtish eighteen-year-old went to see *Rebel Without a Cause*. 'It was the first time I had seen what it really felt like to be an adolescent. Up to then all the movies and ads showed what fun it was to be a teenager. There was this really unhappy, miserable person up there, and I said "That's me! That's me!"' The eighteen-year-old was Dustin Hoffman, and he would never have believed that, twelve years later, post-pubescent moviegoers would be looking up at him in *The Graduate* and saying the same thing.

But while Brando, Dean and Newman were broodingly handsome nonconformists, Dustin was a *nebbish*, a loser in a success-struck society. It was not the bikers or hippies that rallied round the awkward figure of Ben Braddock in *The Graduate*, but middle-class college kids, one of whom wrote to *The New York Times*: 'I thought of him as a spiritual brother. He was as confused about his future and about his place in the world as I am.' A decade later, the same group identified with Ben when he grew up and became advertising executive Ted Kramer, going through divorce.

It was only after Dustin Hoffman came along that the names and faces of current movie stars reflected more accurately the diversity of ethnic groups in America, opening up the floodgates for the likes of Al Pacino, Robert De Niro and Richard Dreyfuss. They also inherited his obsessive striving for perfection, the meticulous researching and living of parts.

4

The King of Acne

I never got looked at.

'SO WHAT ARE you going to do for a living?' asked Aunt Pearl of nineteen-year-old Dustin during a Passover dinner at the Hoffmans' Los Angeles home. Those around the table, including his mother Lillian, his father Harry, elder brother Ronald and Aunt Pearl herself, all fixed the *nebbish* boy with expectant and probing eyes. Dustin looked down at his square of matzo and snapped it violently in two.

'I want to be an actor,' he said defiantly.

There was a long pause. Aunt Pearl scrutinised him again before saying with some relish, 'You can't. You're not good looking enough.'

Dustin's ears glowed crimson with embarrassment as he continued to look down at his plate. The worst part of it was that, despite his strong determination to become an actor, he felt that Aunt Pearl was probably right. She shared the popular misconception that a prerequisite of becoming an actor or actress was good looks. Of course there had been Wallace Beery, Victor McLaglen and Marie Dressler, but they were larger and uglier than life. Small, shy, big-nosed, acned Jewish boys like Dustin Hoffman did not become actors.

From as far back as he could remember, Dustin was unhappy with his physical appearance. Did he not have a face that not even a mother could love? When still a child, Dustin used to stare at his face in the chrome toaster in the kitchen. 'Dusty, Dusty, Dusty,' he said to himself, trying to understand that the puffin's face he saw glaring back at him was his. He was skinny, short and spotty, and wore a set of braces on his teeth. 'I was the King of Acne, and the braces were my crown.' As a result of the braces, Dustin developed a smile that kept the lips tightly closed so as not to reveal the unsightly teeth. Thus the origin of the Hoffman smile.

He was also extremely self-conscious about his nose, and for years would always look people straight in the face, never allowing his profile to show. Apart from the problem of his looks, the little boy was a late developer who could hardly talk until he was three and a half, a handicap he made up for later as a loquacious adult.

'I was the baby of the family, always pushing out to get attention. I always felt like an intruder. I came along years after it started. I needed every inch I could get just to be myself. I was always the black sheep of the family. My brother was the brilliant one. A straight-A student, and a good athlete.'

It is quite possible that Dustin's desire to be an actor was merely the logical conclusion of 'always pushing out to get attention', a phrase reminiscent of Linda Loman's plea for her husband in *Death of a Salesman*: 'Attention, attention must be finally paid to such a person.'

Dustin's connection with Arthur Miller's classic American play goes back to his seventeenth birthday when Ronald gave him John Gassner's volume, *Best Plays*. With some prescience, Ronald had inscribed it: 'Loin all the voids, Dusty, so you can recite real nize when company comes.' *Death of a Salesman* had first been produced in 1948, just four years earlier, and Ronald knew that his younger brother would respond to it in much the same way as he had. When Dustin read the play he 'was just destroyed by it. It was like finding out something terrible about my family. I just shook. I felt like my family's privacy had been invaded. I couldn't even talk about it for weeks.'

One of the first roles he played when he took acting classes at college was Biff in the confrontation scene with his father. 'Pop! I'm a dime a dozen and so are you!' 'I am not a dime a dozen! I am Willy Loman, and you are Biff Loman!' 'I'm one dollar an hour, Willy! I tried seven states and couldn't raise it. A buck an hour, do you gather my meaning? I am not a leader of men, Willy, and neither are you; you were never anything but a hard-working drummer who landed in the ashcan like all the rest of them!'

The scene had great significance for Dustin because 'I felt like a dime a dozen. It was true.' And like Willy Loman, Harry Hoffman, also a father of two sons, was a travelling salesman who had gone 'way out there in the blue, riding on a smile and a shoeshine'. Harry 'was always working, always trying to get ahead and not being appreciated. I loved him like we all love our fathers, but we had some bad times; guys coming while he was at work, pulling the furniture out, and then he'd get into fights at the finance departments. I think my father was very conscious of being a little guy.'

Harry was the model for Dustin's portrayal of Loman over a quarter of a century later, just as Lillian provided her son with the inspiration for Dorothy Michaels in *Tootsie* towards the end of her life. Far from being role models, his parents were models for roles.

Lillian was a devout fan of the movies, and like many such fans, dreamed of becoming a film star herself. She was a good enough dancer to pass an audition once for a stage show, but her strict orthodox Jewish mother forbade her to take the job. As so often happens, her thwarted ambition was transferred to her first child, whom she named after suave British actor Ronald Colman. When her second son was born six-and-a-half years later on 8 August 1937, at Queen of Angels Hospital in Los Angeles, Lillian, going down the social scale somewhat, named him after Dustin Farnum, a cowboy star of silent films.

However, Lillian, who was not short of vanity, once denied that the name of her second son had anything to do with the hero of Westerns. 'I'm not old enough to remember Dustin Farnum. I just liked the name; that's why I called him Dustin.' Yet she would most often refer to him as 'Dustala' or 'my little Tootsie Wootsie'. He would also be known in later life as 'Dusty', 'Dust' and 'Dustbone', the latter courtesy of Robert Duvall.

In fact, Lillian Gold was already in her early teens when Dustin Farnum became a movie star. Farnum's most famous role was the lead in *The Squaw Man* in 1913, Cecil B. DeMille's first film as director, and the first major movie to be made in Hollywood. Farnum's last screen appearance was as General Custer in *The Flaming Frontier* in 1926. (Dustin Hoffman later played the only living survivor of Custer's Last Stand in his sole Western to date, *Little Big Man*.) Lillian could never have imagined that *her* Dustin would become a far bigger star than Farnum. It was hardly likely that Dustala, a little unprepossessing shrimp, would fulfil his mother's dreams of having a show-biz celebrity in the family. If one of her sons was going into the movies, it would certainly be Ronald. And that he did, in a way.

In 1939, when Ronald was eight years old, he had a walk-on as one of the newsboys in Frank Capra's *Mr Smith Goes to Washington*. The film was about political chicanery in the capital and, ironically, many years later, when Ronald went to Washington as an economist with the US Treasury, he saw worse corruption at first hand than the film had depicted. Capra's films, from 1936, glorified the 'little man' (only figuratively in the case of Jimmy Stewart and Gary Cooper) fighting for what is right and decent and losing the battle until the hectic rush to achieve the happy ending; not all that distant from Dustin's own Washington film, *All the President's Men*.

One of the reasons Ronald got the job in the movie was because Harry was prop supervisor at Columbia Pictures at the time. But Ronald's acting career did not advance beyond that one film. The elder Hoffman son plainly was not going to follow Ronald Colman into show business, and later took a PhD in physics and an economics degree. Both sons had been in continual conflict with their father, but Ronald suffered more from parental nagging because Harry's ambitions for him were higher than those for Dustin. 'Dusty as the youngest was always better able to deal with my father,' Ronald admitted.

Dustin explained that, 'Ronald, rather than making money and being in business like my father had wanted him to do, went into universities and taught. So my father knew Ronnie had done well but he wanted him to have done well in Depression terms. It was the same kind of thinking that Arthur Miller's family had.' Ronald felt he was 'as unsuccessful at dealing with my father as anyone could possibly be'.

In 1984, when Dustin was playing Willy Loman, Ronald remarked, 'I was brought closer to experiences I've had. It was exhausting, it gave me insights. It was disturbing emotionally. When I left my seat, I continued to be moved and still am. I got a view of some major problematical aspects of my life.' Despite his worldly success, he had always seen himself as Biff through his father's eyes, while Dustin identified with Happy, the ineffectual younger brother in Miller's play.

Before the play opened in New York, Harry had to have a serious heart operation. Both his sons rushed to his bedside. The elderly man had just had a five-way bypass operation which he called 'nothing, just a plumbing job'. Yet, according to Dustin, 'the first thing he did when he saw Ronnie standing there was to pick a fight with him! It was unbelievable. The man wasn't even conscious – he had all these tubes and wires sticking out of him, he was hooked up to monitors – and he started criticising my brother's children. My father almost started shouting in intensive care. Later I said to Ronnie, "Well, he almost got you again this time."'

Both Harry and Lillian Hoffman were first generation American Jews. In the early part of the century, Harry's parents had come over from Romania to Chicago, where his father literally scraped a living as a barber. A devout man, more interested in studying the Talmud than cutting hair, he virtually left the running of the barber shop to his wife, nicknamed 'Red'. Knowing that the customers liked to talk about sport, she genned up on baseball, especially the legendary Chicago White Sox, and could carry on a knowledgeable conversation about the game. The cultural transplantation from the Jewish ghettos of Bucharest to the clamour of the 'Windy City' might have been a contributing factor in unhinging her husband's mind, because he died in a mental hospital when Harry was only nine. As the eldest son, Harry had to go out and work and take responsibility for his family. He had contracted TB as a child, but had managed to overcome it. A tough little five-foot-two-inch man, even shorter than his illustrious younger son would turn out to be, he was industrious, resilient and stoical, and had turned against his father's orthodox Jewish faith, which was further eroded when he met and married the free-thinking Lillian Gold.

Despite being a carpenter by trade, he came under the influence of his new wife's ideas about the glamour of Hollywood, and she persuaded the young man to leave Chicago and go West, where he would become a movie-producer. After all, Louis B. Mayer, Samuel Goldwyn, Jesse Lasky, Harry Cohn and the four Warner brothers were all Jews from poor backgrounds who made it big in Hollywood, virtually creating the movie business there.

Franklin D. Roosevelt had not been in office very long when Harry and Lillian Hoffman, just preceding those Okies who inspired Steinbeck's Joad family, left for California in an old Model A Ford, carrying with them five-year-old Ronald, and not much more than their dreams of wealth and fame. Although a character in the 1934 Fox musical *Stand Up and Cheer* rushes into an office towards the end and announces, 'The Depression is over!', the country was still firmly in its grip.

Hollywood, which Fred Allen once described as 'a great place to live if you're an orange', was at the peak of the studio system in the thirties, although the suburb itself had a mere 153,000 inhabitants. Unfortunately, for the handful of Mayers and Selznicks, who struck gold, there were thousands of people who came to Hollywood and struck dirt. One of Harry's first jobs in California was digging ditches on the newly created freeway system. However, it wasn't long before he was working at Columbia Pictures . . . installing sewerage pipes at the studio. Gradually, he worked his way up from the drains into the props department. He seemed to enjoy his job there and used to come home from work with a wealth of stories about the stars (Jean Arthur, Cary Grant, Irene Dunne, etc), with which he would regale Lillian. Among the actors he met was Lee J. Cobb, who would become, a decade later, the first Willy Loman, at the time when Harry was struggling as a real-life salesman. But the future seemed rosy to Lillian, who was busy preparing herself to be a movie producer's gorgeous wife. She spent a great deal of time trying to look as attractive as possible and encouraging her husband to get friendly with the top brass and work his way up.

When Harry Hoffman arrived at Columbia, the studio was just emerging from Poverty Row, that group of small B-movie studios on Gower Street always in the shadow of the Big Five: MGM, RKO, Fox, Warner and Paramount. Under Harry Cohn's dictatorial rule, it began to gain prestige and make money, mainly with Capra's popular social comedies such as *It Happened One Night* (1934) and *Mr Deeds Goes to Town* (1936). Although the company continued to operate out of Poverty Row, it gradually took over most of the area between Sunset Boulevard and Fountain Avenue, and Gower Street and Beachwood Drive, as well as acquiring a 35-acre ranch near Burbank on which the studio's large output of B Westerns was filmed.

Harry, who had watched hack directors churning out quickies on the back lot, as well as Capra, George Cukor (*Holiday*), Rouben Mamoulian (*Golden Boy*) and Howard Hawks (*Only Angels Have Wings*), felt he could do as well himself. One day, he expressed his ambition to become a director to a studio executive. 'Harry, you'll never make a director and you'll never make an assistant director,' stated the man bluntly. Despite this putdown, Harry continued happily enough in the props department, daydreaming of directing a film. At least he had a salary and some security. But it did not last. Harry was laid off when Dustin was still a toddler, following Capra, the linchpin of the company, who had just left after making *Mr Smith Goes to Washington*, which received acclaim but made little profit. Forty years later Dustin returned with some satisfaction to the studio where his father had failed to take over from Cohn or Capra; Columbia produced two of his greatest triumphs, *Kramer vs Kramer* and *Tootsie*– and, just for good measure, his biggest flop, *Ishtar*.

Lillian continued to keep a tidy house and saw to it, within their limited means, that there was always enough food on the table. But financial insecurity, Harry's feeling of failure, and Lillian's shattered dreams of becoming a producer's wife caused some friction in the Hoffman household. Harry got a job as a travelling furniture salesman working on commission for Barker Brothers, a California department-store chain, and he would come home weary and irritated after a fruitless day.

'A salesman is an it that stinks excuse', is the first line of a poem by e. e. cummings, who was to become one of Dustin's favourite poets. When he read the poem years later, it had a certain personal resonance:

> a salesman is an it that stinks to please
> but whether to please itself or someone else
> makes no more difference than if it sells
> hate condoms education snakeoil vac
> uumcleaners terror strawberries democ
> ra (caveat emptor) cy superfluous hair
> or Think We've Met Subhuman Rights Before

Harry realised when his sons had grown up that he had been so busy trying to make money that he never spent enough time with them. There were constant rows between the parents, and between mother and children, and father and children. Harry was a stubborn little man and would never apologise even if he was wrong, so there were days when there was no conversation during meals. A great tension hung over the dinner table. As Dustin says in *Lenny*, 'I was eight years old before I found out my name wasn't Shut Up.'

'Sometimes Ronnie and I used to fight during the day and drive my mother crazy, and she'd finally say, "I'm going to tell your father when he comes home." That was bad. When he came home from being an unsuccessful travelling salesman filled with tension, he would say, "Your mother told me that you weren't respecting her, and I'll take your heads and crack them together till your brains splatter on the wall." Lillian would say, "That's enough, Harry." And he would say, "If you don't respect your mother . . . Shut up, Lil!"' This eerily echoes Willy Loman's continually telling his wife not to interrupt him in *Death of a Salesman*.

Harry (Willy):	Will you let me talk?
Ronald (Biff):	Don't yell at her, Pop, will ya?
Harry (Willy):	I was talking, wasn't I?
Ronald (Biff):	I don't like you yelling at her all the time and I'm telling you, that's all.
Harry (Willy):	What're you takin' over, this house?
Lillian (Linda):	Willy . . .
Harry (Willy):	Don't take his side all the time, god–dammit!
Ronald (Biff):	Stop yelling at her!

Five-year-old Dustin (Happy) used to memorise this kind of dialogue, and suddenly, by the third day of silence at the dinner table, he would start throwing back the lines that he remembered during the fight, and it would break the tension. At least Harry and Lillian had the capacity to laugh at themselves. Lillian once described Dustin as 'a clown from the word go'.

But the tension over the dinner table obviously had a detrimental effect on the sensitive young boy. For a period, he hardly touched the food on his plate during dinner at home. He would never go to other children's homes or birthday parties for fear of having to eat what was put before him, a situation that did not help overcome his inability to make friends. Finally, Lillian took him to the doctor, who told her, 'When the boy needs food, he'll eat it.' Lillian followed his advice until a week later she noticed Dustin's tongue was discoloured. On a return visit to the doctor, Dustin was found to be suffering from serious malnutrition. From then on, Lillian provided him with whatever he wanted to eat at any hour. (Some years later, in *John and Mary*, the situation is shown in reverse. John's mother is

too busy with political activities to feed him properly, except for frankfur-
ters.) As further encouragement to get Dustin to eat, she bought him a
huge part-Alsatian mongrel, called Buffy, which was allowed to sit next
to Dustin at the dinner table with a napkin round his neck, and eat off a
plate like the rest of the family. This did the trick, although Buffy's presence did nothing to improve the atmosphere, and Harry positively
disliked the animal.

One thing, more than anything else, that managed to draw the Hoffmans
together was television, contrary to fears that the device would kill off
family life. Dustin belonged to the first TV generation when the one-eyed
monster began proliferating throughout the USA in the early fifties. As
Sam Goldwyn commented, 'Why should people go out and pay money to
see bad films when they can stay home and see bad TV for nothing?' Because
the Hoffman family were constantly making ends meet, going to the
movies became a rare treat, and, as there was virtually no theatre available
and barely a book in the Hoffman household, TV was Dustin's only entry
into 'culture'. For him, as for most viewers, the highlights were the comedy
programmes. The family would sit in front of their 12-inch black-and-
white set and watch Dustin's favourites; Jackie Gleason and Art Carney in
The Honeymooners, Uncle Milty (Milton Berle) and Jimmy Durante. It was
on TV that Dustin first saw Abbott and Costello's 'Who's on first' routine,
which he used so effectively in *Rain Man* in 1988.

'They were great clowns. I didn't know I was watching greatness.
Durante was a wonderful music-hall comedian. At the end of his show,
which you'd been laughing at all through, he would finish off by stepping
into a white light, he'd turn, look at the camera, push his straw hat back,
and he'd say, with a very sad look on his face, "Goodnight, Mrs Calabash,
wherever you are." No one knew who Mrs Calabash was. It was a Shakespearean moment. Like all great clowns, he had different levels. It gave
you goosebumps when you saw it, because you didn't know whether to
laugh or cry. I had a great love for him.'

The self-conscious boy's love for the gravel-voiced bulbous-nosed
comedian was engendered, in part, by the famous proboscis. And this
identification led to a pivotal experience for the young Dustin.

Scene: 1953. Classroom of LA High. The pupils are giving an oral presentation of books read at home. Sixteen-year-old Dustin Hoffman, short,
big-nosed and acned, waits his turn. He is the class jester. A boring little
girl is giving her views on *Jane Eyre*. He pulls faces and imitates the teacher
behind her back. 'Hoffman,' she calls. 'You're next.' The book he has been
given by the teacher to expound upon is Gene Fowler's biography of

Jimmy Durante called *Schnozzola*. The class laughs because Dustin's nose is the butt of their jokes. Dustin launches into it by imitating Durante, ending with 'Goodnight, Mrs Calabash, wherever you are.' Applause. The teacher tells him to get on with talking about the book. Dustin begins to describe Durante's childhood in the lower East Side and how the comedian had felt about being a short, ugly kid with a big nose.

He reads in a simulation of Schnozzle's voice: 'I had a feelin' everybody was looking at me an' makin' cracks about me. I was afraid to take girls out. My nose made me a shriekin' violet [*sic*]. Every time I went down the street I'd hear, "Lookit that big nose kid." I'd just sneak off. I'd shrivel up. "What an ugly kid! What a monster!" I'd go home and cry.' Then Dustin, whose voice is beginning to quaver with emotion, reads a letter Durante received from a big-nosed kid thanking him for making him proud of his conk. Dustin finds he cannot go on. He begins to cry. The class laughs. Dustin fights back his tears. The class continues to laugh. Dustin looks around and flees the classroom.

As Dustin told it later: 'There were twenty-five kids in the class. I was not popular. I'm looking at these kids who aren't my friends, because I don't really know them. Maybe it was the first book I'd read in my life, and I'd start crying, and I had to leave the room, while everybody was laughing. But at that moment there seemed to be a fusion with that and my wanting to become an actor.'

The acting career of Dustin Hoffman had begun inauspiciously as Tiny Tim in *A Christmas Carol* in the seventh grade at John Burroughs Junior High. He was chosen for the part because he was the smallest boy in the school. In fact, there might have been another shorter, but Dustin wanted to be in the play so badly that, when the teacher studied the line-up of boys, he made himself look even smaller by dipping down slightly. His acting debut was cut short, though, because an older student dared him to replace 'God bless us all, every one of us', at the play's end, with 'God bless us all, goddamn it!'

'I was a skinny little runt, and a coward, who was intimidated by the older boy, a kind of hero of the school.' Therefore, on the night, when Dustin in his timorous voice ended the play with the expletive, the curtain came down rapidly, and he was promptly suspended from school.

But, like Charles Dickens's Jo, Dustin was always being moved on. Because of Harry Hoffman's fluctuating fortunes, the family had moved some six times to various LA addresses before Dustin was twelve. Relieved as he often was to leave an environment of children who were hostile towards him, each time he had to face another group of strangers.

One year, they would be living in a pleasant neighbourhood, the next in a rough downtown area, and then back to Beverly Hills just as the boy was adjusting to his new surroundings. Actually, he preferred the less salubrious neighbourhoods, where children were not judged by their fathers' bank balances.

In one of the downtown areas, Dustin made friends with a Mexican and a black boy, and became part of a gang which had a feud with a rival faction called 'pachuchos' (a Mexican word that means a flashy dresser). For safety, the very un-*pachucho* Dustin kept a knife taped to his leg, although he made sure he never got into a fight. As the new kid on the block, he constantly had to prove himself. Wherever he lived, however, he always felt an outsider. He was seen by other kids as a little rat with his dark, ever-moving eyes, tiny body and big nose.

It was in one of the better areas that he heard the word 'kike' used against him for the first time. 'I was the only Jewish kid in the neighbourhood. I used to deny being a Jew and just say I was an American and get out.' Although the Hoffmans were Jewish, Harry professed atheism, and Lillian was no Yiddisher momma. They had no time for the rituals of the religion. Although both the Hoffman sons had been given a *bris* (circumcised by a rabbi), neither Ronald nor Dustin had bar mitzvahs, nor did they ever go to the synagogue or observe a Jewish holiday. Christmas was the special family time when Lillian put a tree up in the living room and presents were exchanged. The dichotomy was well illustrated one year when Dustin imaginatively decorated the Christmas tree with bagels. It would be some time into the future before Dustin would be less ambiguous about his Jewishness.

It was only through humour, always his saving grace, that he was able to make some contact with others. Once, during a geography class on the Rocky Mountains, Dustin's mind was elsewhere. The teacher recognising this pounced on him. 'Hoffman, what is the name of those mountains?' she asked. The boy sitting behind Dustin leaned forward and whispered 'George Washington' in his ear. Dustin happily announced, 'The George Washington Mountains!' and the class went wild. 'I had this terrible feeling of humiliation and at the same time I was delighted.' He gradually turned himself from the dunce into a clown.

'I remember Miss Goodman, a little four-foot-ten-inch Jewish woman. She used to say, "Shut up everybody. Stop talking. We're going to loin this." She'd turn round and write on the blackboard and I'd say in her high voice, "You hear what she said, we're going to loin this." And she'd turn around and say, "Hoffman, go right away to the principal's office."'

A favourite prank of his was getting the other pupils all to cough on a given signal. When campaigning for president of his ninth–grade class, he pasted a picture of his face over the poster of a biceps–flexing Mickey Mouse. He was not elected, but he gained some laughs, this time not at his own expense. The other kids used to tell him, with some disdain: 'Dusty, you're a real comedian. You're going to be a comedian.' They never said that he would be an actor. That was something far too grand. The idea occurred to Dustin that if he was going to be anything, he would be a comedian like Uncle Milty on TV.

However, when Dustin was ten years old, he revealed another of his talents, one that seemed a more practical possibility for a profession. Someone gave the Hoffman family an old piano and Dustin immediately found he had a natural feeling for it. Encouraged by his mother, who saw the chance of bringing some 'class' into her younger son's life, Dustin started to have a number of piano lessons a week with a very old-fashioned music teacher who imposed a rigid formula on him. 'There were times I really wanted to play something, like I'd see Cornel Wilde as Chopin playing a Polonaise and I'd go home and really want to play Chopin and get carried away. But that wasn't in the teacher's programme and he wouldn't let me.'

In 1952, after some years of private lessons, he took up classical piano at LA High, practising every day once home from school, and dreaming about making it one day as a concert pianist. More often than not, Dustin was called upon to play in school assemblies and at school parties. His big number was 'Bumble Boogie', which he was requested to play over and over again. 'I was a Bumble Boogie ace in the hole,' he commented. Though his piano playing brought him a measure of popularity, it failed to bring the girls flocking as he had hoped. He would play song after song just waiting for that special girl to come and sit alongside him and tell him how gifted he was.

'At parties, the first thing I did was find the piano. I would sit on the edge of the bench, leaving room for the right girl to sit down next to me, and say, "Boy, do you have sensitive hands." She never did. I had small hands and couldn't reach beyond an octave.'

If one looked carefully at that time, one could see that Dustin's fingernails had been bitten unevenly. His first memory was of having his hands tied to the side of the crib so he could not bite his nails. The cruel cure was ineffective, and he continued to be a compulsive nail-biter into adulthood.

'I remember dialling the number of a girl and not being able to get to the last digit, I was so afraid of rejection. I was never able to make the bridge from "he's cute" to "he's sexy".' At school proms, he would choose the ugliest, heaviest girl to dance with in order to get a laugh. The girls were happy to be picked off the wall, while he never dared ask any girl he fancied. However, there was a pretty girl called Fran who was friendly towards him. There was nothing more, but a female friend at that stage was more than he expected in his waking life. Unfortunately, a tall school bully called Perry, sporting an ugly mole on his neck, considered that she was wasting her charms on a wimp when she could have the benefit of his masculine beauty. One day, Perry and his cohorts spotted Dustin coming down the street. The mindless youth found it easy to grab Dustin and pull his low-slung jeans to the ground, while a crowd of other boys stood around and laughed, calling 'Fight, fight'. Then Dustin's assailant got down on his knees, looked up at Dustin and said, 'Come on, little Dusty. Fight me – now I'm even shorter than you.' It was the sort of humiliation one carries around for the rest of one's life. It also led to a determination in the ambitious Dustin to do the humiliating rather than ever be its victim again. Fame as revenge . . .

When he was younger, it was always a traumatic experience going down to the beach with his brother, mainly because it happened to be the famed Muscle Beach, where all the weightlifters congregated to flex their muscles to impress the bikini-clad girls. Dustin imagined himself getting smaller and smaller as they approached the sands. At the time twelve-year-old Dustin was going to the beach, Joseph Strick and Irving Lerner were making their documentary *Muscle Beach*. It is quite possible that somewhere in the background of that film is the future movie star.

Determined never to have sand kicked in his face by a bully, Dustin saved up his allowance for several weeks and sent off for the barbells advertised on the back of a comic book. He weighed 90 lb at the time, and lifted weights in the privacy of his own room for the next two years. There he would fantasise that he was a great prize-fighter, bravely coming back from knockdowns to knock out his opponent. (In a way, this brutal fantasy was later fulfilled in *Straw Dogs*.)

Despite his lack of prowess, Dustin was extremely keen on sport, although he claims to have been the last boy in High School to have got pubic hair, a situation which necessitated his waiting for all the others to leave the gym class before he could go into the showers. Perhaps because it was a lonely pursuit, he was best at marathon running, though without making much impact. When jogging became fashionable in the sixties, Dustin was out there with the sweatbands and running-shorts brigade, a habit that later stood him in good stead for *Marathon Man*, and for general fitness needed for other arduous roles. He also played tennis, but that did not do much for his school image, because in the fifties 'tennis was considered pretty much a sissy sport'. Tennis and running continued to be passions throughout his adult life. Dustin Hoffman expending his energy by running regularly in Central Park is one of the early-morning New York sights. (One can also catch a brief glimpse of Dustin's tennis abilities in *John and Mary* during a game played in Central Park.)

At one stage, he owned a Schwinn bicycle, but it was used mainly to go on Peeping Tom exploits. With a flashlight and binoculars, he attempted to spy on girls in states of undress. 'A lustful nerd' is how Dustin described himself at high school, and quite a few women who came in contact with him then and in later years would concur. But if anything was going to attract the opposite sex, which was the only goal Dustin could see in life, it was going to be neither sport nor music.

5

In Pasadena

I got into acting so I could meet girls.

'I WAS ALWAYS hanging around with the tangential element in High
School, the twenty per cent of black kids, because I wasn't accepted by the
white community. I wasn't a football star, I wasn't good-looking, I wasn't
a good student. I was not political. I didn't fit in anywhere except amongst
the black students in the fifties. They were into jazz and no one else was.
Three of us formed a trio, but I wasn't any good. They only let me play
piano because I had a car and they didn't. I would drive and they would all
pile in the 'thirty-seven Pontiac and we'd go to the LA Shrine to listen to
jazz.'

At sixteen, Dustin was 'torn between wanting to be a musician and
being told I should be a doctor'. He was floundering and had no concentration. Being overshadowed by his brilliant older brother did not help his
confidence either. Ronald had been captain of the school baseball team and
a barrel-chested lineman on the football team. He would also get nothing
less than Grade As. As Ronald was kept busy with all his accom-
plishments, Dustin would often sit on the side of the bathtub while his
brother sat on the toilet, just to steal a few minutes to talk to him. From all
this, one might get the impression that Ronald towered over his father and
brother, but he was as close to the ground as they were.

After graduating from High School, Dustin worked towards a degree in
music at Santa Monica City College, which he entered on 30 September
1955, significantly the day his future idol James Dean was killed in a car
crash. During his second year, a fellow student told him, 'Take acting. It's
an easy three credits. Nobody ever fails acting.' Dustin took the advice.

The class was on the fundamentals of acting, and the initial experience
made him begin to wonder if this were not an alternative to a career in
music. The teacher would write various scenes to be acted on pieces of
paper, then put these into a hat for pairs of students to draw out, rehearse
together and act out for the class. The first scene Dustin remembers getting was the one between Jim, the Gentleman Caller, and the crippled
Laura in Tennessee Williams's *The Glass Menagerie*. 'As I was into jazz at the
time, we rehearsed it to Stan Kenton's *City of Glass*. I thought that was

very clever – *City of Glass/Glass Menagerie*. I never went to the theatre, so I didn't have much comparison. There was no theatre in LA. I only remember seeing Fanny Brice on stage when I was a kid. My theatre was TV.'

The scene has Jim remembering having called Laura 'Blue Roses' at school, because he had mistaken the name of her illness, pleurosis. She recalls his beautiful voice. Then he lectures Laura on her inferiority complex and urges her to be more confident. They dance, but accidentally break the horn of her glass unicorn. Nevertheless, she is elated. 'The horn was removed to make him feel less – freakish. Now, he'll feel more at home with the other horses.' Then, much to his delight, Dustin got to kiss the girl playing Laura, before explaining to her that he is engaged and 'not in a situation to do the right thing'. At that stage, Dustin was closer to Laura and the unicorn than to the more self-assured Gentleman Caller.

With salesman Harry Hoffman struggling to make enough to put his two sons through college, Dustin sold newspapers across the street from Rexall Drugs on Beverly Boulevard in Hollywood in order to supplement the family income. After some years, however, things picked up in the Hoffman household when Harry began making a moderate success in the furniture business by designing his own Danish-style tables and chairs. Dustin inherited his father's feel for the aesthetics of wood. 'I love pine. I love wooden chairs. If I see a wooden chair with its seat worn into a curve from generations of use, I think to myself, ten thousand asses sat on that chair and wore it into that curve – and that knocks me out!'

As a result of the new prosperity, Lillian felt it was time to expand her own horizons and decided to enrol for some courses at the same college as her son. Looking much younger than her age (and more attractive than Dustin's later semi-impersonation of her in *Tootsie*), her presence on the campus embarrassed Dustin. At home, Harry was none too happy having his wife seemingly searching for a new lifestyle, an attitude that Dustin was to echo during his first marriage. There was relief all round when Lillian quit school just before Dustin graduated.

On leaving Santa Monica City College, he signed up at the LA Conservatory of Music to study classical and jazz piano, still confident that he could make it as a professional pianist. But, early on in 1956, doubts crept in again when he began to realise that acting gave him the greatest joy. 'Before I went into acting, I didn't know who I was. I would feel something I didn't get in life.' Yet he told himself that he was not being practical and that his sole reason for wanting to act was that it was the only way for him to get into close contact with girls. For Dustin, at the time, acting was far more of a vacation than a vocation.

'First I wanted to start with someone with two legs, who would smile and look soft. When I took a girl out, my impulse was to kiss her, but I never would. I was King of the Never Kissing. Then, in acting class we would do scenes where we were supposed to follow our impulses. My impulse was to take a girl in my arms and kiss her. I would pick certain acting classes just because of the girls in them.'

So, despite his Aunt Pearl's disparaging remarks about his looks being an obstacle to life upon the wicked stage or screen, and much to his parents' disappointment, Dustin left the LA Conservatory to join the Pasadena Playhouse, a theatrical college whose sanguine motto was, 'Work with the stars, become a star.' (Sadly, it went bankrupt in 1969.)

Despite the impact of Marlon Brando and the new wave of anarchic performers, the top ten box-office stars of 1957 were Rock Hudson, John Wayne, Pat Boone, Elvis Presley (already sanitised by Hollywood), Frank Sinatra, Gary Cooper, William Holden, James Stewart, Jerry Lewis and Yul Brynner. Dustin was only interested in acting that reflected 'reality', and, apart from performers who had trained at the Actors Studio, such as Brando, Paul Newman, Rod Steiger and Eli Wallach, that meant off-Broadway. He viewed the rest with scorn.

It was the time when James Dean, 'the first teenager', caused a frisson to run down the backs of the nation's youth, and the beatniks were proclaiming their credo. Dustin, in sympathy, wore a tattered sheepskin jacket, no shirt, and shredded blue jeans, while playing the bongo drums and trying to look as James Deanish as possible. It is significant that in the class's commencement programme, in a page of photographs of the students (whatever became of William Hogoplan, Sue Ginsberg and Steiner Kulseng-Hansen?), there is one blank space. It reads: 'Dustin Hoffman. Picture not available.' The omission is probably not accidental.

Fellow student Judi Clutinger met him for the first time while they were standing in line to register. He had on tattered trousers, a T-shirt with a cigarette packet in the sleeve (he smoked a great deal then), and rubber sandals. His scruffy hair was shoulder-length. But she found him attractive and they dated for a while, although they never slept together, she being 'a good girl'. Judi introduced him to her mother, who wondered what on earth her daughter saw in this unprepossessing young man.

At the time, Dustin shared an apartment in a stucco Spanish-type building with Steve Ihnat, a young Canadian at the college. When Judi's mother discovered that Steve and Dustin had no plates in the kitchen, she brought them some. Dustin immediately showed his gratitude by serving his guests the dish he most liked to cook – noodles with cottage cheese.

Ihnat was a rugged Steve McQueen type, who was to make it in films just before Dustin, notably as the heavy opposite James Coburn in *Our Man Flint* in 1967. Five years later, while attending the Cannes Film Festival with his wife, he suffered a fatal heart attack in the bath tub of his hotel. He was 38.

One weekend in the winter of 1956, Dustin invited Judi to visit his parents' comfortable new home high up in Beverly Hills. There was a freak snowstorm that year, and the two young people went out to romp in the snow. They also played pranks by phoning up people and pretending to be stars, on one occasion playing at being Dewy Martin and Peggy Lee, who were married at the time.

Although Dustin was always willing to play practical jokes and fool around with friends, he didn't socialise much. For instance, during the lunch break, Dustin would sit alone, usually barefoot, eating sandwiches he had brought in a brown bag rather than buy food as most of the other students did from the cafeteria on the roof of the playhouse.

He would really only come alive on stage. Most of his contemporaries recognised even then that he had 'something'. Judi and Dustin were cast in a production of Ibsen's long poetic drama *Peer Gynt* in which they each played a variety of roles, with Dustin especially effective in the madhouse scene. The couple sometimes disagreed over the value of film acting (which Dustin claimed to despise), particularly when Judi, who wanted to get into movies, went up to audition for a role in Warner's *Marjorie Morningstar*. The part went to Carolyn Jones.) They eventually broke up when she got involved with more of a 'pretty-boy type', but they nonetheless remained friends. (She later married Don Record, the renowned designer of film titles, and is now a lawyer in Las Vegas.)

In Dustin's first year at Pasadena, the teachers, with one notable exception, did not really respond to his rebellious attitude. 'They taught all the things I only became interested in subsequently. I hated a lot of what they were teaching. There was a speech class, movement and fencing. I said, what am I going to do with fencing? There was also costume history. I loved the acting class, though.'

One of the few students at the college who seemed to share his views was Gene Hackman. It was inevitable that the two most obvious misfits at the college would find themselves drawn to each other and form a lasting friendship. Dustin looked up to Hackman, admiring his maturity and experience, and identifying with his anti–Establishment image that set him apart from the Californian 'walking surfboard' types around them.

The contrast between the tall and burly Hackman and the small and skinny Hoffman was not only physical. Hackman was six years Dustin's senior and had already knocked around the world, while Dustin had never left Los Angeles; Hackman was already married, but Dustin had rarely dated a girl. When Hackman was sixteen, he quit school and served three years in the Marines before being discharged. He then drifted from job to job, working as a truck driver, soda jerk, shoe salesman, and doorman at a Times Square restaurant. Thanks to the GI Bill, he was able to study draughtsmanship, journalism and TV production, and for a period moved across the country from one small town to another, holding temporary jobs as floor manager or assistant director in small TV stations. Finally, at the age of 26, he decided to realise his dreams of becoming an actor, and joined the Pasadena Playhouse school at the same time as Dustin. He and his wife, Fay, lived next door to Dustin and Ihnat.

Unfortunately, Hackman, Dustin's best buddy, was kicked out of the school after merely four months, and was advised, for his own good, to give up acting. It was not the first or last time that Hackman was given the theatrical boot. Disappointed but not discouraged, Gene and the pregnant Fay took off for New York, while Dustin continued at the Pasadena Playhouse for another year.

Legend has it that Dustin was thought to be the second least-likely-to-succeed student after Hackman. In April 1989, after Dustin had won an Oscar for *Rain Man*, and Hackman was nominated for *Mississippi Burning*, the Pasadena Playhouse Alumni and Associates Newsletter put out this disclaimer: 'There has been considerable publicity concerning this year's Academy Award winner for Best Actor, Dustin Hoffman, and his fellow nominee, Gene Hackman . . . The publicity states that these very success-ful Alumni were both voted the "least likely to succeed" by their classmates. We wish to state that there was no such vote, nor was there ever in the entire history of the Pasadena Playhouse College of Theatre Arts. We believe this puts both the College of Theatre Arts and its students and alumni in a very demeaning light. Whoever perpetrated this mythical story should be informed that nothing like this ever happened. We who were there *know*, the general public does not.'

Actually, when a producer from NBC's Matinee Theater came to see a couple of shows, he remarked rather depressingly to the assembled com-pany that in his opinion only one of their number would become famous. He said this staring directly at Dustin. (Of Dustin's contemporaries, apart from Hackman, Ruth Buzzi made a name on stage and in films, and Lisa Lu played the old dowager empress in Bernardo Bertolucci's *The Last Emperor*.) Dustin had made an impression as the narrator in a production of *A View from the Bridge* by Arthur Miller, the playwright who already meant so much to him and would come to mean even more. Almost unrecognisable in a sober grey suit, and with his hair neatly combed back, he brilliantly held the play together.

When the school put on Georg Büchner's *Danton's Death*, Dustin wanted to tackle the title role. He was far from the physical type to play the largely-built, hedonistic and passionate French revolutionary leader, and yet he managed to be convincing. This was largely due to Barney Brown, the only teacher at the college for whom Dustin had any respect. Dustin didn't seem to care about the praise of others: he only wanted Barney Brown's approval.

Brown was himself a graduate of the Pasadena School, and had served on the faculty for ten years after having worked as actor, teacher, director and producer for theatrical groups in New York and LA. With his thick, round glasses, unruly mop of hair and gaunt features, he looked rather like a mad scientist. He would push the students to their limits and beyond. He could be very serious and very funny. He loved to mimic the actors and then do the part the correct way. As this suggests, however, he could also be cruel. Once he solved the problem of an actor's very loose walk by shoving a pencil between his buttocks and having him squeeze it in place while he walked.

One of his most acclaimed productions was *Inherit the Wind* in February 1958 at the Pasadena Playhouse, with Sidney Blackmer in the Clarence Darrow role, an evening that deeply impressed Dustin. Because Brown had certain radical ideas and was a follower of the Russian actor-producer-teacher Konstantin Stanislavsky, who died in 1938, he was labelled a Red by certain 'patriotic' Californian citizens in the Communist witch-hunting atmosphere of the times. But he managed to hold on to his job.

One of the principal tenets of Stanislavsky's teachings, much of it laid out in his book *An Actor Prepares* (1926), was that the actor must give the complete illusion of reality, doing away with all theatricality and stereotyped mannerisms. In his productions of Chekhov, Stanislavsky transferred the external to the internal, rejecting the truth of history, manners and customs for the truth of feelings, moods and expressions. He concentrated on the psychological internal development of the roles with greater simplicity of external expression. This became absorbed into the system taught by Elia Kazan and Lee Strasberg, among others, at the Actors Studio in New York, which emphasised the need for the performer to use his or her imagination to recreate a personal experience in the same or a similar situation. Although Dustin later spent some time at the Actors Studio, the foundation stone of his approach to acting was laid by Barney Brown at Pasadena.

Brown was the first person to recognise talent in Dustin. 'You'll probably be thirty before it happens to you, but you have something unique,' Brown told him with uncanny foresight. (He would not live to see fame come to his protégé. He died after heart surgery in 1961, aged fifty.) Brown also advised Dustin to leave California and take his chances in New York, where there would be more opportunities to get stage work. Dustin was aware that there would be little chance of finding employment as an actor in LA; he knew he certainly was not the type to appear in the many soaps and cowboy series on TV, and as for Hollywood . . . How could he hope to compete with WASPish macho action men like Rock Hudson and Tab Hunter? What Jews there were, were hidden behind Aryan names like Kirk Douglas (Issur Danielovitch Demsky) and Tony Curtis (Bernard Schwartz). He could, of course, have changed his name to Dustin Mann, but he always felt he was 'Jewish looking'. He therefore decided to hop on a Greyhound bus and join his friend Gene Hackman in New York. Besides, he commented, 'it's easier to fail three thousand miles away from home, and I was sure I would fail.'

The unknown Dustin Hoffman arrived in New York in 1958, aged 21, and remained unknown and undiscovered until Barney Brown's prediction was fulfilled.

6

New York, New York – a Wonderful Town?

I was committing a kind of chronic suicide in my early days in New York.

DESPITE BEING BORN and bred in California, Dustin is a New York person. He is more himself there; he looks New York, he talks New York. 'I love New York; I consider it my home, I love being able to walk to museums, theatres, restaurants. Every time I go out of the city and fly back, and take a cab in from the airport, I get the same thrill out of being here.

'I wouldn't have been such a misfit if I'd grown up in New York. What a wasted childhood! The only thing I'd change in my life, if I could, is that I'd have myself born in New York . . . I hated LA. I never really felt I belonged there. I was always an outsider.'

Dustin never got much of a kick out of living in the proximity of Hollywood. When he was at Pasadena, Dustin had imagined himself on stage, not in the movies. There was experimental theatre in New York and, most importantly, it was the home of the Actors Studio, which he was determined to enter.

For those brought up in LA, Hollywood was just another sprawling suburb without much mystique. For people brought up elsewhere, especially abroad, Hollywood represented a glamorous way of life unobtainable in other countries. It is inevitable that visitors arriving in Tinsel Town for the first time are invariably disappointed by its tattiness. What they fail to realise is that Hollywood is not a real place but a state of mind, a mythical kingdom, like Disneyland, in which America likes to see itself reflected. Dustin had no such illusions.

'You'd see a movie star now and then. I think one time I was playing baseball when I was about eleven years old and Robert Young passed by and we'd hit a ball that had gone over the fence and he threw it back. I remember thinking, "Gee, Robert Young threw the ball back."'

When he was growing up in Los Angeles, Dustin dreamed of living an exciting existence in New York (filtered through Hollywood) in the manner of Leo Gorcey and the Dead End Kids. It is typical that his attraction to New York was the urban low life he saw depicted in the movies and not the Park Avenue plush. As befitted his adherence to the Beatnik philosophy, to which his appearance testified, Dustin reacted against the swimming-pool and surf ethos of California, water not being a prime element among the Beats. Although there were times when the Hoffmans could afford the obligatory swimming pool, Dustin never used it much. He later commented about his unexpected return to LA for *The Graduate*, a movie that echoed many of his own attitudes, that, 'They had to shoot all the pool scenes underwater. That's the only way I can swim.'

It is not difficult to see why Dustin was attracted to the Beat Generation, who, according to *The Literary History of the United States*, 'spoke primarily for the beleaguered self, for the holiness and spontaneity of the natural man'. Like Dustin, the beatniks were not political, but they despised square suburban America, its plastic values, its empty goals, its sexual repression. There was a kinship between the stream-of-consciousness Beat writers such as Jack Kerouac (whose novel *On the Road* was published in the year Dustin arrived in New York), Allen Ginsberg and Kenneth Rexroth, Method acting, and the new experiments in theatre, film and jazz. It was not long before Dustin was able to see Jack Gelber's extraordinary junkie drama, *The Connection*, produced by The Living Theater, as well as Robert Frank and Alfred Leslie's film, *Pull My Daisy*, with 'cool' jazz and Kerouac's ironic monologue on the soundtrack.

The nine years in New York during which he worked, absorbed, struggled and strove to make a name for himself were, to a less elevated degree, like Maxim Gorky's early life, his 'university days'. They also turned him into the sort of movie star he was to become.

On his arrival by Greyhound, he headed straight for Gene Hackman's sixth floor, $22-a-month apartment in the East 20s. It consisted of a bedroom and a kitchenette where Hackman, his wife Fay and baby Christopher lived. The last thing big Gene needed was another person, no matter how small, to move in with them.

'They let me sleep on the kitchen floor. They thought it was just for a few nights. They couldn't get rid of me. I was too scared to leave. This city was cold, lonely and terrifying. I slept on the floor next to the fridge. Every night at two and four a.m., it would have a heart attack, and wake me up.'

Hackman introduced Dustin to a friend of his, another aspiring actor called Robert Duvall. Duvall and Hackman were both born in January 1931, had both been in the services, and had done things and been places, and vice versa. The son of a rear admiral, Duvall, with his stern features, fixed gaze and gleaming forehead, seemed born to play psychotic soldiers, gangsters or cops. There has always been a recognition in American films that the line between the military, the mobsters and the police is a fine one, and Duvall was later to walk it with perfect equilibrium. Hackman and Duvall, the two prematurely balding would-be actors, took young Dusty or 'Dustbone', as Duvall called him, under their wing. 'I really admired Gene and Bobby. If they wanted a girl, they just went right after her. I'd be totally paralysed at the thought of making the right move.'   .

Duvall, on the other hand, claimed that 'Dustin has had more girls than anyone I've ever known – more even than Joe Namath ever dreamed about.' He recalled Dustin's technique. 'We'd be in a coffee shop when the waitress came over for the order. "How would you like your coffee?" she'd ask Dustin. "Black, with sugar and a kiss," he'd reply, fixing her with those big eyes of his. Occasionally he would get the kiss and sometimes even more.' It is true that New York released a sexual confidence in him that was lacking in California, and he was determined to make up for lost time.

Sometimes, Dustin would sit out on the windowsill of the apartment and shout out to any passing girl he fancied, 'Do you know you've got a great ass?' and other similar flattering remarks. He once successfully convinced a girl he had known in LA that he had become an artist and wanted to see what she looked like in the nude in case he wanted to paint her. According to a semi-serious Ronald Hoffman, the rumour that Dustin was a pre-med student 'got started because he was always looking up the girls' skirts'. Dustin later admitted that, 'as an unemployed actor, I used to take girls to bed in order to perform'.

But he didn't always score. When Dustin, on being refused a date by a sculptress named Marisol, asked why, she replied, 'Because I think you're a creep.' On the whole, Dustin, whose self-esteem was very low during that period, agreed with her.

After some months on the Hackmans' kitchen floor, Dustin moved into Duvall's Hell's Kitchen railroad apartment with three others. They were Vladimir Kostinoff, a Russian emigré who was studying choreography, and the brothers Richard and Robert Morse. Only the latter had already made it. He had been a hit in his New York debut as Barnaby Tucker in a long-running production of *The Matchmaker*, and was, at the time, in a Broadway musical about the making of a musical called *Say, Darling*. Morse's brother Richard later formed his own mime company.

The group of unknown actors got together regularly for a series of poetry and play readings which were followed by parties. Among those at the gatherings were Dustin, Duvall, Hackman, Elliott Gould (also in *Say, Darling* with Robert Morse), James Caan and Jon Voight – the last two studying at the Neighborhood Playhouse with Duvall's teacher Sanford Meisner. At these bohemian affairs, Duvall would often play the guitar, while Dustin would sing and dance to Ray Charles records and, when a piano was available, belt out jazz numbers. Sometimes Duvall and Dustin would act out dirty jokes.

When Dustin first arrived in New York he auditioned for the Actors Studio. Unfortunately, he found it difficult to relax and it was a 'disaster'. He was rejected four more times, and was never told why. Finally, two years after his first audition, he was accepted. Apart from his classes with Lee Strasberg, Dustin worked under the tutelage of Lonnie Chapman.

Geraldine Page, an actress Dustin admired more than any other at the time, believed that, 'Stanislavsky was trying to get down what the best actors do anyway: he didn't invent anything. So even actors who sneer at the Method, are militant against it, or, conversely, have never heard of it, when they get up and act they use themselves. What happens when you study that aspect of acting is that you find more analogies between yourself and the material than you thought you had. The Method allows you to discover less obvious connections between yourself and your character . . . It opens up a whole field of connections you can consciously bring from yourself. You bring a lot unconsciously and automatically, but the Method widens your perception: you can then add more of your own colours to the tapestry of your character.'

Bruce Dern, another disciple of the Method, stated that it 'enables you to find the things which will relax you, unlock you, and let all the private emotion come out. It has to do with being able to recall the emotions and sensations of a particular incident, but it takes about five years of total concentration to learn how to do it.'

Dustin spent two years in Lee Strasberg's class. 'I wasn't one of his "followers", but he was great to listen to. I always thought it was terrible the way they'd follow him around like he was God and could make them be Jimmy Dean or Marlon Brando.' Strasberg taught him that the causes of people's individual rhythms may be the opposite of what they appear. A slow deliberate rhythm may be masking a lot of inner conflict. 'This was the most important thing I ever learned from him. We used to watch animals. He said watching animals, how they eat and move, all the movements of their living would help us move. We used to spend hours at the zoo, all us actors watching some damn penguin.' He would also spend his time studying the faces of people on the subway or on a bus.

In answer to the once-popular question in the USA, 'Where were you when you heard of the assassination of John F. Kennedy on 22 November 1963?', Dustin could answer, 'On a bus coming from a Strasberg class.'

If part of the Method was to delve into personal experiences to bring reality to a role, then Dustin would have plenty to give to the theatre when he finally got the chance. The parade of jobs he took to survive, many of them perfect candidates for 'What's My Line?', make a remarkable montage . . .

Dustin is playing piano at a dance studio run by Daniel Nagrin and Helen Tamiris, a couple he met some years back when he was teaching drama and they were teaching dance at a summer camp in Colorado. He tours with their small ballet company, acting as stage manager and general dogsbody in return for food and lodgings and no wages. Helen Tamiris, a follower of Isadora Duncan, is a woman with a forceful personality, who trains her dancers to observe and emulate rhythms as part of their daily routine, just as Strasberg has got his actor-students to do. Dustin and the dancers sit in a Greenwich Village café watching people go by and studying the rhythms of their walk and observing how someone is reading a newspaper. 'Everyone has his own individual rhythm,' says Madame Tamiris. Back at the studio, the dancers reproduce that rhythm, with Dustin at the piano taking notice of the way movements change personality.

Dustin is janitoring at another dance studio; clerking in the offices of the City Morgue; stringing Hawaiian leis in a small, sweaty factory in the flower district.

Cut to Dustin as a waiter in a French restaurant, where he affects a French accent when dealing with customers, a performance which works until a real Frenchman wants to pursue the conversation in his own tongue. Dustin suddenly develops a cough and has to be escorted back into the kitchen by fellow waiters. One day, Dustin is told that Sam Spiegel is eating there. In a flash, Dustin sees his chance of being discovered! Resurrecting his French accent, he nervously serves the big movie producer until he spills coffee on his famous client's expensive suit. 'I'm not really a waiter,' he splutters in explanation. 'Actually I'm an actor.' 'No,' protests Spiegel, 'You're neither an actor nor a waiter.' In the next shot the snooty maître d' is telling Dustin that he has been demoted to dishwasher.

At The Premise, the Greenwich Village improvisational club, Dustin is washing dishes again, and sometimes getting tips from the customers by playing the piano on occasions. One day, he summons up his courage and approaches Joan Darling (born Joan Kugell), who runs the show, and asks her to let him audition. Although Dustin has not seen Lenny Bruce, the outspoken nightclub comedian whom everybody is talking about, ('I never made the nightclub scene, because I didn't have the money'), he knows some of his routines from a record a girlfriend has played to him, which 'turned me on to him'. Dustin stands on stage in front of Joan

Darling and other members of the club and spills out his repertoire of
filthy jokes. They are impressed by his *chutzpah*, but feel his act would be a
little too vulgar even for their hip clientele. Back to the kitchen sink. It
looks as though his epitaph will read, 'Here Lies Dustin Hoffman –
Dishwasher'.

Cut to Dustin as a waiter at another establishment, Rudley's on
Columbus Circle. He is told by the generous manager that all his food is
free during working hours. Taking him at his word, Dustin proceeds to
down six thinly-sliced steak specials – and then is promptly fired. Now he
is a waiter at the Village Gate, where he is making $40 a night in tips, until
he is dismissed for standing around listening to the live music too much.

Suddenly we see him in a twenty-room town house. Has he struck it
rich already? Is this a flashforward to the seventies? No, he is a companion
and honorary uncle to the lonely child of a 70-year-old multi-millionaire
and his much younger wife. Dustin and the kid go on outings to the zoo,
the top of the Empire State and on the Staten Island Ferry. Dustin's
comment: 'When the day came that I actually had to go, both of us cried. I
was determined that, when I did become a father, no child of mine would
have to suffer for lack of parental guidance.'

Cut to Dustin typing rapidly in an office, having been sent there by the
Manpower agency. 'In high school if you got kicked out of class, you were
sent to study hall, and if you got kicked out of study hall, you were sent to
typing class. Consequently I became a very good typist. I could type sixty-
five words a minute. I was usually the only male in the offices they sent me
to.' There he is at a typewriter, just as he will be many years later as reporter
Carl Bernstein in *All the President's Men*. Rapid montage: Dustin typing for
the Yellow Pages, filing *Time* magazine cuttings, and soliciting for charity
over the telephone.

(But Dustin hated the confined space and atmosphere of office work. He
walked out of so many jobs by not coming back after the lunch break that
after a while he began to bring his own lunch to work just to stop himself.)

Extended sequence: Dustin working as a psychiatric attendant in a mental hospital, the New York Psychoanalytic Institute on West 168th Street.
On his first day in the men's ward, he meets a middle-aged man charging
down the hall. 'I'm getting out next Sunday . . . my wife's an old Dutch
cleanser . . . you got nice teeth, sonny boy, are they yours?' Rambling on
senselessly, the man, without warning, suddenly starts making the noise
of an electric razor. Cut to Dustin in Lonnie Chapman's Method class at
the Actors Studio being an electric razor. He then becomes a pinball
charging around the room, hitting chairs and going 'Ping!'

Cut back to the mental hospital. Dustin watching the patients with the rapt intensity of someone who believes he will one day use it as raw material in his work. The bones of Raymond Babbitt in *Rain Man* are forming even now.

Dustin observes the effects of illness on the loved ones left behind. The wife of a doctor arrives to visit her husband, now a patient, and Dustin witnesses the temporary transformation of the stroke-stricken man back into the person he was before. In the past, he has not recognised his wife at all, but this day, for a few fleeting seconds, he does, yelling, 'I can't help it, I'm trying,' before reverting to the stranger his illness has made him.

At the piano, Dustin is entertaining the patients. They are beating him at Scrabble. He is playing volleyball with them. (Ken Kesey is writing his counter-culture bestseller *One Flew Over the Cuckoo's Nest* around this time, based on *his* experiences of the inanities of psychiatric treatment at a state mental hospital.) But there is distaste on Dustin's face as he has to hold down patients during electric shock treatment (EST).

Dustin says: 'I've always been attracted to mental illness, that's why I really enjoyed the job until it got to me, so I quit after eight months.' (Years later, in the 1980s, a successful and much older Dustin dines out on the comic and tragic stories that he witnessed at the hospital.)

Christmas. Dustin is working in the toy department at Macy's department store, a job he does each Christmas for three years. He is selling hockey games which retail at $16.95. In an attempt to boost sales, Dustin comes to work one morning dressed in a Montreal Canadian's hockey sweatshirt and fakes a French-Canadian accent while demonstrating these games for customers.

Shop-assistant Dustin is looking after Gene Hackman's eighteen-month-old son Christopher while his father is at an audition. He sits the child on the counter-top, tells him to stay dead still and sells him to a woman as 'a life-size doll' for $16. Just as she is to take the kid away, the joke is explained to the gullible and humourless customer. Cut to Dustin accusing innocent women of shoplifting, and insulting others. When they become furious and threaten to report him, he smiles broadly and tells them they are on *Candid Camera*. So great a desire does Dustin have to act, that this form of 'street' theatre gives some satisfaction.

Now he is walking up and down Times Square in a Paul Revere costume reading the news. He is not certifiable, but has been employed by Modell's Army and Navy store during the New York newspaper strike as publicity. He is paid $15 a day, most of which he uses to buy himself some army-surplus clothes at the store.

In the meantime, Hackman was working as a furniture remover and Duvall was sorting letters on the night shift at the Times Square Post

Office. In the wee small hours of one December morning, Duvall returned to the apartment and shook Dustin awake. 'Dusty, I've just seen Sir John Gielgud,' enthused Duvall. Gielgud was in New York doing his Shakespeare recital, *The Ages of Man*, at the 46th Street Theater. Duvall explained that he was stumbling home from the Post Office when he came across Gielgud leaving a restaurant with some friends. Through the steam that was coming up from the snow-covered ground, Duvall saw them hail a taxi, and before Sir John, who was a little drunk, stepped into the cab, the great actor held his arms out in an expansive gesture, and in his most mellifluous tones addressed himself to the vacant New York spaces.

'Does anyone want to fuck an actress?' he demanded. Then he got into the taxi and drove off. Duvall was left in the snow, lost in amusement and admiration.

The story allayed Dustin's annoyance at being woken up at such an unearthly hour, and he thought, 'I like this man. I'd like to see him.'

Despite Cole Porter's advice that brushing up one's Shakespeare would wow the women, the Brandophile Dustin was never interested in classical acting, especially not of the English variety. 'Huh! The English – they're just technical actors,' was the received opinion; the not unjustifiable feeling being that English actors were taught to create characters from the outside in, which made it more mechanical. Nevertheless, not long after Duvall's nocturnal encounter, Dustin went along to see Gielgud give readings from T. S. Eliot one Sunday night.

'I went and sat in the fourth row. I didn't know anything about Eliot. Gielgud was doing *The Waste Land*. I found myself laughing at a poet I'd never heard of. I didn't even understand half of it. Suddenly, it was the first time it ever happened to me in my life, I realised that I was crying after I was already crying. He caught me right down to the marrow of my bones. He did that beautifully. Shit! It was a revelation to me. He got to me. He connected. I knew he connected with it, and he connected with me. I said, Man, you can be moved by this stuff! That stuff that was always so intimidating. Yet I did remember Brando making me cry when he did Mark Antony in the film of *Julius Caesar*. When he cried over dead Caesar, I cried. I learned later that Gielgud, who was Cassius in the same film, taught Brando the metre. Brando was no fool and went to Gielgud to ask him to do so.'

Out of the montage of jobs Dustin did, only one got him close to where he wanted to be – the stage. He worked as a hatchecker and orange-drink seller at the Longacre Theater where Zero Mostel was starring in *Rhinoceros*, Eugene Ionesco's parable of conformity. Blacklisted from films by the House Un-American Activities Committee (HUAC) in the fifties, Mostel had become a Broadway hit throughout 1961. After dealing with the customers, Dustin would sneak inside the theatre and observe the great comic performer evoking a rhinoceros every night, studying, comparing acting styles, and absorbing.

One evening, Eleanor Roosevelt, well known for her liberal views and homely looks, handed him her coat, which he sat looking at throughout the performance in case it should escape. On another occasion, Dustin was walking near the theatre on West 48th Street, when the rotund Mostel came huffing and puffing past him. Desperate to make contact with greatness, and without thinking, Dustin shouted, 'Lewis Gilbert [the British film director, who had visited the theatre the night before] says to give you his best.' 'And give it right back to him,' Zero bellowed back, waving his fist in the air as he continued on his way. Dustin was shaking with humiliation for some hours afterwards.

Sometimes, after unsuccessfully searching for a job off-Broadway, he would wander over to Central Park on Thursday afternoons and enviously watch the Broadway Show League playing baseball. One day, Dustin watched Paul Newman, playing left field, completely miss a high-flier hit in his direction. An immense feeling of satisfaction came over Dustin, seeing this superstar failing at something. 'It made my whole day,' Dustin recalled.

In the meantime, Harry and Lillian continued to send their son $200 a month to help him out for at least two years. Without their support, Dustin admits, 'I wouldn't have made it.' However, they decided to cut him off at one stage in the hope that he would give up his 'meshuggener' idea of becoming an actor, come home and be the doctor they still dreamed he would become. But they underestimated his staying power.

7

The Ugly Kid Next to the Lead

I'll never forget that period in my life. I learned more than I can say.

IN THE EARLY sixties, Dustin and his two closest friends, Hackman and Duvall, did not have the sort of faces that fitted the time, a message that came through to them as they did the rounds of the agencies.

'I couldn't stand the rejection,' Dustin recalled. 'They were looking for faces, photogenic faces . . . If you didn't have the face, you slipped your photo under the door and ran away. I worked and I studied and I cried and I slept a lot.'

'Even though I know they're stars,' says the now-renowned Hackman, 'I still can't picture Bobby and Dusty except as living in those cold-water flats in New York that I lived in too . . . In those days it was a question of which was the more broke right then, and the other two would help him out.'

'If you had come up to any of us and said we were going to be successful or famous, we would have laughed at you,' claimed Dustin. 'We never thought of it. We expected with a little luck to be working actors, not even on Broadway. Get character roles. We knew we weren't leading men. If I woke up tomorrow and I was told I was in a coma, and had dreamed all this, I would believe it.'

However, Hoffman, Hackman and Duvall gradually started getting sporadic parts. Duvall's first roles were all psychotics in TV shows. In fact, he made his screen debut as the simple-minded recluse in *To Kill a Mockingbird* in 1962. The year before, Hackman had appeared briefly as a cop in his first movie, a B feature called *Mad Dog Call* (1961). His first good part off-Broadway was in Irwin Shaw's *Children at Their Games* in 1963, which won him the Clarence Derwent Award for a supporting actor, followed by Muriel Resnik's *Any Wednesday* on Broadway in February 1964 at the Music Box Theater.

Hackman nearly lost the *Any Wednesday* part, however, when Sandy Dennis, one of the cast of four, had an initial meeting with him. She told the director she found Hackman repulsive, and that, when he came into the room and she had her first look at him, she had almost died. George Morrison, who was scheduled to direct, managed to get the reluctant Dennis to accept his former pupil.

With his two actor buddies beginning to make names for themselves, Dustin saw himself lagging behind. He had to wait until his second year in New York before he was offered his first professional acting job; in Gertrude Stein's *Yes Is for a Very Young Man* at Sarah Lawrence College in Bronxville. 'I paid my own train fare out there, got thirty dollars and ended up with three'. However, it gave him a chance to act, and meet the girl students.

In the cast was a student at the college called Jane Quigley, who was to become the actress Jane Alexander, later to appear with Dustin in *All the President's Men* and *Kramer vs Kramer*. Strangely, neither Dustin nor Jane remembers the other in the play, which is even more curious on the actress's part because there are only two male roles. As she describes her stay at Sarah Lawrence as a 'stressful period in her life', this amnesia might be understandable. It was directed by Will Leach, the respected drama lecturer at the college.

The elusive plot of the play, coincidentally first performed in 1946 at the Pasadena Playhouse just after Gertrude Stein's death, concerned the bitterness and division that wrenched French families during the war in France. It is a play not with rounded characters but instead with various types who represent different reactions to the Occupation. Dustin's role was of a young man infatuated with an American spinster, whose maternal protectiveness he later rejects to join his brother in the Resistance. At the Liberation, he realises the war is not over. 'For me it is just beginning, yes is for a very young man,' he tells the spinster. 'I won't have time to think so I won't think about you and the quays of Paris and roast chickens . . . no I won't have time to think. Goodbye.' The play ends with his going off to continue fighting.

After this short but sweet taste of acting in front of an audience, Dustin was given the chance to emulate one of the Dead End Kids he had so envied as a child. It was in a one-week showcase revival of Sidney Kingsley's 1935 play *Dead End* performed by the Equity Library Theater, which staged shows for agents to come and spot talent. Dustin played Spit, the hardboiled, fast-talking but basically kindly slum boy, originally portrayed by Leo Gorcey on Broadway and in the Warner Bros movie. (The production also featured another struggling newcomer, Bill Macy, later to gain TV fame as the husband of 'Maude'.) 'We put it on at the Forty-First Street Theater and I got an agent out of that. I needed a job to get an agent, and I needed an agent to get a job.'

The agent got him a small but meaty part in an episode of the popular TV series *Naked City* in June 1961. Entitled *Sweet Prince of Delancy Street*, it guest-starred James Dunn and Robert Morse as father and son covering up for a crime neither of them committed. The culprit turns out to be Morse's friend, played by Dustin, an apprentice car mechanic. Dustin's face was seen for the very first time on a screen, albeit a TV one, behind protective goggles as he worked on a lathe in a garage, his first words being 'Hi, Richie!' Looking about nineteen years old, Dustin immediately displayed many of the later mannerisms that would one day be famous. The smile, switched quickly on and off, the charm, the sudden intensity, the modulated voice. The role gave Dustin an emotional final monologue, facing Morse's mother (Jan Miner, who was to play his mother over a decade later in *Lenny*): 'Listen Mrs Wilkin. Nothing is as simple as it seems. What do you know what a hunger I've got to get out of this rat-trap of a place I'm stuck in . . . Now I've got to go to jail and I'm afraid. I'm really afraid.'

It was the kind of 'character juvenile', defined by Dustin as 'a euphemism for the ugly kid next to the lead', he thought he might be able to get his career going with. Given the excellence of his performance, it is surprising that he was not picked up straight away for other TV work or even recruited for one of the many juvenile delinquent roles that filled a number of Hollywood movies in the early sixties.

Instead, Dustin went on to make his Broadway debut (before Duvall and Hackman) in the brief role of Ridzinski, a nutty soldier in *A Cook for Mr General* by Steven Gethers. The play was a knockabout GI farce set in an army rehabilitation centre in 1944 in the wartime Pacific, about a Greek cook's attempts to become an American citizen and his disruption of an inspection of the centre by the top brass. The all-male cast was led by a former Charlie Chan, Roland Winters, together with brawny British actor Bill Travers, and John McGiver (who would later appear in *Midnight Cowboy*).

Sometime movie director Fielder Cook first directed it, but it was in such a shambles on the road that David Pressman was brought in to get it into shape for Broadway. The first day, he called a 10 a.m. rehearsal to inform the cast of how much work was needed in a very short time. He was about fifteen minutes into the talk when Dustin rushed in. Pressman demanded an explanation. 'My alarm clock didn't go off,' Dustin offered lamely. 'This better not happen again or you're through,' warned the director. 'No, sir.' Dustin was determined not to blow his first Broadway chance. 'He looked really nothing; a pipsqueak of an actor,' Pressman later recalled.

When the company got to New York, Dustin invested in a motor scooter so he could get from his room in the Bronx to the theatre on West 48th Street to save subway fares. On the day before the opening, there was a technical run-through of the show, starting at 2.30. Determined not to be late, Dustin left the Bronx early enough to find he had a little time to kill, so he scooted around Central Park. Suddenly, he ran out of fuel. By the time he had got some, he realised with horror that he was not going to make the theatre on time. Remembering the threat of dismissal if he was late again, he decided to do something drastic. He therefore tore his shirt and put dirt all over his clothes so that when he arrived about 30 minutes into the rehearsal, he was able to stammer out that he had been in an accident. 'What happened? Are you okay?' Pressman asked. 'I'm fine,' said the brave Dustin. 'I don't want to talk about it.' Five years later, when Dustin was a star, he met Pressman at a New Year's party and confessed: 'You scared the hell out of me, but I've been feeling guilty ever since.'

A *Cook for Mr General* opened at the Playhouse on 19 October 1961. Dustin's only line was 'Yes, sir!', spoken during a roll call. On the opening night, he choked up and it came out something like 'Caw, caw!' One reviewer referred to a strange sound coming from one of the actor's mouths. Dustin cut out the review, underlined the passage and stuck it in his scrapbook.

Uneven, and occasionally very funny, the play achieved, according to the critic in *Best Plays of the Year*, 'the funniest single moment of the season when a group of rehabilitation camp soldiers are thrown into such chaos that a sergeant's "Attenhut!", automatically barked at the sight of an entering general, causes two stretcher bearers to drop an unconscious lieutenant on the ground and salute. With a slightly better cast this comedy might have been a hit.' As it was, it closed on 11 November 1961, just 28 performances after its opening, throwing the large cast out of work. It was the only Broadway play by the author, who subsequently went into TV. Steve Gethers died of lung cancer in December 1989 aged 67, the month Dustin returned to Broadway a bigger star than ever in *The Merchant of Venice*.

Dustin's first Broadway role went unnoticed by the theatre world and, as acting jobs were hard to come by in New York, he decided to take up an offer to work on community theatre productions in Fargo, North Dakota, in the winter of 1962. In the three months there, he gained valuable experience in acting as well as directing. Among the plays he relished directing was William Gibson's *Two for the Seesaw*, the first piece Arthur Penn directed on Broadway and in London, and in which Anne Bancroft made her entry on to the New York stage. The comparative security of being a big fish in Fargo made him consider staying there, but his ambitions still lay in the big pond of New York.

Among the things he discovered about himself in North Dakota was his ability to communicate his enthusiasm and skills to others. On his return to New York, he put these talents to further use by starting an acting class at New York's East Harlem Boys' Club, located on West 110th Street. The club was a haven of culture for the deprived children who joined it, and they warmed to Dustin's personality and perceptions. A rapport was created between the boyish 25-year-old unknown actor and the teenagers, whom he directed in several plays. They were busy months as he bounded from classes to the club and worked through various part-time jobs to feed himself.

This part of his life would be well depicted, rather more glamorously, in the first section of *Tootsie*, which sees the actor Michael Dorsey/Dustin Hoffman working as a waiter, between auditions and teaching an acting class. At a birthday party given for Dorsey, a friend makes the toast: 'To Michael Dorsey who, like it or not, makes you remember what acting's all about . . . being unemployed.' Dustin was sure even then that 'there wasn't an actor at the Actors Studio who wouldn't dress up as a woman to get a year's contract on a soap opera'.

On the principle that it was better to take any theatre job outside New York than wait on tables on Broadway, Dustin strayed from Manhattan again. He directed a production of *Death of a Salesman*, the key play in his life, at a small summer stock company in New Jersey before joining the Theatre Company of Boston in January 1964. This was a smart move. Although he earned only $65 a week, he did ten plays in nine months. It could be argued that this intense exposure to a range of modern classics educated him far more in acting skills than if he had got into movies earlier in his career. Among his wide-ranging roles were Clov in Samuel Beckett's *Endgame*; Dunlavin in Brendan Behan's *The Quare Fellow*; C. Couch called Babboon in Bertolt Brecht's *In the Jungle of the Cities*; Dr Nicholas Triletski in *A Country Scandal* (Alex Szyogt's adaptation of Anton Chekhov's *Platonov*); Ben in *The Dumb Waiter* and Bert Hudd in *The Room* (two one-act plays by Harold Pinter); Zapo in Fernando Arrabal's one-act play *Picnic on the Battlefield*; Hugo in Jean-Paul Sartre's *Dirty Hands*; and Peter Quilpe in T. S. Eliot's *The Cocktail Party*. The last character ends up in the film business in Hollywood. 'What a metier! I've tried to believe in it so that I might believe in myself. I thought I had ideas to make a revolution in the cinema, that no one could ignore – and here I am, making a second-rate film!'

He got great personal satisfaction when, one evening after a performance of *The Quare Fellow*, a woman came backstage and asked him if she could meet the man who played the overweight old Irishman who had reminded her of W. C. Fields. He told her that it was he. She did not believe him and left in a huff.

The Boston experience was followed by a short stint as Frankie McCarter, a professional gambler, in John Cecil Holm and George Abbott's 1935 comedy *Three Men on a Horse* at Princeton, New Jersey. One of the plays from Boston, Beckett's *Waiting for Godot*, in which Dustin played Pozzo, had a one-night performance at the Circle-In-The-Square in New York. It was curious casting in a role usually portrayed as a large, voraciously-eating, bald, fat man in a greatcoat, whip in hand, driving his servant Lucky to exhaustion. It seemed the least suitable of the four roles for Dustin, but the play's director Ulu Grosbard claimed that 'until Hoffman did Pozzo, I never understood the role'. It is certainly true that Dustin's slight stature in the part of a brutal master was nearer the short dictator images of Napoleon and Hitler than the usual interpretation of a big bully more in the line of Mack Swain, the heavy in Chaplin movies. Robert Duvall played Lucky, Pozzo's slave, and Dustin recalled that it was 'great keeping Duvall on a rope'.

Ulu Grosbard, who was to play both friend and foe in Dustin's life, was born in Antwerp, Belgium, in 1929, the son of a Jewish diamond merchant. In 1943, his parents fled the Nazis and began to perilous journey through France into Spain, before boarding a refugee boat bound for Cuba. Grosbard spent five years in Havana cutting diamonds until he finally received a visa for the United States in 1948. He immediately entered the University of Chicago, where he gained a BA and then an MA in English before going on to graduate study at Yale. There in 1953 he met the actress Rose Gregorio, whom he later married.

Although impressed by Dustin's performance as Pozzo, Grosbard next offered him the non-acting job of assistant director and stage manager on Arthur Miller's *A View from the Bridge*, which he and film producer Joseph E. Levine were backing. It was Grosbard's second attempt at it. The first was a 1957 Long Island production, the first time he had directed professionally. The play was originally produced in one act, but now, at the Sheridan Square Playhouse in New York in January 1965, it was expanded into two acts with an interval. Robert Duvall got the lead as the long-shoreman Eddie Carboni, the part that proved a breakthrough for him. Though disappointed at not acting, Dustin did begin a friendship with Grosbard and one of the play's young stars, Jon Voight, who played Rudolpho, the man Eddie's niece (Susan Anspach) falls in love with. He also got to meet Arthur Miller.

Arthur Miller often visited the theatre during rehearsals. One day Grosbard took the playwright aside and told him that there was a member of the company who would be perfect for Willy Loman in a few years. Miller looked around at Duvall and Voight and the others, until he realised that

Grosbard meant Dustin. Miller wrote in *Time Bends*: 'My estimate of Grosbard all but collapsed as, observing Dustin Hoffman's awkwardness and his big nose that never seemed to get unstuffed, I wondered how the poor fellow imagined himself a candidate for any kind of acting career.'

However, it was not long before Dustin was playing the role of Bernard, the 'anaemic' bespectacled good student in a recording of *Death of a Salesman* with Lee J. Cobb and Mildred Dunnock, the original Willy and Linda Loman. Grosbard, the director, had Dustin read the part of Willy with all the actors auditioning for lesser roles. Dustin also got to rehearse for three weeks with Cobb. In 1984, when Dustin was preparing to tackle the title role on stage, he remarked, 'Watching Lee J. Cobb and his sixteen-inch guns as Willy was the most intimidating factor for me taking the role. Cobb's scenes are there – playing in my mind.'

A View from the Bridge ran for 780 performances, but Dustin was not there on the opening night, because he had auditioned for and won the second lead in a new off-Broadway play, *Harry, Noon and Night*.

A curious piece set in Munich in December 1955, it featured former Our Gang child actor Robert Blake in the title role as a psychological misfit American in Germany, who gets involved with an American soldier and a limping, hunchbacked German homosexual, a juicy part for Dustin. The director George Morrison (Hackman's one-time teacher) recalled that, 'Dustin's audition was the most brilliant I've ever seen. It was incredible. He started grabbing props and improvising. One day, during rehearsals, Dustin just disappeared before my eyes, leaving behind the character.' Ronald Ribman, the author of the play, said, 'Dustin had the ability to annihilate his own ego and become the character he was looking for. He studied the German accent, and worked on the limp, and the homo-sexuality.' How he worked on the homosexuality is not recorded.

The play, which opened at the Pocket Theater off-Broadway on 5 May 1965, got Dustin noticed by the critics for the first time. 'With a part like that you just have to get attention,' he claimed. Despite some good reviews, *Harry, Noon and Night* only managed six performances.

Later in the year, Dustin got a role as a petty crook in an episode of *The Defenders*, coming to the end of its four years on TV, for which Dustin pocketed $500, the most money he had made as an actor. Because he looked such a slob, a fellow actor said, 'Jeez, you're never gonna get work unless you look right!' So with his new wealth, Dustin went into a smart clothes shop to get a new coat. He liked the way he looked in one that cost $150, a price he had never paid for any clothes before. Sweating and trembling, he handed over the money at the counter. A feeling of guilt came over him at buying such a luxury. When he stepped out of the shop, everything went black. He thought, 'What's happening? God is punishing me.' There was no light to be seen. He had not gone blind, but the world had gone dark. Fear gripped him. People scurried by. He soon learned that there had been a huge electricity failure in the city, and New York had been blacked out. It was 10 November 1965, the night of the biggest power cut in American history, which plunged New York City and parts of nine states into darkness. Dustin's experience could have been a sketch in the 1968 movie 'inspired' by the events of that night called *Where Were You When the Lights Went Out?* (Many years later, as Ted Kramer in *Kramer vs Kramer*, he started to relate this story to his boss. Dustin wanted to tell it all, but it was truncated in the finished film, thus rendering the anecdote pointless.)

At the time, one of the most successful plays on Broadway, *The Subject Was Roses*, Frank D. Gilroy's Pulitzer Prize-winning drama of an Irish family, was recasting. It had been running at the Royale since May 1964, and the cast were going with it to Los Angeles. Ulu Grosbard, who directed, got Dustin to audition. Gilroy was pleased with what he saw and asked if Dustin would be interested in understudying and then taking over Martin Sheen's role of Timmy Cleary, the twenty-year-old son of John and Nettie Cleary (Jack Albertson and Irene Dailey), who tries to adjust on returning home after three years in the army during World War II. He answered with a resounding 'Yes', and studied the part all summer. It was to have been his first major Broadway role, but Fate had other plans for him.

8

Hoffman/Burns/Terminal

I was my very own would-be killer.

FOLLOWING THE FIRST day of *The Subject Was Roses* rehearsals, Dustin went over to a girlfriend's apartment for dinner brimming with enthusiasm and confidence. Things looked rosy. The rehearsal had gone well, and it seemed as though he had successfully jumped the chasm between off- and on-Broadway. He had promised to cook his hostess a speciality of his – beef fondue. Then, after a few glasses of wine and dessert, who knows, he might be able to have his way with her. But when he tossed the beef into the sizzling oil, it somehow exploded out of the pot 'like a canister of napalm', splashing over his arms and starting a kitchen fire, which Dustin promptly and stupidly tried to put out with his hands. The fire finally doused with water, a young doctor across the hall was called and he advised Dustin to go immediately to the hospital. The putting out of the fire had not only dampened any prospects of seduction, it could seriously jeopardise his chances of performing on Broadway in an award-winning show. There was no way Dustin was going to hospital. What if they kept him there? What if he couldn't get to rehearsal next morning? So hungry was he for the role that, instead of going for treatment, he went home to bed.

Despite being in extreme pain and feeling ill, he turned up the following day at rehearsals with long sleeves disguising his burns. He continued to hide this condition for almost a week, until he collapsed during a break in rehearsals, and was rushed to hospital. His injuries were far more serious than he had imagined; he had incurred third-degree burns on his hands and a serious infection had spread into his bloodstream. An urgent operation was necessary to save his life. In fact, doctors listed his chances as 'touch and go'.

Because Dustin had eaten a few hours previously, the anaesthetist had to insert a tube in his mouth to stop him choking on his own vomit. 'How will I know when it's in the right place?' he asked. 'You won't be able to talk,' said the man. The anaesthetist tried three times to insert it. The fourth time, he said, 'That's it.' 'No it isn't,' said Dustin. 'I can still talk.' Owing to fears of the anaesthetist's incompetence, Dustin insisted on having the operation the following morning. Despite being told he might die, he decided to take the risk. By 'willing myself to do so', Dustin survived the night and the operation. When he came to, the doctor who performed it admitted to Dustin that he might have choked to death had he undergone it the night before. Dustin later discovered that his admission card read: Hoffman/Burns/Terminal.

While in hospital, in order to stem the agonising pain, he was given three or four shots of Demerol a day. 'Every morning I'd get a beaut before they changed my bandages. And every few hours I'd get more shots. I felt I knew what addicts' lives are like and what they think they're getting from dope. My euphoria was complete. I had no sex drive, of course, because drugs take its place. In a sense, taking drugs is very sexual. Perhaps what I mean is you have a powerful feeling of love, and while you're on drugs, you experience no hate or fear.'

He left the hospital weighing 110 lb, 30 less than when he came in. 'My life was unbearable. I didn't feel pain from the burns any more, but that had been replaced by a pain a thousand times worse. I felt as if hordes of people were constantly shaking me, shaking my whole insides, shaking me until I'd cry in anguish. But gradually I beat my craving for the drug.' The experience was later dredged out of his subconscious when he played drug addict Lenny Bruce. Dustin always had the consolation that any painful period he lived through could be used to inject reality into a role.

Thanks to proper medical care, the infection was cured, but he needed a convalescence of four weeks under medical guidance, a time which cost him the part of Timmy Cleary that he craved. Going down to the Royale Theater with his hands still lightly wrapped in gauze bandages, Dustin found out that Walter McGinn, who would have been his understudy, now had the role. When Gilroy explained the commercial necessities of having to recast, and offered him the job of understudy and assistant stage manager, he stormed out of the theatre in a rage. But after he had simmered down and contemplated his parlous financial situation, he returned a few hours later to accept Gilroy's offer. For the next month or so, Dustin sat backstage ambivalently waiting for Walter McGinn to break a leg. However, when McGinn heard that Harry and Lillian, on a short visit to New York, were coming to see the show, he feigned illness to allow Dustin a chance to perform in front of his parents.

Despite his one night on Broadway, Dustin felt bitter, betrayed and disappointed. He contemplated becoming a teacher and giving up acting, except he could not shake off the desire. He continued to go to auditions weekly, yet failed to meet the directors' requirements. Though in a vulnerable position, Dustin was never afraid to speak his mind in a forceful manner, often having an alienating effect on directors. One of them was British director John Dexter, who was casting Peter Shaffer's *The Royal Hunt of the Sun*, to be performed at ANTA in October 1965. Dustin managed to get a part, but then the brittle Dexter, not known to suffer actors gladly, told him to kindly leave the stage. Then he landed the role of Sparky in John Arden's *Sergeant Musgrave's Dance* (produced in London seven years previously in 1959) for Peter Cook's company at the Theater-de-Lys in Christopher Street, Greenwich Village. Sparky, the youngest of three deserters from the Victorian army, flees his comrades when he falls in love, but is killed in a fight. Dustin kept changing his concept of the part, and in addition he threw several temper tantrums, none of which pleased the generally unflappable Stuart Burge, another distinguished British director. On the sixth day of rehearsal, Burge decided that Dustin would never 'find' the role, and asked him to make way for another actor.

The now-famous Dustin Hoffman has this advice for a young actor: 'Don't be afraid to be fired. Fuck it! Why be bad? The director wants you to do it a certain way, and either you don't feel that he's right or you feel that he's right but he's forcing you to be a square peg in a round hole. You can't fit in. Quit. Better to be fired than to look bad. It's very hard to get work, but it's a very small community and if you're bad word gets around. It's easy for me to say that now. I never felt I had the choice. I couldn't help it. Unfortunately, there are not a lot of good directors around. There are more good actors. Actors have to learn acting and study it. I'm not sure directors have the same kind of background always. I never understand why they haven't tried acting. Why aren't they closer to what it is to be an actor? It's very easy to tell an actor that it's no good. It's a terrible thing to be told that and then to do what the director says and it feels like shit. I'm not taking it away from directors. They're on a liferaft, where the thing isn't going to float if it doesn't get good notices. "Are you going to be able to do it? Because if you don't do it, they'll replace me." And the actor is going around saying, "I'm going to find this thing. I don't want to fake it. Because it's going to taint it. It's going to screw it up."'

Being fired by two British directors in two British plays did not put Dustin off the British. As will be seen, a British play was to be the making of him. Angry as he was at the directors for failing to appreciate his talents and not understanding what he was driving at, Dustin was angrier with himself for losing jobs. He felt he needed professional help, and entered into analysis that would continue for many years to come. 'I went into analysis because I realised I was a dangerous character – I mean this suicidal, self-destructive instinct I had. It was suicidal trying to put out that fire . . . I couldn't control myself . . . I kept losing jobs.' As the agent in *Tootsie* tells Michael Dorsey/Dustin Hoffman, 'You're a wonderful actor, but you're too much trouble. Get some therapy.'

The analysis helped him work through his anguish and temper his ego to the point that, when he heard of auditions for another play by Ronald Ribman, he felt ready to try for it. But he was almost canned again, this time because the director Larry Arrick thought Dustin was not giving enough of himself at rehearsals. 'Where is the character?' Arrick asked. 'I haven't found him yet,' replied Dustin.

The Journey of the Fifth Horse, partially adapted from a Turgenev short story called *Diary of a Superfluous Man*, was staged by the American Place Theater at St Clement's Church off-Broadway on 21 April 1966. The play portrayed the life and fantasies of Zoditch, a crusty, lonely old publishing clerk (played by Dustin in a high-pitched nasally projected voice), responsible for reading the diary of Chulkaturin, a nineteenth-century Russian landowner who died young. The theme of the drama – that timid people are apt to lead empty lives – must have appealed to Dustin, who was determined to overcome an inherent timidity and lead a fuller existence.

The critics were more enthusiastic about Dustin's performance as the eccentric clerk than about the play, which limped through eleven performances, although it and Dustin won Obie awards – off-Broadway's equivalent of the Tony. Stanley Kauffmann in *The New York Times* thought, 'Dustin Hoffman's performance of Zoditch has the vitality of the born actor and the fine control of the skilful one. With sharp comedy techniques, he makes this unattractive man both funny and pathetic. Mr Hoffman is only in his twenties. Perhaps – the insanities of the theatre world permitting – we will be allowed to watch an extraordinary career develop.'

9

Eh? Dustin Who?

As soon as things are really good, I always have a feeling the rug is about to be pulled out from under me.

IT COULD BE argued that Dustin owes his great fame, in part, to the Lancashire playwright Henry Livings. Having just lost out to Alan Alda in 1966 for the forthcoming Broadway comedy *The Apple Tree*, directed by Mike Nichols, but nonetheless now confirmed as a top off-Broadway character actor, Dustin landed the lead in Livings' *Eh?*, which had had a great success at the Aldwych Theatre, London, in Peter Hall's Royal Shakespeare Company production exactly two years previously. It was the 37-year-old writer's fifth play after *Stop It, Whoever You Are*; *Big Soft Nellie*; *Nil Carborundum* and *Kelly's Eye*, none of them making the voyage across the Atlantic. *Eh?* seemed just as unlikely to find itself transported to America. The title alone would give Americans some trouble. Why did it have a question mark? Eh! meant ugh!, not, as in England, hey? or ay? (In France it was called *Hein?*) There was fear that their indifference to the play might be expressed as 'Eh! Who cares?'

But a few months before its off-Broadway opening, *Eh?* had had its successful American premiere at the Playhouse in the Park in Cincinnati, Ohio, in which 26-year-old Sam Waterston played the lead to the author's supreme satisfaction. However, Livings was not in the USA to see Dustin and a cast which included Dana Elcar, Elizabeth Wilson (who would play Dustin's mother in *The Graduate*) and Carl Gabler when it opened at Circle-In-The-Square at Bleeker Street on 16 October 1966.

Again it was touch and go whether Dustin would be fired before the first night. Theodore Mann, co-founder and producer of Circle-In-The-Square since 1951, had seen Dustin on stage and wanted him badly enough to have dismissed two directors instead of the actor. Melvin Bernhardt, who had directed the show in Cincinnati, was sacked after differences of opinion with Dustin. The conflict with the second director derived from his wanting Dustin to play the role of Valentine Brose just as David Warner had done in the London production. Dustin refused, not only because he had not seen the very different Warner, which the director had, but he justifiably felt he had to find his own direction, even if he had to

47

make a number of detours on the way. (Some years later Dustin would work with Warner on *Straw Dogs*, and they were able to compare notes.)

Enter Alan Arkin. Although Arkin, who had created the role of Harry Berlin in Murray Schisgal's *Luv* in 1964 (in Mike Nichols's production), had directed sketches in revue, he had never directed a legitimate play before. Because of his inexperience and the firing of the two previous directors, he asked to do it under another name, not wanting to take the rap for a flop. So he called himself Roger Short.

Dustin was a jazz enthusiast and found out that Arkin was too. 'So I went up to him. It was the first time we made a connection. And I said, "I know why you picked the name Roger Short, because Shorty Rogers did an album once on a label he wasn't supposed to, and changed his name from Shorty Rogers to Roger Short." [Rogers was to provide the music for Dustin's very first film.] We had the same sense of humour. We had a lot in common and we liked each other and he was one of the best directors I ever had.' Arkin allowed Dustin time to find the character himself. 'There are two kinds of difficult people in the theatre,' Arkin pronounced. 'Those who are passionate about their work, and those who are passionate about themselves. Dustin is passionate about his work.'

In order to try and get a 'Northern English accent', Dustin went to see the Beatles in *A Hard Day's Night* about a dozen times determined to 'sound like those guys'. No matter that his approximation to Liverpudlian was not what Livings had in mind for the character: it made no difference to American audiences who were not well up on the variations of British speech patterns. Actually, Dustin, although masterful in changing the timbre of his voice to suit different parts, only rarely attempts to put on anything other than an American accent.

Henry Livings describes the character of Valentine Brose as 'pale and totally lacking in human fire. He behaves excitedly on occasion, even frenetically, and he wears gaudy cheap clothes with some dash . . . It's as if he were giving a performance of some character he's dreamed up, and his pale eyes wander in search of effect even in his apparently wildest moments.'

The play revolves around Brose, a harebrained nonentity machine-operator, who runs a boiler room of a semi-automated antiseptic dye factory, having taken the job because it was easy work and non-union, and who manages to annoy everybody except his fiancée. He has brought with him some psychedelic mushrooms to grow at work. When his superior comes across the boxes clearly marked 'Mushrooms', Brose replies that this actually means M. U. Shrooms (Mervyn Ulrich Shrooms), seed merchant. By the end, people have 'turned on' and the boiler room blows up.

Eliot Fremont-Smith, normally the book critic of *The New York Times*, wrote that, 'All involved deserve laurels. But because it is essentially Brose's show, the biggest should go to Mr Hoffman, who must be reckoned one of the most agile and subtly controlled comedians around. He carries the show and even if *Eh?* still doesn't sound enticing, he should be seen.'

On the Sunday morning after the opening, Dustin spread out *The New York Times* on the sidewalk, and saw a half-page picture of himself illustrating a long article by Walter Kerr, the most esteemed American critic of the day, then only doing weekend pieces. In glowing terms, Kerr equated Dustin with Buster Keaton. Stunned, Dustin felt it was 'the single greatest moment I had as an actor.' Dustin, who had barely seen Keaton, tried to catch some of his films. Fortunately, it was the period when Keaton was just being rediscovered. (There are some moments in Dustin's films that could be called Keatonesque – the blankness of his face at the beginning of *The Graduate*, some of the comedy in *Little Big Man*, and the office party scene in *Kramer vs Kramer* – without his face ever resembling Keaton's handsome 'stone-face' features.)

British playwright John Arden (he of *Sergeant Musgrave's Dance*) accepted the Obie on Henry Livings's behalf, though, commented Livings, 'In his mild way John hinted I might well not have enjoyed the way it was done in New York, but I never argue with box-office returns.' Livings thought it might have lacked the English music-hall style of comedy he wished to capture. One adverse critic of Dustin's performance was the young and eccentric English actor Victor Henry, who, on seeing Dustin in a bar after the show, emptied a glass of beer over his head. Henry was a great friend of the playwright and decided that Dustin had misread a line. (Tragically, Victor Henry died in 1985 aged 42, his last fourteen years spent in silence after a street accident.)

Dustin never forgot the importance of Henry Livings's play in his career, and many years later, when he was making *Agatha* in England, he sought the modest playwright out and took him to lunch at a smart restaurant. Dustin introduced Livings to his business manager, the London boxing promoter Jarvis Astaire, 'who took me into his offices,' recalled Livings, 'and *en passant* introduced me to a chap standing at a window ledge in a corridor, typing: "This is one of our writers", says he. It seemed a good time to make my excuses and leave, and I did both.'

Almost immediately following the opening of *Eh?*, Dustin was given his first chance to be in pictures. 'I got there at ten a.m. and was done by one p.m. Then I phoned everybody and said, "Well, I just finished my first movie."' *The Tiger Makes Out* was a fleshed-out version of Murray

Schisgal's one-act play, *The Tiger*, about a sexually repressed New York mailman, played by Eli Wallach, who attempts to kidnap a 'sexy swinger' only to end up capturing Anne Jackson (Mrs Wallach), a socially repressed Long Island housewife. Wallach and Jackson repeated their stage roles, while cameos were taken by stars and friends of the writer. Filmed on location in Manhattan, this shoestring Columbia Picture comedy provided a modicum of wacky New York humour. It was released on 19 September 1967, with a nineteenth-billed Dustin Hoffman. As long-haired 'Hap', one of a pair of beatnik lovers, wearing a polo-neck sweater and a raincoat, Dustin's 45-second moment comes when he is seen breaking up with his girlfriend (Mariclare Costello) before she wanders off to be almost grabbed by the preying Wallach. 'It's no good any more, Rosie,' Dustin moans. 'You mope around the house.' 'I'm not going to any more,' she pleads. 'It's just no good, Rosie,' he continues. 'You fill me with guilt.' 'I'm not asking you to marry me,' she insists. 'I'm perfectly content to go on living with you under the original terms. We split all the expenses and live together. What's so terrible about that?' 'What's so terrible?' Dustin protests. 'I'm the one who has to carry the guilt around. I'm the guilty one. Goodbye, Rosie Kriger.'

The film's director, Arthur Hiller, had previously seen Dustin in *Journey of the Fifth Horse*, and 'was bowled over by how convincing and skilful he was playing an elderly man. Needless to say, he showed those special talents again playing a young man in his twenties in our film. Indeed, I remember Murray Schisgal saying to me, "That man will be a major star."'

Dustin and Schisgal had met earlier in August 1966 at the Berkshire Theater Festival in Stockbridge, Massachusetts, where Dustin acted in a number of Schisgal plays – the Old Jew in the play of that name, Max in *Reverberations* (changed later to *The Basement*) and Jax in *Fragments*. (Gene Hackman was to feature in the plays when they got to New York.) It was the start of a beautiful friendship – Schisgal was to become godfather to two of Dustin's children (Jacob and Rebecca) some years hence – and they would also form a long-standing working relationship.

Murray Schisgal was born in Brooklyn in November 1926. After serving in the navy during World War II, he performed as a musician with small jazz groups, practised law for several years, then taught in public and private schools. His career as a playwright began with three one-act plays, *The Typists*, *The Postman* (later changed to *The Tiger*) and *A Simple Kind of Love Story*, which was first produced by expatriate American Charles Marowitz at his tiny Open Space Theatre in London and then off-Broadway. When *Luv* opened at the Booth Theater in 1964 (with Wallach,

Jackson and Arkin), Walter Kerr over-enthusiastically claimed it was better than *Waiting for Godot*.

During the theatre festival, the author liked to take early-morning walks, and every day when he left his hotel Dustin would be waiting for him. 'He'd have the script and a million questions to ask: "What's your thought here? What's your thought there?" I had never worked with an actor like that. He is eternally dissatisfied with what he has achieved.'

While *Eh?* was still running, Dustin signed to star in the low-budget Italian–Spanish *Madigan's Millions* (*El Testamento de Madigan/Un Dollaro per 7 Vigliacchi*) to be shot in Rome from April 1967, for which he would receive $5000. George Raft, originally set to take the non-speaking title role, turned down the offer before shooting, reportedly because of ill health, and was replaced by Cesar Romero, in what was barely a cameo. Dustin played Jason Fister, a bumbling undercover Treasury agent sent to Italy to locate gangster Madigan's ill-gotten millions, thereby becoming embroiled in a series of slapstick mishaps. Amidst the unhilarious mayhem, a bespectacled and wide-eyed Dustin managed to time a few gags well, but became swamped by the strained and desperate elements of the ridiculous plot. The draggy love interest was provided by Elsa Martinelli, who plays Romero's daughter, although Dustin thinks she was his lover.

This schlocky international movie, photographed in eye-straining colour, cashing in (figuratively speaking) on the craze for James Bond pictures, was shot in three languages with a different director credited for each version – Stanley Prager (English), Dan Ash (Italian) and Giorgio Gentil (Spanish). Prager (who died aged 54 in 1972) had been an actor in Fox films in the forties, directed Neil Simon's first Broadway play, *Come Blow Your Horn*, and had helmed the popular TV comedy *Car 54, Where Are You?* Who the other two directors were and whether they were justifiably hiding behind pseudonyms is a matter for conjecture.

Madigan's Millions was held back from release until American International Pictures decided to take advantage of the success of *Midnight Cowboy* by foisting it on to the public in 1969 in a double bill with Jon Voight's early indiscretion, *Fearless Frank*, also made in 1967. Shamelessly, AIP publicised it as 'The Two Most Incredible *New* Comedies Ever Laughed At!' Voight came off the better of the two, because *Fearless Frank* (originally called *Frank's Greatest Adventure*) was the more interesting in being Phil Kaufman's debut as director, and having the author Nelson (*The Man with the Golden Arm*) Algren playing a gangster called Needles. *Variety* commented on *Madigan's Millions* that, 'had it been released earlier, it might have finished him . . . Hoffman plays the part like an Occidental version of Charlie Chan's number one son.'

Dustin then returned to the play in New York, and to the woman he was living with. Dustin had first met nineteen-year-old ballet dancer Anne Byrne in 1963. 'I was playing piano, for free, at the Premise Club in Greenwich Village. She had a date with my roommate and he brought her there. He went to the bathroom and I said, "So, you're a dancer?" and she said "So, you're an actor?" and we both looked at the salt shaker and that's how it started. I said to my friend, I really like that girl. He said, "Tell you what. Give me the week to score. If I don't score I'll turn her over to you." He didn't like to spend more than a week at it. That was the limit of his patience. He didn't score so he turned her over to me.' Presuming, of course, that Anne had no say in the matter.

She was five feet nine inches, some three inches taller than Dustin, who was especially attracted to 'long-legged, intelligent, artistically ambitious women'. Anne certainly fitted the bill. Wanting to impress her, Dustin bought a suit for their first date and, on the second date, they went to the beach. They were dozing happily side by side on the sands, when a jet plane roared overhead, waking them with a start. As if in a corny love story, they found themselves in each other's arms. They both liked it, and began going out together for about a month until he left to do summer stock in Fishkill, NY, and she went to Philadelphia where she was chosen as a principal dancer with the Pennsylvania Ballet. The short romantic idyll was over.

It was revived four years later when they ran into each other again in the unromantic setting of a Greenwich Village laundromat. Her first reaction on seeing the tousle-haired bejeaned actor was that he looked like a slob, but 'I thought he was very sexy.' To the background of chugging washing-machines, Dustin discovered that Anne had been with the ballet company for three years, had married and divorced financier Winfried Schlote, and had a small three-month-old daughter, Karina.

Born in New York City in 1944, Anne, the daughter of a schoolteacher mother and a father who was an assistant librarian in the business section at Columbia University, was raised in Chappaqua, NY, where she attended the Horace Greeley School. She seemed a typical product of her upper-middle-class background in Westchester County. But her desire to be a ballerina was more than just an adolescent fancy and she returned to New York to study at the American School of Ballet. 'It was understood that women dated, went to college and married. My dates used to ask me why I was always hanging out with faggots.'

Her first professional appearance was in Montreal with Les Grands Ballets Canadiens, with whom she stayed for two years before returning home to use her classically trained talents in summer stock productions of

Bye, Bye, Birdie; *Fiorello*; and *Blossom Time*. She also danced with the Frankfurt Ballet and the New Jersey Ballet.

When she and Dustin were reunited in the laundromat, he was beginning to be noticed off-Broadway and she was an established dancer. They began a three-year love affair, but were not to marry until he had enjoyed the full fruits of the fame that was just around the corner.

10

My Son, the Movie Star

Looking back on The Graduate, *I have no sense of achievement.*

WHEN CHARLES WEBB'S novel *The Graduate* was first published in 1963, Lawrence Turman, a 37-year-old independent producer with a couple of films to his name – *The Young Doctors* and *I Could Go On Singing* – read it, liked it and managed to acquire the rights in 1964 for $20,000 from the ingenuous author. The book, written when Webb was only 24, crystallised many of the emotions of sixties youth, something Turman was smart enough to recognise. Having just produced the film of Gore Vidal's political play *The Best Man*, Turman started to consider making the movie from Webb's book. Some of its humour happened to remind him of his friend Mike Nichols, who had just begun making a career directing plays on Broadway with the hit Neil Simon comedy *Barefoot in the Park* and Murray Schisgal's *Luv*. Turman sent a copy of the book to the former comedian for his opinion on its filmic possibilities. The next day, Nichols awakened Turman with an early morning call. 'I like the book. Let's talk,' he stated.

They soon talked and agreed that the shortish novel had the potential to make a good movie. At that stage, Nichols had yet to direct a film. *The Graduate* looked all set to be his first, but Ernest Lehman, who was producing and adapting Edward Albee's acid drama of marital non-bliss, *Who's Afraid of Virginia Woolf?*, persuaded Warner Bros to hire the untried Nichols. It was a baptism of fire for the 35-year-old, who had to control the monstrously sacred couple, Elizabeth Taylor and Richard Burton. After the three less-than-convincing films they had previously made together, *Who's Afraid of Virginia Woolf?* brilliantly restored their credibility as performers, and Nichols's essentially theatrical but competent direction was nominated for an Oscar.

In his satirical cabaret days, Nichols used to do a sketch with Elaine May about a Jewish mother's shock at her son's choice of profession: 'Can you imagine me saying, "There goes my son the nurse"?' Now Nichols's mother could say, 'There goes my son the movie director.'

Born Michael Igor Peschowsky in Berlin in 1931, Nichols arrived in the USA at the age of seven with his family after fleeing the Nazis. When he was twelve, his doctor–father, a Russian-born Jew who had changed his name to Dr Paul Nichols, died of leukaemia, leaving the family financially destitute. A bright and ambitious lad, Mike was able to continue his studies due to scholarships and almost as many odd jobs as Dustin would later have. While at the University of Chicago (where he met Ulu Grosbard), he made his living as a night janitor, hotel desk clerk and delivery truck driver. It was at university that he first began to perform, and he later went to New York to study acting with Lee Strasberg. After some years in theatrical revue and improvisational comedy in the Second City troupe in Chicago, he gained wide fame when he teamed up for a double act with Elaine May from 1957 to 1961, before becoming a successful Broadway director.

Turman, having finished producing the entertaining but flimsy *The Flim Flam Man*, was now ready to embark on *The Graduate* with Nichols as director, and Calder Willingham writing the screenplay. Because the novel is written mainly in dialogue, a spurious impression was given that it would be easy to adapt. But Willingham had delivered an unacceptable script which was then completely reworked by Buck Henry. Nevertheless, the 45-year-old Willingham, co-writer on Stanley Kubrick's *Paths of Glory*, who made his name with his 1947 novel *End as a Man* (filmed as *The Strange One*), was later asked to do the screenplay of *Little Big Man*. Henry (born Buck Henry Zuckerman) who, like Nichols, had been a performer in an improvisational theatre group in Chicago, had written only one film, the offbeat and unsuccessful *The Troublemaker*, three years previously. *The Graduate* would be financed and released by Embassy Pictures, the company Joseph E. Levine had formed in the late fifties to exploit cheap European spectacles such as the *Hercules* films with muscle-man Steve Reeves, which brought in millions of dollars. Levine later went upmarket by helping to finance De Sica's *Two Women* (1961) and Fellini's *8½* (1963), but with Mel Brooks's *The Producers*, and *The Graduate*, he was taking a chance on relatively new film talent.

Casting for *The Graduate* began in late 1966. The role of Elaine Robinson went to the pretty, auburn-haired, hazel-eyed 25-year-old Katharine Ross, an up-and-coming star. She had made four previous films: *Shenandoah* (1965), *The Singing Nun* (1966), *Mr Buddwing* (1966) and *Games* (1967), but only the first of these had any merit. Dustin's buddy, the little-known Gene Hackman, who had appeared briefly in three previous films, was cast as her father, and William Daniels and Elizabeth Wilson were to play Mr and Mrs Braddock, the graduate's parents. Others chosen were Brian Avery, Norman Fell, Elisabeth Fraser, Alice Ghostley and Buck Henry in the small part of the suspicious hotel clerk. ('Are you here for an affair, sir?') Momentarily glimpsed would be nineteen-year-old Richard Dreyfuss appearing in his first movie as a Berkeley student, with one line: 'Shall I get the cops? I'll get the cops!'

For the role of Elaine's mother, known only as Mrs Robinson, the sexy older woman who seduces the young hero, Nichols wanted the semi-retired 48-year-old Susan Hayward. According to her biographers, Robert Laguardia and Gene Arceri, however, Hayward 'wasn't anxious to do with her career what now had to be done: modify her image away from the old-guard glamour to fit the concepts of new directors like Mike Nichols . . . repulsed at the semi-nude hotel-room sex scenes she would have to play, she did not consider it.' It might have revived her career, as it certainly would have done for the 42-year-old Doris Day. It was an inspired idea to offer the part to the 'eternal virgin' of the fifties and early sixties, but Day, nearing the end of her career, turned it down because, 'It offended my sense of values.' Hayward and Day were obviously actresses who still clung to a perception of Hollywood stardom that no longer existed.

The contrasting Jeanne Moreau, once the darling of the then exhausted French *nouvelle vague*, was also considered, but Nichols and his team decided, after some thought, that her European quality might unbalance such an essentially American story. They finally came down on the side of 36-year-old Anne Bancroft, although she had seldom played comedy, having made her name in such powerful dramas as *The Miracle Worker* and *The Pumpkin Eater*. Born Anna Maria Louisa Italiano, the daughter of Italian immigrants, she had two Hollywood careers. The first – from 1952 to 1957 – was so undistinguished that it was difficult for filmgoers to believe that she was the same actress who returned to movies after five years on Broadway.

The main difficulty was in finding the right actor to play the title role of the 21-year-old Benjamin Braddock.

While Dustin was doing eight shows a week in *Eh?*, Mike Nichols and Lawrence Turman, who were still struggling after six months to find their leading man, took in the show one night. They had read the reviews, and they wanted to see this new Buster Keaton for themselves. In fact, Dustin was not unknown to Nichols, who had seen him in *Journey of the Fifth Horse* and had auditioned him for the Broadway musical *The Apple Tree*. After the performance, they felt they might have found someone who could fit the part. Nichols went to see the play a second time, then a call went out to Dustin's agent, and arrangements were made to fly the actor out to his home town for a screen test.

Originally Nichols and Turman were going to cast Benjamin Braddock to type – a tall, sun-bronzed Californian – although the hero is never described in the novel. Nichols got Robert Redford to read the script and take a screen test, but it was agreed that, because most of the story concerns Benjamin's hesitancy with women, Redford was too dishy to be convincing. Redford had previously turned down Nichols's offer to play Nick (eventually taken by George Segal) in *Who's Afraid of Virginia Woolf?* the year before. So Nichols began to think that it might be more interesting to cast against the 'walking surfboard' kind of guy that Dustin had always envied.

But Dustin was racked with doubts about himself and the part. When he was approached, he said, 'I don't think I'm right for the role. He's a kind of Anglo–Saxon, tall, slender, good-looking chap. I'm short and Jewish. I'm getting scripts now, I'm doing better than I've ever done in my life, Kerr says I'm as funny in *Eh?* as Buster Keaton.'

'Believe me, Benjamin is Jewish inside,' replied Nichols persuasively.

Dustin flew to LA in late February 1967 (being replaced by MacIntyre Dixon in *Eh?*) in a state of anxiety and self-doubt. He arrived jet-lagged, tired and jumpy. 'I felt people were nudging each other and pointing at me and saying, "Him, the juvenile lead?" I was sitting in the make-up chair and I felt like the ugliest piece of shit there ever was. I mean, I always felt like that but this time was worse. And Nichols kept saying, "What are we going to do about his nose?" He wanted me to look as good as I could. He'd seen me read. He knew I could act. He wanted me.'

Dustin was one of a long line of candidates being screen-tested in a ten-minute scene with Katharine Ross. Of Dustin, Ross said, 'He looked about three feet tall, so dead serious, so humourless, so unkempt. I thought the screen test was going to be a disaster.' At one point Dustin reached out and grabbed her behind. 'Don't you ever touch me again!' she yelled, rather inauspiciously if they were to be cast as lovers.

'I was so nervous and fatigued that I couldn't concentrate. I blew lines repeatedly and did a terrible job, and I knew I wouldn't get the part.' Dustin was doing so badly that Nichols decided to allow the actor time to learn his lines and then redo the test. When Dustin returned, he fluffed more lines than before. 'I can't figure it,' Nichols sighed. 'You study the lines, and then you're *worse*!' After the screen test, Dustin approached the director. 'Well, you've seen me at my worst.' 'God, I *hope* so!' came the reply. As he dejectedly left the huge shed-like building that housed the sound stage, he slipped and a New York subway token fell out of his pocket. A crew member picked it up. 'Here, kid,' he said. 'You're gonna need this.'

He returned to New York under a cloud of gloom and despair, though relieved in another way. 'I went back to *Eh?* after the screen test and said, "Don't worry about nothin', folks. I'll be here. I ain't getting that job."'

A day or two later, when Dustin was wending his way home over West 11th Street, he bumped into his neighbour Mel Brooks. They had often crossed paths until Dustin decided to introduce himself, having regained his confidence since his put-down by Zero Mostel. Dustin admired Brooks, who had yet to make a movie, for his TV work. Brooks, soon to marry Anne Bancroft, talked about a film he was planning called *The Producers*, for which he wanted Dustin to play the crazy Nazi playwright. When Dustin told Brooks that he was up for the part in *The Graduate*, Mel said, 'But you're an ugly little rat. You're not going to get it.'

It was not long after the test that Nichols called Dustin from Hollywood to say, 'I've seen the rushes. They're not so bad.' Dustin replied, 'I'm not right for the part physically.' 'Yes, there is the nose. But we'll let you know very soon.'

True to his word, Nichols was on the phone to Dustin again to tell him he had got the part. Nichols had seen, beneath Dustin's nervousness, the exact kind of confused, panicky character he wanted. He thought Dustin would understand the sufferings of Ben. 'It didn't seem good when we were making the test. He didn't know his lines terribly well and he was nervous. But it was good on film. It was special – he made us laugh. He had a kind of pole-axed quality with life, but great vitality underneath. On screen he appeared to be simply living his life without pretending.'

'I later saw the screen test,' commented Dustin. 'I was terrible. I always thought I got cast in *The Graduate* because I was one of the last ones to be seen. I mean, Nichols was very pressured. In those days I don't think there was an average looking or homely looking person playing romantic leads. I mean, Alan Arkin had done *The Russians Are Coming* but that wasn't the romantic lead. No other director would have cast me, no other.'

Curiously, Larry Turman told Arthur Hiller that the thing that finally swayed them towards Dustin was his 45-second spot in *The Tiger Makes Out*. Thus can a minuscule particle tip the scales one way or another.

Certainly, Joseph E. Levine would not have considered him. When Nichols brought Dustin along to be introduced to the mogul in his imposing New York office, Levine, after greeting Nichols, turned to Dustin and said, 'The windows are over there.' 'What do you mean?' asked a nervous Dustin, suspecting the producer was suggesting suicide. 'Aren't you here to clean the windows?' Apparently he had mistaken the small man in jeans for the window cleaner he had sent for. It had rained very hard the night before and the windows of the office were extremely dirty. Dustin, realising the error, decided to play along. He just smiled, took a handkerchief out of his pocket and started cleaning them. Nichols, watching this pantomime, quickly explained that this was the guy he had picked for the lead in *The Graduate*. '*Him!*' shrieked Levine. 'You picked *him*?' Then the producer studied the actor more closely. Dustin became the 'incredible shrinking man'. After a long pause, Levine said, 'I'm beginning to see it. Yeah, I see why you picked him!' Yet, Levine, who died in July 1987, aged 81, could not have realised that he was making one of the best investments of his life.

The screenplay of *The Graduate* followed the novel in most of its essentials. Benjamin Braddock, who has just graduated with honours, flies back to his wealthy family in Southern California suburbia. On his first night back, his parents give him a party, to which they invite their circle of middle-class, middle-aged friends. Ben escapes to his room, but he is observed and followed by Mrs Robinson, the wife of his father's partner in a law firm. She asks Ben to drive her home. She explains that her husband is away for the evening and she doesn't want to return to an empty house. Once there, the woman starts to make a play for the young man but, before a seduction can take place, Mr Robinson returns. Ben and Mrs Robinson arrange an assignation a few days later at the swanky Taft Hotel, where, after initial naivety and clumsiness almost make the occasion a farcical disaster, they end up satisfactorily in bed with one another. 'You're the most attractive of my parent's friends,' he confesses to her. They drift into an affair until the Robinsons' daughter, Elaine, returns home from Berkeley. Ben, at his parent's insistence, takes her out. Mrs Robinson warns Ben against seeing Elaine again, but he is now in love with her daughter. When Elaine returns to college, Ben follows her, taking a room there. However, he learns to his anger and dismay that she is to be married. On the day of the marriage, Ben arrives just as the couple are pronounced man and wife, taking the unreluctant Elaine away with him. They jump on a passing bus and head towards a new life.

Charles Webb, the author of the novel, who was not much more than Benjamin's age at the time of writing, had fashioned a different ending. In the book, Benjamin arrived at the church in time to stop the wedding and there was no further 'moral transgression'. Webb was disturbed by the changed ending. In a letter to *The New Republic*, complaining about critic Stanley Kauffman's view of the film's 'moral stance', Webb wrote:

'As a moral person, he [Benjamin] does not disrespect the institution of marriage. In the book the strength of the climax is that his moral attitudes make it necessary for him to reach the girl before she becomes the wife of someone else, which he does. In the film version it makes no difference whether he gets there in time or not. As such, there is little difference between his relationship to Mrs Robinson and his relationship to Elaine, both of them being essentially immoral.'

But Webb's strict ethical judgement that, once the couple had been pronounced man and wife, Benjamin was not entitled to put them asunder, disregards the fact that Benjamin has rescued Elaine from a loveless marriage before it is consummated. In contrast, Mrs Robinson is trapped in an unhappy marriage. 'It's too late,' she screams at her daughter, at which Elaine cries, 'Not for *me*.' More importantly, the ending escapes the cliché in countless films of a marriage being halted in the nick of time although it most resembles the climax of a 1928 Harold Lloyd comedy, *Speedy*.

Nichols claimed unconvincingly that, 'I think Benjamin and Elaine will end up exactly like their parents; that's what I was trying to say in that last scene.' What we see, however, is nothing of the kind. It is a happy but open ending, as the young couple, like most others, face an uncertain future.

Some adverse criticisms of the film's content came from The National Catholic Office for Motion Pictures, which gave the film an A-4 rating for Catholics as 'morally objectionable for adults, with reservations'. Another hostile group was Americans of Italian Descent (AID), which objected to the use of the word 'wop' in the movie. Nothing came of AID's protest, however: the film still contains the word 'wop', although you have to listen very hard for it. Dustin made dubious reparation to the Italian community by playing the slimy Enrico 'Ratso' Rizzo in his next movie, *Midnight Cowboy*, an adulterous Italian bank clerk in *Alfredo Alfredo*, and Vito, a thief of Italian extraction, in *Family Business*.

Just as for a play, Nichols had the luxury of three weeks' rehearsal on *The Graduate* before shooting began on location in Los Angeles, Berkeley and San Francisco. During filming in LA, Harry and Lillian would go down to the set and watch their son perform. (Dustin was not prepared to stay with his parents and had rented an apartment.) When on a shoot at the Taft Hotel, Dustin warned the Hoffmans, who were standing behind the ropes, to keep behind the barrier and also, knowing of his father's blighted ambitions to be a director, not to say anything. Nevertheless, after the day's filming, Harry introduced himself to Nichols. 'How do you do, I'm Dusty's father.' He then went on to congratulate Nichols on the job he was doing. 'That's a good shot you got there, but, you know, on the next one, I'd shoot it like this . . .' Needless to say, Nichols was unappreciative of the advice.

It rained on days when they needed sun and it blazed when Nichols wanted a rain sequence. Dustin had to drive a convertible in the pouring rain on a sunny day, rain being supplied by a water-spray truck driving along behind. Benjamin's parent's home was created by Richard Sylbert on a sound stage, but the underwater sequences, which Dustin practised for a week, were shot in a real outside pool with a glass wall for photographic purposes. For the opening party, Nichols and Turman rounded up some of Hollywood's partygoers.

Given Nichols's theatrical background it is not surprising that some of the best things in the film came out of improvisation. 'He makes you feel kind of like a kite. He lets you go ahead, and you do your thing. And then when you're finished he pulls you in by the string. But at least you've had the enjoyment of the wind. It was Mike Nichols's point of view that you should always be close to yourself in the most personal way to convey not only truth but humour. Real humour perhaps is the purest truth when it works.'

For the scene when Benjamin is trying to get a room key, Nichols suggested that Dustin find in his life what was the most painful thing for him to do that had a sexual connotation, in a public way. For some reason. Dustin could never go to a chemist and ask for condoms, although he had no difficulty in buying women's contraceptives. 'Although I had not had a sexual experience when I was at high school, I thought I should be ready, if and when it came, and so I thought I should stock up. I would always plan on a day when I felt brave and I would walk into the drugstore and see who was behind the counter. This was very important – if it was a woman I would walk right out again – I wanted someone young – a kind of "big brother" image. I would ask for some Kleenex, some razor blades and I would get to that word and I couldn't do it.' So when he rehearsed the scene he based it on his experience at the chemist's, an example of his always having to make contact with a real, lived emotion.

'Everyone seemed to think Benjamin was a virgin, but I never thought of him as that, but that it was the first time he was making love to a woman who was old enough to be his mother, and who was his mother's friend.'

The fact that Dustin was only six years younger than Bancroft never seemed to bother anyone. 'Actually, it wasn't hard for me to play a man ten years my junior, because I was not only physically younger but I've always been emotionally immature.' The respected Broadway actress Elizabeth Wilson, who was playing his mother, was twelve years his senior. They lived in the same apartment block and often dined together, creating unfounded rumours that they were having an affair. In fact, they had already become good friends when she had played Mrs Murray in *Eh?* with him at Circle-In-The-Square, and she had also been in *The Tiger Makes Out*.

During the third week of rehearsal, Gene Hackman was fired and replaced by the extremely different Murray Hamilton. 'We were urinating together, and Gene looked at me and said, "I think I'm going to get fired today."'

'That was a painful experience . . . I think it was my fault,' said Gene. 'I just wasn't capable then of giving the director what he wanted.'

Ironically, the sacking proved to be the turning point in Hackman's career. A week later, Warren Beatty grabbed him for the role of Clyde's brother Buck in *Bonnie and Clyde*, for which he would gain an Oscar nomination. Beatty remembered him from three years before, when Hackman had a small but impressive scene in *Lilith*, Robert Rossen's final film, which starred Beatty.

After Hackman's departure, Dustin felt even more insecure, remembering that he had himself been fired a few times for not satisfying the director. Dustin never had the feeling that Nichols was pleased with his performance. Once the director took Dustin aside and said, 'This is the only day we're ever going to shoot this scene and, no matter how exhausted or lousy you feel, I want you to remember that what you give me is going to be on celluloid for people to see for ever and ever. I know you're tired, but when you go to see this film, if you don't like your work in this scene, just remember always that this was the day you screwed up.' A somewhat sadistic variation on Warner Baxter's famous speech to Ruby Keeler in *42nd Street*: 'You're going out there a youngster, but you've got to come back a star.'

Whereas on *Who's Afraid of Virginia Woolf?* the first-time director had been constricted by the wishes of the starry couple and the confines of the Albee play, Nichols now had far more power to exercise. He used it more on the unknown Hoffman than on the others.

'I hated making that film. I thought, if this is what movies are like in Hollywood, I never want to make another one. I never felt so inadequate. If there is any victory in this film it's not mine. It has nothing to do with me. The film belongs to Mike Nichols. At the beginning everyone said it would get better as filming progressed. It got worse. Nichols knew every colour, texture and nuance he wanted and worked like hell to get it. Of course I resented it.'

It is difficult to tell how much of Dustin's discomfiture during the making of the film seeped through into his portrayal, but it might have added something uneasy to the character of Benjamin.

'All through *The Graduate* Nichols thought he'd made a mistake in casting me. I wasn't allowed to see the rushes. No one was. You're no judge of your own work. If you can't look at the rushes, you come in every day wondering. They look at you and you know they've seen the work the day before. I asked Ulu Grosbard, who knew Nichols, to ask him what he felt about me: "I think he feels he has made a mistake. I can feel it." Grosbard told me, "You're not paranoid. Nichols does feel he has made a mistake."' This was hardly reassuring.

Lawrence Turman, years later, admitted that when there were screenings at his house people would come up to him and say, 'It's a shame. You have a great movie here if only you hadn't miscast the lead.'

As it turned out, it was Dustin's performance that was the film's greatest coup.

11

'Movies Aren't Made For Tuxedos'

I'd wake up in the morning and find a line of girls outside my front door.

AFTER *THE GRADUATE* finished shooting, Dustin returned to New York to live quietly with Anne and her daughter Karina in his small Greenwich Village apartment on West 11th Street, having absolutely no conception of how his performance or the film would be received and not fully realising that the long days of anonymity would soon be over for ever. Because the $17,000 Dustin received for the picture was not enough to ensure any real security for himself, let alone Anne and the child, he was still not prepared to get married. In fact, when all his debts were paid off, the money was quickly spent and he soon found himself waiting to collect his $55 a week on the unemployment line at 75 East 13th Street, where he happened to be caught by an eagle-eyed *Life* photographer before the film's release. As for work, he had auditioned for the role of the Dauphin in Anouilh's *The Lark* at the Lincoln Center, but he did not get the part. It seemed that nothing had changed. One day, in Times Square, Dustin looked up and saw his face for the first time on a billboard. 'I looked up and saw this person – I didn't think of it as *me*. My first thought was, "That person up there is more successful than me. He's working, and I'm not."'

During the promotion of *The Graduate*, Anne and Dustin had visited Hollywood, and she made the rounds of studios and talk shows with him. 'I was intimidated by the extravagance,' said Anne, who had never even contemplated the possibility of Dustin's becoming a movie star, an occupation she then professed to despise. 'Everyone had their own hairdresser and make-up artist. As a dancer, I was used to making $125 a week. We had to wash our own hair and mend our own clothes. I was sure that everyone in Hollywood knew I had holes in my shoes and my underwear. I felt like Plain Jane, and Dustin felt they had made a mistake in choosing him for the film in the first place. We were both nervous wrecks and we started fighting with each other.'

The first inkling Dustin had of the film's effect on audiences was when it was previewed before the general public. It was in a cinema on 86th Street where he sat in the balcony, wearing an old sports jacket and open-necked shirt. He was recognised by only a few, including columnist Sheilah

Graham. She wrote that he went into the theatre as an 'unknown boy beatnik', and came out 'mobbed by the crowd'. Miss Graham, who was taught fiction by F. Scott Fitzgerald, got it wrong. Dustin was neither a boy nor a beatnik, nor was he mobbed.

'It was the first time I'd ever seen myself on screen. And the audience really went with it. There were laughs and cheers at the end when the character I was playing is running to the church. Then a few days later we had opening night, and I was in my first tuxedo. It was rented. I never returned it either. And the women were in their formals and they all sat down and there was not a laugh in the entire show. And all the openings nights since then have been the same. Movies aren't made for tuxedos.'

But it did not matter one iota what the stuffed shirts, or even that first audience of regular people, thought. It was the critics that counted. Never before had Dustin been so exposed or felt such trepidation while awaiting their verdict on him.

As if realising that these were the last days of his anonymity, he took to walking the New York streets at night, staring into people's faces. He got some kind of perverse pleasure out of this, thinking at the back of his mind that when *The Graduate* opened in the movie houses around Manhattan, the face would be seen magnified on a big screen and imprinted on audiences' minds.

In March 1812, the 24-year-old Lord Byron woke up the morning after the publication of his poem *Childe Harold's Pilgrimage* to find himself famous. The rather un-Byronic 30-year-old Dustin Hoffman must have had a similar experience on the morning of 22 December 1967 when he opened the newspapers.

'An amazing new young star', wrote the veteran Bosley Crowther in his final review for *The New York Times*. 'He gets a wonderfully compassionate sense of the ironic and pathetic immaturity of a mere baccalaureate scholar turned loose in an immature society.'

'He is the best American comedian since Jack Lemmon,' raved *New Republic*. The *New York Daily News* proclaimed Dustin a new star but stated, 'He is rather plain-looking, resembling both Sonny and Cher,' and, missing the point entirely, 'In addition, he'll never threaten Rock Hudson's image.' More perceptively, Lloyd Shearer in *Parade* wrote, 'With his short stature, hook nose, beady eyes, unkempt hair, he looks like a loser, and it is precisely because of that loser image that the younger generation have made him their winner.' There is actually nothing 'unkempt' about the squeaky-clean Benjamin in the movie. So 'kempt' is he, in fact, that he is thought to be a guest at a formal reception held at the

Taft Hotel on his first visit. *The New Yorker* thought *The Graduate* merited 26 pages, and it provided a springboard for endless discussions about modern youth.

Whatever the views of the predominantly middle-aged critics had been – and they were mostly favourable – audiences in their teens and early twenties would still have found the film out and responded to it. From the opening, during the cold New York winter of 1967, the queues extending round the block outside Manhattan cinemas consisted mostly of young people hugging themselves and each other, and stamping their feet to keep warm, full of the expectation of seeing a movie that addressed them and their problems. Audiences grew when older people went to see what was attracting these young, mostly middle-class, college kids.

It is significant that, at the height of the student protests in America, Benjamin neither joins nor identifies with the draft dodgers, hippies or Yippies (the movement started by another more radical Hoffmann, Abbie). Why didn't Benjamin demonstrate against the Vietnam War instead of just lying around in his parents' swimming pool? For all his seeming rebellion against middle-class values, he remains essentially middle-class. He is just a confused young man going through a postgraduate crisis; a rebel without claws.

Richard Corliss in *Time* magazine recognised that, 'The most reactionary middle-American could sit back comfortably and think that, if marrying a pretty girl is all my subversive son wants, maybe the kid isn't so bad after all.' Pauline Kael in *The New Yorker* felt that if Ben, who had nothing to communicate, had 'said anything or had any ideas, the audience would probably hate him . . . It's almost painful to tell kids who have gone to see *The Graduate* eight times that once was enough for you because you've already seen it eighty times with Charles Ray and Robert Harron and Richard Barthlemess and Richard Cromwell and Charles Farrell . . . What's interesting about the success of *The Graduate* is sociological: the revelation of how emotionally accessible modern youth is to the same old manipulation.'

Only in a Hollywood context could the film be called daring in its sexual attitudes and moral position. The older woman is the villainess of the piece and true love triumphs in the end. Compared with the anarchy of *Bonnie and Clyde* of the same year, *The Graduate* was rather cosy.

Six years after the film's first run, Andrew Sarris in the *Village Voice* of December 1973 took another look at it. 'Nichols and his writers wanted it both ways. They wanted Benjamin to be fuzzy enough as a fantasy figure so that everyone in America could identify with him without joining the Movement. On the other hand the Movement itself is placated by incidental jabs at square right-wing America, an easy target for Dustin Hoffman's off-Broadway theatre timing. Without putting down the West Coast loonies in so many specific words, Hoffman seemed to be putting them on with his canny deadpan expressions. They scrupulously avoid jabs at hippies, junkies, minorities, militants and any other sacred cows of the Counter Culture. With nothing but *The Graduate* to go on, one would think, for example, that Berkeley was ideologically indistinguishable from Pasadena and that California was one vast, overflowing, suburban swimming pool. . . . Some movies age and some movies date. I would hazard the guess that *The Graduate* belongs in the second category.'

With the deradicalising of students in the Reagan years, Sarris's criticisms seem less relevant, and the film is less dated now than those made at the same time or a little later that *did* reflect the Counter Culture, such as *Alice's Restaurant, The Strawberry Statement, Getting Straight* and *Zabriskie Point*. Nearly a quarter of a century on, the philosophy of *The Graduate* now seems as touchingly ingenuous as its hero, but the situations are still delightfully humorous in the best traditions of romantic comedy, tinged with a certain sadness. The seduction scenes are beautifully timed by Dustin and a super-cool Bancroft, but they have enough ambivalence to suggest his guilt and her loneliness, and the emptiness that brings them together. It is also rather moving today to see Dustin easily managing, with some help from adept make-up, to look far younger than his years, at the dawn of stardom.

The director plunges into the movie immediately with a huge close-up of the unknown Hoffman, as if to say, 'This is the new face of the movies. Look at it. Get used to it. This face belongs to a great movie star, although you don't know it yet. It will be around for a long time. Future movie stars will resemble him more than those you have been used to.' Dustin's face stares wide-eyed, unblinking, unemotionally ahead of him while on the soundtrack Simon and Garfunkel's 'Sounds of Silence' takes up the theme: 'People talking without speaking. People hearing without listening.' The use of songs, including 'Mrs Robinson' and the irrelevant 'Scarborough Fair', instead of the usual music score, added to the film's attraction for young people, and started a never-ending and much-abused spate of movies which are virtual illustrations to albums of pop songs. (Simon and Garfunkel were used as models for the untalented couple of nerds played by Dustin and Warren Beatty in *Ishtar* twenty years later.)

Although Dustin as the glum insecure centre of the film is amusing – looking rather like Eddie Cantor on tranquillisers – he is directed to within an inch of his life. Only rarely does one feel Dustin's personality breaking through the rigid mask Nichols has constructed for him. The face is continually seen hiding behind dark glasses, underwater goggles, and through a goldfish bowl, cutting himself off from those around him.

Mike Nichols stated that one of his ambitions behind the movie was 'to stop the Los Angelesisation of America', although it only added to the Los Angelesisation of American movies. Yet, the unambitious satiric intentions are fulfilled, the most successful sequences coming in the first fifteen minutes. The most widely remembered is the pithy and witty exchange that plays on Ben's alienation from the materialistic world of his parents and their friends. 'Ben.' 'Mr McGuire.' 'Ben.' 'Mr McGuire.' 'I just want to say one word to you.' 'Yes sir?' 'Are you listening?' 'Yes, I am.' 'Plastics. Think about it. There's a great future in plastics.'

The most telling symbol of the young man's alienation, which Nichols lightens and makes funny, is Benjamin standing awkwardly in the rubber underwater suit his father has bought him. A subjective camera, filming through goggles, picks out the inane faces and soundless mouths of his elders as he descends to the bottom of the pool where he stands silently and alone, away from the pestering people above. Skilful and creative editing enables Nichols to show a time-passing sequence as Benjamin moves smoothly from his bed to Mrs Robinson's, from stretching out on a raft in the pool to stretching out on top of her.

Unlike his hero and Dustin, Charles Webb and his wife Eva (nicknamed Fred), protested against the Vietnam War and rebelled against their affluent background. Webb's father was a wealthy LA doctor who was outraged by the novel, which he considered mocked his lifestyle. Who was the model for Mrs Robinson? 'That bit was not autobiographical, but a lot of the rest was based upon my own experiences,' Webb stated. Absent from the screenplay was an exchange between Benjamin and his father in which the former expresses his desire to live among 'ordinary people who don't have big houses. Who don't have swimming pools.' The film was made some months before the establishment of the Gay Liberation Front, and the passage in the novel where Ben describes his adventures on the road to shock his dad was omitted from the screenplay. 'What kind of people stopped to give you rides?' 'Queers.' 'What?' 'Queers usually stopped,' Ben says. 'I averaged about five queers a day. One queer I had to slug in the face and jump out of his car.'

Webb had sold the film rights for only $20,000, but the movie made his book a bestseller and, over the next fifteen years, five more novels brought him $150,000. But Charles and Fred were flower children who never wilted. Sickened by the sterile goals of the middle-class life into which they were born, they gave up everything and took off in a mobile home, fighting to be entitled to educate their two sons themselves.

'Fred and I were never interested in money,' the writer explained. They twice tried owning houses but found it too expensive so they gave them away, and Charles refused to accept any of his estranged father's estate. When money became scarce, he tried to go on welfare, but the woman official said, 'What's your problem, Mr Webb? You're a famous author – the writer of *The Graduate*, for goodness sake, a book I love – how can you possibly be broke?' So, for many years, the couple made their living as hired help, and were doing so at the time of the film's success.

On 19 February 1968, the nominations for the Academy Awards were announced. *The Graduate* was up for Best Picture, Best Director, Best Actor, Best Actress (Bancroft), Best Supporting Actress (Ross), Best Screenplay (based on material from another medium), and Best Cinematography (Robert Surtees). Dustin commented: 'I hope to God I don't win an Oscar tomorrow night. It would really depress me if I did. I really don't deserve it. It wasn't that important a part anyhow.'

The Oscar ceremony on 10 April was held under unusually sombre circumstances. The assassination of Martin Luther King six days before, only one of a tragic series in recent American history, had caused the event to be postponed for two days. The funeral had in fact been held only the day before. For the same reason, the annual post-Oscar ball sponsored by Pat Brown, the Governor of California, was cancelled altogether. Oscar night did not seem particularly relevant to those uncertain days of vague social unease, political upheaval and, of course, the Vietnam War rumbling away inconclusively on the other side of the globe, yet brought home with a vengeance to the American people on nightly TV news broadcasts; and accordingly the attendant razzmatazz of the movie industry's Night of Nights was reduced to what was considered a decent minimum.

Despite his later expressed views about the distastefulness of holding the ceremony so close to the death of the Reverend King, and his saying that 'movies aren't made for tuxedos', Dustin, in hired white tie and tails, was there to present the best cinematography award with Katharine Ross. He retained his liberal credentials by escorting Mary Abigail McCarthy, the daughter of the anti-war Senator Eugene McCarthy, to the shindig, despite being warned by the Hollywood imagemakers not to ruin his box-office potential. (Anne was in New York with Karina.) McCarthy's bid to become the Democratic nominee for president was getting up steam, and his following included the liberal Hollywood establishment, among them Paul Newman, Joanne Woodward, Robert Redford and Warren Beatty. On the other hand, John Wayne was enthusiastically campaigning for George Wallace, the segregationist governor of Alabama. 'The Duke' had sent Wallace three $10,000 cheques, the last one inscribed 'Sock it to 'em, George!' It was the time when many stars started to come out of the political closet and openly voiced their support for one candidate or another. This was nothing new, as movie stars had supported John F. Kennedy when he ran for the White House. Nor is it very daring in the monolithic two-party system of the USA, where the narrow choice is between two rich, conservative (in a wide sense) white men, to offer allegiance to one or the other.

Bob Hope, the master of ceremonies for the umpteenth time, unfunnily and inaccurately joked about Dustin's youthfulness, saying, 'They nominated a kid like Dustin Hoffman – he made a picture he can't get in to see.'

The winners were *In the Heat of the Night* and Rod Steiger for his performance in it, Katharine Hepburn (*Guess Who's Coming to Dinner?*), George Kennedy (*Cool Hand Luke*) and Estelle Parsons (*Bonnie and Clyde*). Mike Nichols grabbed the film's sole award as Best Director (he was also similarly awarded by the New York Film Critics and the Golden Globe). Among the Best Actor losers, Dustin was in the prestigious company of Paul Newman (*Cool Hand Luke*), Warren Beatty (*Bonnie and Clyde*). Spencer Tracy, who was also nominated, for *Guess Who's Coming to Dinner?*, had died the year before.

After the ceremony, at around one in the morning, Dustin rang his friend, actor Stanley Beck (who would later appear in *John and Mary* and *Lenny*, and co-produce *Straight Time*), telling him he had nowhere to stay the night. Dustin asked if he could sleep at Beck's apartment, and if he would come and pick him up at the hall. Beck, who had been woken up by the Oscar-nominee, offered him a bed in the living room but told him to take a cab over. As Beck recalled, 'He came, he slept, he left without making the bed and I never saw him.'

Dustin's parents were thrilled by the reception and the money the film was making. After years of subsidising their son, they were enjoying his fame. 'I never earned more than $3000 a year before I was thirty-one. If my parents hadn't sent me money every week, I couldn't have survived.' Harry and Lillian subscribed to the movie trade papers and began tracing the film's grosses as it climbed upward towards an eventual $40 million. Harry would often call his son in New York to tell him how much money the film was making in various cities, while Lillian phoned local LA cinemas to see how long the ticket queues were.

Dustin seemed to behave towards fame with a certain cynicism, rather like Ben Braddock at the party thrown for him by his parents to celebrate his graduation. But he was, in Alexander Pope's words, 'nor yet a fool to fame'.

There were disadvantages he had to get used to. He found that the plastic namebar on his mailbox kept being pinched by fans, so he bought a hand label machine to replace it daily. He also read all his fan mail each evening, and answered all of the letters, by hand, except the cranky ones. One was a brief note from a girl in Duluth who wrote: 'Please come and share Passover with me and my family. P.S. If you're not Jewish tear this up.'

Only a day or two after *The Graduate* opened, someone came up to him in the street and said, 'You know something? You look just like Dustin Hoffman!' It was just a step away from the immediate public recognition that he had to learn to live with. 'If I passed a group of people on the street, I could usually count three before I heard it – "Eeeeee!" Wham! All of a sudden you're on everyone's brain. You're offered everything. A clothing company (Petrocelli Suits) want to give me $2000 in clothes. Me, a stump of a man and they wanted to make me Cesar Romero. I said no . . . My biggest pitfall would be to grab the fat movie contracts, do commercials and go on talk shows and be a pompous ass who pretends he knows everything about sex, religion, philosophy, you name it.'

It was obvious that Anne had adjustments to make in accommodating his success in her life. She had since left the New York City Ballet, and was working as a counsellor for the blind at both the Lighthouse and the Jewish Guild. 'The enormity [*sic*] of it scared us both. I wasn't ready for people to shove me aside. I was terrified I'd lose him to a starlet.' Her fears were justified and, initially, Dustin's relationship with Anne did suffer. They therefore decided to break up for a while because, Dustin said, 'I wanted my fling. I discovered that being a celebrity meant I had acquired power over women.'

As well as being a revenge on others and on mortality, fame is equally an aphrodisiac, not only for the possessor of it, but for those in contact with it. The fact that many more men resembled Dustin than ever resembled film stars like Cary Grant or Gary Cooper was irrelevant. The cities of America were full of Dustin Hoffmans – just as every young woman seemed to bear a likeness to Barbra Streisand around the same time.

In May 1968, a young man registered at the Las Vegas Sahara Hotel under the name of Dustin Hoffman. He was given VIP treatment and was besieged by the media. He told the press that he attributed his sudden success in the movies to his parents for their unwavering support throughout the years. The interviews were already published when it was discovered that he was an impostor. His real name was Harvey Pepper, a 23-year-old native of Montreal, who was a dead ringer for Dustin. Pepper explained in an interview, 'When I came to the hotel I was sort of looking for work. Then everybody said they saw *The Graduate* and I said I was Dustin Hoffman. So I let them think it and played the game.' He was arrested and spent twelve hours in Clark County jail. His sentence was terminated when Sahara officials bailed him out and said they would pick up the tab for the room but he would have to pay for his food and drink himself. Perhaps, when people have expressed negative views of Dustin's behaviour and personality, we can charitably assume that his *Döppel-gänger*, Harvey Pepper, has been at work again.

A few years later, a homosexual friend of Anne's said that he had come across a man who looked like Dustin, who hung out in gay bars, telling everyone he was Dustin Hoffman.

Meanwhile the real Dustin Hoffman was waiting for a role to prove that he would have a post-*Graduate* career.

12

Dustbin Hoffman

Some people are waiting to see me fall on my ass.

F. SCOTT FITZGERALD, in the notes to his Hollywood novel, *The Last Tycoon*, wrote, 'There are no second acts in American lives.' Dustin was determined to prove that he was no seven-day wonder whose promise would remain unfulfilled: the history of American culture is already littered with enough of these. Although he now had the potential earning power of any major movie star, he nevertheless remained on unemployment benefit while waiting for his agent to find the right new vehicle for him. Not that he was short of offers, but most of them, before the banal fashion for numbered sequels, were on the lines of *After the Graduate, Another Graduate, Shadow of the Graduate, The Graduate Comes Home* and *Song of the Graduate*, leading inevitably to *Son of the Graduate*. Unsurprisingly, there was talk that Dustin was being considered for the title role of *Portnoy's Complaint*, the film version of Philip Roth's novel of a Jewish mother-dominated boy with masturbation problems. The joke around at the time was that it would be filmed with a hand-held camera. (It took another four years before it limply reached the screen with Richard Benjamin.)

Instead, after the first flaring of fame had died down to a steady glow, and he had enjoyed the sexual fruits that it offered, he stayed in his two-room West 11th Street apartment, together with Anne and Karina again, dressed in the faded jeans and threadbare leather jackets he had always worn.

Every time Dustin saw his name in block letters on the marquee of a movie house, he was assailed with thoughts of his own mortality, a subject that constantly obsessed him, especially as he had already seen into the abyss. 'It was like death – with my children already grown up, tired of watching my movies at my own request, with my ex-wife at my side and my faithful dog.'

Dustin seemed to need his shrink sessions more than ever. He had first gone to a psychotherapist because he felt he was a failure, and now he was going to help him cope with success. All actors should be so lucky! He went five times a week at $200 a session. 'I find analysis essential to get me through the day. It helps to break down tension and get everything into proper perspective,' he explained later. 'It also helps me to make the right decisions . . . When I'm working, I'm very hard to live with. I don't drink and it's very difficult to shut out the stresses of the day. I work hard, it's sheer panic.'

While his mind was being massaged on the couch, he continued to keep his body in good shape by working out strenuously every morning. As could be seen in *The Graduate*, Dustin had a compact and well-built body. He may not have been too keen on his height or his face, but he was proud of his physique. He also took ballet lessons to improve his posture and bal-ance, and singing lessons to aid his breath control with a view to being called upon to star in a musical. He knew that the more strings an actor had to his bow, the wider the possibilities there were open to him. He would soon use these newly acquired talents in the play *Jimmy Shine*, but the only time in which he has attempted to sing on film were in his two biggest turkeys – *Who Is Harry Kellerman and Why Is He Saying Those Terrible Things About Me?* and *Ishtar*. If in the latter one could not tell whether his voice was as bad as it was supposed to be, the former gave ample proof. (As the autistic Raymond/Rain Man, he also manages a few unharmonious bars.) However, neither a good physique, nor ballet or singing skills, would be particularly evident or useful in his next film role.

As far back as August 1965, when James Leo Herlihy's novel *Midnight Cowboy* was first published, it had done the rounds of every major studio, all of which turned it down. UA reported, with a certain amount of acuity, that the action 'goes steadily downhill'. In October 1966, however, one year after the decision not to take up the option on the book, David V. Picker at UA bought the movie rights. It took another two years before Picker offered it to English director John Schlesinger.

The former actor and TV documentary director had made his feature film debut with *A Kind of Loving* (1962) followed by *Billy Liar* (1963), two modest pictures set in accurate British working-class surroundings, which introduced fresh, young players such as Alan Bates, Tom Courtenay and Julie Christie. As the 'kitchen sink' was replaced by 'Swinging London', Schlesinger moved into the upper echelons with *Darling* (1965), an attempt at a cynical morality tale about the society its director and writer (Frederic Raphael) seemed to relish. It gained three Oscars (Julie Christie, Raphael and the costume designer Julie Harris) and brought Schlesinger a nomination. Although *Far from the Madding Crowd* (1967), which seldom got beyond being a plodding, picturesque illustration of Thomas Hardy's novel, failed to make an impact in the USA, Picker somehow had confi-dence that the cultured, softly-spoken, bald 42-year-old Englishman would be able to make a good job of the essentially New York story of *Midnight Cowboy*. 'I thought I could do it as an outsider, as an Englishman coming in,' Schlesinger claimed.

Schlesinger's agent tried to dissuade him from taking it on, advising him rather to direct Jack Lemmon in *The April Fools*. This put him in a quandary. He was anxious to make the right choice with his first American movie, and Lemmon was his favourite actor. 'I'd had a flop, which unnerved me a bit. You're expected to have smash hits all the time in America. Frankly, that old adage about only being as good as your last picture was totally the attitude, I'm afraid. I half-believed things people were saying and yet I also knew that *Midnight Cowboy* was a damn good project.' (Schlesinger had made the right decision, because *The April Fools*, finally directed by Stuart Rosenberg, was a real failure.)

Waldo Salt, who wrote the completed screenplay of *Midnight Cowboy*, had been blacklisted in 1951 after refusing to testify on Communist affiliations before the HUAC. His best writing credits were the sentimental *Shopworn Angel* (1938), the romantic comedy–drama *Rachel and the Stranger* (1948), and the tongue-in-the-cheek Burt Lancaster swashbuckler *The Flame and the Arrow* (1950). It was not until the early sixties that he was able to resume his film career, but his post-blacklist work had been undistinguished by two top-heavy Yul Brynner spectacles, *Taras Bulba* (1962) and *Flight from Ashiya* (1964). *Midnight Cowboy* was to give him his first chance in over fifteen years to regain respect in the business.

The screenplay focuses on the incongruous and interdependent friendship between a dimwitted stud and a petty con man. Joe Buck, a handsome hick from Texas, comes to New York dressed in leather cowboy gear, hoping to make a living by servicing wealthy Park Avenue ladies. However, he is reduced to sleazy encounters with both men and women in 42nd Street grindhouses and hotels. His only friend is the tubercular and crippled Ratso Rizzo, who dreams of getting to the sunshine of Florida one day. Joe steals two bus tickets to Miami, but Ratso dies just as they reach the place of his dreams.

Dustin was the first actor to receive the script, and he immediately accepted the role of the miserable gammy-legged sleazeball Rizzo, against the advice of friends and agents. They did not consider it good for his image. An image is to the movie star, as distinct from an actor, what a brand name and logo are to merchandise. One film had already given the industry the right to talk about Dustin's image, which they defined as a slightly anti-Establishment romantic young man. There was also still a feeling in the Hollywood colony that as he had established himself as a star he should not play an unattractive character, and, what is more, he would only be the second lead and not appear for the first twenty minutes. (He was to keep audiences waiting almost the same period in *Rain Man* many years hence.) But to Dustin's credit he recognised it as a role in which he could immediately dissociate himself from the whole 'image' concept of acting, as well as prove that, 'I was a character actor, not just this nebbish kid that Nichols found. People have me in a little pocket of their minds in that role [Ben Braddock] and they don't want to see me get out of it.' The magazine *Harvard Lampoon*, in fact, presented Dustin with The Wilde Oscar: 'to that performer who has been willing to flout convention and risk worldly reputation in order to pursue artistic fulfilment'. Andrew Sarris accepted that, 'By following up the glamorous *Graduate* with the dreggiest drop-out imaginable, Dustin Hoffman has achieved his aim of not becoming the Andy Hardy of the sixties and seventies.'

The producer Jerome Hellman had seen Dustin in *Eh?* and had thought of him for the part way back then. Schlesinger first thought him wrong for Ratso, but changed his mind when they met in New York. After spending some time in an all-night diner on 42nd Street, a calculatedly unshaven Dustin just melted into the atmosphere.

'Dustin made extraordinary sense the first time he ever read the script. He also seemed to have the right physical image to play Ratso. Jerry Hellman felt the same. Now I can't imagine anyone else playing Ratso,' said Schlesinger.

'It was not so much of a stretch for me to do that role as people might think,' Dustin explained. 'It was a character that I felt to be a very basic part of me and when I read it I had that immediate connection with him. I had for many years had this feeling about myself – that I looked like that – not literally, but in an inner way I felt I did. I felt a combination of unattractive and anonymous and I felt that the way to play that part was to forget about what he was and to think about what he wanted. I feel that we are all partly Ratso and partly J. F. Kennedy if you like – a most successful, attractive person. It always strikes me when you see meths drinkers and imagine those people as children – they were all beautiful then, and it is simply an inexplicable phenomenon which makes me sit here and that other person is out there on the street. Much of it has very little to do with what you are, and that is an emotion I have always felt and will always feel. I'd always been fascinated by the people who live on the skid rows of our cities – the ones we regard as the scum of the earth. They're really no different from us . . . only their circumstances. I wanted to get inside one of the those people.'

Typical of the kind of pain Dustin would put himself through, in order to get 'inside' a character, was the way in which he developed Ratso's limp by placing stones in one shoe and then walking on them for a day. He remained unshaven for days and wore brown and rotting snap-on teeth. He also spent a great deal of time strolling around New York's back streets observing down-and-outs to see if he could steal anything from them – for the role, that is. Fortunately, his fame had not yet reached the gutters so the winos were not aware that they were providing material for a movie star's performance.

In order to seep up the fetid atmosphere of the New York streets, a hidden camera was used to track Dustin's peregrinations. At one moment, a taxi cab almost hit him as he was crossing the street. Remaining in the character of Ratso, Dustin yelled to the driver, 'I'm walkin' here! I'm walkin' here!' It was kept for the finished film. Dustin has always believed that some of the cinema's best moments have come out of improvisation. One of his favourite instances is the scene in *On the Waterfront* when Brando, thinking he was between takes, idly tried on the glove that Eva Marie Saint had dropped. Elia Kazan kept the cameras rolling and caught it for posterity.

Four actors were initially tested for the lead role of Joe Buck, among whom Michael Sarrazin was first choice. The gangling, boyish 28-year-old Canadian actor had made some impression as an innocent in *The Flim Flam Man* (1967) and as a Malibu beach bum in *The Sweet Ride* (1968), and seemed to have promise. But he was under exclusive contract to Universal, and they wanted a prohibitive amount of money to loan him out. Instead, he was put into Sydney Pollack's *They Shoot Horses, Don't They?*, in which he played one of the many self-pitying characters struggling through a marathon dance contest. It did not do as much for his career as *Midnight Cowboy* did for Jon Voight.

The blond, six-foot-two, eyes-of-blue actor, born on 29 December, 1938 in Yonkers, New York, had made three films previously (all in 1967) – *Hour of the Gun* (a bit-part), and two low-budget movies, *Fearless Frank* and *Out of It*. In *Fearless Frank*, Phil Kaufman's first solo feature, Voight played a country bumpkin who comes to Chicago, gets shot by mobsters, and wakes up to find he has the powers of a superman. In *Out of It*, he portrayed a stupid high-school football hero. There was an element of Buck in both roles, and Voight already had experience in the wearing of Western gear because he had also been featured in the TV cowboy series *Cimarron Strip* and *Gunsmoke*.

Many of Voight's films have cast him as a none-too-bright but likeable hunk. In contrast, his stage work included a role in *The Sound of Music* on Broadway in 1961, in which the baby-faced 22-year-old sang 'Sixteen Going On Seventeen' to Laurie Peters, who was to become his wife, and

Romeo and Ariel at the California National Shakespeare Festival. He also won a Theatre World award for his performance opposite Irene Papas in *That Summer, That Fall* in March 1967 (directed by Ulu Grosbard).

Voight first got to know Dustin well when he was playing Rudolpho in *A View from the Bridge* in January 1965, on which Dustin had been assistant director. Their friendship had always been tinged with rivalry, something which helped each to bounce off the other's character in the movie. 'It wasn't a case of upstaging one another, but it was let's see who can really act better in this scene,' commented Dustin. There was a moment during the shooting of *Midnight Cowboy* when Dustin gave so much energy to the character's cough that he fell down in the street vomiting. Voight commented that there was no way he could 'upstage vomit'.

The supporting cast was made up of Sylvia Miles, Brenda Vaccaro, John McGiver, Barnard Hughes (film debut), Ruth White and Jennifer Salt (the screenwriter's 25-year-old daughter with whom the divorced Voight was living at the time).

Filming began on location in New York in April 1968 with a budget originally set around $2 million. Dustin was offered $250,000 – fifteen times more than he earned on *The Graduate*. This tidy sum enabled him and Anne to move from the tiny Village apartment which they rented for $125 a month to a much larger air-conditioned place for $400 a month, a brownstone directly across the road from 16 West 11th Street, just off Fifth Avenue. 'It gives me the willies to even think about the rent,' Dustin averred.

At the same time, Dustin hired a business manager. 'The idea is to save as much as you can and not let it go to the government. I don't need yachts and mansions but you do have to live.' The first object he bought with his *Midnight Cowboy* money was a $700 antique desk, declaring: 'It's the most important thing I ever bought. It's a lifetime item.' (Later events would prove otherwise.) He also hired himself a cook-housekeeper-secretary, Cathy Allen, the wife of an actor friend.

If he began to live more in keeping with his stature as a movie star, there were some indications that fame was going to his head. In the past, he had always been particularly solicitous towards any small-part player or struggling actor. Donahue Silvis, an exact contemporary of Dustin's at Pasadena Playhouse, had a bit-part in *Midnight Cowboy* when the team moved to Florida. 'After a few days of production I had the opportunity to approach Dustin,' Silvis remembered. 'He was sitting by the water of Biscayne Bay just a short distance from the set. I walked over to say "Hi". He pretended he didn't know me or didn't want to. He asked the director to get me away from him. It was very embarrassing and I was shocked at this behaviour from a person I had thought of as kind of shy and introverted.'

Meanwhile, the shooting and budget on the movie were starting to go over schedule, forcing UA seriously to contemplate not sinking any more money into the production. UA officials had a conference at which doubts were expressed about the possibility of the film's being able to recoup its investment if the budget was extended. The issue was resolved when they agreed that filming should continue. The movie was completed at the final cost of $3 million.

David Picker recalled, 'When we first saw the film one afternoon, we were stunned by its magic and the magic of Hoffman and Voight together. So we decided on a special release pattern – an opening in New York a couple of months before any place else, play-off in small theatres with long engagements, letting word of mouth build an audience.'

There certainly was an audience, and they paid $16.3 million to see it in the USA alone. So popular was the film that, a month after its opening, AIP decided to release *Madigan's Millions*, two years after it was made, to cash in on Dustin's name, double-billing it in the USA with *Fearless Frank*, films both actors rather hoped had been dead and buried.

The Oscar nominations *Midnight Cowboy* received were Best Picture, Best Supporting Actress (Sylvia Miles), Best Director, Best Screenplay adaptation, and both Voight and Dustin for Best Actor, forcing each of them to practise their smiles for the possibility of losing out to the other. In the event, the award went to the veteran midday cowboy John Wayne for his performance in *True Grit* and/or for never having won an Oscar before. *Life* magazine ran an article entitled 'Dusty and the Duke' in which they contrasted the poles-apart stars with photos of Wayne in colour and Dustin in black-and-white. Later, both Dustin and Voight avowed they were rooting for Wayne, despite the wide political divergence between them and the older star. (The same year, Wayne had acted in and directed the gung-ho *Green Berets*, which supported US military involvement in Vietnam.) 'I thought Dusty and I would cancel each other out, anyway,' remarked Voight. Given the propensity of the Academy jury over the years to equate serious acting with stars' willingness to make themselves unattractive, it is surprising that Dustin did not win hands down. Didn't Grace Kelly win an Oscar for *The Country Girl* for having the courage not to wear elegant clothes or much make-up?

Many years later, in the mid-eighties, John Malkovich, who was rehearsing *Death of a Salesman* with Dustin, remarked, 'One night we were playing Trivial Pursuit. There was a question, "Who won the Best Actor

Oscar the year of *Midnight Cowboy*?" Well, the answer was John Wayne in *True Grit*! The next day, I'm in rehearsal, Dustin whispers, "Why don't you try this?" I said, "Why should I listen to an actor who lost the Oscar to John Wayne in *True Grit*?" He screamed, "A lie! A lie! Voight and I split the vote. I was so depressed, I went to Europe for three months." '

Midnight Cowboy won Best Film, Director and Screenplay. (The other screenplay award was given to another 'buddy-buddy' movie, *Butch Cassidy and the Sundance Kid*, written by William Goldman, who was to write two of Dustin's future movies.) The film was a significant Oscar-winner because it was the first X-rated film to do so. It was a belated acknowledgement from the Academy that the 'permissive society' had arrived. *Variety* trumpeted: 'It's a new ballgame; the artists and scientists of the world's cinema center are unhesitant about saying to all the world that there's to be no hesitation about subject matter. As a matter of fact there's pride, pride in that a picture can get away from the lollipops and still be inoffensive and commercially pleasing. *Midnight Cowboy* . . . deals, among other things, with male whoredom. The voting majority of the Academy said yes, this is the legitimate victory.'

Actually, for all the film's surface modernity, sexual frankness and jaundiced eye, it is essentially an old-fashioned movie about an innocent coming from the sticks to the big city and not finding the sidewalks paved with gold. Had it been made in the 1930s, Jimmy Stewart would have played Buck and Margaret Sullavan would have taken the Hoffman role, dying in the arms of the man she loves just as she reaches Miami. (Remember Waldo Salt had written the Sullavan–Stewart weepie, *Shopworn Angel*.)

On the way to the East coast by Greyhound bus, Buck passes typical and very carefully selected places like 'The Biggest Hot Dog in the World' and 'Jesus Saves' signs. Then Schlesinger, through his foreign eyes, sees New York as a rotten Big Apple, over-emphatically capturing the city's brashness and indifference. A man lies on the sidewalk outside Tiffany's, passers-by just stepping over him. This is the director's immediate and obvious way of telling us (and Buck) that New York is a dog-eat-dog society. Everything and everybody in the city is depressing and vulgar. When Buck goes to a diner, he sits at a table opposite a creepy woman with a nervous tic who keeps running a grey rubber mouse over her face. When Buck and Ratso go to another greasy spoon, a crazy is ranting in the background. While watching TV, Buck sees a show in which a poodle is made to wear a wig, false eyelashes and panties. Despite Schlesinger's claims that 'there wasn't anything in the movie that I hadn't seen in some way somewhere' and 'one was always confronted by something worse on the streets than one was putting into the film', they were attention-getting elements, unabsorbed into the texture of the film.

There is not one person (including extras) in the movie who is not a 'character'. Ratso gets Buck an introduction to a man (John McGiver) who is supposed to put him in touch with some rich ladies, but he begs Buck to get down on his knees and pray with him under a kitschy lit-up Jesus on the bathroom door of his hotel room. Buck's other contacts include an ageing hooker whom he mistakes for a society woman ('I'm one gorgeous chick,' says the ungorgeous non-chicken Sylvia Miles); two weak and whining homosexual pick-ups; and a couple of weirdos who invite him to an 'underground' party. His main companion is the pathetic dreg of society, Ratso Rizzo.

Dustin starts by playing Timothy Mouse to Voight's Dumbo, although his voice seems to be dubbed by Mel Blanc, first as Daffy Duck (whom he resembles somewhat with his beak and slicked-down black hair), then as a consumptive Bugs Bunny. When people cough in the movies, it is usually a sure sign they are going to die. In a number from *Funny Girl*, Barbra Streisand sings 'As Camille I just feel, I've so much to offer. I know I'd be divine, because I'm a natural cougher.' More chameleon than Camille, Dustin proves himself just as natural a cougher.

But the heart-of-gold whore and the con man are sentimentally conceived. Ratso takes Buck to visit his father's grave, and a series of frenetic flashbacks and nightmares reveal Buck's past in a superficial attempt to explain his character. 'You're gonna be the best lookin' cowboy in the whole parade,' his bible-bashing granny tells him when he is a child. These flashbacks to his past in Texas show him making love to a girl whose family seems to object to him, then (in an obliquely filmed sequence) he is gang-raped by a group of yobs.

There are occasions when the relationship between Voight's big, blond, likeable dimwit, ludicrously decked out in cowboy gear, and Dustin's small, greasy-haired, pallid, crippled down-and-outer is touchingly and humorously portrayed, particularly the moment when Buck's face lights up on seeing an unshaven Ratso eating alone in a diner. Although he has been looking for the little creep to beat him up for having steered him wrong, he realises that it is better to be with someone, even someone like Ratso, than to be alone.

Actually, Voight is rather too old for the role, and overdoes the wide-eyed innocence, especially in the last twenty minutes when the movie gets as soft as an overripe Florida plum. As in *The Big Street*

(1942), in which a soppy busboy Henry Fonda gets money to take a crippled Lucy Ball to Florida, Voight manages to take his friend to Miami, a place already glimpsed in Ratso's (and Schlesinger's) sub-Fellini-esque dreams. Again, as in *The Graduate*, it was a hit song on the soundtrack, in this case, Fred Neil's 'Everybody's Talkin'', that gave the film a contemporary resonance, lodging itself more in the ear than in the eye or mind.

The critic David Thomson thought Schlesinger, 'too sloppy an artist to let Ratso emerge as less than adorable, but Hoffman was probably capable of nastiness had he been trusted.' Although Dustin is perfectly able to portray nastiness, he has never allowed himself to be other than sympathetic to audiences in whatever he has done. (He has come closest to an antipathetic character as the ex-con in *Straight Time*, and as a crook in *Family Business*, two of his biggest commercial failures.)

The *New York Times*'s Vincent Canby wrote: 'There is nothing obviously glossy in *Midnight Cowboy*, but it contains a lot of superior laughter that has the same softening effect,' yet he found the central relationship was 'as honest and affecting as anything you're likely to see in a movie, and more than compensates for those moments when the film seems to be exploiting its cheap, gaudy locale as might the director of a sight-seeing bus cruising through West 42nd Street and Greenwich Village'.

Wim Wenders, when a 24-year-old film student, thought, 'Schlesinger misses the opportunity to make a film about America. He makes a tortured film about European visions of America; he wants to demonstrate the "melting pot" in the film, plaster it with psychology and try not to miss any aspects of it. It gets more and more embarrassing to watch Dustin Hoffman coughing and limping as if he'd come straight to the film from a Broadway theatre.'

For the party scene Schlesinger got Paul Morrissey, the film director in Andy Warhol's Factory, to round up a number of Warhol's friends and stars, including Viva, Ultra Violet, International Violet, Taylor Meade and William Door. Morrissey made a short, silent movie that was shown in the background, along with the obligatory psychedelic projections on the wall. (There would be a similar scene in Dustin's next picture, *John and Mary*.) Warhol had been asked to play himself but he was still in hospital recovering from the attempt on his life. The involvement of members of the Factory enraged Warhol's gay militant friend Ondine who confronted Morrissey: 'How dare you accept the $25 a day in blood money to go and make fun of Andy? He's the reason why you're even here! Don't you have any feelings?' She might also have been incensed by the negative portrayal of homosexuality in the movie. The Factory, which had some influence on *Midnight Cowboy*, then decided to make their own picture about a male hustler. *Flesh*, starring the hunky Joe Dalessandro, was shot over two weekends at a cost of $4000, and is arguably the better film.

13

John and Mary; Dusty and Anne

I knew that if I got married and concentrated on that, I could kiss my career goodbye.

WITH *MIDNIGHT COWBOY* in the can, Dustin was given the opportunity to return to the stage in the title role of *Jimmy Shine*, a Broadway-bound play by his friend Murray Schisgal. Some months previously, in London, a small film called *John and Mary*, based on a novella by Mervyn Jones, was being set up to be directed by Anthony Harvey, whose first film, the modest but impressive *Dutchman*, had just opened. Glenda Jackson had already been approached for the female lead. However, when Harvey went on to direct *A Lion in Winter*, Mia Farrow, fresh from *Rosemary's Baby*, was sent the screenplay, written by John Mortimer. At the time, Farrow shared an agent with Peter Yates, who was now to direct it. She liked the script about a young couple in the then fashionable Swinging London, but did not feel it was quite right for her. When Yates suggested transferring the action to America, she agreed to become involved. The producer Ben Kadish thought that if he could get the 'hot' Hoffman to play opposite her, he would be able to convince Twentieth Century-Fox to put up the money and release it. Yates was happy with the possible casting. 'I knew John Schlesinger very well and he told me Dustin could play almost anything.'

Dustin knew he was coming in to Broadway with *Jimmy Shine* and did not relish the idea of making a film and simultaneously appearing in a play, especially as the production was having problems on the road. In order to cajole him into accepting the role, the British tandem of Peter Yates and John Mortimer were asked to fly out from London to Philadelphia, where the play was trying out.

After the performance of *Jimmy Shine*, the two of them made their way from the theatre to the hotel where Dustin was staying. Zev Bufman, the Israeli-born producer of the play, had had a pool table hoisted up the side of the hotel and installed in a room adjoining Dustin's suite, to help him relax. 'You want to please these people,' Bufman commented. 'Limos, aides, redecorating dressing-rooms, flowers and champagne go without saying. It pays off in the end.'

Mortimer, who was still a practising barrister, was due back in court in London the following day. Therefore, he had to get a connection to New York in order to catch his 6 a.m. plane. It was already past midnight when they got to see Dustin, who was playing pool by himself, while a huge party for the cast was going on in another suite. With the noise of jollity in the background, Dustin talked endlessly about everything except the film, while Mortimer watched the clock ticking away. Dustin then started asking Mortimer and Yates what they thought of the play. In a rather tentative manner, they made some suggestions on how they thought it could be improved. It was not long before Mortimer was drawing diagrams with the cue chalk. Whereupon, Dustin, at around 3 a.m., phoned Murray Schisgal's room to tell him to come down to hear what the Englishmen had to say about his play. A very tired and dishevelled Schisgal appeared and they spent an hour discussing the problems with him. 'I didn't think we helped much on *Jimmy Shine*,' said Yates. 'Coming down in the middle of the night like that probably muddled the hell out of them. Schisgal was terrific, perhaps because he was so beaten into the ground by that time, I don't know. But Mortimer said that if it had been him he would have hit the roof.'

Finally, when Schisgal had returned to his interrupted slumbers, Mortimer and Yates brought up the subject of the purpose of their visit. 'I was hysterical,' recalled Mortimer. 'I still had to get to New York where my plane was due to leave in about two hours.' After what seemed ages, Dustin thought he might be willing to co-star in *John and Mary* if only in gratitude for the bit of play-doctoring the two visitors had done. Mortimer left in a hurry, caught his plane, and was standing bewigged at the Old Bailey the next day.

There were further archetypal all-night sessions, rewriting the play in smoke-filled hotel rooms. Yates, who was busy setting up *John and Mary* in New York, went down to Baltimore two or three times to participate in the nocturnal meetings. According to Dustin, Yates 'made some excellent suggestions. He seemed more involved in helping the play than with planning his movie, and I thought, "This is a really genuine guy."'

Dustin declared that he had accepted the part, not because of the screenplay nor the $425,000 he would receive, but as a favour to Peter Yates. 'It was not the script. I'm not even sure I understand the character. I mean, his life is ordered, he's a good cook, he's aware of clothes, he has a neat apartment. I never lived that way. But when I saw *Bullitt*, I thought, "This wasn't the script either, it was all in the director's head." With a play, it seems to me you go for the text, with a film you go for the director.'

The 40-year-old British-born Peter Yates had gone to Hollywood the year before to direct Steve McQueen in *Bullitt*, the movie with 'the car chase to end all car chases'. (It didn't; it only began a spate of them.) He had been a motor-racing driver and team manager, and his best films have been concerned with cars, bikes and heists, rather than boy meets girl. *John and Mary*, his second American film, did not satisfy his love of action, nor did it provide him with the opportunity to demonstrate his fine sense of place.

The interior filming of *John and Mary* took place at the old and dilapidated Biograph Studios which were at 174th Street in the Bronx. On the sound stage, the production designer John Robert Lloyd built a huge apartment containing a workable kitchen to represent John's 'pad'. Yates wanted it realistically built 'because I wanted the duplex feeling without faking a big place like this.' In fact, it was copied almost entirely from an apartment in the Dakota building, outside which John Lennon was shot some years later and where Yates himself would live.

Meanwhile Dustin was concentraing on *Jimmy Shine*, a whimsical episodic comedy about the reveries of an unsuccessful 30-year-old Greenwich Village artist who maintains his essentially sunny disposition despite life's vicissitudes. Using a flashback technique, Schisgal's Jimmy moves back to his school and college days, allowing Dustin to play younger again. At one stage, he is told, 'The main thing is that you have innate ability, talent, genius, something that's born inside you; it has nothing to do with studying. Some people got it; some don't.' Schisgal obviously had Dustin in mind when he wrote this.

The role gave Dustin plenty of scope to demonstrate his versatility, even allowing him to warble a few songs, including a vaudeville fish ditty, and to dance with beer cans strapped to the soles of his feet. His enormous vitality energised what was a less than satisfying piece. Also in the cast were Rose Gregorio (Ulu Grosbard's wife), Pamela Payton-Wright, Rue McClanahan (much later Blanche in TV's *Golden Girls*) and Cleavon Little, who would play the role of the French-influenced director in *John and Mary*.

In one scene Dustin had to tear into one of his canvases with a palette knife. For the opening night in Baltimore, the prop man had over-sharpened the knife so that Dustin cut his right index finger rather severely during the performance. Nevertheless, he continued with his finger covered in blood, keeping his hand in his pocket. After the final curtain he went to the local hospital to have the wound attended to. But Dustin's confidence in the play was so shaky that he insisted that the stage manager announce to the audience every night that, 'Mr Hoffman is appearing with a cut finger', even after it had healed. It was 'a blatant bid for public

Main picture: Dustin in the stage play, *Jimmy Shine*, New York, 1968

Inset: Dustin (at right) with Fred Ricci in *Danton's Death* at the Pasadena Playhouse, 1957

In *The Graduate*, 1967: (*above*) with Anne Bancroft, and (*below*) in the final moments, with Katharine Ross

Above: In *John and Mary*, 1969, with co-star Mia Farrow and director Peter Yates.
Below: As Ratso Rizzo in *Midnight Cowboy*, 1969, with Jon Voight

As the young Jack Crabb, with Faye Dunaway, in *Little Big Man*, 1970, and (*right*) as the 121-year-old Jack

Left: In *Midnight Cowboy*, 1969

In *Alfredo, Alfredo*, 1971, with Stefania Sandrelli

Left: In *Who Is Harry Kellerman and Why Is He Saying Those Terrible Things About Me?*, 1971

Dustin as Dega with Steve McQueen, in *Papillon*, 1973, and (*inset*) Dustin's first wife, Anne, in the small part of Mrs Dega

As Lenny Bruce in *Lenny*, 1974

sympathy', according to the director Donald Driver, who had walked out on the production in protest at the way Dustin had taken over.

When *Jimmy Shine* opened on Broadway on Thursday, 5 December 1968, at the Brooks Atkinson Theater, the New York critics showed little sympathy. *Newsweek* called it 'the baddest bad play possible to conceive . . . a mess, an incredibly hackneyed, shamelessly exploitative farrago . . . The play itself is a monster.' Of Dustin's performance, though, Clive Barnes in *The New York Times* wrote, 'He has the strange ability to be himself on the stage. Or, at least, if that is not himself he is playing, then some aspect of himself. He must be so unnaturally talented that he is practically monstrous.'

For John Simon, it was 'so puny a play that if it were not extended in all directions by Dustin Hoffman's life-giving performance, it would barely be discernible to the naked eye. Mr Schisgal, whose fame rests on his ability to infuse bloodless old contrivances with the plasma of pseudo-modernism, specialises in the portrayal of loveable failures . . . Of course, the whole (apart from not being a play but a series of more or less laboured skits) is a huge lie. If Jimmy Shine were so loveable and bright, he could not be such an ecumenical failure at everything from school to girls, from New York to San Francisco, from painting to living. And if he were pro-pelled by such categorical imperative to fail, he could not reek love-ableness out of every pore . . . As Jimmy, Hoffman elaborates the film role that made him famous, Benjamin in *The Graduate*, and he is a thoroughly charming actor with sufficient off-beat idiosyncracies to make him a spiny delight. He has his own truth, but the role is merely a Jewish fantasy figure: the successful failure, the yearned for anti-self of all dissatisfied successes, a figure to cosset as well as patronise.'

Favourable reviews came from *Women's Wear Daily*, who considered it 'a funny, lovely, painfully gentle play that manages – without being fake-sensitive or psychedelically souped up – to understand just the thinking of today's young people'. It reminded Frank Marcus in London's *The Sunday Telegraph* of Molnar, Saroyan, Fellini and the paintings of Chagall.

Thanks to astute advice from his business manager, apart from $4500 a week and ten per cent of the gross box-office receipts, Dustin also received half of the profits from every souvenir programme sold. At one dollar a programme, he was reaping in as much as an extra $100 a week. This pleasant perk was gained from Zev Bufman because the Broadway com-pany had not been given Dustin's permission to use certain material on him in the programme.

While Dustin was appearing in his first lead role on Broadway, he was filming at the Biograph Studios in darkest Bronx, thirty minutes by limo (laid on nightly by Twentieth Century-Fox) from the Great White Way. This committed him to a punishing schedule for the next eight months, from the time the play went into rehearsal until it closed on 26 April 1969 after 161 consecutive performances. Each night, behind the peeling facade of the studio where D. W. Griffith worked before World War I, filming would go on until early in the morning. In order that Dustin could sleep late and rest during the day, Fox bought him out of Wednesday matinees of the play.

There were rumours that stimulants or 'poppers' were the only things that kept Dustin going. Yates discounts this. 'I read somewhere of how Steve McQueen had been on drugs the whole time we were shooting *Bullitt*. I must say I never saw any sign of it at all. I feel exactly the same way about Dustin. I think he was working far too hard. He was going to the analyst every morning. I don't see how you could do a show, go to an analyst, work on a film and take 'poppers' or 'coke' or anything like it the whole time.'

Dustin relied mostly on coffee and aspirins while shuttling between the theatre and the studio. Although he felt under pressure – Dustin is an actor who always commits himself totally to what he is doing – he enjoyed having to make the adjustment from Jimmy to John and back again.

His role in the film was one of his most difficult because there was nowhere to hide – neither behind make-up nor behind a character younger or older than himself. 'The tough thing for me is not to have a particular voice or gait for a part, to have to play a guy like John, who is close to me physically and in age and so on. I have this strong fear that if I am just myself, I'm going to be dull. I don't have the leading man's charisma. I mean, I've always felt that I had better do a helluva lot of acting.' Yates felt that, 'Dustin didn't relate to the character because I don't think Dustin likes to be thought of as nice and charming. Playing a character role is often more interesting for an actor, secondly you've got something to hide behind and thirdly you're not exposing anything about yourself.'

The teaming of 'Benjamin Braddock' and 'Rosemary' seemed to make perfect box-office sense. In 1968, the boyish 31-year-old Hoffman and the girlish 23-year-old sixties flower child Farrow were two of the most talked-about 'young' stars. She had recently emerged from a much-publicised divorce from Frank Sinatra and a month's transcendental meditation with the guru Maharishi Mahesh Yogi in India. The down-to-earth Hoffman and the ethereal Farrow got on reasonably well during the shooting. 'Mia's fine,' said Dustin, 'except that she talks a lot about meditation. I tend to avoid those conversations.'

One day, much to Dustin's irritation, she asked the driver of the limo that was taking the two of them back to Manhattan to stop because she saw a wishing star in the sky. 'I can't pass up a wishing star,' she chirped, bouncing out of the car. After standing silently looking up at the Brooklyn sky for a few minutes, and reciting a poem, she then jumped back into the car.

Dustin, who, according to Yates, had 'the biggest supply of dirty stories that I've ever known', was in the habit of trying to shock everyone. 'This stream of obscene language was all the more strange coming from such a seemingly innocent-looking person.' The even more innocent-looking Mia, however, was unshockable.

On the set, Dustin cast himself as the sensible person, whereas Mia was busy 'talking to the spirt of Mozart', perhaps under the influence of André Previn (still married to Dory Previn), the conductor of the London Symphony Orchestra, with whom she had recently fallen in love. (They would marry two years later, some months after she had given birth to twin boys.) Not wanting to be away from Previn for long periods, Mia crossed the Atlantic on a few weekends during the shooting. Sometimes, when it snowed heavily, the filmmakers were terrified lest she would not get back from London in time. But she always made it.

Yates used the off-camera relationship of the two stars to establish a rapport between them on screen. For example, in the scene where John first meets Mary, 'I didn't have the attitude right, and Peter said, "Do you remember how you were when I first brought Mia backstage to meet you?" I was very nervous, and I found myself coming on very strong and direct with her, and saying, "I liked *Rosemary's Baby*, but the picture bothered me for this reason . . .' Peter said, "Use it." It worked perfectly.'

The setting of the original novel by Mervyn Jones was shifted from London to New York because, says Yates, 'I didn't want any of this dreadful, clichéd Swinging London business creeping in. I had never believed in Swinging London in any way, and always felt it was a figment of *Time* magazine's imagination.' Other considerations were his wanting to make another American film and because the project had got off the ground due to its big Hollywood stars. In order to make sure the dialogue had the authentic American tone, Mortimer had two American actors read it aloud and make comments before the script was given to the two leads.

Mervyn Jones, in an article in *The New Statesman* in October 1969, commented on how the short novel he wrote during four months in 1965 became a Hollywood movie outside his control. 'It is a trivial little book, the product neither of serious thinking nor of deep feeling. My purpose was to see if I could write a novel with only two characters, preserving the unities of time, place and action (it all happens in one day in John's London flat), without any cheating through long flashbacks or such devices. For

what it is worth, I brought off this trick – something of interest, I should
suppose, only to other writers . . . In 1966, soon after the book appeared,
my agent told me that someone wanted to make a film out of it. This
amazed me. I thought and still think that *John and Mary* is the least film-like
of novels; most of the wordage is devoted to the thoughts of the characters, and the most dramatic piece of action is the accidental breaking of a
glass . . . I asked if I could see the screenplay on which the film was now
based. My agent explained that it was a highly secret document, but that
he had a friend in the London office who might be able to sneak out a copy
. . . Orienting myself through a large cast of characters, several long flashbacks, and a variety of thrilling events in New York and Jamaica, I came
across occasional reminders of the novel . . . The shooting of the film
began early this year. Mr Hoffman or Miss Farrow or both were the
subjects of long articles in the American press, of the cover story in *Time*,
and then of another cover story in *The Observer*'s colour section. They also
gave interviews. Miss Farrow was fairly reticent, especially about *John and
Mary*. Mr Hoffman made it clear that the subject did not interest him and
that he wanted to work with Mr Yates.'

The refashioned story relates how two young people, both just over
affairs, pick each other up on a Friday night at a swinging Manhattan
singles bar, the then modish Maxwell's Plum. John has been brought to
the bar, 'a paradise for bachelors', by his randy friend Ernest (played by
Dustin's real friend Stanley Beck). She goes back to his four-room bachelor apartment at 52 Riverside Drive. They go to bed as strangers and then
spend the weekend alternately insulting each other and making up, trying
to find out if they are fond of each other. We learn with them that he
designs furniture (as Harry Hoffman did) and she works in a gallery of
primitive art on Madison Avenue, but only in the end do they reveal their
names to each other. When they first meet at the bar, he says to her, 'What
did you say your name was?' 'I didn't say. What's yours?' But they are
interrupted and they do not bother to ask the question again during the
whole weekend. Obviously, unlike the bar in TV's *Cheers*, Maxwell's
Plum was not a place 'where everybody knows your name'. The idea that
two people could spend two days in such intimate proximity and not
know each other's names is impossible to swallow, even though it is
meant as a metaphor for their relationship. Although it is too fanciful to
believe that the later *Last Tango in Paris* could have been influenced by *John
and Mary*, there are nonetheless similarities between the two seemingly
worlds-apart movies. In the 1972 Bernardo Bertolucci film, Marlon
Brando and Maria Schneider as Paul and Jeanne embark on a series of erotic encounters in an apartment, agreeing never to reveal their names to

each other, in order to keep their relationship anonymous and exclusively physical. There also happens to be a young TV filmmaker (Jean-Pierre Léaud, the *nouvelle vague*'s fetish actor) similar to the one played by Cleavon Little in Yates's picture.

To show how adult even a major Fox movie could be in the late sixties, the credit sequence has the two lovebirds in bed together, cutely sleeping side by side and back to back. Dustin's neat Beatle cut is slightly tousled and there is a close-up of a mole on his right shoulder. Mia, waking up to find her companion still sleeping, hardly gives the impression that she has spent a passionate night. Her hair, slightly shorter than his, earrings, make-up and false eyelashes are all perfectly in place. He, however, looks rough before he shaves and dresses, demonstrating the still prevailing differences between the way men and women are treated aesthetically on screen.

His scrupulously tidy, chic apartment, a converted artist's studio, contains furniture of his own design, pop art on the walls, a bookshelf prominently displaying the very latest Tom Wolfe volume, *The Electric Kook-Aid Acid Test*, and, on the coffee table, a copy of the prestigious British film magazine *Sight and Sound*. This is contrasted with her noisy, untidy, 'funky four-storey walk-up' on the East Side which she shares with two other girls, one of them being Tyne Daly, the future Mary Beth Lacey of TV's *Cagney And Lacey*. The couple's recent past is filled in by a series of 'flash-ins', influenced by the French *nouvelle vague*.

This influence is acknowledged when Dustin meets Mia at the bar and overhears her discussing what is obviously (though it is coyly not named), Jean-Luc Godard's *Weekend* of 1967. One of the men in her party considers it was made by a madman. 'I like a film to have a beginning, a middle and an ending, preferably in that order, so I can follow it,' he says, Mortimer's screenplay knowingly making him paraphrase Godard's view that a 'film must have a beginning, a middle and an ending, not necessarily in that order.' Although Yates freely admits he was happy to pinch from the French New Wave – voice-over, jump cuts, freeze frames and a certain improvisatory quality – the techniques as used here are too self-regarding. The director also seems to be trying to satirise the fashionable filmmaking of the day by having Cleavon Little play a French-speaking director with a hand-held camera. As he films Mia, she tells him, '*Cinéma vérité* is just an excuse to follow little girls into the ladies' room.'

The slick editing and second-hand New Wave tricks cannot save the film from being too thin and too contrived, and rarely amusing or touching enough. 'What happens now?' Mia asks at one stage. 'What a day it's been and we haven't really done anything at all. Nothing at all.' Unlike

Godard's intellectual young couples in a confined space, these two people spend the weekend together communicating on as superficial a level as the movie itself.

Yates is almost desperately aware that 'there's a whole world outside this little egg box you inhabit', as Mia tells Dustin. He feels so restricted by the screenplay that he has to break away from the apartment at every opportunity. Even a slight anecdote of her as a sixteen-year-old girl guide being seduced in a tent by a boy scout is illustrated. The voice-over device (their spoken thoughts) only works intermittently because much of what they are thinking could be spoken. Their visualised thoughts, however, communicate far more to the audience. We learn that John has had an affair with a fashion model (Sunny Griffin), who moves in with her dresses, wigs and dog, but decides to leave after she has made a mess of the kitchen by boiling the spaghetti over. Mary has had a relationship with a married US senator (Michael Tolan).

Because her life is a little more vividly described than his, Mia's character exists less in a vacuum than Dustin's, and as a result her performance is more satisfactory. It has to be said that when Dustin has co-starred in a movie with as big a star as he – McQueen, Redford, Beatty or Connery – he has come off second best. He works much better when he has plenty of space around him, and when his name is, metaphorically or literally, the only one above the title. Here, Dustin generates a little warmth, but not much passion or conviction, and his celebrated off-and-on smile gives the impression that he is not exactly sure what to do with his mouth.

'With it' as the film pretends to be, it is curiously reactionary. The political references seem no more than accoutrements, just another part of the decor of the period. Seemingly irrelevant is the scene in which Mary's liberal Eugene McCarthyite senator lover addresses the University Political Science Club, which makes reference to student protests, sit-ins, Vietnam and black rights. He calms the whole student audience by concluding, 'In my opinion you have coined the great motto of our time: "Make Love, Not War",' and they all give the peace sign. The very real issues of the day are trivialised and the senator, who is cheating on his wife, is seen as a hypocrite. There is also implicit criticism of John's politically committed mother Rosalie (Olympia Dukakis), so busy demonstrating for human rights that she shamefully neglects her son and fails to fill the fridge with enough food for him. As a result, the adult John is obsessed with food, has an overstocked fridge and is a good cook. When he discovers that Mary helps people, collects for Biafra and has protested against the Vietnam War, he is not happy because she suddenly reminds him of his mother. (Flash-in of her leading a march in his mother's place.)

The message of the film seems to be, 'All you need is love and cheese souf-flés.' As well as its rather old-fashioned view of a woman's place, the film represents gays as 'men who walk poodles'. One of them is approached by Dustin, who asks if he knows where three girls live. 'Girls!!!' shrieks the man in horror.

Nevertheless, *John and Mary* is an interesting record of its time, in which Dustin again represents, as in *The Graduate*, the blander side of sixties youth. Hemlines have since come down, and so have many of the buildings. Maxwell's Plum has finally closed its doors. The film was responsible at the time for the tremendous popularity of the bar and, whenever Yates or Dustin went into it, they were sent over a bottle of champagne by the management.

John and Mary opened in Hollywood on 25 November 1969, starting off sluggishly, but ending up making $1.2 million profit. The icons of the period drew the worshippers to the shrine, despite the sacrilegious critics.

'Hoffman, who is so fine in *Midnight Cowboy*,' wrote Vincent Canby in *The New York Times*, 'is here upstaged by interior scenery. He gives a per-formance by combining his mannerisms, including a smile turned tenta-tively on and off like a light bulb and the stooped strut of an over-age Holden Caulfield.' Judith Crist commented that, 'despite all the "now" sets and surfaces, it's like an old comedy of the thirties – minus the comedy'. Pauline Kael admitted in *The New Yorker* that, 'reviewing this perfect nothing of a movie is rather degrading: it's like giving consumer hints on the latest expensive worthless gift for the person who has everything'. David Thomson felt that, 'Hoffman seemed at a loss . . . in one of his few concessions to the big-salary syndrome.' Dustin's salary had certainly gone up in leaps and bounds, from $17,000 for *The Graduate*, to $250,000 for *Midnight Cowboy*, to $425,000 for *John and Mary*.

Before *John and Mary* came into being, Dustin and Anne were the subject of many an article. When a reporter, visiting the couple, asked Anne if she and Dustin would marry, Anne showed her crossed fingers behind Dustin's back. Dustin's macho response seemed to indicate that he would not want his wife to work. 'It's a wonderful thing when you can share a life. I want a wife who can make me laugh, and I would always want her near me.' It was this proprietorial attitude that was later to be one of the elements that would alienate Anne, who wanted to pursue her own career in parallel with her husband's. (The education of Dustin towards some understanding of feminism, even though mainly in theory rather than in practice, was only to come after his divorce, the making of *Kramer vs*

Kramer and *Tootsie*, and marriage to a woman who did not put his ideas to the test.)

One could easily imagine that a visit by Dustin to Anne's parents in Westchester would be similar to the scene in *Annie Hall* when Woody Allen has Easter dinner with his girlfriend's cold and formal WASP family, who he imagines see him as a rabbi. However, despite being raised a Catholic, Anne had no qualms about a Jewish marriage, nor did her open-minded librarian father and schoolteacher mother. Therefore, after the stint on Broadway, Dustin married the woman whom he called 'my shiksa goddess' on 8 May 1969 at Temple Beth El Reform synagogue at Chappaqua, New York. About thirty-five close friends and relatives attended the wedding and the reception in Anne's home town of Mount Kisco in northern Westchester, NY. After the celebrations were over, the couple took off for a honeymoon retreat in Asia. One of the first stops on the way was London, where *The Graduate* was yet to become a hit, so Dustin was able to walk the streets in peace. Not for long, though.

14

One Little Indian

The key to the character was that he hadn't had a decent bowel movement in forty-six years.

IF ONE HAD been going to cast anyone in the title role of a movie called *Little Big Man*, there would not have been many actors in Hollywood one could have thought of besides Dustin Hoffman. (This was a few years before little actors such as Al Pacino, Richard Dreyfuss or Dudley Moore became big.)

The Western was in its dying throes, but *Butch Cassidy and the Sundance Kid* in 1969 kept it hanging on by a thread. Director Arthur Penn had bought the rights to the Thomas Berger novel *Little Big Man* in 1965, and MGM had originally planned to produce it as a multimillion-dollar epic before the deal fell through. In June 1969, Cinema Center Films agreed to finance the film, and Jack Richardson, who had started to write the screenplay, was replaced by Calder Willingham (who co-wrote *The Graduate*).

It was inevitable that the actor that seemed to epitomise the new Hollywood of the late sixties should work with one of the most fashionable filmmakers attuned to young audiences. Arthur Penn's strong sympathy with the outsider and an anti-Establishment stance made an impact on the anti-draft, anti-Vietnam, middle-class college students of that tumultuous period. His first feature had been a Western, *The Left-Handed Gun* (1958), in which Paul Newman played a crazy mixed-up Billy the Kid with Method mannerisms. *Bonnie and Clyde* (1967) was one of the most influential American movies of the last decades in its amoral attitude to 'the outlaw', seen from a modern psychological and social viewpoint. Another of his significant outsiders was the blind, deaf and dumb Helen Keller in *The Miracle Worker* (1962), and *The Chase* (1966) was linked in a plodding way with the law/outlaw theme of *Bonnie and Clyde*. *Alice's Restaurant* (1969) had an obvious appeal for those who could identify with a communal haven for hippies, and *Little Big Man* would continue to reveal his preoccupation with the outsider by seeing the Cheyenne as 'ethnic' hippies who contrasted favourably with white civilisation. Curiously, it was Penn's last success to date. From there it has been downhill all the way.

Penn described the anti-hero of his Western as 'a man who gets rid of his history like a snake sheds his skin . . . A man who is essentially passive in an activist's role, a man willing to let the tides of history dictate his actions.'

This man, played by Dustin, was Jack Crabb, a 121-year-old survivor of Custer's Last Stand, who reminisces over his long and eventful life. In 1859, as a ten-year-old abandoned orphan, he is found and adopted by the Cheyenne, and is made a brave called Little Big Man by Chief Old Lodge Skins (Chief Dan George). Aged sixteen, he rides into battle against white soldiers but is captured, and taken in by Reverend Silas Pendrake (Thayer David) and his wife (Faye Dunaway). He soon learns that the latter is not as pure as she makes out. In his mid-twenties, he joins Custer (Richard Mulligan), but during an attack on an Indian village he meets Sunshine (Amy Eccles) who becomes his wife. Shifting loyalties once more, he determines to kill Custer, but cannot do the deed when he has the chance, and becomes a vagrant. One day, just as he is about to throw himself off a cliff, he sees Custer riding for Little Big Horn. He offers himself as a scout. At the battle, Jack is saved by Younger Bear (Carl Bellini), who owed him a life from childhood.

Before shooting could begin, producer Stuart Miller had to sign a treaty permitting the use of Custer's Last Stand battlefield in the movie. Agreement had to be reached with the Northern Cheyenne to film scenes at Lame Deer, Montana, and with Scarvee and Stony Indians for the use of land in Calgary, as well as a contract drawn up for forty Crow Indians to appear in the film. These agreements not only had the effect of gaining the Indians' approval of the film but also lent it a greater authenticity. The days of using Jeff Chandler, Rock Hudson and Burt Lancaster supported by Debra Paget, J. Carrol Naish and Ricardo Montalban as Indians were virtually over. To quote Kurt Vonnegut in *Bluebeard*: 'In the movies back then, just about any big-nosed person whose ancestors came from the shores of the Mediterranean or the Near East, if he could act at little, could play a rampaging Sioux or whatever. The audiences were more than satisfied.' Despite the use of assorted Caucasians as some Indians, two of the leading roles were played by Chief Dan George and Robert Little Star.

The movie was originally set to be produced on a budget of $5 million to be filmed at such diverse locations as California, Montana, Colorado, Nevada City and Calgary, Canada. But a range of climatic difficulties from the blistering heat of Colorado to below-zero temperatures in Canada spectacularly doubled the picture's original budget. Despite the problems with the elements, however, Penn's 114-person cast and crew brought the film in on schedule.

Because of the extensive location work, Dustin, who disliked being away from his family for any length of time, insisted on Anne and Karina joining him at a house he had rented in Billings, Montana. He needed their support after a hard day's work in often uncomfortable conditions. Horse riding did not come easily to him, and he had to bathe in Epsom salts every night to soothe his acting legs and behind. Dustin also found that firing a gun was not something he was adept at, and would often burn himself with the powder from the blank cartridge. In addition, he insisted on doing the stunts that were in his power himself, like lying face-down in freezing mud for a scene that would take almost two days to shoot. But it was on his return to the West Coast that he was to suffer most discomfiture. It was there that the scenes of Dustin as a centenarian were to be filmed.

Long gone were the days when an actor could, like Paul Muni, have his hair powdered and his face lined, and put on a wavering voice and a stoop to represent ageing. Even as recently as *Giant* (1956), Rock Hudson, Elizabeth Taylor and James Dean undermined the later part of the movie by their inability to age convincingly. When Dustin played old, as in *Little Big Man* and the later *Death of a Salesman*, he *really* played old, and aged everyone around him.

With the meticulousness with which he was to become associated on each project, Dustin decided that he had first to get the voice of the 121-year-old man right. Some actors find the character initially in the posture, the clothes, or the make-up, but Dustin almost invariably works from the voice, perhaps because his own is rather nasal, flat and nondescript. Like an ordinary face that one can build a character upon with multiple disguises, Peter Sellers's for example, Dustin draws on the blank score sheet of his voice.

He worked and worried about this long before he got to play the old man. 'I first tried to get that kind of raspy voice that comes when the vocal cords have broken down. A doctor friend of mine found this home on Welfare Island where I could just observe old people. I found one guy and talked to him for a while on tape. He wasn't right – just wasn't old enough – and I was very depressed afterward. Then, another doctor told me there was a drug that dries out alcoholics and makes something very raspy happen to the voice. But I chickened out.'

Then one day Dustin got laryngitis, and promptly put his crackling voice on tape. It was exactly when he wanted. Still, there was one small problem. He could only really recapture the timbre if he had laryngitis when the time came for shooting.

In Montana, he visited a number of old age homes for someone to supply him with the right voice, but to no avail. Eventually, when they were in Canada, in the fifth month of the picture, Dustin got friendly with an Oriental man who claimed to be 104 years old. Dustin spent hours watching and listening to the old man.

However, when the production shifted back to Los Angeles, the day before shooting started, he lost the kind of gravelly voice he had been working on. 'I still didn't know what to do about the voice. So in a panic I went into a room, closed the door, and started screaming until I got hoarse. The next day my voice was okay again. So I screamed while I got dressed, I screamed leaving the room. In the car I rolled up the windows and screamed all the way to the Sawtelle Veteran's Hospital in Los Angeles where we were filming. I screamed vowel sounds and different registers more delicate than the others that would get me hoarser.'

Actually, the voice was the least of his problems. Dustin had to suffer under a fourteen-piece latex mask, which took five hours a day to apply under the hot, steaming make-up lamps. (Far worse torture was to come in *Tootsie*. Playing old was child's play compared with acting a woman.)

'I defy anyone to put on that make-up and not feel old,' Dustin explained. 'I couldn't see too well with my contact lens cataracts, and the crew would walk me over to the wheelchair where they had to wheel me on to the sound stage. Everybody was very gentle. That really helped me believe my fantasy world.'

It was the process of his metamorphosis from a 33-year-old into a 121-year-old that got most of the film's pre-publicity. Legendary make-up artist Dick Smith's creation ranks with some of the most celebrated elaborate make-up jobs in the past, such as Lon Chaney's thousand facial transformations, Boris Karloff's Frankenstein's monster, and Bette Davis as Queen Elizabeth I.

Little Big Man was released in 1970 and took a healthy $15 million at the box office. The reviews were less perky. *Variety* commented that, 'Hoffman's prior films show up in marked contrast. To be sure, the characterisations are low key, but in other pix they have manifested depth, plot propulsion and story meaning. *Little Big Man*, in contrast, is rather like documenting the US space programme by following the janitor in the NASA HQ . . . The show is advanced so sluggishly and episodically that, apart from first and last reels, there could be a mix-up in reels without much comment.' As for the famous make-up, 'It is a technical achievement but, for all anyone knows, it could have been Stacy Keach in such a rig.'

Vincent Canby in *The New York Times* felt that the film was often 'not terribly funny, at just those moments when it tries the hardest, and it sometimes wears its social concerns so blatantly that they look like warpaint', but concluded that it 'is an important movie by one of our most interesting directors'. Of Dustin, he surprisingly found peculiar traces of both Ben Braddock and Ratso Rizzo in his Jack Crabb, but thought him 'fine'.

John Simon found Dustin 'always endearing with that sour-grapefruit face and voice of his, both of which, paradoxically, ooze the juice of human kindness', while David Thomson thought that Dustin 'was near his best, managing old age easily and riding the picaresque adventures of a put-upon outcast all the better because of his own denial of starriness. Still, it was easier to accept Hoffman as Penn's spokesman than as someone actually living through the film. His very intelligent scrutiny of a role can make him seem too detached, too much the performer of a plan.'

The one hundred and fifty minutes has its entertaining chunks but *Little Big Man* too self-consciously views the past from a modern standpoint (there is even a gay Red Indian and bluesy music), and the demystification of legends, such as Custer, is done in too simplistic a manner, a process Penn had begun in *The Left-Handed Gun*. As Robin Wood has noted, 'The presentation of the Cheyennes is confused and blurred by the divided impulse, the desire to recreate an "ideal" alternative to the white world.'

Although his voice and the accent change slightly when he becomes the narrator, Dustin was brilliantly convincing as a very old man, as well as managing to look and behave like a very young man when necessary. However, after many experiences and two marriages, the character still comes on like an idiot boy during the second meeting with Dunaway in a brothel, making Benjamin Braddock seem like Don Juan by contrast.

The tone of the picture is unsure, veering from broad comedy – Dustin as Bob Hope in *Son of Paleface* – and burlesque of the *Blazing Saddles* type to an attempt to make serious comments about Indian culture, and analogies between their treatment by the whites and the Vietnam War. A sequence when Custer attacks an Indian village could not help but stir vivid memories of the My Lai massacre and the photos of Vietnamese on fire that were seen in all the newspapers and on television during that dark period in America's history. At the time, student audiences were in no doubt as to the intentions of the scene, and would chant 'My Lai! My Lai!' as well as cheering the death of Custer, whom they identified as Lieutenant Calley.

Little Big Man was certainly not the first Hollywood movie to attempt to redress the balance in favour of the Indians. There had already been examples in the fifties, notably Delmer Daves's *Broken Arrow*, Robert Aldrich's *Apache* and Sam Fuller's *Run of the Arrow*, but it began a new trend in which the Western was appropriated by directors in order to express their liberal views. Indians were seen as representing the Vietcong, nineteenth-century negro slaves spoke like members of the Black Power movement, and detailed blood-baths were presented as condemnations of violence. The Western was moving out of its frame, until it disappeared altogether.

Despite the mixed response from critics, Dustin felt pride in his achievement and confidence in the film itself, so he expressed his anger when *Little Big Man* was not nominated for any Oscars. 'Sure I would like to win an Academy Award,' the twice-nominated actor told *Daily Variety*. 'I realise that intellectually it doesn't really mean very much. But it is a means to more power, which in turn enables you to be choosy about your scripts. And it makes you more money – which you can put away toward the day when you won't be in such demand!'

In stark contrast with Dustin's ambition, this was the year that George C. Scott won and refused the Oscar for *Patton*. 'Life isn't a race,' he stated, 'and because it is not a race I don't consider myself in competition with my fellow actors for awards or recognition.'

Ignored by the Academy, *Little Big Man* was acknowledged by The New York Critics and The National Society of Film Critics, who selected Chief Dan George as their Best Supporting Actor, and *Harvard Lampoon* presented the picture with their annual Twenty Cent Token 'to that film which does the most fashionable injustice to a minority class'.

Although Dustin took no awards for the movie, he took away fond memories of the Indians. 'To the Indians, death was a very simple thing, for life was just an appetiser. The ideal way would be to call your own death, to fear it all through life, and then reach an age where fear disappears, when you could say, "I'm ready now. I'm tired, I've had my life."'

But just around the corner, Death was lying in wait for Dustin once again.

15

Bombs Away!

Film is a personal effort and if you fail, you should fail for the right reasons.
And the only way you're going to fail is if you get out on a limb.

AFTER THE FIVE months on gruelling location and the inconveniences
of the long make-up sessions, Dustin took a rest with his family in New
York. In early 1970, he met the Italian director Franco Zeffirelli to talk
about his playing Francis of Assisi in *Brother Sun and Sister Moon*. He was
almost on the point of signing before his better judgement saved him at the
last moment from the emetic flower-child rompings of this 1972
Paramount flop.

A few weeks after his escape from a film disaster, Dustin came shat-
teringly close to a disaster of a more fatal kind. On the morning of
5 March 1970, a white station wagon delivered some cartons to the
elegant townhouse at 18 West 11th Street, next door to the Hoffmans.
The cartons contained dynamite, blasting caps, sections of metal pipe,
and several cheap alarm clocks. Gathered in the house were members of
the Greenwich Village group of young Weathermen revolutionaries,
including Diana Oughton, Kathy Boudin, Terry Robbins, Ted Gold
and Cathy Wilkerson, the teenage daughter of the wealthy new owners
of the house. James P. Wilkerson, president of the Star Stations of
Indiana Inc – a chain of five radio stations in the mid-West – had no
idea of his daughter's political leanings, and was on vacation with his
wife in the Caribbean. With her family absent, a meeting was held in
the basement to discuss the making of bombs. A few days before, one
of the male members of the group had bought two 50 lb boxes of
dynamite from the New England Corporation of Keene, New
Hampshire, for $50.

Dustin had been working at his antique desk all morning on contact
sheets of his wedding pictures, taken almost a year before, trying to pick
out the ones to develop. Karina and Anne, now two months pregnant, had
left for downtown New York. It was Karina's birthday, and they had
gone shopping for candles for her cake. Dustin left to join them at 11.30.
About forty-five minutes later three huge explosions went off in the
Wilkerson house, the force of which blew Dustin's $700 desk through a

hole in the wall. He would certainly have been killed instantly had he still been at it.

When Dustin heard news of the ensuing blaze, he rushed back to the scene, and was able to push through the gaping crowds to pull three of his modern paintings and a Tiffany lampshade from the smoke-filled Federal-style building, before the police prevented him from re-entering the house. Sadly, the rest of his collection of paintings and furniture had been badly charred or destroyed. The basement of the house had sustained heavy damage and part of the ceiling on the top floor had collapsed. All told, three people died and twenty-three were left homeless. After he and Anne had gone to the Red Cross centre to help comfort some of his neighbours, he told a friend, 'Thank God, I'm not poor!'

At first the explosions were thought to have been caused by a gas leak, but gradually the police were able to piece together evidence linking the disaster to the Weathermen, one of whom had attached a wire to the wrong terminal. The fatalities were three of their number: Terry Robbins had been virtually obliterated in the blast, Diana Oughton was mangled almost beyond recognition and Ted Gold, on the first floor, was killed by falling beams. Another three of them, never identified, escaped by crawling out of the back of the house. Cathy Wilkerson and Kathy Boudin, the latter totally naked, stumbled into the street and were taken in by a neighbour who offered them a shower and clothing. The two young women quickly washed and dressed before taking flight, not to surface again for over a decade. (Boudin was finally arrested in October 1981 while fleeing an armed robbery.)

The Weathermen, about whom the underground filmmaker Emile De Antonio made a sympathetic documentary in 1977, took their title from the protest song by Bob Dylan: 'You Don't Need A Weatherman To Know Which Way The Wind Blows.' In June 1968, they produced a document that announced that young Americans must accept the need for 'armed struggle'. Their credo was: 'Kill all the rich people. Break up their cars and apartments. Bring the revolution home, kill your parents, that's where it's really at.'

After fights with Mayor Daley's police on the streets of Chicago, they decided, at a 'war council' in Flint, Michigan, in December 1969, to go underground and become urban guerillas. The Weather People, as they later called themselves because of the number of women in their ranks, were led by Bernardine Dohrn. It was she who, commenting on the Sharon Tate murder in August 1969, said 'Dig it, first they killed those pigs, then they ate dinner in the same room with them, then they even shoved a fork into a victim's stomach! Wild!'

If the explosions had happened a few weeks later, the Hoffmans would have been living somewhere else. They had decided to move to an apartment opposite Central Park because Karina had been molested in Washington Square Park. Not very seriously – just a hand up her dress – but they felt they would prefer a better neighbourhood. It would have been tragically ironic if one of the Weather People's victims had been the actor, however bourgeois in their minds, who had been associated with a certain rebellion against the exploitative capitalist system they wished to destroy.

Death had brushed Dustin's cheek twice, threatening to take him first by fire and secondly by a bomb. Later, in the mid-70s, while on holiday in the Caribbean, he switched on a lamp that had frayed wiring and he received a terrific shock. 'I got so angry. I had a picture of myself standing barefoot in my swimming trunks, screaming and thrashing in a motel room, and I thought, "This isn't the way I'm supposed to go."' When the time comes, Dustin has expressed his desire to depart in the style of the actor David Burns, who suffered a fatal heart attack in the middle of a performance. Because he was a comic actor, he got a laugh. 'It was the perfect exit. He died the death of an actor.'

His life spared once more, Dustin signed to star in *Who Is Harry Kellerman and Why Is He Saying Those Terrible Things About Me?* for Cinema Center Films. The project attracted Dustin because he felt comfortable with the director Ulu Grosbard, his friend since 1962; it was to be filmed on his doorstep in New York, and the off-beat fantasy-comedy-drama which dealt with psychiatry, the price of fame, the fear of ageing and dying, and the need for love, struck a personal chord. It also seemed terribly contemporary in a society where pop singers were becoming the spokespeople of the age. The screenplay was written by Herb Gardner, a cartoonist who made his name with *The Nebbishes* and the 1962 hit Broadway play, *A Thousand Clowns*, filmed in 1965. The latter told of a hack TV gag writer (Jason Robards Jr) trying to prevent his precocious twelve-year-old nephew from being taken away from him by a Child Welfare Officer (William Daniels). It contained enough witty lines to keep the creeping whimsy, indicated in the title, at bay.

Who Is Harry Kellerman . . . ? was only Grosbard's second film as director, although he had previously assisted Elia Kazan, Robert Wise, Robert Rossen and Sidney Lumet. His debut had been *The Subject Was Roses* for MGM in 1968, the film of the Frank D. Gilroy play which, along with a plum Broadway role, was plucked away from Dustin by a pyrotechnical fondue pot.

The first shot in the movie is of Dustin writing a suicide note on the rooftop of the General Motors Building in New York. 'There was a time when I planned to live for ever, but the time has come to change those plans.' He finishes the note, sticks it on a pole and then jumps off the building, floating delightedly in slow motion behind the credits. It is probably the best sequence in the film. There was something suicidal about the whole pretentious enterprise, which Dustin should have been talked down from before he leaped.

Dustin, with an unbecoming Mexican bandit moustache and frizzy hair, mercifully covered by a cowboy hat for most of the time, is the vastly successful multi-millionaire Bob Dylan-type rock composer George Soloway (soul away, solo way), whose suicidal fall is broken on the couch of his psychiatrist Dr Moses (Jack Warden with a ginger beard and, naturally, a German accent). The consoling shrink tells George that, 'We must not rule out the possibility that you are a bird – a loony bird. A crazy, nutty loony bird.' What is George's problem? His main one seems to echo another interrogatorily titled film, *Will Success Spoil Rock Hunter?* Fame has made the former rebel into a smug, uncommitted and corrupt member of the musical establishment. Apparently, someone called Harry Kellerman has been phoning people up about George, and giving him 'the bad mouth all over town'. Warden then starts miming to a Ray Charles number, 'Don't tell me your troubles,' in the manner of a Dennis Potter TV play.

It is unfortunate that Dustin did not similarly mime the songs he sings while strumming a guitar (an instrument he studied for the part), because his singing voice is strained and uncomfortably high. By the end, we discover that of course he himself is Harry Kellerman, his alter ego and conscience. Before the audience learns the truth, they are subjected to a depressingly muddled, self-conscious wallow on the theme of fame, time and death which, for some obscure reason, eventually ends with George and his psychiatrist skiing down a slope.

When Dr Moses appears in one of George's hallucinations as Santa Claus, he asks George what he wants for Christmas. 'I'd like a new life and a day without fear,' his patient replies. Gardner's script contains other doubtful gems such as, 'I keep thinking, how come I've got kids and I'm only eighteen years old. Those kids are like clocks ticking away', and 'Time is not a thief, it's an embezzler.'

About midway through the film, a long sequence is given over to Barbara Harris, auditioning for a show by singing, intentionally weakly, 'Painting The Clouds With Sunshine'. 'I feel I've just auditioned for the part of a human being and I didn't get the job.' Throughout her self-pitying monologue (for which she received a Best Supporting Actress Oscar nomination), all Dustin has to do is stare at her while his moustache droops in sympathy.

The 33-year-old Dustin once again tries to run the age gamut, this time from 17 to 42 years old. He just about gets away with it as a teenager in long shot and make-up, but mostly he is heard (putting on a 'young' voice) and not seen. Firstly, Dustin is hidden under a folding bed which he is repairing in readiness for his first sexual experience, and then he is off-camera, talking to his parents, in the one comic-satiric scene that Woody Allen might not have disowned. But this tone soon dissolves into a miasma of melancholy. Neither Grosbard's direction nor Gardner's script is able to come into focus and, as a result, Dustin's character remains blurred. Is he sympathetic, comic, grotesque, touching? In the attempt to be all these things, he achieves none of them.

The crude satire seems to be directed at the fashionable protest singers of the time, who, while singing songs against the materialistic values of American society, are worried about the receipts from their concerts. George Soloway has been so busy making money that he has been unable 'to commit himself to another human being'. Was it more than just an in-joke to make George's chauffeur go under the name of Chomsky? (At the time, Noam Chomsky, the anti-Establishment linguistics professor, was a prominent critic of US intervention in Vietnam.) Or did it reveal a conservative attitude at the heart of a movie that is dressed up in hippie garb? Perhaps this contradiction contributed to its failure.

The producers, Grosbard and Herb Gardner, should have known that as a general rule films with long titles have short runs. Previous verbosely titled flops had been *Oh Dad, Poor Dad, Mamma's Hung You in the Closet and I'm Feelin' So Sad* (which also had Barbara Harris in it) and *Can Heironymus Merkin Ever Forget Mercy Humppe and Find True Happiness?* As far as audiences and critics were concerned, the answers to the two questions in *Who Is Harry Kellerman and Why Is He Saying Those Terrible Things About Me?* were 'Frankly, I couldn't give a damn.'

The picture was thought by *The New York Times* to have 'a flat, tinny sound', apart from the several scenes shared by Hoffman and Harris that were 'as touching as they were funny'. *Variety* found that it 'fails to engage any sympathy or interest: entire reels could be interchanged without it being evident'. (The same critic said the same of *Little Big Man*.) 'Hoffman's shy-guy ability to reach an audience is completely perverted; to say he is miscast is an understatement.'

On top of the unenthusiastic reviews for his last three movies, there appeared, at the same time, an article by Pauline Kael called 'Notes on

New Actors, New Movies' in *The New Yorker*, in which she wrote: 'Dustin Hoffman has become such a culture hero that one hesitates to point out that he's more relaxed and likeable on TV talk shows than when he's acting. In his screen roles, he hasn't yet found the gift of moving into a part and then just going with it. I love to watch him, because he's intelligent and he has extraordinary drive and he takes us by surprise, but he isn't an intuitive actor, and we're aware of how cleverly he's playing the part.'

In the meantime, Dustin was being honoured in other quarters. He was selected as the winner of the annual William J. German Human Relations Award, sponsored by the American Jewish Committee's Motion Picture and Entertainment Division in November 1970. Others who had received the award included Sidney Poitier, Stanley Kramer, Paul Newman and Joanne Woodward. Over five hundred directors and producers gathered at a luncheon to pay tribute to him. Gordon T. Stulberg, president of Cinema Center Films, in presenting the award cited his work to 'further human understanding to achieve a better society through the political process'. For *John and Mary*? *Midnight Cowboy*? *Who Is Harry Kellerman . . . ?* It turned out that the encomium had little to do with these epics, but for his generous economic support of the New York Psychoanalytic Institute, where he had once worked as a lowly attendant.

In the same year, Dustin was in London again as one of the guests at the Royal Command Performance of *Love Story*, where he was to be presented to the Queen Mother. 'I could hear the assistant quickly telling her about the person she was being introduced to. It was a lot of work for her. I think I was at the end of the line. So the first thing I said was, "You don't have to talk to me. I know you're very tired." That was the first mistake. She asked me what I was doing there. Tony Curtis was standing next to me so I said I was there to try and collect money from Mr Curtis. I said I'd been chasing him all over the world. She was stunned. I didn't get any laughs out of her.'

At that period, despite a postbag of film offers, Dustin tried to put his pregnant wife and his stepdaughter before everything else. To prove this, he turned down the role of the American archaeologist in Ingmar Bergman's *The Touch*, because the shooting would coincide with the birth of his child. How Dustin would have managed to submit himself to a real *auteur* like Bergman must remain a matter for conjecture. He would have been the first non-Scandinavian to star in a Bergman film, an honour which went eventually to the more laid-back Elliott Gould. He did, however, lend his now recognisable voice to an animated ABC feature called *The Point*, shown on 2 February 1971. Based on a story by Harry Nilsson, it told of a father competing with a TV set for his son's attention.

Meanwhile, Dustin, who has said that he envies pregnant women, followed a natural childbirth course with Anne, doing all the exercises she did. Dustin imagines himself angrily taking his case for male pregnancy to God, a bureaucrat behind a desk. 'I don't understand. Why don't I get to carry it?' But God brushes him aside. 'I don't want to talk about it. I've spent a lot of time on this.'

On 15 October 1970, Dustin had a photographer stationed outside the delivery room of the hospital ready to film the first moments of his first child's life. Anne, on cue, gave birth to her second child, Jennifer Celia (nicknamed Jenna), who weighed 8 lb 3 oz. 'I was there for her birth and it was the most exciting thing I have ever experienced!' exclaimed the father of the baby, and the owner of a home movie of strictly limited appeal.

16

'Jesus, I Got 'Em All!'

I'm not a violent person. I don't shoot guns, don't fight, but I get excited by violence.

THE DAY AFTER Anne went into labour, Dustin signed to do *Straw Dogs*, due to start production in England on 3 February 1971. The original title of the film was *The Siege of Trencher's Farm*, the name of the novel by Gordon M. Williams (a pseudonym for novelist J. Anderson Black), which was adapted by David Z. Goodman and the director Sam Peckinpah.

The plot tells of David Sumner, an introspective mathematician (changed from a professor of English in the book) who moves to a Cornish village with his sexy wife in order to escape violence in America. She attracts the attentions of the local yobbos and he the suspicions of the villagers. One day, while Sumner is out duck shooting, his wife's ex-lover bursts into the house and rapes her, followed by his friend. After the simpleton Henry Niles (David Warner) strangles the teenage daughter (Chloe Franks) of Tom Hedden (Peter Vaughan) and is given refuge in David's house, Hedden, his sons, and Scutt, the local ratcatcher, try to break into the house and get Henry out. This leads the non-violent professor to take up arms against the thugs to protect his home. 'This is where I live. This is me. I will not allow violence against my house.' After he has killed off the whole lot of them in various ways, he shouts in triumph, 'Jesus, I got 'em all!'

In October 1970, screenwriter Goodman and Dustin started research on the character in New York by going to a couple of universities to observe the behaviour of certain professors, presumably threatening the eggheads with violence to see how they would react. They then worked on the script together for a few months before joining Peckinpah in England, where he was busy with pre-production. Although Goodman and Peckinpah are credited with the screenplay, all three of them hammered out a final script. 'The basic characterisation of David Sumner represented an enormous amount of research and work on Dustin's part, and I think it showed on the screen,' commented Goodman.

Dustin was fond of quoting Cicero's phrase, which his father kept pinned on the wall beside his desk: 'Wise men are instructed by reason, men of less understanding by experience, the most ignorant by necessity, and beasts by nature.' The way Dustin envisaged his character in the scripting stage differed somewhat from what appeared (less subtly) on the screen. 'I saw him as fleeing the violent campus situation in America for the peaceful English countryside on a conscious level, while on an unconscious level he would begin to set up the conflict in the small town he went to. In other words, I saw the town as being completely different towards him at the outset of the film, and then in snide little ways he would turn them against him because he carried his violence with him. That was the thing that I found exciting about the script. The fact that Sam and I differed over this concept doesn't mean we didn't work well together.'

Another initial area of disagreement was over the casting of Susan George as his wife Amy. 'Sam sent me screen tests of her and some other girls, and I went to London to meet her. She seemed very nice and I thought she could act and we had a nice rapport, but I said to Sam, "I just feel she's the wrong type for a guy who's a teacher in college. You're opening up a whole new can of beans as to why he married this young kind of Lolita-ish girl." I could see a woman in her late twenties. Also the whole rape thing. I thought a woman who was a little older and starting to feel a little out of it in terms of being attractive – had the sensuality but was losing it – might be more ambivalent about being raped. Sam said he agreed and that I shouldn't worry because he could get that out of her. He even went so far as to say that he wouldn't do the picture without her. He asked me, "Please go with my hunch." I said, "All right." I still think I was right. Not that it didn't work the way we did it, but it worked in a different way.'

Lolita-ish the twenty-year-old Susan George wasn't! She had been a former child actress, making her film debut at the age of four, and at twelve she appeared in the London production of *The Sound of Music*. Her career in movies from the age of seventeen had not been particularly distinguished. Among the other girls tested for the part of Amy were 23-year-old Judy Geeson, who had already played a number of cock-teasing roles, and Joie Gould, an English secretary who was Peckinpah's girlfriend at the time. When Susan went for an interview for the role, she walked into Peckinpah's office, where Daniel Melnick, the producer, Dustin and Peckinpah were deep in conversation, ignoring her. Suddenly she noticed that all three had their trousers around their ankles.

'I backed towards the door. I was in a terrible fluster.' Then Peckinpah turned round and said, 'Welcome, Amy,' and the part was hers. 'It was Dustin's sense of humour personified,' Susan George says approvingly.

The rest of the cast, which included David Warner, Peter Vaughan and Colin Welland, were greeted more conventionally.

In January 1971, shooting began in what Patrick Agan, a previous biographer of Hoffman, called 'a desolate corner of Britain', a risible if not insulting reference to the county of Cornwall. The cast and crew were situated in the picturesque summer tourist trap of St Ives where they virtually took over the comfortable olde-worlde Tregenna Castle Hotel, while Peckinpah rented a small cottage for himself on the moor.

St Buryan, some twelve miles from St Ives, was selected as the town in the script. The film people wanted to shoot in the local pub, but the landlord refused them permission, explaining that he did not want to inconvenience his regular customers, despite being offered a tidy sum as recompense. As a result of the man's refreshing lack of avarice, a replica of the pub had to be built.

It was a raw, damp and cold Cornwall winter and, not long into the shooting, Peckinpah contracted 'flu which developed into pneumonia. He kept going on penicillin shots, but his condition continued to deteriorate. Finally, clutching Joie Gould with one hand and a bottle of Scotch in the other, he was sent off by train to a London clinic.

Meanwhile the cast and crew occupied themselves as best they could. Dustin, who had arrived with Anne, three-month-old Jennifer, and a nanny, played the piano or sang dirty songs to a guitar accompaniment in the hotel lounge in the evenings and, on one occasion, went into the kitchen to gather a few pots and pans to use as bongo drums in order to entertain his colleagues. Dustin and Anne often had meals with Colin Welland and his wife, or sometimes with Susan George and her boyfriend, the young actor Simon MacCorkindale, whom she was soon to marry. Otherwise Dustin was found swapping quotations with Irish actor T. P. McKenna in the bar or playing endless poker games. He was quite content with the food as long as he could have a plentiful supply of fillet steaks and his daily dose of freshly squeezed orange juice. One morning, Claude, the French maître d', ran out of oranges and had to top up Dustin's glass with some of the tinned variety. Dustin took one sip and told Claude that he was the only man he knew who could get fresh oranges out of a can.

When Peckinpah left Cornwall, he seemed in such a bad way that the possibility of replacing him was discussed. But the hardy director returned to the location four days later propped up by alcohol and Vitamin B12 shots.

Dustin and Peckinpah had a liking and respect for one another. The Western character actor Strother Martin, a friend of the director's, visiting the location, gave an account of their working rapport. 'There was this one scene where Dustin first did it by coming on very strong as the scene opened and then gradually bringing things down until everything was just suggested by innuendo and gestures. "Beautiful. Print it!" says Sam. "Now let's do one the other way, Dustin. Where you start down at the bottom and build it right up to the goddamn, fuckin' sky!" And Dustin says to Sam, "Which one did you like the best?" And Sam says, "Well, in the first one I liked this moment, and in the second I liked this." And Dustin says: "Give me one more! Give me one more!" And he tries to catch what Sam likes in both takes.'

'Dustin was so far ahead of me through the first half of the picture, it wasn't even funny,' Peckinpah confessed. 'Then somewhere about halfway, we were doing a scene, and after we had finished he turned to me and smiled and said, "Got me." That was it. He realised I had finally caught him . . . He forces you to work at controlling the character because he brings so much to the part.'

Dustin recalled that the director drove himself and his crew to the limits of endurance by keeping them up half the night, as he was never satisfied with the outcome of one take. 'It was a tough experience,' admits Dustin. 'But I loved working with him. He had the spontaneity of a child. Suddenly he would come up with things that were very exciting.' Several technical crew members were less enamoured by the director. When they complained of the long hours, Peckinpah had them fired. More friction was created when Susan George refused to play the rape scene all the way to the end. After a number of rows, Peckinpah got a double to complete the scene.

Some of Peckinpah's behaviour arose from his view of himself as a victim of the movie industry, because as much violence had been done to *Major Dundee* (1965) and *The Wild Bunch* (1969) as to the characters in them. For years he had continued a running battle with producers and film companies whom he saw as the bad guys. The 44-year-old director was born and brought up on a ranch in California, before attending military school and a spell in the Marines. His films reflect his background, a masculine world where one's manhood and independence can only survive through violence. Hence the nostalgia for the 'Old West' where men were men and women were nowhere. No matter how unpalatable one may find his vigilante philosophy – 'We're violent by nature. We're going to survive by being violent' – he expressed it with passionate intensity. But away from the controlling mythology of the Western, his blood-dimmed vision lacked the same conviction. Although *Straw Dogs* was his first non-Western, it had a plot that belonged in the Wild West rather than the West of England.

The comparatively gentle Dustin might not fully have realised the movie's meretricious implications. 'The reason I agreed to do the film was because of the script and the potential that I thought was there. What appealed to me was the notion, on paper at least, of dealing with a so-called pacifist who was unaware of his feelings and potential for violence inside himself that were the very same feelings he abhorred in society. The best example of that type of person is the liberal who professes to be anti-war and anti-violence and then goes to the boxing matches or watches the football game and screams his head off. He is totally unaware of that contradiction within himself.'

The first close-up in *Straw Dogs* is of Susan George's nipples, seen through a fetching sweater, which have the male townsfolk, young and old, leering. They act as though no sexy young woman has ever trod those cobbled streets before, although the nubile daughter of the drunken town bully (Peter Vaughan) walks around in the mini-est of mini-skirts especially catching the eye of the long-haired village idiot (David Warner), who has already molested young girls. Neither, it seems, has the population ever set eyes on an American. When the mild-mannered and bespectacled Sumner, who has a nice line in polo-neck jumpers, enters the local pub, they look upon him with suspicion, just like a stranger entering a saloon bar in a Western. He is also the only intellectual in a town full of morons, except for Major Scott (T. P. McKenna) and the well-meaning vicar (Colin Welland). All the same, Dustin does some things that seem strange to the natives, like making the Woodstock peace sign to the yobbish workmen, who return it mockingly, and also by playing loud bagpipe music on the record-player when the vicar and his wife pay a call.

We find out little about his past or where and when he met his English wife. There are only oblique references to the fact that he refused to 'get involved' (in what? the peace or civil rights movement?) in the States. (In this respect, *Straw Dogs* could almost have been called *John and Mary in Cornwall*.) His young wife says, 'You're here because there's no place else to hide.' It seems as though he wouldn't hurt a fly, except there is an inkling that he could become nasty when he starts to throw fruit and vegetables at the cat, who is as suspicious of this 'foreigner' as the natives.

When the cat is found hanged in the closet (the first act of violence after nearly an hour's build-up), his wife reproaches him with being a coward because he will not confront the men she thinks have killed the animal. There is also the suggestion that he doesn't satisfy her sexually. The couple play chess in bed and then, as they begin to have sex, he stops to wind up the alarm clock. He also ignores her during the day when he is busy with his mathematics. She gets bored, disturbs his concentration, and surreptitiously changes a plus sign into a minus to upset his calculations. (Despite the coming horrors, Dustin's most aghast look in the entire film comes when his wife sticks chewing gum on his blackboard.) When Susan exposes her breasts to the already randy workmen by standing topless at an open window, the implication is clear that she is 'asking' for the eventual rape.

Dustin's transition after his wife's rape from passive to active, from Clark Kent to Superman, comes about too smoothly to be credible. And he plays the menacing scenes that follow over-lightly, winking at his wife, giving his half smile and making quips. A greater nervous intensity would have been more convincing than his almost icy calm as the brutes try to break into his home – something Al Pacino, Dustin's near double, might have achieved. There is never a moment when Dustin gets as worried as Gary Cooper in *High Noon*, although, like Cooper, he has to cope single-handedly with a number of killers, and is only saved at the final moment when his wife blasts the last opponent with a shotgun. (Interestingly, Grace Kelly's character in *High Noon* was also called Amy.) However, at the end of the Fred Zinnemann Western, there is calm content at good having defeated evil, no triumphant gloating of the 'Jesus, I got 'em all!' variety.

Using his logical mind, Dustin/Sumner takes them all on, getting rid of them in various ways – with a knife, burning oil, a gun and an animal trap. Audiences cannot help but cheer him on. At almost every showing there are cries of 'Go get 'em, Dustin! Kill 'em, Dustin!' There is no doubt that Peckinpah makes us share the exhilaration of revenge. The quiet American, as usual, comes out on top.

In theory, Dustin's man of reason forced into bloody revenge could be seen as a therapeutic investigation into the nature of violence, making audiences consider their own potential for brutality. But Peckinpah is unable to create any objectivity towards the sadistic spectacle, in the manner of, say, Akira Kurosawa. It is clear that the director relishes the cruel revenge meted out to the crudely characterised Cornish villagers even more than the turned bookworm does, thus inciting the audience to condone the sorry sight. It may also have been reassuring to US audiences, while America was being condemned world-wide for its barbaric acts in Vietnam, to see that they did not have the monopoly on violence, which could even be found in an English village.

J. Anderson Black (alias Gordon M. Williams) was not amused by what had been done to his novel. 'I will never again sell one of my books to an American,' he said. 'It was horrific to see what they have done to my work. They've added a rape scene, an act of buggery, and lots of violence that was not in the book. A girl sitting next to me in the cinema vomited during one of the worst scenes and had to leave.'

Someone might have warned the poor girl that Peckinpah's movies do have that effect on some people. In the 1987 Motion Picture Guide, the unnamed critic of the film goes into an absolute frenzy of hatred. 'A disgusting tale . . . abysmal . . . this pus-oozing open sore of a film . . . All of the actors, especially Hoffman, are nothing more than stooges to Peckinpah's notions of perversity, degradation, and dungheap characterisation . . . this putrid, wholly offensive and nauseating snotball of a film . . . two hours of a running sewer disgorging human waste . . .' And so on.

David Thomson, who found the film 'gratuitous, misogynist, pretentious and repellent', remarked about Hoffman that 'his adoption of violence at the climax is the more troubling because Peckinpah never seems to have explained its need to the gentle and perplexed actor. The gloating contrivance of *Straw Dogs* is accentuated by Hoffman's guardedness. He fights back like someone under orders; he never concedes the thrill of revenge or the trembling orgasm of blood. The one aspect of his character that works is the appeal of mathematics; but the actor's cerebral dimension never appeared to win Peckinpah over . . . Hoffman is as unlikely a killer as he is husband to the very ripe Susan George. The movie might have been truer to the actor if Hoffman had rejected retaliation and been left with physical ruin and intact theorems.'

Pauline Kael, who called it a 'fascist classic', thought that 'Hoffman, notoriously a cerebral actor, projects thought before movement; he's already a cartoon of an intellectual.' According to John Simon, the casting of Hoffman 'strikes me as ill-advised and damaging . . . I do not see Hoffman's hesitancies of speech, his throatbound voice that has to struggle past a colony of frogs, his eyes that crouch nervously in their sockets, as a proof of consequential ratiocination going on inside his head. I see it rather as an actor's bag of tricks, and not a very apposite one for the role. Hoffman is a "character" emanating a naive or crotchety puniness; in this part, however, a more neutral figure, scholarly and aloof but not infantile or even doltish in appearance, would have been vastly preferable.'

Robin Wood, however, defended the film, comparing it favourably with *A Clockwork Orange* ('the ugliest film I have ever seen') of the same year. Wood claimed that 'if one follows the film's narrative carefully, one finds that all the acts of violence perpetrated by the hero are logically motivated – he is forced into them step by step from the moment he determines to earn and preserve his self-respect. Yet the effect of the violence is as much exhilarating as horrifying . . . if one's moral position is the tenable one that violence is intrinsically wrong and must at all costs be held in check, then there is no doubt that *Straw Dogs* is an immoral film. Peckinpah sees life as, inevitably, a bloody struggle for survival – not just physical survival, but the survival of one's manhood. Peckinpah's films implicitly accept violence as a metaphysical fact, a condition of our existence.'

Straw Dogs managed to attract enough blood seekers to put it into the black at the box-office, but this disturbing tale of rural atrocities can scarcely have done much for the Cornish tourist industry.

17

Hoffman – Italian Style

They told me I could do it in Italian. But they lied to me and I had to do it in English.

AFTER THE MONTHS of location shooting in Cornwall, and the completion of the interiors of *Straw Dogs* at Twickenham Studios in London in March 1971, Dustin returned to his New York home, determined to spend as much time as possible with his family, only going down to his production office, SweetWall Productions, on West 56th Street, for a few hours a day. But it was not long before he was off on location again, having accepted an offer from the Italian director Pietro Germi to star in a comedy entitled *Till Divorce Do You Part*. 'I did not offer Dustin the role as insurance for American release,' insisted Germi. 'I thought he was perfect for the story and sent him a script with about as much hope as those who put messages in bottles and toss them in the ocean.'

After the cold of Cornwall, Dustin relished the thought of the warmth of Italy and the making of a genuine Italian film, unlike the bastardised *Madigan's Millions*. With the admirable thoroughness with which he approaches each role, Dustin took a crash course in Italian. Never having had much schooling outside acting, and without knowledge of a foreign language, he had to make a huge mental effort. After some weeks, he had absorbed enough Italian to learn his lines in the lingo, and feel adept at ordering a meal at an Italian restaurant. However, he was only called upon to reveal his prowess in the latter activity. When he arrived in Italy with Anne and the children, Germi informed him that he was to play the role in English, to be dubbed later into Italian. This was (and is) a common practice in Italy, where even Italian actors are dubbed, often by entirely different people, and Dustin was by no means the first English-speaking star to be given another voice. (Luchino Visconti had already used Farley Granger, Burt Lancaster, Michael Craig and Dirk Bogarde. Steve Cochran and Richard Harris had taken leads in Michelangelo Antonioni films, while Anthony Quinn, Richard Basehart, Broderick Crawford and Terence Stamp had been cast by Federico Fellini.) But this was not the sort of thing Dustin was used to. Besides, he always began creating a character from the voice. Yet he had clearly been naive to suppose that his American–accented Italian would be acceptable.

However, so keen was Germi to get Dustin that he had made him co-producer, and allowed him equal say as to how the role was to be played. In fact, it was the sort of autonomy that Dustin had already won on his last two pictures, and would retain, much to many directors' displeasure, in most of his future ventures. A further pandering to the star would seem to have come in the change of title to *Alfredo Alfredo*, repeating the name of Dustin's character, but in fact it was Germi who was not happy with the original title, which sounded as if the film were a sequel to his big inter-national hit of 1961, *Divorce Italian Style*.

The four months of shooting began in October 1972, much of it in the Abruzzi, in the mountain town of Ascoli Piceno (well photographed by Carlo Rustichelli), with studio work at the De Paolis Studio in Rome. Again, as in *Straw Dogs*, Dustin was the only American in the cast. (He would later have the same experience in *Agatha*, and in *The Merchant of Venice* on the London stage.) So Dustin found himself in the odd position of acting in English, while all around him the cast spoke Italian. 'Germi knows exactly what he wants and cuts as he goes along. He doesn't have to take as many shots and gives more time to each one he wants. Everyone around him is like a member of the family. He's worked with them for years. I was the only newcomer to his unit and felt like a boarder in a rooming house until I settled in.'

More difficult than delivering his lines, however, was learning a multi-tude of meaningful Italian gestures. But the gregarious and curious Dustin, after an initial awkwardness, forced himself to fit into the ambience. If only for the veracity of the role, he mixed as much as possible with the cast and crew and with the local population. He also learned a couple of Italian songs, which are sung in the film.

Germi had begun his career directing serious, realistic features on post-war Italy, but in the sixties he changed to broad, satirical sex comedies, the best and most popular being *Divorce Italian Style*, which received three Oscar nominations. (It won Best Original Screenplay.) *Alfredo Alfredo* was to be Germi's last completed film. He died of hepatitis in 1974 aged 60.

Dustin played a timid bank clerk who dreams of being a ladies' man, although he does not seem to be short of girlfriends. When he meets a voluptuous pharmacist (Stefania Sandrelli), he is astonished when she pur-sues *him*. Marriage to her is a dream come true. However, he soon discovers that she has a voracious sexual appetite, which he finds almost impossible to satisfy. When she makes love she screams like a banshee, and things are inclined to get knocked over. As no children seem to be on the way, the doctor recommends that the couple make love from 10.30 to 11.30 in the morning and 2.30 to 5 in the afternoon, as well as in the evening, a situation that causes Alfredo to break out in a rash. When his wife becomes pregnant, he is confined to a room in the cellar while her parents move in upstairs. This gives him the chance to escape at night while *The Count of Monte Cristo* is on the radio. On one of these escapades, he meets and falls in love with a landscape architect (Carla Gravina), a far gentler woman. When his vixen wife's pregnancy turns out to be a phantom one, and he has to return to her bed, he runs away from home, taking refuge in his girlfriend's apartment. 'You have transformed a poor runaway slave into a man still capable of being happy.' He now finds he cannot get a divorce. He is labelled a criminal because of his extra-marital affair, although the legal system sanctions his wife taking a lover. But, with the help of the changing law, a divorce is eventually granted, which allows him to marry again. At the wedding, he wishes his bride would say 'no', but he's trapped again. The film ends with Dustin's fixed grin, while audiences are left with fixed frowns.

Dustin, with darkened eyebrows, oily black hair smoothed down on either side of a central parting, dark sunglasses and Italian gestures, wastes much of his talent in this frenzied, intermittently funny satire on Italian customs. But it is difficult to imagine how Dustin could have felt any involvement in the picture. Here, in a role that might have better suited Peter Sellers, or, more authentically, Alberto Sordi, he goes through a few variations on Ben Braddock and Jason Fister, the agent in his first Italian misadventure. He is neither comic nor romantic enough for the role. But it is difficult to blame him. The film is like a light pizza piled with heavy dressing, and it sags under its burden. Whereas the satiric intentions of *Divorce Italian Style* were pointed and comic, *Alfredo Alfredo* gets unduly preachy as Dustin and his mistress join the four-year fight to change the Italian law on divorce. 'We want divorce and we want it now,' they shout on a march. However, because the absurd law, Germi's principal target, was changed at the time of the film's release, the message was rendered almost meaningless.

Variety thought that the 'fact that so many of these gags depend on ill-concealed misogyny soon stifles the laughs that flowed more easily in a pre-women's liberation era. Now, all the simplistic stereotyping of the femme characters is fairly distasteful . . . Hoffman mugs satisfactorily in the leading role, but his voice has been dubbed by an Italian actor. Since the choked delivery has become one of his trademarks, it's not a little disconcerting to hear a smooth vocal style accompanying his post-*Graduate* body movements. With his own voice as back-up, the 36-year-old actor might not seem quite so strained in still milking certain "boyish" manner-isms.' Nora Saye in *The New York Times* found him 'Passive as a potato, timid as a fawn . . . Despite his efforts to tear into his food with Latin gusto, or the slicked-down hair above the urban American face, he simply can't appear to be a native of a provincial Italian town.'

Pauline Kael, on the other hand, thought that although 'dubbing is an abomination', the 'stranger's voice does wonders for Hoffman – it brings him out. In American movies, he's the perennial urban weakling-adolescent, doomed to swallow spit forever, but here, rid of the frightened, choked-up voice that constricts his characters, he gives a softer-edged, more relaxed performance. Maybe the director, Pietro Germi, put him at his ease; Alfredo, Hoffman's bank clerk, is warm and friendly and likeable. Hoffman's face has never been very expressive (sometimes his rabbit stare makes me think that the great Maureen Stapleton has spawned an emotionally retarded son), but he has always been able to get our empathy.'

Disgusted by the reaction to his last few films, Dustin locked himself in his New York home and became a virtual recluse. When scripts arrived he sent them back unread. He seldom ventured out. 'I'd always told myself that if I dried up creatively I'd walk away from acting. So I thought I'd had it. It wasn't easy, but it's better than burning yourself out making pictures you don't like for people you don't respect . . . I've never turned down a film I've wanted to do because the money was too small. If I believe in a film I'll do it. On the other hand, of course I ask for as much as I can get.'

18

Heat and Dustin

There are actors who like making movies, but I've never enjoyed it.

'SO THE LUNATICS have taken charge of the asylum,' remarked Richard A. Rowland, president of Metro Pictures, on hearing of the formation of the United Artists Corporation in 1919 by D. W. Griffith, Charles Chaplin, Mary Pickford and Douglas Fairbanks, the four biggest names in motion pictures at the time. If so, it was inspired lunacy, for it led to the creation of such classics from the Big Four in UA's first decade as Griffith's *Way Down East*, Fairbanks's *The Thief of Baghdad*, Pickford's *Little Lord Fauntleroy*, and Chaplin's *The Gold Rush*. UA was idealistically founded to act as a distribution agency to give independent producers freedom of expression away from the restraints of the major studios. The films were not only to be self-produced and self-distributed, but self-financed as well.

Half a century later, in 1969, First Artists Productions, a new independent film company, was set up by Paul Newman, Sidney Poitier and Barbra Streisand, with a similar aim – a balance between mammon and idealism – to that which led to the formation of UA. The idea of First Artists was to offer each star, tired of bureaucratic controls at other major studios, a rich financial package – including creative control. The idea was that each film should have a $3 million budget limitation, be in colour and not exceed one hundred and forty minutes, have a rating of G, PG or R, and star or co-star the actor or actress involved. It was just the sort of set-up that attracted Dustin, who had been itching to have more power over his films for some time.

So, on 12 September 1971, at National General Pictures' international conference for foreign film distributors in Hollywood, Dustin signed to become a partner, following Steve McQueen, who had joined the same year. His contract contained a clause granting him creative control over the films and a final say on editing, and a salary of over $1 million per film and 50 per cent of each film's box-office revenue, a profit participation scale somewhat higher than the others'. 'I always felt it was difficult for me to find films. I'm not someone who's going to be the same person in every film.' (Implying that Newman, McQueen, Poitier and Streisand might be.) 'One of the selling points when I joined was that I'd be privy to scripts that I was never exposed to because I never had an agent.'

As with the Fairbanks–Pickford–Chaplin–Griffith studio, the dream would turn sour, and the participants would all too soon realise they had mistaken Hollywood for Cloud-Cuckoo Land. This rude awakening was, however, still a few years away at the time when Dustin joined.

Three of the principal shareholders were already producing films for release at the time of Dustin's signing, and unfortunately proving that artistic liberty was not synonymous with artistic quality. Sidney Poitier directed and starred in the yukkie *A Warm December*; Barbra Streisand played a rebellious housewife in *Up The Sandbox*, a garish comedy-drama; and Steve McQueen produced and starred in the brutish Sam Peckinpah heist movie *The Getaway*, which grossed more than $36 million world-wide despite mixed reviews.

Meanwhile, a screenplay was being concocted from Henri Charrière's 1969 semi-autobiographical bestseller *Papillon*. Ex-convict Charrière found himself a huge celebrity when the book sold a million copies in France, two-and-a-half million in America and ten million throughout the world. The film was independently financed by French producer Robert Dorfmann, who had bought the rights to the novel. When it came to casting, it was thought that Jean-Paul Belmondo would be the best choice to play the Charrière role, although his international renown was beginning to fade a little. But in order for Dorfmann to get the money to produce it, an American superstar was needed. It was Steve McQueen who was picked to play the French criminal determined to escape from Devil's Island where he has been sentenced to life imprisonment for the murder of a pimp, of which he claims he is innocent. The title derives from the nickname of the hero, who has a large butterfly (Fr. *papillon*) tattooed on his chest.

Franklin J. Schaffner was contracted to direct the $13 million movie. The 53-year-old director was no tyro in turning millions of dollars into celluloid and possibly gold. In the early part of his career he had made a number of smaller, better films such as *The Stripper* (1963) and *The Best Man* (1964), before embarking on bigger and more portentous projects such as *The War Lord* (1965) and *The Planet of the Apes* (1967), both with Charlton Heston baring his teeth and chest; *Patton* (1969), an ambiguous biopic about a modern war lord (for which he won Best Director Oscar); and *Nicholas and Alexandra* (1971), a tedious and simplistic Tsar-trek.

Over the two years of preparation for *Papillon*, the screenplay went through the hands of four writers. The successful screenwriting team of Robert Benton and David Newman (*Bonnie and Clyde, What's Up Doc?*)

did a treatment that was discarded by Schaffner. He turned to William Goldman for help. Goldman's prime input was his suggestion that the film should end with the first part of the book, before Papillon arrives in Venezuela and settles down. Goldman worked on the script from October 1971 to April 1972, submitting three drafts, but all that remains of his contribution to the film is the last line, 'Hey, you bastards. I'm still here!' spoken by McQueen when he finally escapes on a craft made of coconut shells – an attempt to round off the story as a paean of praise to survival.

Before leaving to begin *The Great Waldo Pepper* for George Roy Hill and Robert Redford, Goldman later recollected in his *Adventures in the Screen Trade*: 'I was present at a meeting at which some guys said, "Dustin Hoffman is getting hot. If we only had a part for Dustin Hoffman, that would be terrific." And we scoffed because there was no part.'

At the time, Dustin was looking for a role that attracted him. He had recently shown interest when Paramount wanted him to play a homosexual murderer in a drama called *The Witness*, to be directed by Milos Forman. But the project was scrapped at the last minute. When he heard that a role in *Papillon* would be especially created for him, he was not only flattered but asked for (and got) a salary of $1.25 million. (McQueen received $2 million.) Steve McQueen and Dustin Hoffman were to be billed always on the same line. 'Dustin was bought – not brought – into the film,' said Schaffner.

Lorenzo Semple Jr came in to spend six weeks writing three quick drafts to create the character for Dustin – the wimpish, thickly bespectacled Louis Dega, 'the best counterfeiter in France', who did not exist in the Charrière book. According to Schaffner, Dega was essential because the book contained no real human relationships. When Semple departed, Dalton Trumbo came in to build up the Dega character in line with the buddy-buddy movie trend.

The filming began with only 57 pages of script and the rest of the story was simply blank. Therefore Schaffner was forced to take the unusual step of shooting it mostly in sequence, getting on with what had already been written. Trumbo continued writing on location in Spain and Jamaica. (He is seen briefly, with his snowy moustache, at the beginning of the film, addressing the convicts in the role of the commandant.) But when he suddenly took ill and returned to Hollywood to undergo surgery for lung cancer, his son Christopher helped polish up some of the last few scenes. Dalton Trumbo, who was one of the Hollywood Ten, jailed and blacklisted in 1947, reappeared as a screenwriter in the sixties. *Papillon* was his last film, and he died three years later in 1976, aged 70.

The production was plagued by money troubles from the start. The film subsisted on funds that Dorfmann would gather along the way by showing ten or fifteen minutes of cut film to prospective investors. There was a period when only McQueen and Dustin were getting their per diem allowance, something they did not need as much as the rest of the cast and crew. When McQueen discovered the situation, he refused to work until everyone was paid. Not surprisingly, they were.

The first parts of the picture were shot in Spain before the company moved to Jamaica for most of the rest of the location work. The filming in the tropics was 'just nerve-racking', prompting Dustin to say that 'all pictures are hard work, although some actors have an easier time than others. I've got a calendar from the day I start shooting, and I start crossing off the days the way I did at high school, waiting for summer vacation to begin.' On screen, the locations certainly seem rough enough to give the impression that much of the filming must have been genuinely unpleasant, and the physical and emotional demands of the film, shot in high temperatures, led Dustin to lose twenty pounds by the time it was completed. (He had in fact put on weight while resting after *Alfredo Alfredo*, and needed to lose it for the role anyway. Ironically, it was a case of an out-of-work actor getting fat, then starting work and starving.)

McQueen was accompanied on location by Ali MacGraw, whom he had met on *The Getaway*, and whose presence he admitted saved him from going round the bend. Both his and her children were there too. It was in that tropical setting that Steve and Ali were married. Accompanying Dustin on the trip were his wife and two daughters. Anne is glimpsed briefly at the beginning of the film in the role of Dega's wife. Wearing a chic black costume and white fur wrap, she is seen waving to him as he departs for the colony before walking away to a smart car beside which stands a chauffeur.

The relationship between the contrasting Hoffman and McQueen was an uncomfortable one. Dustin had a certain envy of McQueen's looks, self-confidence, physical prowess and rebellious nature. On the other hand, McQueen, seven years Dustin's senior, envied the other's reputation as a fine actor, something he had always wanted for himself. Dustin privately entertained his friends with a wickedly accurate imitation of superstar McQueen attempting to upstage little Dustin.

'Maybe what upset Dustin was that he knew that, although he was the better actor, Steve's performance in *Papillon* was superior,' commented Norman Jewison, who had directed McQueen in *The Cincinnati Kid* and *The Thomas Crown Affair*, but who never worked with Dustin. 'Like Bogart, Steve brought himself to each part he played and something of each of them rubbed off on his personality. He was the quintessential film

star in that he never played anyone else. A strong persona is the difference
between a film star and a theatre star. You'll see Dustin's acting, but you'll
never see Steve's.'

Further differences between the stars were underlined by Schaffner. 'I
would always shoot on McQueen first to make him commit and then turn
around and shoot on Hoffman. It seemed to work better that way because,
if I covered Hoffman first, Steve would become restless about what he was
doing. The quicker you got him comfortable, the better the scene would
play. Hoffman, on the other hand, is a totally electric performer. He
comes in with ninety-nine ideas of how to approach a scene. And you're
prepared to say, "Hey, look – here in my view is the approach." Usually,
he'd say, "Okay, let's go right away."'

Though McQueen collected cars and motorcycles while Dustin was
interested in antiques and art, they respected each other's acting abilities.
Actually, they came from similar traditions. McQueen learnt his acting at
New York's Neighborhood Playhouse, making his professional debut,
somewhat surprisingly, at a Yiddish theatre on Second Avenue. He also
attended classes at the Actors Studio, before replacing Ben Gazzara in the
leading role of the junkie in *A Hatful of Rain* on Broadway in 1956.

McQueen's most fruitful period in films had been in the sixties while
Dustin was still unknown outside off-Broadway. In the seventies,
McQueen's appearances became more intermittent, and it was reported
that he had turned increasingly temperamental, rejecting more scripts than
he was prepared to accept. But he still conveyed an easy-going personality
and had a deceptively casual acting style that differed from Dustin's volatile nature and the nervous intensity he invested in each role.

Dustin as Louis Dega (pronounced, most of the time, as Lewis Dega),
unshaven, thickly spectacled, in red striped pyjamas, with his head shaven
on either side of his ears, spends most of the film with his mouth agape.
Limping behind McQueen, he has resurrected Ratso from *Midnight
Cowboy*, and the performance also looks ahead to his mentally handi-
capped *Rain Man* character. With his whining, nasal, urban voice, there are
moments when he is the weedy boy at the summer camp or Woody Allen
finding himself in the South American jungles in *Bananas*. Dega is so
myopic that he never takes his glasses off – there is a nice touch when Dustin
holds his hand over his spectacles as he is showered down. Nevertheless,
he is not so short-sighted that he cannot catch a butterfly between his
fingers.

Despite Dustin's worries over the script – 'I learned not to try to build
more of a character than the text can support' – his performance is one of
threads and patches, full of actorish tics and attempts at pathos. Next to

Dustin's overacting, Steve McQueen's acting is almost naturalistic. Although McQueen is too lightweight a performer for the part, he occasionally reaches moments of tragic agony. One cannot help imagining, however, what Jean Gabin and Marcel Dalio would have made of the roles.

McQueen is happiest in the action sequences such as the exciting 'Great Escape' from the prison during a concert of French ballet music, and his subsequent flight through the jungle, surviving snakes, crocodiles, Indian blowpipes, and a leper colony until he gets himself to a nunnery and is betrayed by the Mother Superior.

Much of McQueen's acting was done for him by the make-up of Charles Schram, who effectively ages him over his years of solitary confinement. (Yet despite leaving his cell quite old and grey after his first five-year stint there, he seems to shed almost ten years within weeks.) The scenes in solitary are especially well depicted, as the prisoners react to a shrill whistle when it is feeding time, but Schaffner's tone, like McQueen's personality, lacks the austerity needed for such a subject. Perhaps he should have watched Robert Bresson's *A Man Escaped* before embarking on the picture.

Although *Papillon* has rousing and touching moments, the whole enterprise meanders on too heavily for too long. Unusually for a Hollywood film, the only glimmer of sex in the movie, until near the end – a hackneyed Polynesian idyllic interlude with a willing bare-breasted native girl – comes in a strangely Genetesque moment when a pretty young boy prisoner is fondled by the turnkey, who puts a rose in his mouth. The only real kiss is the platonic one between Dustin and McQueen on the cliff top, before McQueen dives into the sea and escapes, swimming surprisingly powerfully for a man of his age and condition.

The movie opened on 19 December 1973 to less-than-glowing reviews, although it made over $22.5 million, becoming one of the year's top moneymakers. (*Alfredo Alfredo* was also released nationwide on the same day, but the public obviously preferred Hoffman French Style to Hoffman Italian Style.) In *The New York Times*, Vincent Canby thought McQueen was 'as all-American as a Rover Boy' and Hoffman was 'not especially convincing', but he enjoyed it as the sort of 'escapist movie we used to go see on Saturday night without even bothering to read the marquee'. *Variety* thought it 'impact numbing and stunning', and Hoffman did 'an excellent job'. Pauline Kael was less than flattering: 'Why does he go through the picture with his mouth open, like some adenoidal chinless wonder? Is he trying to be helpful by making himself different from McQueen? (He really doesn't have to worry about that.) This co-starring arrangement between men needs the right chemistry, but McQueen doesn't supply for Hoffman what Voight did in *Midnight Cowboy*. The reverse happens. McQueen seems to inspire Hoffman to underplay, too. When Papillon prepares for his final escape and Louis says he's not going, he sounds as if he had decided not to shave that day.'

Harvard Lampoon gave Dustin the Worst Supporting Actor award and the movie received the Please-Don't-Put-Us-Through-DeMille-Again award for the film which 'best embodies the pretensions, extravagances, and blundering ineffectiveness of the Screen Spectacular'.

Anne's non-verbal bit-part as Mrs Dega was not even credited. More importantly, she continued to struggle with the increasingly demanding role of Mrs Hoffman.

19

Lenny

It was the most difficult part I have had to play.

THE OUTRAGEOUS CULT nightclub comedian Lenny Bruce died of drug abuse in 1966 two months before his 44th birthday, after being harassed by the police and the courts for years. His longtime friend, film producer Marvin Worth, had been trying since 1968 to set up a screen biography. Three years later, in May 1971, Julian Barry's play *Lenny*, of which Worth was co-presenter, opened to acclaim at the Brooks Atkinson Theater, with Cliff Gorman winning a Tony in the title role. Because the subject dealt with strong sex, strong drugs and strong language, film companies, even in the early seventies, were rather timid about handling it. Worth eventually sparked the interest of Bob Fosse, who managed to get United Artists to throw timidity aside and product it.

Fosse's first choice for the role of Lenny Bruce was Dustin, to whom he sent Julian Barry's script. It was based on the stage play, which used actual material from the trials, and took the form of flashbacks spoken into a tape recorder by various people who knew Bruce. Although Dustin liked it, he felt he could not accept the role. He had seen the Broadway play and was so impressed by Gorman's performance that, initially, he felt no one else could play the part, which is what he told the film's producers when they approached him. Fosse wanted Dustin so badly that, if he saw the actor at a party or a restaurant, he would half-mockingly fall to his knees and crawl towards Dustin, imploring him to take the role. Gorman had been considered but was not a big enough 'name'. (As some consolation, Fosse would later cast him in *All That Jazz*.)

Then it was announced that Al Pacino was close to signing. The Bronx-born Pacino, two and a half years Dustin's junior, resembled Dustin, and could be cast in similar roles. In fact, he seemed to dog Dustin's footsteps throughout the early part of his career, which led both men to make defensive jokes about their likeness. In the mid-seventies, there was a cartoon that read: 'If Al Pacino and Dustin Hoffman aren't the same person, then howcum they are never in the same film together?' (Many years later, they did appear together briefly in *Dick Tracy*, though, because they wore such heavy make-up, it was not enough to allay doubts among cynics as to their oneness.) Pacino was another alumnus of the Actors Studio, and came to films via off- and on-Broadway. When he was approached to do *Lenny*, he was at the height of his popularity after *The Godfather* and *Serpico*. Mainly because Gorman was out of the running and because of the unspoken rivalry between Pacino and himself, Dustin now immediately committed himself to doing the picture.

As part of his build-up for the role, Dustin bought a number of index cards, on which he jotted down any significant information that came to him about Lenny Bruce, as well as observations as to how he thought he should play the real-life character. These cards he stuck all over the walls of his office. Some of them read 'Leo Gorcey', 'Charlie Parker and Miles Davis', 'Brando', names that he felt might bring him closer to a style that he was aiming for.

Dustin had never met Lenny Bruce or seen him work in the flesh so he spent about six months prior to the filming listening to records, watching films, and reading books on the comedian, as well as interviewing over sixty people who knew Bruce intimately, including his ex-wife, Honey, his daughter Kitty, and mother, Sally Marr. Invaluable, too, was *The Lenny Bruce Performance*, an unedited film record of a routine in a San Francisco nightclub in August 1965, which included a savagely funny attack on his trial in New York for having performed obscene material. Other film footage was his pilot for a TV series, the tape of the cleaned-up monologue he did on the Steve Allen Show, both of which censored his vigorous language, originality and spontaneity, and some home movies which he and his mother made.

'His mother and I talked at lot in LA,' Dustin stated. 'She said that there was a certain spontaneous side to him, strange things he might do in public. In the middle of a meal in a restaurant he might get up and go into the kitchen and talk to the guy washing dishes. I tried to close in on those things in me that they said were reminiscent of Lenny.'

Dustin was inclined to do similar things. Once, in a New York restaurant with British journalist Clive Hirschhorn, during a conversation on fame, Dustin claimed that it meant nothing to him. He then got up and went round to each table in turn asking astonished people what they thought about the subject. The verbal filth with which Dustin enjoyed littering his conversation was another point of similarity.

Contradicting his negative opinion of filmmaking, expressed during the sweltering period of *Papillon*, Dustin commented: 'The obsession with his work is a central thing. I know from my own experience that I'm most happy when I'm deep into my own work. Working was very, very important to Lenny. And that's why when the work was taken away after all the busts, he began to fall apart. He couldn't get on the stage and it really hung him up. For the research I did, and I must say that I am not an authority on this man, I feel that he would have had his self-destructive problems no matter what he was – he was a man who used drugs, needed drugs as an addict. From what I understand, that was a part of him and was not tied into persecutions he suffered. It worried me primarily because [he] had been a real person and he had only been dead eight years, and there were people who loved him still living . . . I was sensitive to the danger of misrepresenting a man who'd been misrepresented enough already.'

For the part of Bruce's stripper/drug-addict/bisexual wife, Honey, Fosse spent weeks testing up to thirty women. Dustin said that he did not mind testing them in the love scenes as it gave him the chance to kiss 'about ninety of the best-looking girls in town.' The role went to 30-year-old Texan Valerie Perrine. After studying for a short period at the universities of Arizona and Nevada, she got a job as a topless dancer in a Las Vegas nightclub. Like many other young people in the sixties, she went hippie, embarking upon drugs, communes, the novels of Herman Hesse and all the assorted rites of the cult before finding herself in LA on welfare. Perrine made her screen debut in *Slaughterhouse Five* (1972), the film of the sci-fi novel by Kurt Vonnegut, one of the literary heroes of hippy culture. In it, she made an impression as a beautiful, outerspace Hollywood starlet named Montana Wildhack.

In *Lenny*, she is first seen as Hot Honey Harlow doing her sexy disrobing act in a smoky, small-time strip-joint in Baltimore in 1951. Lenny Bruce is working a club nearby as a second-rate stand-up comic. They meet, start an affair, marry and do a comic double-act. But the routines get a bit raw for the audiences and they are asked by the then-reigning Mr Entertainment, Sherman Hart (Gary Morton), to tone it down and apologise. Instead, Lenny ends up telling the audience he will piss on them. The couple take off for California to begin a new life. There they start to take heavy drugs as the double act gets nowhere. Honey returns to stripping and they spend their evenings at heroin parties. They have a child, but the marriage deteriorates and they divorce two years later. Lenny's material becomes more political and socially satirical, and by 1960 he is earning big money. A year later he is arrested for obscenity, but he gets off and finds himself more famous than ever. At the age of 36, Lenny is arrested again and decides to defend himself. His final arrest brings him to trial in New York where he is cited for contempt of court. One of his lungs collapses, he is under pressure from Honey, and has drug and doctors' bills to pay. One night in 1966, he is found dead on his bathroom floor, a dope needle nearby.

There were eight weeks of rehearsal before shooting started in Miami on 21 January 1974. It began pleasantly enough. Perrine, who had to shave for the stripper scenes in which she would wear only a G-string, sculpted out a neat little pubic heart which she told Fosse was his Valentine's Day card.

But the early antics and high spirits gave way to depression. In order to conjure up the atmosphere of Bruce's shows, Fosse decided to stage some scenes in several Miami nightclubs with a live audience invited in to watch the proceedings. 'It is much easier for performers to become actors. It is more difficult to make an actor become a performer,' explained Fosse. Dustin admitted that he was petrified over performing the material in front of a real audience. Although he had seasons of stage work behind him, being a stand-up comedian required different skills of timing. 'The audience was making him nervous, so I put the cameras on him,' said Fosse, 'and we rapped back and forth like a TV warm-up.' This led to a sudden outburst from Dustin.

'He had me doing this routine where Lenny is talking lickety-split. Take after take, he said, "Faster, faster." I said nobody talks like this. I got very angry at him. It was like twenty takes. He'd break you down after a series of takes so you didn't know which end was up, and he'd always get what he wanted. And he was absolutely right. He wants you to do your best. He's an obsessed leprechaun; I think he is always sitting on your shoulder, whispering in your ear.'

For Fosse the ends justified the means. And the means were pretty mean. In one scene, Perrine was supposed to break down and cry. Fosse was not happy with it, so he used one of the oldest ploys in the book. He told her that her dog had been hurt, which turned her next reaction into grief-stricken pain. Just before shooting a courtroom scene, Fosse reminded her of a boy whom she loved very much who was killed in a hunting accident. 'Valerie, I want you to think back to the time when you were going to get married. I want you to remember how you felt when that boy was shot. You loved him and suddenly he's dead.' Fosse gave her a minute for this to sink in, then just before the camera rolled he hissed at her, 'You'll never see him again.' (Rumour had it that the director also informed her, just before a take, that her current boyfriend had been killed in a plane crash.)

Fosse's harsh methods were even extended to the lowest form of creature in a movie – the extras. Once, Fosse harangued one of them for not giving him the facial expression he wanted. As he shouted at the poor man, he kept the cameras rolling in order to get the required shocked expression.

During one afternoon, Perrine and Dustin were to play a love scene in a hotel room with a temperature of 105 degrees Fahrenheit. 'They had to seal up the room and air conditioning couldn't be used, because it would hurt the sound,' Dustin complained. 'Here we were baking and sweating and doing this love scene together, and we couldn't even see straight. I kept wishing that I was back in a studio that was silently air-conditioned. Here you couldn't think about anything except the weather conditions.'

The movie kept dropping behind schedule and the crew worked six and seven days a week, ten to sixteen hours a day. At the beginning Fosse had been simultaneously rehearsing the Broadway musical *Chicago*, which he directed and choreographed. This required working in the theatre all day and on the film all night. He just about managed four hours' sleep a night. Resentment focused on Fosse's demands. 'He'll do twenty-five takes then walk over and move a glass on the table – move it half an inch – and do it all over again,' said one crew member. 'The guy is overrated and he knows it,' said another. 'He knows the critics will be gunning for him, so he's trying to cover his ass. He's already shot seven hundred and fifty thousand feet of film. He'll do a master shot and thirty different angles with thirty different takes per angle. He wants it all. And he's hard on the actors and people behind the camera. It's like he's always saying, "I don't think you have it. I think you're shit. Show me what you can do, but I don't expect much."'

Once a svelte, simpering, boyish, blond dancer in fifties film musicals such as *Give a Girl a Break*, *Kiss Me Kate* and *My Sister Eileen*, Bob Fosse was now a 47-year-old, chain-smoking, overweight, thrice-married, extremely successful Broadway choreographer and director, whose second film, *Cabaret*, had won eight Oscars (including Best Director) at the 1973 Academy Awards ceremony. In the same year he won an Emmy for *Liza with a Z* and a Tony for *Pippin*.

His first film, *Sweet Charity* (1968), had an over-reliance on stage-structure, and the vulgar performances and strident direction showed inexperience of the medium. Wisely jettisoning most of the stage musical and refusing to 'open out' the numbers by keeping the sleazy nightclub at the centre of the film, his *Cabaret* was far more successful, and almost eliminated the suspicion that a slick Broadway musical, despite its Brecht-Weill pretensions, is not the best vehicle to comment on the rise of Nazism. *Lenny*, which is also set in the cabaret world, was a further advance, yet all Fosse's films are simultaneous condemnations and cele-brations of his profession with the narrow philosophy that, 'There's no business *but* show business.'

By April, while filming in the Catskills, the atmosphere on the film had turned ugly. The Catskills, a holiday resort in upper-state New York, sprang up in the late thirties and early forties catering to a mainly Jewish

New York City clientele. The room rates at Brown's, a seen–better–days Borscht Belt resort hotel, proclaiming itself 'Jerry Lewis's Favorite Resort', where they were filming, included three meals a day and the nightly entertainment – usually a singer and a stand–up comic. Comedian and trumpet player Gary Morton, married to Lucille Ball since 1961, used to perform regularly in the Catskills. Most of the elderly hotel guests knew him as well as they did Dustin. In *Lenny*, Morton is excellently horrible as a fictionalised comic who advises Lenny to 'work clean'. The fact is that when Lenny Bruce worked there in the early fifties, he did work clean, doing impressions of movie stars.

Rolling Stone magazine's Tim Cahill, following the shoot, witnessed a meal that Dustin was having in the huge dining room, after six hours of shooting that day: 'Enter a cheerful elderly widow from an adjoining table. She's got rhinestone cat's eyeglasses and the white shawl opened down the front but buttoned at the neck. "Mr Hoffman, may I have your auto-graph?" She's holding out a soggy napkin and a ballpoint pen. "It's not for me, it's for my daughter." Dustin doesn't look up. "Can't you see I'm eating?" The woman thrusts the napkin in his face. Hoffman picks up the vegetables on his plate with both hands and stuffs them into his empty water glass. Next, he pours his wine into that glass, then dumps it all on his plate. "I'm eating," he shouts, and several people at other tables turn to watch the little drama. "Oh, I see," the woman says, smiling uncertainly. "You're acting for me." Dustin splashes his right palm into the mess on his plate. "I'm eating. Can't you see I want to be left in peace?" "Well, I'll come to see your movie anyway." Exit the old woman limping slightly. There is a leaden silence at the table, then the tired sad truth from Hoff-man's own lips. "She'll never see any movie I ever make."'

The scene finds echoes in Woody Allen's later *Stardust Memories*, one of the few movies that subjectively portrays how the famous see the fans, bores and sycophants that pester them.

Looking back on the filming of *Lenny*, Dustin considered that the best part of it was when shooting was over. 'My memory of that whole thing is working nights . . . It was a very hard film to do. There was a tremendous amount of hours put into it. I mean it was depressing. A bummer.' The finished film, however, was far from a bummer.

Although it opens with a huge close-up of Perrine's sensuous lips, it would have made more sense if they had been Dustin's, because the subject of the film is what issues from those lips. Some of the routines give a pretty fair idea of what offended the guardians of American morality at the time. In one of them, Bruce explains that because fucking is such a pleasant experience, 'Fuck you!' should not be considered an insult. One should be able to say, 'Hi Mom, fuck you!' People should get angry if you said, 'Unfuck you!' to them. What emerges is that Bruce was the most moralistic of comedians. Every one of his routines illustrated in the film has a moral point to make, especially in the act where he asks how many niggers, kikes, wops, spiks and grease-balls are in the audience, to deflate the meaning of these words.

Unfortunately, Fosse weaves relevant extracts from the act into the narrative, artificially using them to comment on Bruce's life, but despite this, the film manages to serve the function of Bruce's humour – to shock audiences into questioning their prejudices. With the jazz of Miles Davis on the soundtrack, *cinéma vérité* camerawork, and Bruce Surtees's sharp black-and-white photography, Fosse captures the feel of the fifties. (*Lenny* was one of the rare films being made in monochrome at that period and is the only non-colour movie Dustin has made.)

'The Trials of Lenny Bruce' might have been a more apt title, because the film's main impetus derives from the tragicomic court cases. It is here, even more than in Lenny Bruce's performances, that the movie becomes a powerful attack on American hypocrisy and puritanism. As Bruce points out, the war in Vietnam is far more obscene than any 'dirty' words of his. There are, however, two important elements lacking in the screenplay: there is too little attempt to understand Bruce's psychology and how he developed his act, and there are far too few laughs in what is, after all, the life of a comedian, so that the film hardly justifies Honey's claim in the end that, 'He was just so damn funny.'

Biopics work least well when the subjects are available for comparison, such as movie stars. Rod Steiger's W. C. Fields, Donald O'Connor's Buster Keaton, Keefe Brasselle's Eddie Cantor, Faye Dunaway's Joan Crawford, Carroll Baker and Carol Lynley's Jean Harlows, and Jill Clayburgh's Carole Lombard fail to convince because the originals still exist to be appreciated in the same medium. The majority of audiences in 1974 were not able to compare Dustin's Lenny Bruce with the original.

Lenny was a perfect vehicle for Dustin who loved being foul-mouthed himself, and he gave his most daring and self-stretching performance to date. His bravura playing gets to the heart of the man without attempting a straight imitation, presenting us with some idea of Lenny Bruce's real talent on stage, though a greater impression of Dustin's genius comes across than Bruce's.

For David Thomson, 'Hoffman was overawed by the mixture of show-off, paranoid, poet and self-destructive in Bruce. It is his most sentimental performance.' John Simon thought that Hoffman 'manages very little. As young Lenny in love, he is the bumblingly coltish Graduate again, quite out of tune with the sleazy nightclub atmosphere, which Fosse goes to excessive lengths to establish . . . As the adult Bruce, Hoffman is still too nice, cool, and lucid, with little of the madness and meanness that were mixed in with the messianism.'

The New Yorker came to the conclusion that the film was 'for audiences who want to believe that Lenny Bruce was a saintly gadfly who was martyred for having lived before his time.' Critic Ralph J. Gleason thought, 'Lenny was never the offstage klutz and onstage whiner that director Bob Fosse and Hoffman make him out to be . . . Hoffman runs into another problem best delineated by Dr Louis Gottlieb, the eminent folklorist, when he testified at Bruce's San Francisco trial. Asked if he considered a particular passage [quoted] by the DA funny, Gottlieb replied, "When Mr Bruce said those words they were funny, when the prosecutor says them, they are not." I hope I have the exact quote correct, but that's the gist of it and it applied to almost all of Hoffman's performance. . . . So to me, as someone who saw Bruce hundreds of times, the film is disappointing as a film about Lenny Bruce.'

The writer points out many factual errors, among them being that, 'Lenny never, ever, did a show so stoned out he was unable to talk coherently. Not in my experience nor in the experience of dozens of others I have talked to who saw his shows in other parts of the country. And only once, to my knowledge, did he ever forget what he was saying onstage, and that had nothing at all to do with drugs and a great deal to do with Freud. He lost his train of thought when he mentioned his father's name one night in San Francisco. Above all, Lenny was charming and he was funny . . . The tragedy of this film is that Dustin Hoffman's Lenny is not funny at all. Only limply, petulantly, almost high-schoolily, simperingly droll.'

Pauline Kael thought Hoffman 'makes a serious, honourable try, but he's the wrong kind of actor to play Bruce. Hoffman ingratiates himself with an audience by his shy smile, his gentleness, and his insecurity. He wins people over by his lack of physical confidence; you pull for him because he's non-threatening . . . But that clenched, nasal voice of his is the voice of someone trying to get along in the nervous straight world Bruce fled; his putziness is just what Bruce despised.'

But Bruce's nineteen-year-old daughter Kitty said, 'It shows my father's life with all the nastiness, the good times and the injustices. I'm so pleased with the film for telling just that. When I saw the film for the first time I gasped. I could not imagine anyone getting so close to my father on film. That is how good Dustin is. I cried when the bad things happened, they were so real. I felt the pain when he died.' She was, however, only eleven years old at the time of his death.

Prior to the November release of *Lenny*, Bob Fosse was admitted to a New York hospital with a severe coronary condition. He was operated on several days later for a blocked artery near his heart and was immobilised in hospital for four weeks. He was in the habit of going through about five packets of cigarettes a day, worried constantly, and also confessed to other addictions. 'I did cocaine and a lot of Dexedrine. I'd wake up in the morning, pop a pill. After lunch, when I couldn't get going, I'd pop another one, and if I wanted to work all night, still another one. There was a certain romanticism about that stuff. There was Bob drinking and smoking and turning out good work. Still popping and screwing around with the girls. "Isn't it terrific macho behaviour," they'd say. I probably thought I was indestructible.'

Dustin had a gorgeous flower arrangement delivered to Fosse's room and also kept in touch by phone. 'Fosse's a very fair man. He's a very hardworking director, and there are some things he doesn't tolerate. He drives himself to death literally. He doesn't tolerate it when a person doesn't do his job. He's not only someone who's gifted but someone who works hard.'

In 1979, Fosse was to use his experience as a heart-attack victim as the basis for his cynical, clinical, razzle-dazzle autobiopic, *All That Jazz*. He was finally to succumb in September 1987 just following his sixtieth birthday. He bequeathed $25,000 to be divided among 66 of his friends, including Dustin, Jessica Lange and Liza Minnelli, so that they could all go out and have a terrific dinner to honour his memory.

The LA premiere of *Lenny* was a benefit for the Southern California American Civil Liberties Union, which had paid many of Lenny's legal bills during his lifetime. Dustin, Fosse, David Picker, the executive producer, Marvin Worth, the producer, Lenny's mother, daughter and exwife all had a share in the profits from the $3 million movie. The production, which earned $11 million, could not have been made in the less permissive days of Lenny Bruce. It is ironic that Dustin's saying Bruce's words on screen was acclaimed and Oscar-nominated, while the comedian was arrested and charged with obscenity for his performance.

Later in the year, during an interview with critic David Sheehan on CBS, Dustin lambasted the Academy Award ceremonies. He referred to the postponement of the 1968 Oscar awards when over one hundred and sixty nominees had urged that the show be delayed out of respect for civil rights leader, Martin Luther King, killed that day. What upset Dustin was that, when the awards show was finally aired two days later, Bob Hope, the master of ceremonies, was making jokes about the postponement and never said a word about Martin Luther King. 'That's what I found ugly and grotesque. After that, I said I didn't want to come any more. It was as simple as that.'

In addition, Dustin complained about the amount of politics behind the selection of the Oscar winners, saying the Academy did not try to fulfil the purpose for which it was established. He pointed out that the Academy was originally formed to honour those in the industry whose work was exciting – whether they were electricians, make-up artists, directors or actors. In other words, it was the industry's way of saying 'thanks for a job well done'. He also disliked the fact that the Oscars event had turned into a contest rather than an honour. 'The Academy Awards are obscene, dirty and no better than a beauty contest.' Four years earlier George C. Scott had made a similar remark, calling the ceremony a 'meat parade', when he refused his Oscar for *Patton*.

As Dustin was known for his competitive nature, and had yet to win one of these coveted statuettes, his remarks were considered by many commentators as sounding suspiciously like sour grapes. In fact Marvin Worth said later, 'I know Dustin wanted to win.' Dustin would also have achieved more credibility had he, like Woody Allen, who always stayed away from these annual rituals, shut up about them. (Barely two years were to pass before Dustin would put on his tuxedo again to attend an Oscar ceremony.)

Although *Lenny* was nominated for Best Picture, Best Director, Best Actor, Best Actress, Best Screenplay (from another source), and Best Cinematography at the 1975 Academy Award presentations, Dustin decided to give his tickets to his parents. But he was certainly conspicuous by his absence. The ceremony took place during a torrential downpour, which prompted Bob Hope to quip, 'I didn't know Dustin Hoffman had that much power. If Dustin Hoffman wins, he's going to have a friend pick it up – George C. Scott.' When Frank Sinatra came on to present an award, he also got in a dig at Dustin. 'Contrary to what Mr Hoffman thinks, it is not an obscene evening. It is not garish and it is not embarrassing.'

Up against Dustin this time was Art Carney, his childhood comic hero from TV's *The Honeymooners*, for *Harry And Tonto*; Jack Nicholson for *Chinatown*; Al Pacino for *Godfather II*, (which grabbed the Picture and Director awards) and, ludicrously, Albert Finney as Hercule Poirot in *Murder on the Orient Express*. Once again Dustin was passed over. Sinatra later remarked that he was glad Dustin did not win. 'After those cracks he made, I'd have torn the place down.' At least the Best Actor Oscar was given to Carney and not Pacino, his near contemporary. Valerie Perrine, whose touching and funny performance was not outshone even by

Dustin's virtuosity in the title role, lost to Ellen Burstyn in *Alice Doesn't Live Here Any More*. Since then, Perrine has made a living playing various sexy, dumb broads, without being asked to stretch herself again.

For competitors in the Hollywood rat race, the New York theatre seems a comparatively civilised place. So, after the laceration he underwent as Lenny Bruce, and the lashings he received from the industry for his blasphemous remarks on the Great God Oscar, Dustin turned once more to the stage as balm. The month after *Lenny* was released, Dustin began his first assignment as a Broadway stage director.

All Over Town, a typically whimsical Murray Schisgal comedy set amidst Manhattan neurotics, found difficulty in attracting backers. For one thing, the play had sixteen major characters. Dustin got a list of potential angels from the Kennedy Center in Washington, only to be turned down flat by each and every one. If he had starred himself, it might have elicited a different response. Dustin described the process of searching out backers as like 'being at a crap table'. Finally, he obtained $100,000 from film producer Joseph E. Levine, and a large amount from Adela Holzer, who had financed *Hair*. Shortly afterwards, however, Levine withdrew when he found himself in disagreement with Dustin over the production. Dustin was then required to raise at least half a million dollars, part of which he got from his old friend Gene Hackman, and part of which he found in his own (reasonably large) pockets.

The playwright and director then spent weekends auditioning over one thousand five hundred actors, not all of them professionals – cab-drivers, janitors and shoeshine men. His motivation for such unorthodox methods was the feeling that some of the non-actors might give a clue as to how the part of, say, a cab-driver, janitor, etc. should be played, and also because he liked to think that 'real people' brought a greater sense of reality into the theatre by being themselves. Though disabused of this notion, he repeated the same ritual when casting for *Death of a Salesman* years later.

Among the many hopefuls was 23-year-old unknown Meryl Streep. She already had over forty productions behind her at the Yale School of Drama, and was hoping to make it on Broadway. Streep does not remember her first meeting with Dustin at an audition with any pleasure. 'He came up to me and said, "I'm Dustin – burp – Hoffman," and he put his hand on my breast. "What an obnoxious pig," I thought.' She did not get the part, but less than a year later she was to be nominated for a Tony in Tennessee Williams's *Twenty-Seven Wagons Full of Cotton*, and would, of course, co-star with Dustin in *Kramer vs Kramer* in 1979.

Around the same time rumours were circulating that Dustin was about to divorce Anne, and that he was living with an art student called Patty in an Oakland commune. Dustin said the whole thing was a concoction. 'Why, the night before I even got a call from a man who said he was going to be my father-in-law. I started wondering what my wife was thinking of me.' But these rumours of womanising were all over town. Dustin admits that he is an inveterate flirt, claiming that it's an involuntary reflex. 'I'll die wishing I had learned more about what I feel and fear about women. I think I fear my own vulnerability. A woman is a prime example of what will open up my vulnerability. Womankind occupies my thinking most of the day. I don't think that I think about anything else more.' An example of how his vulnerability expressed itself was his cornering women in lifts to solicit sex ('I must have your answer now. Is it yes or no?') and even unzipping one woman reporter's blouse to peek down her chest during an interview. Once, in a hotel lobby, he blocked the way of a long-legged beauty. 'Give me five minutes of your time. Please! It's a once-in-a-lifetime opportunity. Hear me out!' She listened to him, and agreed to all his proposals. But he just left her standing there. 'I was embarrassed,' he explained. 'She said yes too quickly.' This was not the sort of behaviour to appeal to Anne, who was getting increasingly insecure and restless.

But Dustin claimed: 'My wife and friends tell me I'm more relaxed here than in any acting job I've done. There is a certain pain that I always feel when I'm acting that I don't feel now. I don't know how this will turn out. Maybe you have wonderful times doing things that turn out terrible and terrible times doing things that turn out wonderful.' He was right.

As Dustin was becoming more and more involved in the creative side of movies, and was an actor himself, he seemed to be the ideal man to direct a large cast in a play by a good friend of his. Like a new teacher or parent, determined not to make the same mistakes as his own teachers or parents, Dustin started off in an idealistic and optimistic frame of mind. He did bring sensitivity and understanding to the task, refusing to be like the many directors he had suffered under, but as always ideals often clashed with reality.

'I did find things I didn't like about the experience: having to work with so many actors. Next time I would prefer a half-dozen actors who were really together. The way Broadway is set up, an actor can't think of it as just a job. Everyone has to work more hours than there are in a day to make it.'

The part of the ingenue who grows up in a hurry – the role that might have been Streep's – was given to Pamela Payton-Wright. The farcical mixed-identity action centres around an eminent but senile psychiatrist (Barnard Hughes), who is certain that California will fall into the Pacific

Ocean one day, and who confuses a black delivery boy (Cleavon Little), called Lewis, with Louis Lucas, a young, unemployed and white ladies' man (Zane Lasky), who has fathered nine children from five different women.

All Over Town opened at the Shubert Theater, Chicago on 19 August 1974, to distinctly chilly reviews. Then the team got down to making 'emergency repairs', but the show still was not a success when it arrived at the Booth Theater in New York on 29 December 1974. Although it ran for 233 performances until 20 July 1975, it lost $300,000 on its $275,000 investment.

A few months later, Schisgal asked Henry Livings (author of *Eh?*) if he would 'English' *All Over Town*. Livings, who was still attempting to repeat the theatre successes of the early part of his career, was pleased to take up the challenge. In fact, he made such a good job of converting it that Schisgal acknowledged it was even better than his American version. But the world at large has never had the chance to judge it, as it has never been staged.

20

Bernstein

A newspaper office is the pleasantest environment I've ever spent any time in.

AFTER THE RELATIVELY early exit of *All Over Town* from the Broadway scene, Dustin became interested in Bob Woodward and Carl Bernstein's Watergate exposé book, *All The President's Men*, as possible movie material. He had a personal interest in the affair, because his economist brother Ronald, although a Democrat, was one of twelve Nixon advisers, and the only one who had voted for McGovern. John Ehrlichman and the CIA had the entire Hoffman family investigated for three months because they wanted to keep Ronald away from the White House. In the end they could find nothing incriminating so they had to let him in.

Dustin made an offer to acquire film rights for the book from the two *Washington Post* journalists, but the more politically-minded Robert Redford had beaten him to it. In fact, the perspicacious Redford had bought an option on it prior to publication early in 1974 for $450,000. When Redford called Dustin and asked him to co-star, Dustin replied, 'I thought you'd never ask.' It seemed a natural choice, one reason being that Dustin bore a striking physical resemblance to Bernstein. Dustin was also pleased to be playing 'a nice Jewish boy' after his portrayal of the 'naughty' Jew, Lenny Bruce.

Just as Robert Duvall and Gene Hackman had been born in the same month of the same year and emerged as stars at the same time, so Dustin and Redford were both born in August 1937, the latter being the younger by ten days. All four stars were born within spitting distance of each other in California: Duvall in San Diego, Hackman in San Bernardino, Hoffman in LA and Redford in Santa Monica. Like Dustin, Redford was given his first big chance by Mike Nichols. He played the lead in Nichols's Broadway production of Neil Simon's *Barefoot in the Park* in 1963, remaining with the play for the first year of its four-year run, and never working in the theatre again. Although Redford started in pictures before Dustin, they became box-office stars at about the same time.

Generously, Redford gave Dustin top billing, although he had headed the list of top ten box-office stars for 1974 and 1975, two years in which Dustin did not figure at all. Backing up the two million-dollar stars was a strong supporting cast, including Jason Robards as Ben Bradlee, the *Post's* executive editor, Jack Warden as metropolitan editor Harry Rosenfeld, Martin Balsam as Howard Simon, the managing editor, and Jane Alexander as the book-keeper at CREEP (Committee to Re-elect the President).

William Goldman, who had previously written three buddy-buddy movies in a row for Robert Redford – *Butch Cassidy and the Sundance Kid* (with Paul Newman), *The Hot Rock* (with George Segal) and *The Great Waldo Pepper* (with Bo Svenson), was contracted to supply another one for the reserved blond star. But the script that Goldman delivered was a sort of 'Butch and Sundance Bring down the Government', as one *Washington Post* wit described it.

Asked to make it more of a semi-documentary, Goldman supplied another screenplay which satisfied both Redford (the co-producer) and Warner Bros, so he was therefore greatly surprised when Bernstein turned up one day at Redford's New York apartment, shortly before filming began, with a screenplay of his own, written by himself and his soon-to-be wife Nora Ephron. Goldman was appalled by the script attempt, finding it little more than a personal account of Bernstein's romantic adventures. Rumours started going around that Goldman's script was unacceptable, and it took several weeks to cool things down. Redford openly admitted much later that he thought that the Bernstein–Ephron script showed the journalist as 'the great lover hopping in and out of bed', making Woodward appear dull and grey. 'I had to tell Carl that Errol Flynn is dead,' said Redford.

Nevertheless, Redford wanted Goldman to give him some love interest because Dustin had a scene with a woman. Goldman then set about writing in boy-girl scenes without much conviction or the belief that they were good for the movie. In the end, however, the script avoided any romantic involvement for either Dustin or Redford. A major strength of the movie was that nothing compromised or deviated from the monothematic structure, a rare occurrence in Hollywood. Love scenes would definitely have worked to the disadvantage of the film by slowing its impetus.

Warner Bros extravagantly erected a $450,000 replica set of the *Washington Post* newsroom which took up 33,000 square feet of two sound stages combined. The set was so authentic that the phone number of Woodward's telephone was the same in the film as it had been in 1972, not that anyone would have noticed. Warners proudly unveiled their set at the Burbank Studios on 2 July 1975 by giving a shindig for over one hundred unreluctant journalists. Only members of the *Washington Post* staff had qualms about the enterprise.

Ben Bradlee, the *Post*'s executive editor, told Redford, 'Just keep this in mind, pal. Whatever you put up there on the screen stays. Whatever I am on that screen is for ever in the minds of people when they hear the name Ben Bradlee. You can always ride off into the sunset in a Western or jump in the sack with some good-looking girl in your next film, but I'm forever an asshole.'

Editor-in-chief Katherine Graham had been uncomfortable about the project from the beginning. She felt that Hollywood would trivialise her 'noble' calling, and resented the hullabaloo the book had unleashed. Because of her uncooperative attitude, the filmmakers found many *Post* employees unwilling to talk about the Watergate affair. Dustin became so incensed at one stage at the lack of the *Post*'s collaboration that he went to co-producer Redford and director Alan Pakula, to ask them to rename the newspaper in the film. They managed to calm him down.

Notwithstanding the reluctance and antipathy on the part of some journalists, many of them were flattered by the attention that was being paid them, and went out of their way to be of assistance. Throughout the filming, which began in the autumn of 1975 at the Burbank studios and on location in Washington, Dustin and Redford were on the phone to the *Post* to check details. While Redford quietly developed his character as the story unfolded, and was often on the line to Bob Woodward, Dustin was seeking out Bernstein's advice to settle points of discussion as to how things get done in the newspaper business. He also spent months watching the process of news-gathering from the ground-floor room at the newspaper, especially following a reporter called Fred Barbash, who was investigating a corruption scandal of his own at the time. 'I couldn't get over the fact that the paper really does get out every day. Except for a few flurries of activity, it's as quiet as an insurance company.'

Once Redford played a practical joke on Dustin when he informed the Warner security guards that a scruffy, long-haired weirdo had been bugging members of staff. 'When Dustin turned up, they wouldn't let him in,' recalled Redford. Either the guards were in on the joke, or they were not moviegoers.

The friendly rivalry between the two stars extended to Dustin's obsession with his hair. Dustin wanted his unruly mop to compete with Redford's wonderful head of hair that seemed to fall naturally into place, so he would spend hours blow-drying it and having it groomed by the two hairdressers on the lot, Fern and Romaine, whom he nicknamed the 'salad ladies'.

Although Redford praised Dustin by saying that working with him was like working with 'a stream of electricity', and that, 'He's so intense and fluid you can't help but react,' he felt that Dustin wasted too much time on discussing character motivation. 'Dustin is very much like Barbra [Streisand]. He likes to talk everything to death. I'd always be thinking, "Let's get it over with."' Dustin's insistence on experimenting with scenes and discussing them with anyone who would listen, though of vital importance to him, was costly and time-consuming.

Dustin also argued with Redford about certain aspects of the picture. 'I told Bob that he was drying the picture out. I said he should add a scene where Woodward and Bernstein were really having it out. But he didn't. I would have fought more but, by the time I saw the film, it was too late to make the radical changes I wanted. In my opinion, the film is a little too smooth. I would have left a few hairs on the lens . . . I've read anti-Woodward and Bernstein letters to the editors, obviously from Nixon supporters, saying the film takes cheap shots. They should only know what Pakula as a director *could* have done. I would have been a little tougher.

'Instead, the film is really a landmark inasmuch as it's the first movie that really said anything even half-assedly true about the press. [*The Front Page* and *Ace in the Hole* were no slouches at it either.] Bob deserves this success. Not to take anything away from Alan Pakula, who directed it, but this was Redford's project all the way. He may be the hardest working actor I've ever known.' According to Jane Alexander, Pakula was Buddah-like, sitting most of the time on set very quietly, interpolating advice from time to time.

By November 1975, the movie was 35 days over schedule and $3.5 million over budget. The greatest responsibility rested on the shoulders of Redford, whom one crew member described as 'the wasp of all time' (or was it 'the WASP of all time'?), while Dustin's lesser burden made him 'a delight and very cooperative with everyone'.

Billed as, 'The most devastating detective story of the century!', it was the fifth film directed by 47-year-old Pakula. He had just made another political thriller, *The Parallax View*, an extremely disturbing no-holds-barred look at an assassination cover-up with a down-beat ending. The Watergate movie is a more straightforward view of a complex issue, which does not come to any significant conclusions, and, for obvious commercial reasons, leans more towards the thriller element than the political. Anyone without some knowledge of the Watergate affair would gather the impression that the only factor in bringing down Nixon was the determination of two unknown newspaper reporters.

As a thriller it is also problematic for most clued-up audiences, because the suspense is lessened by a foreknowledge of the climax, and despite

menacing hints that Woodward's life could be threatened in the underground garage during his meetings with 'Deep Throat', these are
weakened by our awareness that nothing in fact ever happened to him.
Still, the one hundred and thirty-odd minutes pass fairly rapidly and a
certain excitement is engendered by the meticulous building up of evidence against the conspirators as the eager-beaver reporters close in on the
president. There is an ironic ending as Nixon is seen at his inauguration
ceremony swearing to preserve the constitution, but the film is more a
celebration of a free press than a condemnation of a flawed system.

Using a smooth, documentary technique, and by filming the discussions on the hoof – in corridors, in cars, in elevators, in streets – Pakula
brings movement to bear on what is primarily a word piece crammed with
a multitude of proper names. For example, to escape the tedium of the
painstaking sorting out of cards in the Congress Library, an overhead
camera moves higher and higher above the scene until the people become
just dots.

Of the two stars, Redford has the edge, managing more successfully to
combine a dry humour, a convincing intelligence and a determined
idealism, while Dustin flits flippantly about on the edges. Often self-
consciously trying to submerge their film star personae, they both play
boyish, but Dustin's efforts, with his shoulder-length hair and his small-
stepped jaunty walk, seem more forced. Dustin's Method training tries to
lend the Bernstein portrayal some reality with hesitancies of speech, but
there is not much for him to play with. He spends his time chain-smoking
('Is there any place you don't smoke?' Woodward asks him once with
slight irritation), or looking serious while hammering away at the typewriter (now a rare sight in newspaper offices), or handling a telephone
receiver with dexterity. Occasionally he shoots out a slightly vulpine grin
at women and a fleeting false one at men. Using his own nasal voice without variation, he is a resolute reporter very much in the mould of *Lou
Grant*'s Rossi, played on TV by Robert Walden, who, incidentally,
appears in the film as a crooked lawyer in a scene with Dustin. In some
ways the movie can be seen as an extended and superior *Lou Grant* episode.

All the President's Men, completed in 96 days at a cost of $9 million, was
premiered at the Loews Astor Plaza on 8 April 1976. It soon became both a
critical and commercial success, grossing $30 million in the year, making
it one of Warner Bros' top earners of all time. It also fared well at Oscar
time, gaining four of its eight nominations. Jason Robards, as *Washington
Post* editor Ben Bradlee, got the Best Supporting Actor award for expertly
putting his feet up on desks, while William Goldman was presented with
his second screenplay Oscar (the first had been for *Butch Cassidy and the*

Sundance Kid in 1969). The art direction-set decoration and sound won the other two awards. (Collectors of trivia might wish to note that it was the sixth Oscar-winning film to have a title beginning with 'All'. The others were *About Eve, Quiet on the Western Front, That Jazz, That Money Can Buy* and *the King's Men.*)

For Dustin, 'the real reason for the success of this picture is that Hoffman's back and Redford's got him. It's what the public always wanted: that beautiful WASP finally wound up with a nice Jewish boy.'

The critical fraternity mostly approved, but David Thomson saw that, 'The disregard for interpretation or political understanding in the movie (and the book) bear witness to the way the media have made justice a theme for entertainment . . . [it] proved that the sense of fiction is now so rampant in America that you can go from fact to legend in three years without passing understanding.'

Pauline Kael pronounced it 'poisonously mediocre and, finally, a celebration of the journalistic benefits of having an informer tucked away in a garage'. But Frank Rich of *The New York Post* lushly described the movie as 'a chilling tone poem that conveys the texture of the terror in our nation's capital during that long night when an aspiring fascist regime held our democracy under siege'.

As for Dustin's own politics at the time, when asked by Andy Warhol whether he was a Democrat, he replied, 'I don't know if I'm a Democrat. I know I'm not a Republican simply because I've never voted Republican so I guess I'm a Democrat. I have a tendency to vote for a person. I think I'd vote for Ford over Carter.' Nevertheless, *All the President's Men* continued to sustain the slightly hazy aura of radicalism with which Dustin had been surrounded since *The Graduate*.

21

What Makes Dustin Run?

The press kill you as much as they can. They always have and they always will. They're the destroyers. They're part of the machine.

EXHAUSTED AS HE always was after the rigours of shooting a movie, Dustin took a short vacation with his family in Florida before returning to sift through the many offers of film work. Because of his portrayal of, successively, Lenny and Bernstein, scripts of biopics fell on his desk. Like clockwork dolls, members of the Hollywood film fraternity are set walking in a certain direction until moved on to another track.

Two scripts got a little way beyond the perusing stage. One was about the flamboyant wrestler of the fifties called Gorgeous George, which UA's president David V. Picker wanted Dustin to do, and the other was based on the autobiography of former bankrobber Willie Sutton, *Where the Money Was*. Producer Robert Serpe forcibly cornered Dustin one day at a party and begged him to take the starring role of the gang leader in a third proposal, *The Great Brink's Robbery*, based on the notorious 1950 Boston heist. What made Dustin think twice (but not thrice) about this project was the prospect of acting for the first time in a film with his old friend Robert Duvall, as well as the possibility of being directed by Hal Ashby, who he suspected was someone he could work with. But Dustin declined, because he was trying to put together a project for First Artists, for which he was yet to make a film. The Ashby–Brinks movie never came to pass but, two years later, Serpe produced *The Brinks Job*, an inferior comedy-thriller starring Peter Falk in the part that Dustin might have made more interesting.

The film in which he was to make his First Artists debut was *Friday, the Rabbi Slept Here*, based on Harry Kemelman's rabbi-turned-detective novel series, to be directed by Ulu Grosbard. But he was diverted instead into making his second film with John Schlesinger, again in tandem with novelist-screenwriter William Goldman. Dustin was especially taken by Goldman's novel, *Marathon Man*, on which the film was to be based. Goldman had already written at least four different drafts of the screenplay before the producers were satisfied, although Robert (*Chinatown*) Towne was later brought in to write the (wordless) ending.

Although Schlesinger had had a comparatively unfraught time with Dustin on *Midnight Cowboy*, the director was not terribly enthusiastic about having the star in the lead. He thought that even the young-looking 39-year-old would be hard put to it to convince as a postgraduate student called 'Babe'. He had wanted 36-year-old Al Pacino or 25-year-old Keith Carradine instead, but producers Robert Evans and Sidney Beckerman insisted on Dustin. Actually, with youthful clothes and hairstyle and boyish mannerisms, Dustin passes easily for a student in his late twenties or early thirties. There are once again elements of Ben Braddock in his portrayal; the character is referred to by his brother as a 'liberal pacifist', who shows his non-conformity by daringly not wearing a tie in the posh Etoile restaurant.

In typically dedicated fashion, Dustin went running every morning for more than six months, under the direction of an Olympic trainer, in preparation for the role of the academic whose passion for fitness helps him escape from assorted baddies in pursuit of a bundle of diamonds. Laurence Olivier portrayed Szell, a vicious Nazi dentist who returns from Uruguay to New York in search of diamonds which have been kept for him by his now-dead brother. However, he is outwitted by Babe Levy, the younger brother of an American agent (Roy Scheider) he has stabbed to death with a flick knife he keeps up his sleeve. The scene in which Szell tries to extract information from Babe in the dentist's chair by using the instruments of his trade as torture weapons is the most memorable of the film, if only for its gruesomeness. In the end, Babe forces Szell to swallow diamonds, before the Nazi is killed with his own weapon.

There was a curious working relationship between the culturally and temperamentally poles-apart Dustin Hoffman and Laurence Olivier, exactly 30 years his senior. In Dustin's opinion, performing with Olivier, whom he called 'Lord', proved that there is no great divide between actors coming from seemingly different traditions.

'After three weeks of working with Olivier, I said, "I've never seen you on stage, only on film. I don't know anything about you, but everyone thought you did a great character job in *The Entertainer*, but that's not a character job, Lord, is it, that's you!" He's music hall. He's a dirty, vulgar, crude music hall performer. That's the best kind of actor there is.' (In *Tootsie*, some years later, a poster of *The Entertainer* is prominently displayed on the wall of the apartment of the struggling actor played by Dustin.)

The reputation Dustin would get for the madness in his Method may have arisen in part from a remark made one day to him by Olivier. At one stage, the character of Babe Levy was supposed to have spent three days and nights without sleep. So Dustin decided to deprive himself of sleep for thirty-six hours. 'I wanted to try and match that crazed state. When Lord heard about it, he said, "You didn't sleep? Dear boy, why don't you try acting?"' Dustin also sat in his personal sauna on the set before takes so that he would look tired out from his jogging sessions, or for scenes when he had to display bodily exhaustion.

The justification for such drastic measures is defended stoutly by Dustin. 'I couldn't have done that on stage. You need the energy. But on films anything goes to get the effect you want, and it's nobody's damn business how you get it. When Bobby De Niro put on eighty pounds for *Raging Bull*, the press forced the audience to think about how much pasta he ate. Imagine if the press had the power in the past, they'd have gone up to Michelangelo and said, "How many years have you been on this now? This is your tenth year. Hey Mike, wait'll we write this. Michelangelo's not done with the Sistine Chapel ceiling yet!" When Brando did the dying scene in *Mutiny on the Bounty*, he had a tub of iced water brought on to the ship and put himself in there for twenty minutes for the close-up, because, as I know, if you're burned badly you feel the shock as if you're in iced water. Charles Laughton had the make-up man twist his ankle before a shot in *The Hunchback of Notre Dame*. Get the press away and they'd never know.'

One day, Dustin held up filming for several hours because his character was supposed to jump out of bed and grab a torch; he felt Babe was not the type to keep a torch by his bed. He lost that battle with Schlesinger. However, a question (among many others) may remain as to why Babe should sleep with a torch under his mattress when he has a perfectly good bedside lamp. No matter how trivial a point this might seem to an outside observer, Dustin's meticulous construction of a character from the inside out makes every element weigh equally importantly with him, and is essential to the kind of actor he is.

Off-camera, Olivier was in great pain owing to a recent illness. He was not only recovering from cancer but had contracted an ailment called dermatomyositis, an inflammatory disease that wastes the body's muscles. Dustin, who was unaware of the seriousness of Olivier's condition, insisted on improvising the penultimate sequence in the movie, where Dustin has Olivier at gunpoint and they begin a long walk round and round a hall. Olivier was not happy about doing it, as improvisation was something he was not comfortable with. But both Dustin and Schlesinger thought it might be worth a try. 'Olivier is obviously of the old school,' explained Schlesinger. 'He likes to have everything worked out in advance. Dustin likes to improvise all the time.'

In his *Adventures in The Screen Trade*, William Goldman related how Olivier tried ad-libbing as the two men walked and walked. 'I think part of this was because of Hoffman's need to put himself on at least equal footing with this sick old man. I don't know why Schlesinger didn't stop it. Perhaps, as he indicated, to see what might come out of it that might help the sequence.

'But I also think that Schlesinger knew that Olivier wouldn't give him any trouble: Hoffman was the star, Hoffman had the vehicle role, if anyone was going to bring him to grief, Hoffman was that man, and to go directly against the star's wishes so early on might not be a move of great wisdom – I'm not talking about improvisation, I'm talking about the walking that went along with it – because, inside of a few minutes, Olivier's ankles were beginning to swell. But on they walked. And improvised. And Hoffman was terrific. And Olivier did his best. And Schlesinger watched it all. And Olivier would not sit down. Would not. Give in. He could have stopped, he could have asked for a chair, he could have requested a break. But he walked. And now his ankles were bulging. Pain is impossible to quantify. What lays me up may be something you can deal with easily. No one can say how much anyone is capable of enduring. But watching it all take place, seeing the old man grow increasingly pale, was something I knew then I'd remember. And I mean forever.'

Actually, Olivier who seldom stands still or sits throughout the film, had enough authority and inestimable prestige to have ended his suffering if he had really wanted to. 'He was very frail when he first arrived for rehearsals,' said Schlesinger. 'But nothing was going to daunt him. He actually seemed to get physically stronger as we went along.'

Marthe Keller, who played an enigmatic German woman (pretending to be Swiss) with whom Babe falls in love, was on the set more than Goldman and never saw any of this cruelty. 'Dustin couldn't have been nicer to everyone off the set. At the wrap party, he was terribly solicitous towards Olivier, making sure he was comfortably seated and was looked after with food and drinks. Dustin loves actors and respected Olivier. But he did believe in a lot of improvisation, which I was not used to, and Olivier certainly wasn't. Yet everybody went along with Dustin's method. Most actors want to be good in a movie. It's more important for Dustin to be in a good movie. There were a lot of fights on the set between Dustin and John, but they were really rows between the director and the character Dustin was playing. Of course, Dustin can be exhausting as well as stimulating. He's a professional who is tough on himself and everyone else.

'It was my first American movie, and he couldn't have been nicer. He gave, gave, gave. For example, there was a scene when I was supposed to be on the phone to him. He needn't have been on the set that day. But when I picked up the receiver he was saying lines to me on the other end. It made it much easier for me to act than it would have been with a dead phone. Another example was in the scene when he tells me that he loves me. They first needed a close-up on me. He was off camera. Yet he started crying facing me behind the camera, and I reacted to that. By the time they got to filming his close-up, he had no further tears and they had to film it the next day.'

In the scene in the restaurant when Babe finds out that his girlfriend has been lying to him about being Swiss, Schlesinger wanted her to be calm. But Dustin thought her character should be more emotional so he kicked Keller painfully under the table during the take so that she had tears in her eyes, and whispered, 'You know how many people wanted this part. You're fucking lucky to be here.' After the take, however, they laughed about it.

Marathon Man kicks off as a good pacey thriller, shifting from a hot summer in New York – where there is a baggage handlers' strike – to Paris, where there are demonstrations and a garbage collectors' strike. Schlesinger uses sound eerily and creatively – the dentist's drill, whispering, hammering – with much oppressive heavy breathing, only some of it associated with sex. But as the film goes on, each image becomes more heavily emotive and significant, the plot gets murkier and murkier and, as knives penetrate soft flesh with greater frequency, the exploitative nature of the enterprise is exposed. Schlesinger's agitated direction allows few moments of repose, and, as with *Straw Dogs*, one could ask, 'What's a nice guy like Dustin doing in a movie like this?'

The film and the role were a retrograde step for Dustin, again not acting his age, this time in a meretricious thriller which unscrupulously uses Auschwitz, the McCarthy hearings, strikes and pollution as grist to its hollow plot – one with as many holes in it as Babe's teeth have after Szell has finished with him in the dentist's chair. Dustin has one effective emotional outburst as Babe, while being questioned after his brother's murder, but elsewhere his range of feelings is limited to expressions of bewilderment and fear. He rarely produces a smile and, when he does, it is of the pursed variety. At the climax, Dustin's usual adenoidal voice becomes cracked and husky. This might have been genuinely produced by his own methods of depriving himself of sleep, but it comes across as artificial, and one feels the effect might have been better if he had taken Olivier's advice and just acted.

With director and long-time friend Ulu Grosbard on location for *Straight Time*, 1978

With Robert Redford in *All the President's Men*, 1976
In Laurence Olivier's grip in *Marathon Man*, 1976

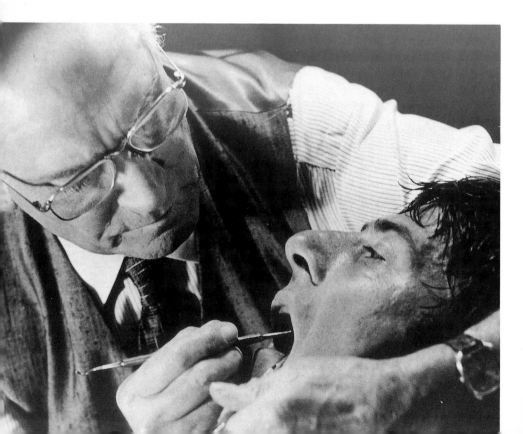

Matching up to Vanessa Redgrave in *Agatha*, 1979

Below: In discussion with director Robert Benton and co-star Meryl Streep during the making of *Kramer vs Kramer*, 1979

In the title role of *Tootsie*, 1982, with Jessica Lange (at left)
Opposite: With Kate Reid in the film of *Death of a Salesman*, 1985

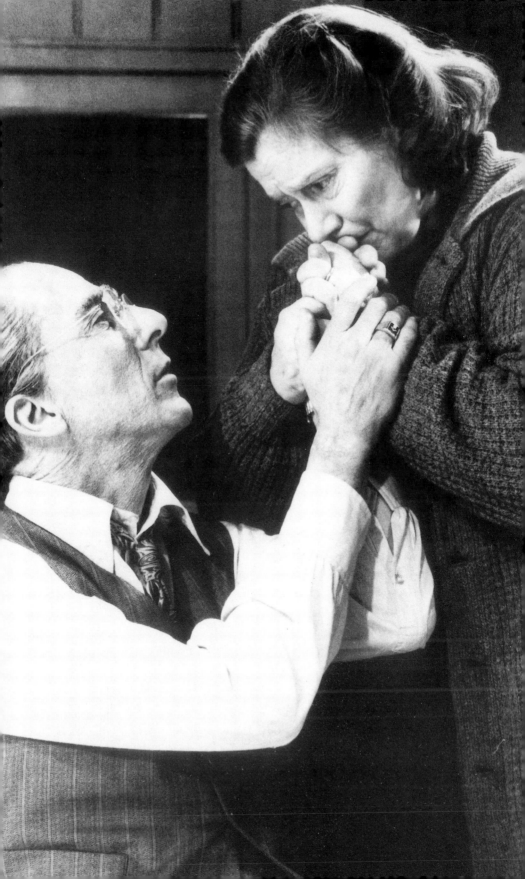

Above: With Tom Cruise in *Rain Man*, 1988, and (*below*) with Matthew Broderick in *Family Business*, 1989

Dustin (at left) in conversation with the author in London, April 1989, and (*below*) with director Sidney Lumet during filming of *Family Business*, 1989

During rehearsals for the 1989 London stage production of *The Merchant of Venice*

Nominated for Best Supporting Actor (in the same year as Jason Robards won that award for *All the President's Men*), Olivier, 'the greatest actor in the world', gives a competent performance in another of the schlocky films he made towards the end of his career, though he unnervingly shifts into various registers and accents, which a feeble attempt in the screenplay to explain away does not justify. And the tall, toothy and toothsome Swiss-born actress Marthe Keller, who was fashionable in the late seventies, does her best with an insubstantial love interest role.

Keller went straight on to make *Bobby Deerfield* for Sydney Pollack, playing opposite Al Pacino, with whom she lived for seven years. Obviously she knew Pacino better than Dustin, but her feeling is that they are complete opposites; Dustin being warm and extrovert, Pacino cooler and more introverted. Energy flowed from Dustin. One had to work harder to get Pacino going. Because *Marathon Man* is so overheatedly filmed, Pacino's interiorisation might have thrown some much-needed cold water on it.

Of the reviewers, Judith Crist of *Saturday Review* was one of the most positive. She considered it 'a film of such rich texture and density in its construction, so fascinatingly complex in its unfolding, so engrossing in its personalities, and so powerful in its performance and pace that the seduction of the senses has physical force'.

The New York Times ended a fairly positive review by claiming that the movie 'hasn't a real idea in its head. It just wants to scare the hell out of you – and it does.' *Variety* thought it 'tedious, dull, violent nonsense', with Hoffman 'reflecting audience dismay'.

John Simon, though disliking the film, thought Hoffman's portrayal was a 'perfect blend of agony and comic absurdity' and 'though the actor specialises somewhat limitingly in unadult bumblers whose humanity must crawl out from under a pile of inhibitions, he comes up here with more searing anxiety, more biting pain than usual'.

The New Yorker's Pauline Kael thought that although Hoffman 'isn't the ideal choice . . . [he] acts young, has never before looked so fit, and there isn't a bum note in his performance. It doesn't come to anything, though . . . Our curiosity is never stimulated. Instead of setting up the situation and showing Babe's encirclement, the director . . . opts for so much frazzled crosscutting that there's no suspense. There isn't the clarity for suspense.' She considered it Schlesinger's 'worst film ever'.

Marathon Man, which cost $7 million, soon drew over $16 million from the US box office alone after its premiere at Mann's Chinese Theater on 8 October 1976. Since 1969, Dustin had been in the annual top ten box-office stars every year except 1973, 1974 and 1975. *All the President's Men* and *Marathon Man*, both released in the same year, put him third behind Robert Redford and Jack Nicholson in 1976. Yet *Marathon Man* began the worst period yet of his life as a star.

22

Little Tough Guy

I sometimes get so wrapped up with my screen character that I forget my true identity.

'I'D REALLY LIKE to play Hitler and I *could* play him, I think. I have always attempted to see Hitler as a human being, an enigma who had enormous theatrical power and a sort of evil charm that seduced an entire nation. But I'd also like to be a director. That way you can *really* be Hitler.' It might have been the filming of the 'fascist classic' *Straw Dogs*, or working with the dictatorial directors Sam Peckinpah and Bob Fosse that prompted Dustin's remark. Regarding directing, he had already had a taste of it on Broadway, but said, 'I've never done a picture of my own vision. Film is a director's medium. It can't be otherwise. It is always the director's vision and his feeling for life and it's never quite complementary to my own.' But he would soon have his chance.

In January 1976, Ingmar Bergman, the great Swedish director, had been arrested for income-tax fraud. Although the charges were dropped, he vowed never to work in Sweden again. In April, he visited Hollywood and announced plans to make films in the USA. One project for First Artists was to be *The Merry Widow* with Barbra Streisand, and another was the possibility of a film with Dustin, who had some regrets about having given up the chance to work with Bergman in *The Touch* five years previously. Nothing came of *The Merry Widow*, and First Artists rejected Dustin's proposal for a low-budget Ingmar Bergman picture. 'They came back and said, "You can't work with Bergman. We've done a check on him, and not one of his films ever grossed more than five million dollars."' So Bergman went off to make his one-and-only English-speaking film in Germany, *The Serpent's Egg*, with David Carradine.

After *Marathon Man*, Dustin had put his energies into finding a film to make for First Artists. He had become 'disenchanted' with what he termed First Artists' 'virtually non-existent story department. I found the scripts I did get from them were scripts I had seen two years before. There was never anything new that came down the pike.'

In 1972, Dustin had bought the screen rights of Edward Bunker's autobiographical novel *No Beast So Fierce*, which he first signed to star in and produce for First Artists. Now he decided to get a script written and direct the movie himself. Neither the company nor his other partners seemed to have any objections. After all, Sidney Poitier and Paul Newman had been able to make the transition from actor to director fairly successfully.

The plot of *Straight Time* tells of Max Dembo, released from prison on parole after a six-year sentence for armed robbery. His only desire is to go straight, but everything seems to conspire against it. His association with an old friend and ex-con leads him into trouble again, and he assaults his bigoted and cruel parole officer. Desperate circumstances lead him to take up a life of crime again, culminating in a jewel robbery that goes wrong.

'I had the feeling that there was a correlation between actors and people in prison. People in prison are not always dumb people, I mean, they're very perceptive, some of them, very bright, and you could almost use the word "gifted". But for happenstance, circumstance, whatever, they got busted. They could have been as gifted as this, that or the other, but they got a shitty run right from the gate and I always felt that's what promotes violence. All my friends . . . Gene Hackman, Bobby Duvall, we couldn't get "arrested". That's the term we used, funnily enough, when we couldn't get a job . . . It's the inability to generate for yourself the creative impulse and to cook it! If you can't do that, you go out and hit somebody!'

Prior to location filming, Dustin had himself booked at Los Angeles County jail to soak up the atmosphere in which prisoners lived. He was given the full treatment, going through the procedure all inmates experience of fingerprints, filling out forms, and having mug shots taken. One cop suggested that, just for a joke, Dustin's name should be put on the police computer board. Dustin blithely agreed. Embarrassingly, the computer revealed he had two unpaid traffic fines, which Dustin made good there and then.

He went on to spend nearly eight months hanging out at prisons and county jails across the country, even managing to get smuggled into San Quentin, where he mingled incognito with the prisoners for several hours to get the feel of prison life. (Imagine James Cagney or George Raft doing the same.) There Dustin took some film footage illegally and later mixed with ex-cons in their trailer-park homes off the freeways of LA.

But the day when Dustin had to put on the mantle and take up the megaphone of a director could be postponed no longer. Rewrites of the script continued right up to the starting date of 9 February 1977, but even after that a group of writers continued to buzz around for several weeks trying to get it into a workable shape; those finally credited were Bunker (who also plays a small role as a con), Jeffrey Boam and Alvin Sargent, the latter having just won an Oscar for *Julie*.

Dustin had assembled a fine cast and an expert crew led by Owen Roizman, as director of photography, all eager to participate in Dustin's directorial debut. But after several weeks of shooting, with the film's budget diminishing rapidly, he began to find the pressures of acting and directing too great. He had underestimated the difficulties of carrying out the double assignment, although a look at the very short list of actor–directors who have done it might have been a pointer. (Of the three films Paul Newman had directed, the only one he also appeared in, *Sometimes a Great Notion*, 1971, proved to be a misnomer.) Dustin was shattered. He therefore decided to hire a director to take over the reins and relieve him of some of the responsibility. A spokesperson for First Artists said that no one forced Dustin to make the decision, but he realised the movie was 'just too demanding'.

'He needs acting to overcome feelings of inadequacy, but acting, by definition, puts you in the passive role of victim of a director,' explained Murray Schisgal. 'He can't do both, because he pours so much energy into acting that there's nothing left for directing.'

Dustin was keen to get his friend Hal Ashby, but Ashby had become ill, his lungs having filled up with the dust he had inhaled during the filming of *Bound for Glory*, his Woody Guthrie biopic. Because First Artists were not willing to wait around until he had recovered, Dustin then asked various other directors – Mike Nichols, John Schlesinger, Alan Pakula and Bob Fosse – to take over from him. 'All those people I'd worked with, which is why they turned me down. Though Fosse later regretted it.' As a result, he called on his steadfast friend Ulu Grosbard, although their collaboration on *Who Is Harry Kellerman . . . ?* had produced his first real failure. Grosbard had not directed a picture since, and agreed to the offer.

Almost immediately, Grosbard realised he had made a mistake in accepting the task. Because Dustin was so close to the movie and had visualised it, he allowed Grosbard very little liberty. 'He had the project for five years, and he controlled it completely. By the time he called me, he had gone through four or five writers and six or seven drafts, and he had some of the best people in the field working for him. He's very bright and very charming, but he can turn it on when he needs something from you and turn it off when he no longer needs anything. It's unconscious. Dustin is a professional victim and, when you put yourself in that position, you can make pre-emptive strikes against everyone and feel righteous. I think he does care about quality, but that is not a licence for his behaviour.'

This behaviour was characterised by the constant dissatisfaction Dustin displayed at Grosbard's handling of the movie, arising from his understandable but obsessive need to get everything right down to the smallest detail. 'I was doing the best work I'd ever done, and I knew the film wasn't supporting the performance,' Dustin commented. Grosbard replied, 'If he's so meticulous and such a perfectionist, why had he created such an enormous mess?'

It was during the shooting that Grosbard asked Dustin, 'What's more important, our friendship or the movie?' 'The movie,' Dustin replied without hesitation. To a certain extent, it echoed the question Jean-Pierre Léaud puts to François Truffaut in *Day for Night*: 'Are films more important than life?' The film is Truffaut's affirmative answer.

Once, in the late sixties, Dustin was overheard in a delicatessen having an argument about Elia Kazan, whose work he greatly admired. Someone said that Kazan could not claim to be a legitimate artist because he had named names before the House Un-American Activities Committee. Dustin responded, 'Elia Kazan is *so* an artist!' The other yelled back, 'You can't be an artist and sell out your friends!' 'You *can* be an artist and sell out your own *mother*!' Dustin retorted.

The finish of *Straight Time* coincided with the end of the long friendship between Dustin and Grosbard, which had begun thirteen years previously. The constant strain of pulling in different directions proved too much for even the strongest bond. The film was also the last straw that broke the back of Dustin's marriage. It was clear that it had been floundering for some time, but Dustin first blamed the break-up on another man . . . Max Dembo.

'I just couldn't get him out of my system. After filming I shaved off the beard [moustache, actually] I grew for the part and scrubbed my face but he stayed with me. I just couldn't get that grimy feeling off.' During filming, Dustin had in fact spent most nights of the week away from his family at a hotel in order to concentrate on the role, returning home at weekends, usually in the worst of moods and more on edge than ever.

'When I'm filming, my working day can start at five thirty in the morning and not end before ten thirty that night. And even when I get home, I still have to study the next day's script before crawling into bed. If you're married and have children and that schedule goes on for sixteen weeks, you are sacrificing your family . . . You can't have a career and a family. Filmmaking is set up so that you don't have enough time. My family suffered.'

The personality clashes became more frequent. Anne took to complaining about her husband's ego, which often revealed itself in small ways. For example, he would regularly visit the New York cosmetician Lia Shorr to have his face massaged, because 'when Dustin's into a part his skin breaks out from stress, and also because he loves being pampered.' This seems a little unfair on her part, considering that an actor's face is his fortune, and bad acne is not an asset in a close-up on the large screen.

More significantly, she found it difficult to cope with his changing moods. His warmth could turn to coolth (in Sam Goldwyn's phrase) in an instant. His roving eye and habitual flirting with any attractive girl that entered his sphere were something few wives would accept, even though to 'flirt', in Webster's definition, is to 'behave amorously without serious intent'.

While her husband was out shooting *Straight Time* or brooding on his part, Anne was getting bored with being solely a wife and mother. She began to take drama lessons and had also started dancing again. One evening, when Anne and Dustin were dining at a pasta restaurant, a woman walking by the table suddenly stopped, turned to Anne and said, 'Excuse me, but weren't you a dancer in the *Nutcracker?*' Anne, used to people pestering her husband for autographs, was taken aback. Jokingly, Dustin piped in: 'Do you realise that your recognising her and not me may lead to a divorce?' 'Oh,' the woman replied shortly, '*The Graduate* was okay.'

Soon after, Anne got a part in Lina Wertmuller's first English-languge film, the tweely titled *The End of the World in Our Usual Bed in a Night Full of Rain*. She was third-billed as the friend of American Candice Bergen, who plays the feminist photographer-wife of macho Italian journalist Giancarlo Giannini. Her scenes were shot in San Francisco which took her away from Dustin. The execrable movie, from which Anne emerged unscathed and unnoticed, happened to open in the USA within months of *Straight Time*.

After almost six months' troubled shooting, there was a hiatus in order to assemble a rough cut, take a look at it, and then shoot whatever else was necessary. Unfortunately, Dustin made the fatal mistake that many unpopular leaders make, of leaving the country for some months, permitting a *coup d'état* in their absence. He should have remembered what happened to Orson Welles in 1942 when he flew out to Rio to make *It's All True*, leaving *The Magnificent Ambersons* in RKO's hands, to await his return to make the final cut. Naturally, the studio cut and reshot it themselves, reducing the film from 131 minutes to 88 minutes, while Welles's back was turned.

Something similar happened to Dustin. He decided to go to England to make *Agatha* in order to fulfil his two-picture contract with First Artists, believing that he would have some months to do the final cut when he returned to LA. By late September 1977, after Grosbard had completed his work, *Straight Time* was 'approximately $1 million in excess of the approximately $4 million budget and exceeded the sixty-one-day approved production schedule by approximately twenty-three days', according to First Artists. They gave Dustin until the end of January 1978 to deliver the finished film. Yet things did not turn out as he would have wanted, and the picture was taken away from him.

Despite Dustin's attempts to stop its distribution, *Straight Time* opened at the Bruin Theater in Westwood on 16 March 1978. 'This is not my film, in any shape or form. I don't want to hurt it, but I don't think it reaches the potential it could have. I hope it's successful but I can't in good conscience promote it,' he stated. Because First Artists thought little of the picture, it was only shown to the press on the morning of its release, in the hope that negative reviews would not impede initial box-office takings. The movie did not do as badly as predicted, but it grossed only $4 million (a little over its original budget of $3.5 million).

Surprisingly, despite the bitterness and turmoil surrounding the film, *Straight Time* turned out to be a sombre, gritty, vastly underestimated thriller. The first half of the film is especially powerful, depicting the humiliation of prisoners being indicted and imprisoned in the LA County jail, and the way in which the end of a prison sentence does not mean the beginning of liberty. 'In a way, it's more frightening outside. Outside it's what you have in your pocket; inside it's what you *are*,' Dembo tells his girlfriend, sensitively played (within the severe limitations of the role) by Theresa Russell. Unfortunately, any criticism of the parole system is rather lessened by the fact that M. Emmet Walsh's character is so cruel and slimy that he cannot be considered representative of parole officers. Indeed, he seems almost to have a personal vendetta against Dembo. The last we see or hear of him is when Dustin blows his top, attacks him while he is driving, and leaves him handcuffed to a fence on the freeway, with his trousers around his ankles, and cars buzzing around him, refusing to stop. From then on, the film loses its tragic dimension, developing instead into a heist thriller, but it is saved from being merely routine by the abrasive quality of the screenplay, by Grosbard's rigorous handling of all the elements with almost documentary realism, climaxing with an exciting slam-bang jewel robbery and, above all, by Dustin's haunting performance.

With a full black moustache, long hair and sideburns and deeper voice, Dustin is compelling and convincing as a tough ex-con battling to go straight in a crooked world, making himself even more effective by dousing his natural charm and refusing to play for sympathy. He is no gentle martyr like Henry Fonda in *You Only Live Once* or Farley Granger in *They Live by Night*, but a brutal killer when necessary. Witness the scene when Dustin confronts the gormless Gary Busey, who has left him and his partner, Harry Dean Stanton, without a getaway car after the robbery. Busey sobs an apology. Dustin relents. 'Gimme a big bear hug,' he says with a smile, then shoots his ex-buddy in the guts while in the embrace.

The film ends with a montage of mug shots of Dustin, going back in time to the first one of him as an adolescent, an unflattering photo borrowed from Lillian Hoffman's family album.

Vincent Canby of *The New York Times* found it 'an uncommonly interesting film . . . It is so cool it would leave a chill were it not done with such precision and control that we remain fascinated by a rat, in spite of ourselves.' *Variety* was less charitable, stating, 'One leaves the theatre hoping the character will die painfully and slowly in a hail of bullets – that's the effect of this nothing film.'

Pauline Kael in *The New Yorker* praised Dustin for giving 'a daring, stretching, self-testing performance . . . He made the character mean and unyielding – a man with closer psychological relations to people from the prison world than he could ever have with outsiders.' David Thomson pronounced the first thirty minutes 'strikingly raw and unusual, and it allows Hoffman to be middle-aged and wearily resentful of a stupid legalistic society . . . the opening of *Straight Time* promises his most powerful and mature performance. Perhaps a business interest in the movie was too much for Hoffman's calm; perhaps he was overwhelmed by the need for a crowd-pleaser. Whatever the answer, it is especially sad that his nerve cracked and deprived us of what might have been a very original picture.'

The Motion Picture Guide admired the film for giving 'no tired explanations for Hoffman's behaviour, no fingers are pointed, no apologies or excuses are offered. Hoffman is a habitual criminal and that's the way he is. Though the parole system is taken to task for the Catch 22-type restrictions given to ex-cons, this is not presented as an excuse for Hoffman's return to crime – only a match that ignites the fuse already inside the man . . . Though *Straight Time* was a financial and critical failure, it stands as one of the finest, most accurate, and honest portrayals of crime and criminals ever committed to film.'

23

Who Is David Puttnam and Why Is He Saying Those Terrible Things About Me?

Once you go to the floor to make a movie, it's crazy time. It's painting a picture on a railroad track with the train getting closer.

IN ENGLAND, WHILE Dustin was doing time as Max Dembo, David Puttnam, the 38-year-old producer who would become the 'white hope' of the British film industry, was busy setting up a 'little picture' called *Agatha*, based on Agatha Christie's mysterious disappearance for eleven days in December 1926, an incident simply mentioned in Christie's autobiography without giving any further information. It was to be a vehicle for two female stars, Vanessa Redgrave and Julie Christie, in the respective roles of Agatha and the woman she befriends at the Harrogate hotel where she has registered under the name of her husband's mistress. When Julie Christie broke her wrist skate-boarding in the USA, she was replaced at the last moment by Australian actress Helen Morse, who flew in from Sydney five days before shooting began.

Puttnam and the director Michael Apted were happy with the script offered them by Kathleen Tynan, who originally wanted to make it as a television documentary. 'With the scaffolding of truth I've filled in the blanks,' she announced. 'Agatha was under enormous strain at the time. Her mother had died and her marriage was breaking up. She had no experience like this at all and was ill-equipped to deal with it. Basically, it's my reading of her state of mind.'

For some reason, Dustin was sent a copy of the screenplay by Jarvis Astaire, his English-based business manager, although there seemed no part for him in it. On reading it, he found the small role of the reporter on the trail of Agatha Christie an interesting one. Why couldn't he do it as a cameo? Kathleen Tynan remembered that Dustin was certainly satisfied with the original size of the role. 'When he first saw it, he said it was one of the best things he had read in years. We formed the impression that he was quite happy to play the cameo role.'

Although Dustin had said that he was pleased to have a small role, he might have had second thoughts. A short while after *Midnight Cowboy*, Dustin commented revealingly, 'I used to say to myself that if ever I became a star, I would still be an artist – I would go after a particular role, and I wouldn't care how small it was if it was really good. But now I see that this isn't going to be so – I do care how small the part is. I saw *Cowboy* recently and sat there thinking, "I wish I was on the screen a bit more. Jon Voight's on the screen an awful lot – this picture is really about *him*." I think now that if a small character came along I liked, I probably wouldn't do it, and I'd rationalise it by saying to myself, "I'd rather save that character for a big part one day, and not waste it now."' (He did eventually take a cameo in *Dick Tracy* in 1990.)

With his marriage in difficulties and the bad taste of *Straight Time* still in his mouth, Dustin thought a short sojourn in England might give him the recharge he needed. He might have had another reason for wanting to do the picture, later imputed to him by First Artists. They accused Dustin and his SweetWall Productions of selecting to do the film 'in bad faith and with improper motives' as an attempt to 'dispose of their commitments to First Artists with the least possible inconvenience to them and in the shortest time possible in order to move on to ventures which would be more lucrative and personally rewarding to Hoffman and SweetWall'. Whatever mixed motives might have been behind Dustin's decision, it proved to be a miscalculation on all counts.

It was not long before Puttnam received a call from Dustin. 'Out of the blue he phoned me. I just picked up the phone, and someone said he was Dustin Hoffman. He told me he'd read the screenplay and thought it was a wonderful piece of work. He said he badly wanted to work in England for personal reasons for a week or so, and was there any chance he could become involved? I thought, well, that doesn't seem too onerous. There was a role for a journalist, and we worked out that we could make the proprietor of the newspaper Canadian, give him a nephew with an accent and make the thing work.'

There was one significant problem, however. First Artists and Warner Bros insisted that under his contract, in any film he did, he had to co-star. This was put to Puttnam and Apted and they agreed to a beefing up of Dustin's role to satisfy the moneymen. According to Puttnam, 'Dustin then literally arrived in England with a writer, a very nice man named Murray Schisgal, who proceeded to rewrite the script! Now that wasn't the deal. On the other hand, as I was very quickly encouraged to understand, the reason that Warners were twice as pleased was that they now had a film starring Dustin Hoffman and felt they had a real bargain. And no matter what Dustin did, it became very clear that he was running the film.'

As in the similar case of *Papillon*, new writers were brought in to 'flesh out' the script and formulate a fuller character, which resulted in Helen

Morse's role being reduced considerably. The first Vanessa Redgrave heard about it all was through ugly rumours emanating from Hollywood about the egotistical Hoffman's demands that his role be made equal to hers. Dustin was furious when he read the stories, insisting that he would have preferred a supporting role, but First Artists would not allow it. However, because of the rewriting involved, he did ask for an extra three weeks of rehearsal. The plea was refused.

'When I wrote the part of the journalist, he was a tall, blond Englishman with a supporting role. Now he's a small, dark American with one of the leads,' Tynan commented. In reality, it was Ritchie Calder, later Lord Ritchie-Calder, then a young reporter, who had spotted Agatha at Harrogate. Dustin's role was turned into the fictional American gossip-columnist Wally Stanton, trying to trace the missing novelist.

While the ever-faithful Murray Schisgal attended to Dustin's lines, Redgrave asked Apted to get Arthur Hopcraft to come in for the British side as her writer. Rumours began to fly around that nothing of the original screenplay remained after Dustin and his cohorts had got through with it, and that the two writing camps – American and English – were not on speaking terms. Yet Tynan claims that a great deal of her screenplay survived the rewriting and that she never blamed Dustin. 'I have nothing but good things to say about Dustin Hoffman: imaginative, fastidious about detail, a perfectionist. I enjoyed working with him on *Agatha*.'

She had always had Redgrave in mind when she began writing the script. 'Agatha was in her mid-thirties, just the same as Vanessa was then.' (Actually, Vanessa Redgrave was nearly 41, a few months older than Dustin.) Although the two stars were not compatible physically, politically or philosophically, they had a professional respect for each other. Vanessa said of Dustin that, 'he's an actor in the truest sense of the word. He sets himself marvellous acting challenges, then pulls them off. He's not content to play the same role, with slight variations, in every film, which can be lucrative, but tedious.' She also found Dustin 'a lovely little mover'. Privately, however, she only had eyes for her lover, 35-year-old future James Bond, Timothy Dalton, who played Agatha Christie's adulterous husband.

Not long after the completion of *Agatha*, when receiving her Best Supporting Actress Oscar for *Julia* at the 1978 Academy Awards ceremony, Redgrave used the occasion to reaffirm her support for the Palestinian resistance to 'fascism and oppression'. She thanked those who voted for her despite Zionist threats against them, while, outside the Dorothy Chandler Pavilion, rival groups of the Jewish Defense League and the PLO held demonstrations. The Jewish Dustin had certain Zionist sympathies and felt somewhat uncomfortable with Redgrave's ideas. ('I wouldn't join the PLO,' he quipped.) It was a pity the two stars failed really to hit it off, because one could have envisaged her Portia taming his Shylock, and her towering Shrew being tamed by his minute Petruchio.

Much of the location shooting took place in Harrogate, where the Old Swan Hotel was taken over by the cast and crew for the month of November 1977. At the time Agatha Christie stayed there, it was called the Hydro Hotel, although it anachronistically remains the Old Swan in the film. 'People in London warned me that it was [like] going from New York to Pittsburgh. I take exception to their patronising words, because I like it here. Apart from anything else, I don't see any evidence of my country hitting it,' Dustin told the local paper. What he found difficult to get used to was British reserve. The natives pretended they did not know who he was, apart from the children who went up to him for autographs. He reacted to this unusual indifference towards his stardom by behaving in a rather flamboyant manner, walking around in a broad-brimmed hat and flowing scarf. However, on the fourth day at breakfast, when he ordered toast, the cook told the waitress to inform Dustin that he would not be getting anything until he gave her an autograph. It pleased Dustin no end. 'Thank God, I thought I was invisible,' he commented.

At the same time, his co-star was very visibly running around in her spare time visiting the picket lines of striking firemen, in order to offer them her support and bring them food parcels.

Despite a bad back caused by attempting a tennis shot beyond his reach, Dustin brought his racquets along. 'It's injuries like this which remind you that you've reached forty. The damp seems to have brought the pain out. But I love tennis so much I would hate to think it was all over. I usually play tennis with club pros. That way I know I'm going to be beaten and I don't feel bad about it.' During the filming, Dustin wore a support around his waist and had an orthopaedic mattress on the floor of the room, which he said 'suited him right down to the ground'.

Dustin also insisted that a shower be installed above the bath, and a piano placed in his three-piece suite. Among the extras on the film was a soprano called Paula Reeves. She had thought her singing career was over because she was having voice trouble, but was helped by a hypnotist and clairvoyant. When Dustin discovered this, he organised a little concert in the hotel lounge where he played the piano, sang and recited poems, as well as accompanying her in songs by Franz Lehar.

On the day they were to shoot in the large ballroom, they discovered that a business conference had been booked into it. In order for the filming to take place there, Dustin persuaded the managing director to hold his meeting in a smaller room, by offering him a walk-on in the film. The man, who had once had acting ambitions, was happy to fulfil his dream to be in the movies.

All very cheery, but the filming had not lasted long before Dustin, who now had top billing, wished he had never got involved in the movie in the first place. He found to his horror that the revised script, which he was responsible for initiating, was unfinished when shooting began.

'*Agatha* was every actor's nightmare. The script was literally being rewritten every day. It was a rainbow of green, yellow, and pink revision pages. The rewriting was done in such a hurried fashion that some pages of dialogue were actually delivered at the last minute before a scene was filmed.' In his opinion, *Agatha* was doomed to self-destruction without some creative control on his part, as his contract stated. 'I literally got on my knees and begged them [First Artists] not to continue with the film.'

However, it was David Puttnam who quit as producer, because of what he saw as Dustin's disruptive attitude. 'As soon as Hoffman arrived as producer on the film, David just ran,' said Michael Apted. 'I don't think David wanted the competition, he didn't want the fact that he was not going to be the sole producer influence. I think this was a ridiculous thing for him to do, for he had been responsible for bringing Dustin into the project. I think if you are taking on a major American star who is bringing the finance with him, you have to acknowledge his existence in other ways than just having him turn up in the morning and act. He's going to have his own people round him and his own demands. David would never acknowledge that. So there was one horrendous punch-up, and David left the film and left me and Vanessa and the project stranded in the hands of Hoffman, who is very difficult to deal with. It was a dreadful state of affairs.'

Puttnam explained. 'My experience with him was an unhappy one. There seems to be a malevolence in him, a determination to make other human beings unhappy. I went through agonising and cajoling and found myself asking if I really wanted to work with this worrisome American pest.'

Dustin was astonished by this remark. 'What's extraordinary is that I've never worked with this man. As far as I know I've met him only three times. And yet he goes around saying these terrible things about me.'

The atmosphere on the set was described by visitors as the most bitter and frenzied they had ever encountered. Despite the bad vibrations, Jim Clark, the editor, had good memories of Dustin. 'I was fond of him. You can't not love Dustin. He's a monster with directors, though. He's a perfectionist – quixotic, difficult, bright, a great guy – but not to direct, I think!'

Paul Brooke, who played a local journalist, was unaware of the alter-
cations behind the scenes, though there were some days when he was left
sitting around wondering whether he would be used or not. He found
Dustin, who had the final say in the casting, extremely helpful. For
example, in a scene in a taxi cab, he said to Brooke, who had not done
much filming before, 'You know there's a very tight lens, so don't flicker
an eyelid.' But everything he said on the set had a strong impact and weighed heavily with (and sometimes on) Apted. The director was, however,
adamant in Dustin's defence. 'He's a very serious and intelligent actor who
valued the views of someone with a detached and overall view of the film.
He would listen to everything I had to say.' With any other actor, Apted's
apparently unremarkable comment would seem only to state the obvious,
but it takes on more weight where Dustin is concerned. He actually
listened to everything the director had to say!

With Christmas approaching, and the shooting dragging on, First
Artists decided enough was enough, and announced that they were termi-
nating the production in three days. Actually, filming ended in London in
January 1978, five weeks late and way over its original $3 million budget.
Dustin argued that they needed two to three weeks more for an additional
scene which would explain why the reporter was so obsessed with
Christie. Redgrave concurred. Had they included the extra small scene, in
which he confesses to her that he is a failed novelist who has grown to
admire her for her success, the focal point of their relationship would have
made more sense. So convinced was Dustin about the importance of the
scene that he offered to pay for an extra day's shooting himself to film it.
Co-financiers Warners and First Artists turned him down flat. On the last
day, he was still begging them for more time to complete it. At that stage,
both Schisgal and Hopcraft had left and the British playwright Christopher Hampton had come in for a short while.

'When Dustin found out that as a producer I was agreeing with First
Artists and not with him,' Jarvis Astaire told Michael Freedland, 'our busi-
ness arrangement and our friendship was over. It's just a shame that the
Hoffman of today isn't the Hoffman I've known in the past nine years.
Puttnam was complaining that Hoffman had too much power. He was
lucky. Hoffman didn't have as much as he wanted.'

Early on during the shooting, a daughter of Agatha Christie tried to get
a court injunction to have the filming stopped. She failed, but this did not
prevent the Christie family peppering *The Times* with letters complaining
about the project. On top of everything, Redgrave took out a High Court
writ against the film company, claiming that £20,172 plus VAT for her
work was still owing to her. The action was by Vanessa Redgrave

Enterprises Ltd, which claimed it was due money from Enigma Productions of London, First Artists and SweetWall Productions. Chris Nixon, publicity officer for the film, said, 'I just don't understand why there should be writs flying around. Miss Redgrave seems to be saying that she has not been paid. This may be true but there is no question of the film being in financial difficulties.' When she was finally paid, Redgrave gladly gave £40,000 from her fee on *Agatha* to the Workers' Revolutionary Party, of which she is an active member.

If *Agatha* was not going to be a commercial success, at least a number of lawyers were going to make a great deal of money out of it.

Leaving *Agatha* behind him in England at the Christmas break like a bad dream, Dustin faced another nightmare in the States. After a stopover in New York to see his daughters, he continued to LA where he began a round-the-clock edit of *Straight Time*. 'I then went directly back to England from cutting to resume the shooting on *Agatha*.' Caught between the twin pressures of completing editing on one film and shooting on the other, he threw himself into a frenzy of activity.

'When we did wrap *Agatha* I said goodbye to everyone and I walked out of the door and started to walk a hundred yards to my trailer. On the way, a man hands me a letter to say they were taking *Straight Time* away from me.' Dustin stood there trembling. He discovered that, while he had been away, the film had been totally removed from his hands into those of First Artists' President Phil Feldman, who took control of the film before release. It was Feldman who had hacked twenty minutes out of Sam Peckinpah's *The Wild Bunch*, cutting out all the flashbacks which humanised the violent characters, thus unwittingly further emphasising the graphic bloodletting.

Furious, Dustin refused to complete the dubbing of *Agatha* unless he got *Straight Time* back. It was an empty threat because, during a trip to Europe, he stopped in at the London studio to dub the necessary dialogue. 'I had always hoped he would loop the dialogue,' said Michael Apted. 'Secretly, I thought that Dustin wouldn't allow the film to go out without trying to make it the best film possible.'

'I had the shit kicked out of me, and that can be very valuable in going through life. I learned not to trust anybody,' Dustin said at the time, echoing Jason Robards's line in *All the President's Men*: 'I hate having to trust anybody.'

Straight Time was scheduled for release on 16 March 1978, but Dustin asked for it to be postponed, in order to give him time to shoot a couple of new scenes at his own expense. When First Artists refused, Dustin filed a multi-million dollar suit against Phil Feldman and his colleagues, thus starting a spiral of legal actions that gave him the reputation for being a litigious individual. In a 32-page document, he complained that his 1972 First Artists agreement granted him the exclusive right to produce two projects without pay, in exchange for creative and artistic control, including final editing. First Artists was only able to take control if costs of these productions became excessive. Dustin did admit that *Straight Time* exceeded its original budget and it took longer than anticipated but, knowing the duration and cost of the production, First Artists elected not to exercise any take-over right (even if they were legally able to do so), and he asked the court for an injunction against any editing, distribution, exhibition, or other use of the movie pending outcome of the trial.

Dustin further claimed that the filming of *Agatha* was extended because of revisions of script and that the studio had stopped the shoot one scene short of completion. He alleged that it would have been completed on time had not Redgrave refused to play certain scenes unless they were rewritten. This accusation was refuted by Jarvis Astaire. Astaire stated that, 'It was he who refused to act in the film as originally written.'

In addition, Dustin complained that First Artists repeatedly interfered on *Agatha* and demanded delivery of *Straight Time* by 15 February, putting him 'under great pressure'. He also said that he agreed to finish shooting *Agatha* before supervising the final editing of *Straight Time*, but that First Artists illegally ordered the final scene editing without his permission. Dustin sought over $2 million in lost salary on the films and over $66 million in damages resulting from breach of contract, with $3 million of that filed in exemplary damages against Feldman and Astaire.

It was a bitter irony that the desire to control his own work was the principal motivation for his joining First Artists. 'I wanted to experience having creative control over a film I was in, and I was willing to forgo salary.' It was not long before First Artists, which in eleven years had completed only fifteen films, was dissolved. Somehow the artists had delegated authority to their attorneys, leaving the company to be run by the studio executives – the very people First Artists was formed to get away from.

The history of artists attempting to control their own affairs in Hollywood was merely repeating itself. By the end of UA's first decade of existence, D. W. Griffith was financially ruined and starting to attack the bottle, Mary Pickford and Douglas Fairbanks were heading for divorce and retirement and, despite further masterpieces, Charlie Chaplin's divorce cases and politics were to tarnish his reputation. Thus the original 'company built by the stars' passed out of their hands into those of producer–businessmen–showmen such as Schenck, Goldwyn, Hughes, Selznick and Korda.

Agatha had a world premiere on 9 February 1979 at New York's Cinema I Theater. As he had done over *Straight Time*, Dustin repudiated the picture. 'If *Agatha* is a great success, so be it. It's not my film. If it's a great success, let those people who are responsible take the credit. If it's not successful critically or commercially, it's also not my film. Either way.'

Disputes between production companies and either writers or directors are not unheard of. Two recent cases had involved imbroglios with Paramount: Richard Bach's over *Jonathan Livingston Seagull* (1973) and Elaine May's over *Mikey and Nicky* (1976), but never before had a star so completely disavowed any responsibility for two major studio releases.

There is a justifiable indignation among the creative members of the film industry about decisions taken by the 'philistines' in the front office. Whenever the top brass gets its way on cuts or additions, the cry goes up that a masterpiece has been ruined. In some cases this has been true, although the greatness of a vandalised film like *The Magnificent Ambersons* still shines through. There are other films that acquire an undeserved mystique by having been mutilated or even altered slightly. But *Straight Time* and *Agatha* are in neither category. It seems highly likely that the two films might have been improved if First Artists had had the confidence to give Dustin the final cut and allowed him the extra scenes, but not substantially so. Unsurprisingly to Dustin, both films received mixed reviews, but he did not get any satisfaction from saying, 'I told you so.'

On the whole, *Agatha*, 'an imaginary solution to an authentic mystery', is a pretty sluggish piece in which there are long periods when nothing much happens. Wally Stanton explains his presence at the spa by claiming to have a constipation problem. There is in fact something constipated about the whole picture. It fills up time with a non-conclusive plan for a murder or murder mystery suggesting that Agatha Christie might have planned to kill her rival. To create some action, Dustin is seen running, like at the end of *The Graduate*, to save the mistress (Celia Gregory) from being electrocuted, but this creates little tension because the audience knows that Miss Christie never killed anyone outside the confines of her books.

There are, however, some visual compensations. Despite often looking as though it were shot through smoked glass, Vittorio Storaro's splendid sepia-toned photography and the sumptuous period settings and costumes by Shirley Russell (then the wife of the director Ken Russell) recreate the time and place immaculately. Only the end title song, 'Close Enough For Love', strikes an anachronistic note.

In the title role, Vanessa Redgrave expertly communicates the slightly nervy and unstable manner of a distressed woman, while Dalton, reminiscent of the young Olivier, cleft chin and all, is the perfect cad with a neat little moustache on his stiff upper lip. Dustin also keeps his lip stiffer than usual, although he injects some much-needed humour and restrained brashness into the over-polite proceedings – overcoming many of the vacuities of the role by playing it passively and tongue-in-cheek. But for most of the time, with his hair slicked down on either side of a parting in the twenties manner, and dressed more nattily on screen than ever before or since, he just chain-smokes, looks very knowing, and stares unblinkingly at his lofty co-star. Although there is some tentatively humorous byplay about the stars' respective heights – she, willowy and untouchable, he, short and sensuous – they are a mismatched pair in a peculiarly lethargic, truncated and irrelevant love affair that merely pads out an extended short story or anecdote.

The New York Times found *Agatha* 'tends to leave us slumped back far from the edges of our seats . . . Mr Hoffman finds a good deal of humour in a role he appears to have made up – his mannerisms anyway – though you never for a moment believe he could have fallen in love with such a desperate character.'

For Pauline Kael, Dustin's was 'just a concoction of a role . . . Hoffman has grown into his older-man's head, which looked a little anomalous when he played youthful roles. Yet he's even less relaxed now and more stage-actorish: you feel that in *Agatha* he has an image of the character in his mind and he's impersonating it. Sometimes he has images of so many characters that he's impersonating a whole gallery of people; at other times, there's nobody there.'

Against the consensus, *Variety* thought the picture 'would do Agatha Christie proud', and for all the acrimony and disputation that surrounded it, the picture was 'engaging and stylish'.

It was the 37-year-old Michael Apted's fourth feature after *Triple Echo* (1972), in which he sensitively handled a cross-dressing theme, *Stardust* (1974), an uninspiring pop musical, and *The Squeeze* (1977), a predictable and sleazy thriller. Despite the setback of *Agatha*, Apted's fifth film, and his first truly American one, *Coal Miner's Daughter*, was nominated for a Best Film Oscar.

After the lukewarm critical and box-office reception of the two First Artists movies, there were still more problems to beset Dustin. The LA Superior Court Judge David A. Thomas rejected his legal suit for seizing control of *Straight Time* and *Agatha*, and Jarvis Astaire countersued the actor for $3.5 million in damages. The suit dragged on for years afterwards. It took over five years for a settlement to be reached, the main condition being that its details would remain undisclosed. 'I'm sure they thought I'd give up. Not me. I felt like Jimmy Stewart in *Mr Smith Goes to Washington*.'

At about the same time, Anne, his wife of nearly ten years, got into the spirit of litigation by suing Dustin for divorce, for 'mutual reasons'.

24

Kramer vs Kramer; Hoffman vs Hoffman

You can't imagine how shattering divorce is until it happens to you. It's like a death in the family. And it's worse when children are involved.

'I WANT TO thank divorce,' announced Dustin Hoffman in his Oscar-acceptance speech for *Kramer vs Kramer*. After the financial and artistic problems on his two preceding films, *Straight Time* and *Agatha*, he said that it was *Kramer vs Kramer* that restored his faith in cinema. Whether it restored his faith in marriage was another question. The two-and-a-half year making of the divorce-centred movie coincided with the breaking up of his own marriage. Life and Art became inextricably linked.

Like Meryl Streep in *Kramer v Kramer*, Anne was tired of only being 'somebody's daughter, wife and mother'. She was struggling to find her personal identity. Because she had passed the stage when she could resume her dancing career, Anne followed up the Lina Wertmuller movie with a role in Woody Allen's *Manhattan*. She was sixth billed (just below Meryl Streep) as the wife of the adulterous and egocentric Michael Murphy, a part she must have found easy to relate to. She has a good scene with Woody in a restaurant, where she is touching about her husband's affair. Curiously, a copy of *Papillon* is clearly visible on Diane Keaton's book-shelf, as if it were a plug for the first film in which Anne appeared. A year later, she had a minor role in the justifiably barely-seen melodrama *Why Would I Lie?* (1980), but it was still work. Dustin took a dim view of his wife's attempts at an independent existence by complaining that Anne's turning to acting did not form part of their original 'marital agreement'.

Dustin tried to rationalise the break-up of the marriage: 'Most separations come from the basic reason: something is structurally wrong in the beginning. The territorial imperatives were wrong and that has come to make things very clouded. But trying to be creative and spontaneous – that's the hardest part. That's one of the things, I'm sure, that prompts a lot of extramarital affairs among people – what we call "cheating". What that comes from, I guess, is that spontaneity breaks down.

'Anne and I thought our fighting was healthy in a sense, even all the *Who's Afraid of Virgina Woolf?* scenes, and we used to brag we weren't like those people who say, "We never fight." But I guess you can't just battle that much over a number of years without ultimately – you know. . . The reason for our divorce had to do with differing viewpoints.'

It was while Dustin was under terrific pressure in LA, struggling to regain artistic control over the two First Artists pictures, that Anne left with the two girls and went to live in their Manhattan home. Dustin begged her to stay with him until he was free to concentrate on the marriage, but Anne decided that, as a final break was inevitable, it was better to separate sooner than later. Divorce proceedings got under way. The split was relatively amicable, and their property was divided up fairly evenly, but the couple never returned to friendly terms.

Dustin went to stay at the cosy Mayfair House Hotel while his new bachelor apartment was being prepared. He had bought a plush three-bedroom apartment overlooking Central Park, large enough to accommodate his daughters whenever they came to visit, usually for overnight stays. One day, Jenna arrived for an appointment with 'Daddy – 3.15' written in green pencil on the back of her hand.

'When the girls visited me, they would test me. Whatever I'd say to do, they'd do just the opposite. Things I knew they'd always liked, they'd say they didn't like. I couldn't please them. They were testing me, you know, like kids will do when they're angry with the people they love the most. It's so frustrating to a parent. You want to scream, to break their necks – God, you just feel so damned frustrated and mad at them, at yourself, at everyone.

'You kid yourself if you think being separated does not have a traumatic effect on children. They are going to feel that it is somehow expected that they favour one parent over the other, and that causes conflict. . . It doesn't sound like something I would want to experience if I were a child. I wouldn't want to experience it as an adult and I don't believe children are much different from adults.'

The actor deliberately used his personal pain in his portrayal of divorcee Ted Kramer, successful Madison Avenue man, whose wife ups and leaves him alone with their six-year-old son Billy. She is no longer in love with him and wants to assert her independence. At first, it is a struggle for Ted to look after the child, but gradually a special relationship begins to develop between them as they grow to understand each other. For Ted, a change of values is necessary too. Initially, a shifty, somewhat bland businessman with an eye to upward mobility, he is forced to reassess himself when he can no longer hold down such a high-powered job because of Billy's demands on his time, and finds himself becoming a much more caring parent. When the mother returns to win custody of Billy, she is accused in court of 'failing in the single most important relationship in her life'. The judge decides in the end to award custody to the mother, but she has come to recognise the bond that exists between father and son, and relinquishes her right to bring him up.

Producer Stanley Jaffe had no problems in buying the film rights of the Avery Corman novel for an unspecified amount. To direct it, Jaffe had François Truffaut in mind, but the celebrated French director was too busy with other projects to consider it, apart from the fact that he spoke little English. It would have been fascinating to have seen what Truffaut, whose films testify to his brilliance with children, would have achieved. How the independent director, master of all he surveyed, would have coped with a star like Dustin in the different world of commercial American movies, is another matter altogether. The French director would never have been as pliant as Robert Benton, whom Dustin described as 'an ego-less person'.

Forty-seven-year-old Robert Benton, who had turned out a screenplay of *Kramer vs Kramer*, was then asked to direct the Columbia picture. He had co-written the script of *Bonnie and Clyde* (1967) – another US movie Truffaut was originally to have directed – as well as *What's Up, Doc?* (1972), and was one of the many hands on *Superman* (1978). His previous two films as director had been *Bad Company* (1972), an arty and artful Western, and *The Late Show*, a mildly amusing and controlled Raymond Chandler pastiche, none of which seemed especially to qualify him for a domestic comedy-drama.

Dustin read the novel, when there was talk of his being offered the lead, and found it 'more contrived than I hoped it would be'. He was equally unimpressed with Benton's script, which had been sent to him while he was in England making *Agatha*. Undeterred, Jaffe and Benton flew to London, in the winter of 1977, to speak to Dustin about it. He was not in the most receptive mood when they visited him at the Inn on the Park Hotel at Hyde Park Corner where he was staying. The last thing he had on his mind was this 'little art movie' about parents battling over child custody. 'I told them I couldn't work. I was quitting movies after *Agatha*. I was going back to the theatre. I had more power there.' But they went on talking, and finally Dustin asked them why they wanted to make the movie. It seemed that they wished to focus it towards their own children. Dustin, thinking of Karina and Jenna, suddenly liked the idea. 'Sometimes when you don't want to do something, you get the best terms in a way. So I asked them, if I agreed to make the movie, could we all agree that we three would collaborate from the very beginning and then with the actress. I'd had the experience of doing my best work those few times that had happened to me. They said, yes. Then I said, can we also agree that the script is crap and we begin again? It's not a piece of crap, but can we treat it that way, so we're quite tough. They said yes.' Dustin then asked them to send him another script before he would make a final commitment.

Meanwhile, Richard Dreyfuss, Roy Scheider and John Voight were hovering in the wings waiting for a decision from Dustin. Al Pacino's name was also sent along the grapevine – an old ruse used by producers who wanted to get Dustin to sign a contract. However, like the Duke of Gloucester refusing to become King Richard III, Dustin turned Jaffe and Benton down three times before finally agreeing to their offer on the terms he had outlined. 'Full collaboration, otherwise I'm going back to the theatre. I've had enough of this business. Okay?'

The threat got him over $1 million salary, a share of the percentages from the film's profits, and final say on editing. He was also free to improvise and request additional takes for alternative ideas he had in playing a scene, and he was given the opportunity to supervise the writing of the screenplay. With the bitter experience of First Artists playing in his mind, for Dustin it was a case of once bitten, twice as bold.

Naturally, all this made artistic sense to Dustin, and it was the start of a period in which he was the prime mover behind his films. In purely commercial terms, his insistence on control paid off. He was unable to justify himself to those who had accused him of being difficult on *Straight Time* and *Agatha*, because they were flops. After *Kramer vs Kramer*, he was able to say (to *Time* magazine), 'People should think twice before they rail against me. They may have done their best work with me. I'm like that clocker who is always saying "Come on! Come on!"'

As soon as he finished *Agatha*, and while caught up in the lawsuits against First Artists (they had issued an injunction to stop him filming *Kramer vs Kramer*, but it was turned down) and the divorce proceedings, Dustin started to work with Benton and Jaffe every day for nearly four months, re-writing, re-working the scenario, going through seventeen drafts. They were to write more once they had picked the actors, again in rehearsal, and yet again during shooting.

'I've never let an actor in on the writing or editing before,' commented Benton. 'I always thought the actors were hired to ruin the writer's lines. When I told people about the movie, they sounded interested. When I told them I had Dustin in it, they blanched and said, "Oh, your poor thing!" But he has an amazing amount to contribute.

'I attempted to write the way Dustin talks, so that, when he improvises, you wouldn't know the difference. We wanted Dustin to draw on his own volatile, engaging personality in creating the character. We tape-recorded our talks and took endless notes on his language. If the film has any truth in it, and I think it does have that quality, it's as much to do with Dustin as with me. And I'm not saying that to be diplomatic.'

Dustin seemed happy with the arrangement. 'I'd turn to Benton and say, "I've got an idea!" And this smile would come on his face. I'd never seen that in so many years. I'd say that to other directors and they'd get green. I'd think they were going to throw up. The worst thing you can say to most directors is, "I've got an idea."

'The directors I like best are the kind who don't march up and down in front of the camera before the take but the kind who get lost, become part of the scenery, and yet are very strongly there because they know where to put the camera.'

With the script at a stage to be tested on the anvil of rehearsal and shooting, a cast began to be assembled. For some months, Dustin had become the constant companion of Kate Jackson, the brunette on TV's *Charlie's Angels*, who was just ending her brief marriage to Andrew Stevens. Dustin considered offering her the role of the wife in the film but ABC TV had other ideas. They would not release her from her contract, and she had to wait three years before the series ended and she had a chance to make a movie – Arthur Hiller's counter-productive gay tear-jerker *Making Love* (1982). Jackson then returned to the small screen. Actually, Columbia executive Sherry Lansing was opposed to Jackson from the beginning, and suggested Meryl Streep instead.

The 27-year-old Streep had come some way since her unsuccessful audition for the play *All Over Town* in 1974. She had made her screen debut, wearing a black wig, in the almost imperceptible role of a vulgar *parvenu* in *Julia* in 1977, but had won an Emmy for her performance in the TV drama *Holocaust* the following year. But none of the three movies she had made since – *The Deer Hunter*, *The Seduction of Joe Tynan* and *Manhattan*, in which she was Woody Allen's wife who leaves him 'for another woman' – had yet been released when she came to audition for Dustin and Benton. 'I thought I was going in for the wife's part. So I launched right into how I thought about her and the film – and they were looking at each other sideways. Nobody bothered to tell me I was there for the smaller part of Phyllis, the lawyer. I only learned that later!' When the audition was over, Benton, Dustin and Jaffe agreed Meryl would be perfect for Joanna, the wife. Jobeth Williams took over as Phyllis (a part that required her to be naked for half of the time).

For the role of the child, Dustin flirted with the idea of using his own daughter Jenna, but felt it might become too personal and touch too many nerves, although he used his experience with his young daughter as a basis for some scenes with the child in the film. The sequence at the dinner table when the kid defies his father by saying he hates Swiss steaks and gets the icecream out of the freezer, derived from something that really happened with Jenna.

The search for the child-in-the-middle took Benton and Jaffe to various schools throughout the country, interviewing over three hundred candidates from twenty-six different schools. The choice fell on seven-year-old Justin Henry, who Dustin thought had 'the poise of Wallace Beery'. About the first thing Dustin said to him was, 'I hope we get along because there are people who definitely don't like me.' The boy looked up at Dustin gravely, saying, 'That's okay, my dad has the same problem.' Someone on the set asked Justin what his favourite film was. '*Jaws 2*,' he replied. 'What about *Jaws*?' 'Oh, that was before my time,' explained the child.

'When we were invited to take Justin to New York for an interview for the film part,' explained his mother Michele, 'we thought why not, how often would we get a chance to meet Dustin Hoffman? We barely considered the possibility that Justin would get the part.'

Before shooting began on 12 June 1978, Dustin insisted on four weeks of rehearsal on the set. 'You can't rush quality. That's the key, but most people who make movies today aren't concerned with quality. All they're concerned about is making money.' Stanley Jaffe stated: 'He is a perfectionist about the craft and the structuring of the film, and his ego is subjugated to that.' Jaffe later admitted to journalist Tony Crawley: 'There were a couple of times when I felt like taking Dustin and putting him right through the window. And I'm sure vice versa.'

To research the role of Kramer, Dustin took an objective look at himself as a husband, a father and an actor. 'Ted Kramer touches on certain parts of myself that interest me. But there's no such thing as yourself . . . I think it was Saul Steinberg who said, "I wake up every morning doing a different impersonation of myself." It may sound strange but to be experiencing in real life what I was portraying on the screen was for me, as an actor, a pleasure I'd never had.'

Robert Benton commented, 'It's the hardest work to go in and use yourself as a character – to do a relentless self-portrait. It's hair-raising, and I think he pulled it off.'

Despite the subject of the film, Dustin never talked about the breakdown of his own marriage on the set. He put it all into Ted Kramer. Jane Alexander, who played his sympathetic neighbour, found Dustin far more hyperactive than he had been on *All the President's Men*. His amount of energy seemed to have increased, and 'he's never wanting in energy'.

He would also, rather bizarrely, rollerskate down the corridors of the buildings they were shooting in. One evening, Dustin and Jane Alexander took her brother and his girlfriend from out of town to a restaurant, and the first thing Dustin asked the rather naive girl was, 'So, is he a good lay?', something which shocked her no end.

Gregarious and effervescent as he often was, at lunchtime he would lock himself in his trailer and stare blankly out of the window until he was taken out of his trance by the call from the sound stage. (Little Justin Henry took to retreating to a dark room to prepare for his scenes as he had seen Dustin do.) Then back he would come, exhausting quite a few people around with his excessive improvisation. Alexander, in particular, found the filming took a lot out of her, mainly because she was appearing at night and in matinees at the Majestic on Broadway in *First Monday in October* opposite Henry Fonda at the same time. The Majestic is one of the largest theatres in New York, so Jane had to project her voice to the back of the one thousand six hundred and fifty-five seater. On the second day of rehearsal, Dustin took Jane aside and merely whispered, 'stage hangover', which she understood immediately as a hint to scale her performance down for the cameras.

During preparation for the film, Dustin kept staring at young mothers and pregnant women. He told *Time*: 'I've always found women very sexy when they're pregnant, unless, of course, they're smoking. That gives me the chills. They have an aura that you don't see in a man with his kids. I hear music when I see them – definitely strings. . . Generally speaking, I don't think it's possible to give a child too much love. I try not to spoil mine, because I'm aware that there is a tendency to overcompensate when you're separated and don't see your children always.'

In one of the rushes that were not used, Dustin improvised a speech on the stand in the courtroom, in a plea to the judge to give him custody of the child: 'I get up when he does, I give him his breakfast, I take him to school, I bring him home at night, I bring him dinner, I'm his mother!. . . He didn't come out of my vagina but I'm his mother!' It was a moment when, Dustin said, 'I could smell it like an animal, smell that I was gonna lose the kid, and it's very emotional for me. I'm going through a separation at the time and it's the first time that what I'm doing as an actor corresponds to what is going on in my life. That's what every artist does. They create something in their art out of the moment in their lives. And people said: "That must have been very hard for you." And I said "No, it's a joy! To be able to get it out. It's what I wish I could do all the time!"'

Benton recognised that Dustin was 'one of those natural fathers. Kids drift to him instinctively and immediately. For that reason I worked out an arrangement. Any time I had direction for Justin, I'd give it to Dustin. Then he'd pass it along to the child. Justin totally believed in Dustin, who was a genuine friend. And Dustin was a fantastic acting coach. He knew what buttons to press.'

'The first few days his concentration was terrible,' Dustin reported. 'He kept looking at the camera. He was like a young colt or, more accurately, he was a normal six-year-old. By the third week, he was becoming an actor.'

Dustin's close work and rapport with Justin were essential to the film's success. Before they did a scene together Dustin would sit and talk alone with Justin, explaining to him what emotions he wanted. In the scene when they clash over the icecream, Justin suddenly improvised, turning it into a real fight by taunting Dustin with an upraised spoon. 'It shocked me when he fought back.' But Justin and Dustin become very fond of one another. While filming the hospital scene, Dustin was away for a short period, prompting Justin to ask Jane Alexander, 'Where's Dustin? Where's my darling Dustin?'

Some time later, on *Good Morning, America*, Dustin, with tears in his eyes, related that, 'There came a day when it was all over and we had to say goodbye. I loved that kid. I said goodbye. . . and I've never seen him since.' Justin Henry, who said at the time that he would hate to become an actor because it was boring 'sitting around and waiting for lighting and cameras to be fixed', did not act again until he was thirteen years old. He co-stared with Roy Scheider in *Tiger Town* for the Disney Channel, and appeared in the John Hughes movie *16 Candles*. The $50,000 he earned for *Kramer vs Kramer* was invested for him by his father, Cliff, an investments consultant.

At one stage during the filming, Dustin asked the child who he would prefer to live with in real life, him or Meryl. 'Her! She's nicer,' Justin replied. The cast and crew burst into laughter. 'Oh, yeah? Work with her five weeks and then see what you say.'

Dustin and Streep had some 'bad fights', but they were always fights over the same thing – the construction or playing of a scene, especially the sequence when they meet in the restaurant, when the mother demands the return of her son. As the cameras rolled, Dustin got more and more caught up in the way his character was being bested by hers, and his anger suddenly manifested itself by his picking up a glass and throwing it against the wall, an unrehearsed moment that caught Streep unawares. She was naturally furious with Dustin. As she picked glass shards out of her hair, she told him, between clenched teeth, 'Next time you do that, I'd appreciate you letting me know.' As a result of that piece of inspired improvisation, the look of astonishment on Streep's face is a genuine one caught by the camera.

Streep was proud of Joanna Kramer, 'because I think I stuck up for her point of view. When they came to my part, Benton and Dustin both would just kind of draw a blank. Really the film is the story of father-mothering a child and they didn't know what Joanna felt. They asked, could I speak from that subjective point of view? I said, Sure. . . but I don't know if you'll use it.' She then had a few days off shooting and went to Indiana to visit her husband's family. Streep had just married New York sculptor Don Gummer, a friend of her brother's, in September 1978, seven months after the death of her lover, actor John Cazale, from bone cancer. On the way back, on the plane, a whole speech came to her, and she quickly wrote it down. She then performed it for Dustin and Benton, who approved of it wholeheartedly. On the last scene, they hit a snag. Everybody went off into their corners and tried to write what she should say at the end. 'Dustin wrote his, Benton wrote his, and I wrote mine. And they used mine!'

For Dustin, Streep is 'an ox when it comes to acting. She eats work for breakfast. It's like playing with Billie Jean King. She keeps trying to hit the perfect ball.' According to her, 'You have to throw a little cold water on Dustin every once in a while. He wants to be the greatest actor of all time. He wants you to be good and, at the same time, he doesn't. I understand him; we play the same kind of ball.'

Despite Benton's praise for Dustin's talent, he was not the first or last director to say he would be hesitant in the future about working with the actor a second time. (In May 1990, however, Benton did not hesitate too long before agreeing to direct Dustin again in *Billy Bathgate*, the film version of the E. L. Doctorow novel.)

'He has the unfortunate ability to smell when something is wrong and to throw himself into the cogs of the machine until it has ground to a halt in order to get it right. This is often the case. Someone as obsessed as Dustin creates a lot of tension and puts a tremendous burden on the people he's working with.'

'Dustin is obsessed with his work. Consequently he is not an easy guy to work with. He wants to examine all aspects of a line before he commits himself to going with it,' says Murray Schisgal.

However, there's nothing like the sound of money pouring into box offices around the world, and recognition from the Oscar-giving American Academy of Arts and Sciences, to convince people working on a film that all the squabbles, back-breaking toil and long hours were worth it. Dustin's faith and confidence in the picture made him more cooperative than usual during its promotion. For example, he was quite happy to pose for twenty minutes for a crowd of photographers, by himself, with his parents, with Justin Henry and Justin's parents. He told reporters, 'My two daughters have seen the film. They were really upset by it but they liked it. And I'm not so sure you should keep kids away from the truth even if it is upsetting.' When *Kramer vs Kramer* was selected for the Royal Command Performance, Dustin went to London for the annual regal hand-shaking ritual.

In April 1980, *Kramer vs Kramer* gained five out of the seven Oscars it was nominated for. Stanley Jaffe collected one for Best Film; Benton got a brace – for Best Director and Best Screenplay; Dustin grabbed his first (after three previous nominations), and perversely, both Meryl Streep and Jane Alexander were nominated for Best Supporting Actress, with Streep winning out. Streep was absent from the ceremony as she had become a mother for the first time just two months earlier, and the baby was unwell.

Little eight-and-a-half-year-old Justin Henry, dolled up for the occasion, sat amidst other supporting actor nominees, among whom were the eventual winner, seventy-nine-year-old Melvyn Douglas (*Being There*), sixty-year-old Mickey Rooney (*The Black Stallion*), and forty-nine-year-old Robert Duvall (*Apocalypse Now*), whom Dustin mentioned favourably in his acceptance speech.

Standing on the stage of the Dorothy Chandler Pavillion, Dustin was treated very much as the Prodigal Son, but he was still able to inject some of his own irreverent opinions into the cosy occasion. Looking at his Oscar, Dustin remarked, 'He has no genitalia and he's holding a sword. I'd like to thank my father and mother for not practising birth control.' He went on. 'I'm up here with mixed feelings. I've criticised the Academy before, with reason. I refuse to believe that I beat Jack Lemmon [*The China Syndrome*], that I beat Al Pacino [*And Justice for All*], that I beat Peter Sellers [*Being There*]. . . We are part of an artistic family. There are sixty thousand actors in the Screen Actors Guild who don't work. You have to practise accents while you're driving a taxicab 'cos when you're a broke actor, you can't write and you can't paint. Most actors don't work and a few of us are so lucky to have a chance. And to that artistic family that strives for excellence, none of you have [*sic*] ever lost and I am proud to share this with you and I thank you.' The cameras showed Lillian promptly bursting into tears.

Dustin was also on stage to present an Honorary Oscar to Alec Guinness, whose films Dustin said he had been seeing in the last few weeks 'to watch his work and be a student of him'. Guinness, accepting the statuette, said 'Thank you, Mr Hoffman, for your over-generous words and all that deep research work you did.'

Dustin's comeback performance is one of his finest. He is warmer and far more instinctual than in previous films. There are no disguises, no overt tricks in building a character out of nothing very much – a conventional, smooth, self-absorbed, Madison-Avenue type suddenly realising what it takes to bring up a child and have a career. There is one strangely Keatonesque moment when Dustin sits unsmiling in the midst of the cheer of a Christmas office party. *The New York Times* proclaimed it 'a delicately witty performance, funny and full of feeling that never slops over into the banal, which is the greatest danger faced by an actor who must play most of his scenes with a small boy who is as down-to-earth and pragmatic as Justin Henry'.

One has only to compare the use of the golden-haired gap-toothed moppet Ricky Schroeder, turning on the waterworks in Franco Zeffirelli's shamelessly sentimental remake of *The Champ* in the same year, to see the relative truth behind Justin Henry's portrayal. Unfortunately, there are still a few scenes that would not have seemed out of place in a Shirley Temple movie, especially the embarrassing monologue Dustin delivers to the child in the bedroom, trying to give an explanation as to why his mother left. However, in the Shirley Temple version, the judge would have been a twinkly-eyed Guy Kibbee or Henry Travers, who would immediately have given the father custody.

The film itself is put together with superb craftsmanship, with the Baroque music (Purcell and Vivaldi) on the soundtrack giving it a veneer of class. Its success indicated a market for well-made, middle-class, tearjerking domestic dramas with a soupçon of feminism. One of the things Dustin tried to do with Ted Kramer was to feminise him; not only politically, but physically and emotionally, without effeminising him. *Kramer* and *Tootsie* could be seen as making up a quasi-feminist diptych, the latter being the natural development from the former.

Yet, as in the later *Tootsie, Kramer*'s feminist claims remain dubious. Although the movie demonstrates that a father can be just as good a mother as the mother can (a theme that dates back to Chaplin's *The Kid*), it seems to suggest that a liberated woman would not be capable of bringing up a child while holding down a top job, as well as implicitly condemning the wife for taking off on her quest for selfhood. It would have been sharper if the mother had taken the child, revealing the consequences of a law that continues to think in gender stereotypes, rather than about which is the better parent, thus creating a more subtle polemic. Consequently, the

happy ending, awash with tears, is far too pat. Despite the many manufac-
tured situations, the combination of role-reversal comedy and the tearful
tug-of-war child custody drama is carried off astutely, mainly because of
the performances of the whole cast.

Kramer vs Kramer was the trampoline that enabled Dustin to bounce
back into the annual ratings of the ten top box-office stars in the USA, and
give his career credibility again.

Among the projects subsequently offered to him was the role of George
Gershwin to Richard Dreyfuss's Ira Gershwin in a Columbia Pictures biopic that remains unborn. The whimsical *The World According to Garp*
might have had Dustin in the Robin Williams role, had he not correctly
realised that he was not right for it. Despite having fired himself from
Straight Time, he still had a desire to direct a movie, but was able to say: 'I
hope I don't act when I do direct. I'm in awe of the few who have done it
successfully.'

After the exigencies of shooting and before the acclaim that greeted him
and *Kramer vs Kramer*, Dustin retreated to the house he was leasing in
Westwood, California, where he went on bike rides to the Westwood
Country Club for some leisurely exercise. However, the cold showers he
took afterwards were insufficient to douse his need for women. With
Anne gone, the vacuum in his emotional and sexual life had to be filled.

'I've always been most attracted to women who were working behind
counters – salesgirls, waitresses, working girls – rather than rich women
who go shopping every day.' And yet Dustin expressed his enjoyment of
women whom he regards as equals – women who challenge him intellectually, nurture his creativity, and keep him on his feet emotionally. 'In a
woman I'm attracted to someone who is sexy and beautiful and exciting
and it's all coming from the inside and the exterior is just secondary.'

One of these women was a tall blonde called Barra Gable, who became
his constant companion for a short while. In the late summer of 1979,
Dustin flew to Cannes with her, but the relationship did not last, though
they kept in contact.

'My friends tell me that I'm getting handsomer the older I get. I have my
doubts that's true. I had nowhere to go but up. When you get to a certain
age and you look around, you see seventeen-, eighteen-, nineteen-year-old
boys who have their whole life ahead of them and you know you're gonna
be dead before they're even forty. They're sexually at such a height and
dynamically. I've felt there's a desire to get rid of them, because there's
nothing more threatening than what happens when you look in the rear-
view mirror.'

Marriage was something he still craved for. 'I get a funny feeling when I walk into a home and there's a family there. It moves me. I haven't given up hope. I know people who are sculptors and painters with a shitload of kids and a wife and they just do their work. There's nothing wrong with that. People who have gone past the part of family and children tend to give me the willies. It's nice to have someone there when you need them, which is many times during the day. As long as there's someone in the house somewhere, it's very comforting.'

Dustin began to see his parents more often at their home an hour south of LA. His father became a favourite tennis partner. 'You never know your children,' said Harry. 'You get a sneak here and a sneak there, but you never really know. We went to hear Dusty speak to an auditorium full of college kids. We were astounded by his knowledge. We sat there and felt like we were listening to someone else. We didn't know how smart he was.'

'I want to see him get what he wants,' mused Lillian. 'I would love to see him have a lot more children. With whoever is his mate – whether it's Annie or anybody else. He wants domestic happiness. He's a homebody. This is what he loves. Family life. I hope he gets it.' He was soon to find the right woman who would give him all of this.

25

Hoffman/Hoffwoman

I haven't changed my perceptions about women. I've deepened them.

IN JUNE 1980, just two months after Dustin won his Oscar for *Kramer vs Kramer*, his mother Lillian suffered a major heart attack, followed within weeks by a stroke which paralysed her right side and rendered her mute. Distraught, Dustin chartered a helicopter to get him from Columbia Studios to Scripps Memorial Hospital at La Jolla as quickly as possible. Like a wild man, his hair all over the place from the helicopter's rotors, he dashed into her room. Harry and Ronald were already at the bedside. As Lillian could not speak, Dustin got her to answer 'yes' with a half-smile, and 'no' by sticking the tip of her tongue out. 'Does it hurt here?' he asked, pointing to her arm. The tongue shot out. 'Here?' to the legs. A half-smile.

Although Harry and his two sons were undemonstrative and rarely hugged or kissed each other, Dustin embraced them both to please Lillian. 'Did you see that, Mom?' he asked her. As she was wheeled away for an emergency operation, Dustin begged her not to give in, to stay alive. 'You gotta fight, Mom,' he cried. 'This is the tough one.'

The crisis brought home how important his mother had been to him in his life. But he had also found another woman who already meant a great deal to him. Back in 1967, before *The Graduate* made him a movie star, Dustin had gone back home for a small family reunion at his parents' Beverly Hills house, where they had been living since his father's furniture-design business took off. Lillian's best friend, Blanche Salter, who lived next door, was at the party with her ten-year-old granddaughter Lisa Gottsegen, a child for whom Dustin had once babysat years earlier. He had known Lisa's mother since they were children, when they used to play 'doctor' together.

Dustin was playing the piano at the party, when little Lisa, in pyjamas, came and sat next to him. Later, when he walked away, she turned to her grandmother and said, 'Nanny, I hope he waits for me, 'cos I'm going to marry him when I grow up!'

Eight years later they met at another family party, when she was eighteen and he was a major star of thirty-seven. But in 1975, he was happily married and Lisa was just starting at law school. At her father's request, Dustin hired her part-time as an assistant to keep his LA affairs in order. 'I began having powerful feelings about her, which made me think, you are sick – this is the child of your parents' best friends.' When Anne and Dustin separated, he and Lisa became closer.

'I fought it. It wasn't incest, but it was probably only one step removed from it. The relationship with Lisa was born out of resistance in a sense because I didn't want my first marriage to end. I didn't get married to Anne until I was thirty-one, and I thought that by holding off so long I had a good shot at making it a success.'

Lisa got a law degree at UCLA in June 1980, but Dustin said, 'Her desire is to have dozens of kids.' When they were pestered by reporters, he'd say, 'She's my attorney – and if you're not careful, I'll have her sue you.'

Dustin proposed to Lisa in Central Park. 'I got down on my knees and, to the accompaniment of a chorus of kids whispering, "Would you look at that dude!", I asked her to marry me.' They made a premarital pact that they would always stay together.

At the time his mother first became seriously ill, they had decided to marry as soon as the divorce papers came through. Dustin had told Lisa that they had to have a baby in order to give his mother a reason to live. In August, Lisa became pregnant. Instead of waiting for the marriage, Dustin and Lisa went to see Lillian at the hospital to announce: 'We're going to have a baby.'

Dustin and Lisa were married on 12 October 1980, just six days after his divorce became official. Dustin brought the rabbi to Lillian's hospital room where he performed the traditional Jewish betrothal ceremony for the bride and groom at her bedside, before they went on to an intimate garden wedding ceremony with only eighteen close relatives and friends. After a honeymoon in Hawaii, her pregnancy was officially announced.

It was early in March, during Lisa's eighth month, that her abdomen suddenly became hard and she began losing consciousness when she lay on her back. There should have been bleeding to warn them of the seriousness of the condition but the placenta was ripping away from the uterine wall and stopping the blood's flow. Unknown to them, if the placenta had continued tearing away, the resultant internal haemorrhaging would have killed Lisa and the lack of oxygen would also have killed the baby. Intuitively, Dustin sensed the urgency, despite the doctor's somewhat unconcerned manner on the telephone.

Reliving the scene in *Kramer vs Kramer* when Dustin rushes his son to hospital after an accident, he put Lisa in a car and sped to Santa Monica Hospital, where doctors in the emergency room promptly assessed the seriousness of her condition. They decided Lisa needed an immediate

Caesarean section. Dr Amy Rosenman, the obstetrician, asked Dustin to leave. No husband had ever witnessed a Caesarean section at the hospital before. He refused. 'Then go over there and don't say a word,' she ordered, throwing him something to put on. He struggled to get them on his head. 'I think the slippers go on your feet, honey,' said Lisa. Dustin stood in the corner of the operating room in quiet shock, watching while the surgeon cut open his wife and took out their baby. Dr Rosenman said, 'He told me later it blew his mind that a twenty-nine-year-old woman was telling him what to do, was operating on his wife and saving his baby. He learned that there are things in life completely out of his control.' Had Lisa gone unattended, she would have died within the hour. Jacob, born in March 1981, almost died a few days after his birth. He had hyaline membrane, an undeveloped lung disease that had killed one of John F. Kennedy's children. The premature baby was moved to UCLA's neo-natal intensive-care unit, placed on a respirator and an umbilical artery catheter that pumped fluid and medicine through his navel. All this was kept from Lillian.

Death was hovering over three generations of Hoffmans simultaneously. During those black days, Dustin slept on a cot next to Lisa at the Santa Monica Hospital, went over to the UCLA Hospital to stroke his baby's head and sing to him, and then would rush over to soothe and bolster his mother's will to live at Scripps Memorial Hospital.

'There's this image that stays in my mind of seeing my mother on the brink of death with her arms stretched out between the bars on the side of her hospital bed . . . and then going to see my baby and his arm reaching out through the bars the exact same way . . . I know this sounds odd but my mother's stroke was one of the best things that ever happened to me. Yes, I got Dorothy out of it, but also we became friends, real friends, and had talks all through her illness that we never had before.' Everything, no matter how private, is there to be used for his work. Even grief can be used at some future date.

For 'Dorothy' was Dorothy Michaels, the 'real woman' Dustin played in *Tootsie*, inspired by Lillian. 'Dorothy has her strength, her vulnerability, her vitality and sexual humour. My mother had the spirit of a chorusgirl. At seventy-two she was playing two sets of tennis a day; she had Ann Miller's legs. The only thing she wanted, more than anything else, was to see this movie happen. Every time I felt physically uncomfortable during the shooting of the picture, like when the wig itched or the shoes pinched, I'd put on a happy face for my mother's sake. I told her I was doing the film before she died and she was very proud.'

He spoke to her by phone every day and visited her bedside in San Diego

– and he learned from her. As she grew weaker, Lillian called up early memories. She became reminiscent, philosophical, yet witty. Then one day, she looked up at her son and said, 'I've got the Big C now. I'm going to die.' 'Don't be frightened. I'll be right behind you. So warm it up, kid, I'll be with you in a finger snap.'

Lillian died in September 1981, a year before *Tootsie* was completed. Dustin reacted in anguish. 'Not to be sacrilegious, but from my point of view, God's a perverse motherfucker!'

Dustin then threw himself more than ever into the part, which was, as Ronald suggested, a way of keeping his mother alive by playing her. Freud got in before Dustin's brother by claiming than transvestism was a way men had of reclaiming the lost feminine part of themselves, the departed Mother – the one way of keeping the mother is to be her: 'The spectacle of the man dressed as a woman is both a re-enactment of the mother possessing a penis and the image which explicitly denies the subsequent knowledge of her castration and all the anxieties that induces.'

We cannot expect to know what emotions about his mother were opened up for Dustin by putting on dresses – after all, as far as anyone knows, he only did it for the benefit of the cameras – but he certainly admitted that the character of Dorothy had affected him emotionally the way no other character ever had before. 'In the past, when a role was over, oh boy, what a relief. But with Dorothy, I felt I was at a loss. I miss her.'

How the cross-dressing movie, inspired by Lillian, came to have the Hoffman mark on it and avoided being the certain catastrophe it looked like becoming, is a tale as convoluted as any in the actor's career.

The original script, entitled *Would I Lie to You?* was written by Don McGuire. McGuire, who had been a bit-part actor in Warner Bros movies in the forties, had written a few minor pictures, and directed a Frank Sinatra Western, *Johnny Concho*, and Jerry Lewis's first solo film, *The Delicate Delinquent* (both in 1956) before going into TV. In 1978, the project came to the attention of Charles Evans, who was looking for a property with which to launch himself as a big movie producer like his brother Robert (Bob) Evans, ex-minor Hollywood actor, ex-executive vice president of Paramount, ex-husband of Ali MacGraw, and the producer of *Marathon Man*.

Charles Evans, who had made his millions in the garment industry, bought the script because 'I thought it was funny. And no one could tell me it wasn't. In talking with McGuire, I knew he'd gone about as far as he could with it. I knew it needed a rewrite desperately. I knew I had to pay for a new script. I met a lot of comedy writers; one of them was Bob Kaufman, whose ideas coincided with mine.'

George Hamilton, who had starred in another Kaufman comedy, *Love at First Bite*, was ready to play the lead, and corpulent comedian Buddy Hackett, who had not made a movie for over ten years, wanted to play the role of the theatrical agent.

Evans showed the McGuire screenplay to director Dick Richards, who was interested, and for fifteen days, Kaufman and Richards, joined by Evans, worked in the Sherry Netherland Hotel in New York. Finally they had a new script. It was about an out-of-work actor who gets a job playing a nurse in a soap opera.

As the script took shape, Evans began to have doubts about George Hamilton's suitability for the role. He started to think of others who might fit the bill better. 'I thought about Chevy Chase; Elliott Gould, who would like to have done it, but he'd be too funny-looking a nurse; George Segal . . . but then I thought he was too old . . .'

Then Charles showed the script to his brother Bob, who was unenthusiastic about it, but liked the plot and subject. Although Charles felt more positive towards the Kaufman script, he was persuaded by his more experienced brother to get someone else in. By dismissing Kaufman, Charles would be able to replace George Hamilton with someone of his own choosing.

When Kaufman departed, Hamilton went on to make *Zorro, the Gay Blade*, and Dick Richards, encouraged by the Evans brothers, showed the script to Dustin, with whom he had formed a company. Dustin read the script on a plane and liked it. Coincidentally, Dustin and Murray Schisgal had been talking for some time about the possibility of Dustin's playing a female character; they shared the notion that inside every man there lurked the woman he might have been. This phantom female was referred to by the friends as 'Shirley'. Said Dustin, 'I was at a friend's fiftieth birthday party and we ended up talking about the women in us. I woke up the next day and thought what kind of a woman I would be.' In fact, Dustin and Schisgal had already begun working on a script about a male tennis player who passes as a woman and gets all the way to Wimbledon before he is finally beaten by a thirteen-year-old girl.

Before committing himself to *Tootsie*, Dustin demanded complete control over the script and other aspects of the movie. 'I didn't care,' commented Charles Evans. 'I was happy having Dustin Hoffman do my first movie. I thought it was quite a coup for me, my very first film. So I made a deal with Columbia where I moved myself back to executive producer.' Dustin was to be paid $4.5 million for his pains.

A short time later, Richards decided not to direct the movie, but remained as co-producer. It needed a director, and Dustin tried to get Hal

Ashby again. He had wanted him for *Straight Time*, but Ashby had been ill. Ashby had wanted Dustin for the Jon Voight role in *Coming Home* (Voight was originally to do the Bruce Dern part), but Dustin was involved with *Straight Time*. Now Ashby was up to his ears in *Lookin' to Get Out*, another Voight movie. They never had succeeded in working together by the time of Ashby's premature death in December 1988, aged fifty-two.

Columbia Pictures suggested Sydney Pollack. They liked him because he had managed to bring in many a movie on time and on budget, and was reasonably consistent at the box office. The 48-year-old Pollack was (and still is) a director of glossy commercial movies about important issues, who wishes to be considered a serious Hollywood artist. Those who believe that to be a contradiction in terms are vindicated by Pollack's results. The basic material of the films is often daring and powerful, but in his hands it turns to pulp. In *They Shoot Horses, Don't They?* (1969), a marathon dance contest is supposed to be a microcosm of the Depression; *The Way We Were* (1973) is the worst kind of radical chic, being neither radical nor chic; and *Bobby Deerfield* (1977) is more mawkish than morbid. As in *Three Days of the Condor* (1975) and *Absence of Malice* (1981), issues are raised in order to be skirted. Robert Redford has appeared in four of Pollack's movies and his good-looking, superficial earnestness perfectly reflects the films themselves.

In November 1981, Pollack took over as director and producer, with a deal that gave him control of casting, the script, and the final cut, something Dustin had to give way on. 'At one time this was Dustin's picture. He fathered it along and he had to live with the idea that I was directing it,' Pollack told *Variety*. The fact that contractually Pollack, and not he, had the final cut, was a source of irritation to Dustin.

Larry Gelbart was brought in to work on the screenplay. Gelbart, who had co-written some pretty crummy screenplays in the sixties, including two movies with Tony Curtis, witlessly entitled *Not with My Wife You Don't* and *On My Way to the Crusades I Met a Girl Who . . .* (UK: *The Chastity Belt*), had been Oscar-nominated for *Oh God!* in 1977. But his best achievement was as creator of the superior wisecrack-a-minute TV series of *M*A*S*H*.

Dustin, Gelbart and Pollack then met for about ten days at Pollack's beach house, where a lot of heat was generated. Gelbart later commented that what he learned from the experience was: 'Never work with an actor who is smaller than the Oscar statuette.' As he has often done since in analysing his work, Dustin resorted to a sporting analogy. 'I'm a certain kind of fighter. So I work best when I work with another guy who's fighting with me in a certain kind of way . . . so you wonder whether this director and you are the right fighting combination. And I feel that all good films have to fight. In other words, it's a good fight . . . You do three minutes. When the round's over, you hope you went at it, you give each other a tap, you go sit down, you rest, look at each other from across the ring, you know, you get the cut man on you, and then you go in and fight again. It's like any good marriage, I think. You're fighting for territory. And you want it to be fifty-fifty.'

Unemployed director Elaine May, still recovering from the flop of her last film, *Mikey and Nicky* (1976), and yet to mismake *Ishtar*, came in for three weeks (for which she was reputedly paid $450,000) to work with Pollack on the script after Gelbart had finished his two-year stint. She fleshed out some of the minor roles, introduced the roommate character (played by Bill Murray), and brought in the concept that *Tootsie* was about a man impersonating a woman and thereby becoming a better man. Robert Garland, who had written *The Electric Horseman* for Pollack, worked *à trois* with May and Pollack, and the then-husband-and-wife writing team of Valerie Curtin and Barry Levinson came in to make suggestions. And, of course, there was the ever-present Murray Schisgal. (He pops up as a party guest in the completed movie.) So many people were involved in the movie that there was talk of forming the 'I Also Wrote/I Almost Directed *Tootsie*' Club. Rumours began circulating in the press that *Tootsie* was very likely to be Columbia's *Heaven's Gate* (the epic that almost ruined UA). 'Hoffman's Gate' was the tag floating around Hollywood at the time.

Meanwhile, casting began. Charles Durning was first picked as the widower who falls for 'Dorothy'. Jessica Lange almost said no to the role of Julie, Durning's daughter, at whom 'Dorothy' makes a 'lesbian' pass. ('I just couldn't imagine having the energy after *Frances*.') Lange, who had been hugely hyped for her part as Beauty to the Beast in *King Kong* in 1976, had to wait five years to prove she could act when she appeared as the adulterous wife in Bob Rafelson's steamy remake of *The Postman Always Rings Twice*, consolidating her reputation as the tragic actress Frances Farmer the following year in the biopic *Frances* (1982). Her co-star in *Postman*, Jack Nicholson, called her 'a delicate fawn, but crossed with a Buick'.

When she started on *Tootsie*, she was just beginning to escape from the adverse publicity that had been dogging her ever since it was revealed that her blind husband, living alone and in poverty in a Bowery slum, was suing her for maintenance after she had borne a child to the exiled Russian dancer Mikhail Baryshnikov. The latter spent a great deal of time watching the filming with their blonde baby in his arms.

Teri Garr, who plays Dustin's actress friend Sandy, dumped by him for the more attractive Lange, first came to filmgoers' attention as far back as 1974 in Mel Brooks's horror spoof *Young Frankenstein*, but it was as Richard Dreyfuss's average middle-class housewife in *Close Encounters of the Third Kind* that she made her name. She had trained as a ballet dancer, and impressed in stage work as well. 'She came from the boards like I did,' said Dustin.

George Gaynes, who had appeared in Pollack's *The Way We Were*, was cast as Dorothy's ageing, horny, hammy co-star. The 64-year-old Finnish-born actor and baritone had worked with Lee Strasberg, and had a distinguished cosmopolitan career in operas, musicals and plays. Bill Murray was Dustin's choice as his struggling playwright roommate, a part which Murray plays with straightfaced detachment. He had come to the fore in the improvisational *Saturday Night Live* on TV, and would eventually become even more famous in the hugely popular and infantile *Ghostbusters*.

Pollack wanted Dabney Coleman, a great friend, to play the part of the agent. Dustin thought Pollack himself would be perfect in the role. 'He said I intimidated him!' exclaimed Pollack incredulously. 'He said: "Dabney is a peer. Dabney is not an authority figure. Dabney is not gonna scare me into putting on a dress!"' But Pollack refused, saying that he did not want to appear in a movie he was directing. However, Dustin persisted. He got his agent and lawyer on to it, and sent Pollack flowers with a note saying, 'Please be my agent! Love, Dorothy.' The director gave in, admitting later that, 'if I'm good in this picture, I have to give Dustin credit. Because he cast me.'

Pollack had trained as an actor, and had appeared on stage and TV, as well as in the 1962 movie *War Hunt* in which Robert Redford made his screen debut. Dabney Coleman was given the role of the insensitive soap opera director.

For many, the outrageousness of the behaviour of Dustin's character before he dons skirts was a huge in-joke. Dustin plays Michael Dorsey, an actor who is such a pain in the ass that he has become unemployable. Dorsey, an out-of-work actor pushing forty and getting nowhere in the New York theatre, loses jobs because he is considered temperamental and difficult. His agent tells him that he is indeed so difficult no one will hire him. Therefore he decides to put on make-up, a wig and women's clothes, assumes the name of Dorothy Michaels, and tries out for and gets a role in a TV hospital soap, *Southwest General*, playing the hospital administrator. He develops a close friendship with a beautiful co-performer, Julie. This is a new experience for Michael; being trusted by and being friends with a woman. Julie's widowed father promptly falls in love with Dorothy, and Michael falls in love with Julie. When Michael (as Dorothy) allows some of his passion for Julie to surface, she concludes that her friend is lesbian. Confusions mount before Michael confesses during a live broadcast of the soap that he is not female. (We wait for somebody to say 'Nobody's perfect.')

Although it is stated in Deuteronomy that, 'The woman shall not wear that which pertaineth unto a man, neither shall a man put on a woman's garment; for all that do so are abomination unto the Lord thy God,' drag has a long and honourable tradition in the movies. Germaine Greer, in her article 'What Turns Women On', analysed the phenomenon of female impersonation in feminist terms: 'Men have for the last one hundred and fifty years gradually been required to suppress all the erotic aspects of their appearance. Beards and whiskers disappeared, hair was cut back to the skull and limbs were hidden in drab clothes which were neither loose and flowing enough to enhance or tight enough to reveal the wearer's shape. For women, the duty to attract is primary. Moreover, strict rules and conventions governing the kind of beauty they must exhibit have been laid down, even though they are not suited to the mass of women. The pleasing procedures of self-expression through adornment have become a relentless discipline of dyeing, depilating, injecting, tanning, cleansing and painting . . . but the functional man and the artificial woman are both unsuccessful sex objects. The man does not know the pleasures of narcissism, while for the woman they have become addiction.' Therefore, many male spectators of drag acts can vicariously enjoy the narcissism that is forbidden them directly.

Most of previous Hollywood mainstream transvestism relied on the Bergsonian theory that laughter arises from incongruity and disproportion. As a general rule, only the most masculine and seemingly straight male stars took to skirts, in order to stress the ridiculous. Any disturbing sexual ambiguity or hermaphroditism were eschewed. *Charley's Aunt*, played by Jack Benny among many others, was the exemplar for many subsequent incarnations. Usually these were maiden aunt types, lacking in any sexuality. Lionel Barrymore spends a great deal of time in drag in *The Devil Doll*, Cary Grant gloomily and unconvincingly submits to it in *I Was a Male War Bride*, while comedians such as Stan Laurel, Bob Hope and Lou Costello often found themselves grotesquely attired in women's clothes. Even more difficult to believe were women disguised as men – Mary Pickford as *Little Lord Fauntleroy*, Katharine Hepburn in *Sylvia Scarlett*, Greta Garbo in *Queen Christina*, and, more recently, the sexually underpowered Julie Andrews in *Victor/Victoria*. The only movie with a cross-dressing theme to gain classic status was Billy Wilder's *Some Like It Hot* (1959), with Tony Curtis and Jack Lemmon as 'Josephine' and 'Daphne' giving Hollywood's best drag portrayals, unparallelled until Dustin's Dorothy. But there was still something profoundly unnatural about them. If they avoided the drag queen accusation, they did seem like transsexuals, making it improbable that even the superannuated Joe E. Brown would make a pass at one of them.

Dustin, more than anyone, knew that his portrayal of a man pretending to be a woman, and fooling everyone on screen, had to be authentic enough for audiences to believe they could have been taken in without foreknowledge. Dustin's contract stipulated that reality had to be achieved before shooting could begin. 'I want people to pass me on the street without saying "Look at that guy in drag." I want to pass, and if it's not possible, I don't want to make the movie.' Thus he spent eighteen months on getting the right make-up, walk and voice. The question Dustin asked was, 'What if I had been born a woman? What kind of woman would I be?' Many attempts were made to find an answer in the months that followed.

For the scenes as the unemployed actor, Dustin did not need too much research besides tapping his memory for what it was like in those early days in New York. But he watched *The Goodbye Girl, Next Stop, Greenwich Village* and even *Stage Door* to see how other films had dealt with struggling actors.

At first Dustin consulted a speech therapist to get Dorothy's voice right. If he used a French accent, it automatically raised the pitch. Southern was also an easier range for a man to get. He was helped by southerner Polly Holliday, a close friend of his, who was in *All Over Town* and *All the President's Men*, who played *Alice* on TV, and whom he had wanted to play the hard-boiled soap opera producer – though Pollack cast Doris Belack, a real soap star, instead. Polly spent hours reading *A Streetcar Named Desire* aloud with Dustin playing Blanche, to help him perfect his Southern accent.

Obviously, it was the way he/she looked that was to be the most difficult challenge on the movie. 'The first thing I said is that we have to do a bunch of make-up tests until we arrive at myself looking like a woman. Let's see if I can look really believable, not camp, not uglified, not denigrated . . . Because if I were a woman, I'd want to look as attractive as possible.' Only someone as confident in his own heterosexuality as Dustin could have taken on the role, just as he had had no qualms about the 'feminisation' of Ted Kramer.

'We started shooting and the make-up, for whatever reason, fell apart. They'd tested me with other actors that had make-up. So suddenly in a month of shooting we were a month behind and I looked like a George Romero movie. They kept saying it wasn't colour-corrected. I said we gotta stop shooting because this is *Night of the Living Dead*. I was green, or else I looked good and they looked green.'

Tony Marrero, the hair stylist, tried every type and style of wig on Dustin. Make-up expert George Masters gave Dorothy the same eyes he gave Bo Derek and Ann-Margret. However, the make-up sometimes took three to four hours to apply and, when it was finally on, Dustin was exhausted. Dustin's beard was a big problem, and would grow during the day. The make-up had to be thick enough to cover the beard, and this meant he had to be lit in a special way. He had to shave his legs, his arms, the backs of his fingers. A female impersonator was consulted to teach him some of the tricks of the trade, such as shaving upwards not downwards, and in damp surroundings. Dustin therefore shaved in a sauna. His eyebrows were bleached; he was getting rashes and pimples. It took over sixteen weeks to get it right.

'I begin to say to myself: If I was a woman, I would not shave, man! I just wouldn't do it. Why do I have to aggravate my skin? Because men go "Yuck" when they see hair under an armpit? I don't think men really have any idea the discomfort women go through to please us when they shave their armpits, shave their legs . . .'

As for the breasts, a variety of falsies was tried. There were rice-filled ones which bounced, and those filled with bird seed, which were liable to attack from swarms of birds *à la* Hitchcock. They settled for a custom-fitted pair from a store that makes post-mastectomy prostheses, which cost $175 each. Dustin had wanted his breasts to be big but settled for medium-sized ones. 'Do you know that a woman with a breast my size is carrying two or three pounds on each side of her body? If you had to carry six pounds around on your chest all day, man, you'd feel it. I thought I would have more trouble walking in high heels than I did. I just did what I do when I ski . . . kind of hug the ground with the toe . . . If I were a woman I'd never wear them.'

When Dustin first embarked on the venture, there was a hope at the back of his mind that, if he was not a beautiful man, at least he could make himself into a beautiful woman. But there was no way he was ever going to be desirable. 'Once I saw I was never going to be pretty, it was painful to me. Then I realised she was probably too old to have kids, and I started to cry.'

All the extraordinary dificulties in getting it right simply prove the unreality of expecting Michael Dorsey, with his limited resources, to have been able to do the same thing. There is no way he could have changed from a man into a convincing woman so quickly. But we suspend our disbelief and accept that he was able to do so every morning before rushing off to work, without the benefit of Hollywood make-up men, costume designers, lighting experts and cameramen.

Just as the actor playing Hitler in a play in Ernst Lubitsch's *To Be or Not to Be* steps into the streets of Warsaw in his disguise to see if he could pass for the dictator, so Dustin decided, prior to shooting, to venture into the streets of New York to explore how it felt walking them as a woman.

Arthur Bell in *Village Voice* related an incident when Dustin/Dorothy was in a lift with a friend when José Ferrer walked in. The friend introduced Dorothy Michaels to the actor, at which point Dustin whispered, 'Oh Mr Ferrer, ah loved you as that little man in *Moulin Rouge*. How'd ya like to have your cock sucked?' Ferrer, aghast, waited until the elevator hit the bottom floor and the doors opened before replying to the friend, 'Who is that scumbag broad?' Later Dustin chortled, 'I fooled Toulouse-Lautrec.'

One day he lunched as Dorothy at the Russian Tea Room with Lisa and Renee Schisgal, Murray's wife and Dustin's business partner. Ms Michaels stopped at the table of John Springer, a seasoned show-business press agent, and introduced herself as 'an aspiring poet-ingenue from Kansas City'. Springer was completely taken in. 'I knew there was something fascinating about the woman,' he said; 'I just didn't know what.' He also fooled Jon Voight at another table. In full drag, he accosted Voight who looked right through him. 'I was a four, and he wasn't interested. Men are shits.' The occasion echoes the scene in the film when he goes over to his agent in the Russian Tea Room, snuggling up to him and saying, 'It's me, George; me, Michael.'

Shortly afterwards, again in character, he visited his daughter Jenna's school, asking to be introduced to her teacher, a woman he had met occasionally over two years. He arrived from the *Tootsie* set during the school's lunch hour, and his embarrassed daughter begged, 'Daddy, please get out of here,' but he persisted. 'Just introduce me as your Aunt Dorothy from Arkansas,' which Jenna proceeded to do. 'And you know, that teacher treated me differently from before. There is a kind of sisterhood among women. I never got that before. Women are wary with men.'

Dustin admits that he has found it virtually impossible to have a friendship with a woman he is attracted to. 'I've never been able to say of a girl, "Gee, we're great friends," and let it go at that. I've always had the urge to make love. I don't know any girl I've slept with about whom I can now say, "She's still a good friend."' Ironically, while working on the movie that ostensibly questions male attitudes to women, Dustin continued to treat them as objects to be aroused or shocked by him. Although he was conscious intellectually that his actions were untenable, his libido forced him to take up another position. Pollack, however, seemed unaware that he would rarely call women by their names, but referred to them as 'honey' or 'dear'. Yet the very title of the movie they were making came from the reaction Dorothy has to the director of the soap. 'My name is Dorothy! It's not Tootsie or Toots or Sweetie or Honey or Doll.'

When filming began on 1 April 1982 at the recently furbished Astoria Studios in Queens, the script was still being worked on by Dustin and Schisgal. Almost $1.5 million had been spent on writers and the script was still changing. Most of the crew members had never seen anything like it before. Dustin would present Pollack with new pages and they would lock themselves in a room and argue about it. When they had finally decided on a compromise, or one of them had given in somewhere, they would emerge and the movie would grind into action again.

'You know what's hard about movies?' hazarded Dustin. 'It's that you've got to start it in two weeks and you don't really have the time to fuck around. Ideally, you would be in a rehearsal room with the actors and you would be . . . fucking around for two months.' On *Tootsie*, Dustin had asked for three weeks' rehearsal in which different views could be thrashed out before shooting. But Pollack fell ill, and they had little rehearsal time.

'It's impossible to work in comedy when there's bad blood and bad air,' said Pollack. 'I can only persuade him. If I push it, I've got a stubborn, angry actor trying to do something he doesn't believe in, and I can't win with that. It's okay for me to be uptight, but it's not okay for him because he has to be in front of the camera and people will see it.

'Every morning we screamed at each other for ten or fifteen minutes, discussing how the scene to be shot that day would go. Dustin is famous for annoying directors. I wish he wouldn't worry himself to death. He basically feels he's alone, that all actors are underdogs and constantly getting screwed by directors and producers. I tried to understand his anxieties, but couldn't find the trick to make him relax. A couple of times I threw my hands up in the air and said, "That's it." He's a suspicious man, maybe for good reason. But I got the performance I wanted. Sometimes you forget he's a man.' Bill Murray described the experience as 'a hell ride!'

Jessica Lange realised one day 'how truly different Dustin is from me. Dustin could one moment be playing his character and the next moment be dealing with Sydney Pollack and the following moment be dealing with the wigs. I'm totally different, and if that means I am aloof, so be it. But there's a reason. I am not, by nature, a performer.'

Dustin worked and developed Dorothy's material even when he was off camera. Between takes, he would play Dorothy with the crew. He blew kisses, he flirted. 'I operate like most men,' he said. 'I'm just as perfunctory as the next guy in terms of showing physical affection. Maybe I'm a little more emotional because I'm an actor, I don't know. But I know when I put on the woman's outfit, when I'm with the crew, I'm very physical. I go put my arms around them. I flirt.'

Lisa was always on the set with their baby son to give Dustin moral support and to prevent him from running off with a man. 'I've been doing this since Jake was eight weeks old,' Dustin commented. 'He thinks going to work means putting on a dress. Luckily we can afford therapy for him later.'

Andy Warhol, who was on the set to be photographed with Dorothy for a *People* magazine cover, which was to be used in the film, noted in his diary of August 1981: 'Dustin was wearing something more gay. And it was going to be Dustin's birthday on the eighth and I told him that was mine, too. (*laughs*) Met Dustin's new wife, very pretty, who looks like Debra Winger. So many of these girls now do. But the baby looks like one of those babies Barbra Streisand would have with Elliott Gould.' (Streisand did have a son by Gould, her first husband.)

Although filming *Tootsie* lasted 98 days, Dustin had invested almost four years in it. The relationship with Pollack was strained to breaking point when Dustin screamed expletives at the director after hearing he had been excluded from a private screening of the movie. Pollack admitted that this outburst was indicative of 'what's been going on for four months'. He told fellow director John Boorman that it was the worst experience of his life, and that if he could get back the eighteen months which were total misery making it, he would gladly give back the money. (Pollack earned $14 million from his share of the profits.) It all helped Pollack put as much vitriol into the role of the agent as he could. 'I'm your agent, not your mother . . You played a tomato for thirty seconds. They went a half day over schedule because you wouldn't sit down,' he says, bitterly reproaching his difficult client. 'Nobody does vegetables like me', Dustin replies.

Asked if he would work with Pollack again, Dustin replied, 'Let me put it this way. I'd work with Yasser Arafat if I liked the script and he gave me total control.'

Finally, 16 December 1982. Mann's Chinese Theater. The premiere and dinner at the Brown Derby with a collection of celebrities such as Jacqueline Bisset and Alexander Godunov, Peter Falk and wife Shera, Valerie Perrine, Barbra Streisand, Shelley Duvall, Christopher Reeve, Tina

Turner, Tatum O'Neal and Michael Douglas. The next day the film opened nationally to the general public. Richard Schickel in *Time* claimed it was 'more than just the best comedy of the year . . . it is an unmelting movie memory', and Vincent Canby in *The New York Times* thought it 'a toot, a lark, a month in the country . . . it restores the original meaning of the term "situation comedy"'. Feminist film critic Molly Haskell thought Dorothy 'the first great feminist character of the decade . . . [she] is neither a doll, nor a mincing, lisping impersonation of a female, but something more wonderful. She is a dignified, rather stolid middle-aged woman with harlequin glasses and a Southern–Baptist plainspeaking sort of con- sciousness that is raised, and outraged, by the sexism around her . . . I'm not sure I want to hear Dustin Hoffman bragging about his education as a woman for the next nine months, but if that's the price we have to pay for *Tootsie*, it's worth it.'

But Haskell seems unaware that the film misunderstands feminism as deeply as *Kramer vs Kramer* does. In the latter, Dustin teaches Streep a lesson on how to be a good mother as well as being able to fulfil oneself as a person. *Tootsie* seems to suggest that it really takes a man in woman's clothing to teach women how to live their lives and become liberated, despite the screenplay's strained attempt to stress that it is the male who breaks the shackles of his gender. Dorothy is the only 'woman' character who is her own person. Michael Dorsey's realisation of what women have to put up with would have been a little more persuasive had he been more aggressively macho before his metamorphosis. He has, after all, already told his actress friend to assert herself. Chatting up girls at a party and giving them a line does not add up to much need of reformation. Anyway, the 'feminism' of Dorothy seems to derive, firstly, from Michael's natural unwillingness to be kissed by John Van Horn, nicknamed 'The Tongue', and, secondly, from being a man in drag. Only a man or a very strong woman would have been able to throw a man out of a taxicab.

The film also makes an inverse anti-egalitarian point by concluding that women are better people than men. In his revelatory moment on TV, Michael explains that, 'I became strong enough to be a woman – that was the best part of my manhood, the best part of me.' After this speech, all that follows is a recapitulation of the theme, and the message is underlined, in case it has failed to get through to the audience; the equivalent of the language tic, in which people say 'You know what I mean?' after the simplest phrases.

As at the end of Jean Cocteau's *Beauty and the Beast*, in which Beauty is slightly disappointed by the Beast turning into his romantic self, Julie seems to prefer Dorothy to Michael. 'I miss Dorothy', says Julie. 'You don't have to, she's right here,' Michael replies. 'I was a better man with you when I was a woman than I was when I was a man . . . I've just got to learn to do without the dress.'

The man inside Dorothy makes sure that almost everybody seems to love this unsexy maiden lady. Julie's father wants to marry her, and Van Horn tries to rape her in a farcical scene after which Michael/Dorothy paradoxically says, 'Rape is not a laughing matter.' There are also moments that collude with the notion that male and female homosexuality is cause for sniggering, such as the scene in the masculine environment of a bar – boxing on TV, beer being drunk – when Michael returns his engagement ring to Julie's father, whose manhood has been put in question. However, any film which, even at the simplest level, has a cross-dressing theme obviously cannot avoid creating some kind of sexual ambiguity. When Michael as Dorothy falls in love with Julie, he is in a position that should make him more sympathetic to homosexuals, who often find themselves in similar circumstances, in which they are restrained from expressing their love or attraction.

Dustin (who claims never to have had a homosexual experience) once said that, 'If one of my children came to me and said "I'm gay," I'd say fine, I hope you find a nice boyfriend. If one said they were lesbian, I'd say fine. But if one said they wanted to be a critic, I'd say let's sit down and talk about it.'

Tootsie, its feminist pretensions notwithstanding, is an enjoyable, light-weight, gender-bender comedy of errors that is certainly closer to *Charley's Aunt* than its makers would like to think. The farcical misunder-standings build up just as predictably, and often as funnily. On the other hand, it offers an acute look at the lower reaches of the acting profession, that hectic life where one is always trying to sell oneself. At one point, Michael, somewhat patronisingly, equates being a woman with being an unemployed actor – both are always waiting for the phone to ring. (He had also compared the life of an actor to that of a convict during the making of *Straight Time*.) In addition – another link with *Some Like It Hot* – *Tootsie* demonstrates the lengths to which performers will go in showbusiness to get a job. Unfortunately Pollack lacks the style and astringency of Billy Wilder, yet, never degenerating into camp, the film does celebrate the possibility of genuine friendship and respect between the sexes.

Above all, Dustin delivers a brilliantly deft comic double, self-mocking as a pretentious out-of-work avant-garde actor; and instantly likeable as Dorothy. It is arguably the most convincing drag portrayal in the history of cinema. With her large round spectacles, tailored suits, flashing smile, and soothing Southern accent (with just the right amount of prissiness in it), Dorothy is a wonderful creation.

When Oscar time came around again, the film was nominated for Best Film and Best Director (the rambling well-intentioned *Gandhi* and the rambling, well-intentioned Richard Attenborough won them), and both Lange and Garr were invidiously nominated for supporting roles. The award was won by Lange, who was also nominated as Best Actress for *Frances*. The part-Indian Ben Kingsley's impersonation of Gandhi won out over Dustin's impersonation of a woman for Best Actor, although it was thought by some that Dustin should have won the Best Actress award instead of Meryl Streep for *Sophie's Choice*.

26

Death of a Shrimp

Death of a Salesman is the reason I've been an actor.

BETOKENING SUCCESS, THE grapevine hung heavy with film offers for Dustin after *Tootsie*. Naturally, one or two required him to slip once more into petticoats, not a prospect Dustin would ever contemplate again with any equanimity, nor did he relish becoming the Jim Bailey or Danny La Rue of the Screen. After Ted Kramer and Dorothy, it was time to think butch.

His brother-in-law Lee Gottsegen, who served as head of his new company, Punch Productions, discussed various movie projects with Dustin over the following months. Apart from the many scripts dealing with mid-life crises, Dustin was offered the lead in *Gorky Park*, but there was no way the producers could have matched his huge previous salary. Another consideration might have been that it was to be directed by Michael Apted, conjuring up bitter memories of *Agatha*. (William Hurt eventually took the role of the Muscovite cop.) It was reported that Dustin wanted Taylor (*An Officer and a Gentleman*) Hackford for a project called *The Glory Boys*, then it was rumoured that Mike Nichols was seeking Dustin to reprise the Carl Bernstein role in *Heartburn* by Nora Ephron, Bernstein's ex-wife. (Jack Nicholson took the part, opposite Meryl Streep.) Ridley Scott approached him for *Blade Runner*, to which Dustin responded, 'What the hell do you want me to play this macho charactor for?' But, as was his wont, he did not turn Scott down right away, leaving the British director suspended for a while. Actually, according to the assistant producer, he put in some 'wonderful ideas' before deciding against it, leaving the way clear for Harrison Ford. He also had a chance to appear in the sequel to *Chinatown*, called *The Two Jakes*, for a reported salary of $5 million, with Marlon Brando, Jane Fonda and Jack Nicholson, but it never got past the talking stage. (It was eventually made by and with Nicholson five years later.)

One project he was especially interested in was Blake Edwards's remake of the 1977 François Truffaut picture, *The Man Who Loved Women*. Preliminary work was even begun on the script before Edwards instead cast Burt Reynolds in the role originally taken by Charles Denner. Dustin was reportedly incensed by the episode. 'All Reynolds has to do is wink at the camera and he's a star – I'm short and ugly and really have to act.' Dustin had actually rejected the $10 million fee, because he claimed Edwards would not let him 'share the paintbrush' on the script, although he accused Edwards of using one of his ideas in the film. Eventually the picture, *sans* Dustin, turned out to be an unmitigated disaster.

The Hoffmans had set up home in Manhattan's swish San Remo apartments, again near Central Park, where Dustin regularly went jogging. This residence cost over $1 million, and was actually two apartments with the walls removed for extra space. Slowly he and Lisa poured another $2 million into renovation and furnishings, giving him a chance to educate her in his hobby of collecting antiques. At the same time, despite her brush with death during the birth of her first child, Lisa became pregnant again. Rebecca's birth in March 1983 was relatively trouble-free.

In order for Lisa to convalesce, and for Dustin to escape the speculation and chatter that accompanied his every move, they decided to spend some time at their 92-acre estate, complete with tennis court and swimming pool, in Roxbury, Connecticut. City boy Hoffman commented, 'In the country, you get a primal view of life; you can't get that anywhere else unless you get mugged going home from work. It is extraordinary. Every time I pull the weeds up there is this nightmare going on underneath – worms and other things screaming around.'

One of his neighbours in Roxbury was the 69-year-old Arthur Miller, who lived just 'a jog away' with his photographer wife Ingeborg Morath, in the same house where he had married (and briefly lived with) Marilyn Monroe. Miller had just returned from a visit to Beijing where he had been invited to direct *Death of a Salesman* with Ying Ruocheng as Willy. For Miller it had been a fascinating, exciting and moving experience; a remarkable meeting between two worlds as the Chinese company struggled to come to grips with the Loman family from Brooklyn. For ten years the Chinese theatre had been closed, the companies arrested or dispersed, and only Madame Mao's eight permissible plays could be staged. Miller had to try to help the actors cope with a style of drama totally alien to their training and tradition.

In June 1983, Dustin visited Miller at his home and mentioned to him his desire to go back to the stage. His old Broadway mentor, Zev Bufman, was tempting him with the Clarence Darrow role in a revival of *Inherit the Wind*. But his eminent host's first reaction to this was, 'You don't want to do *Salesman*, do you?' It had been almost twenty years since the afternoon when Ulu Grosbard had pointed out Dustin to Miller during rehearsals of *A View from the Bridge* and predicted that one day Dustin would play Miller's most famous character. . .

The playwright had originally conceived Willy as a little man and had, in fact, altered a few lines of dialogue to accommodate the burly physique of Lee J. Cobb. In the original, Willy was referred to as 'a shrimp', which became, in Cobb's version, 'a walrus'. Willy would become 'a shrimp' once again if Dustin played him. After all, he was Willy Low Man.

But Dustin told Miller that he wanted to wait ten years before playing Willy, although at 46 he was already eight years older than Cobb was when he created the role. But, as Miller said, 'Cobb was born old. He was lugubrious and depressed. Dustin has always been chippier and full of energy.' Miller advised Dustin not to wait: 'You won't have the physical strength for the role at fifty-six.' That was enough to decide Dustin, who had never before tackled any of the classic American roles. Miller knew that Dustin would bring 'a certain nervosity to the role. He's a little fighter, Cobb was a great whale of a man, and many of the other Willies were large men. Dustin has a meticulous observation of that type.'

The first production of *Death of a Salesman* was Elia Kazan's at the Morosco on 10 February 1949, with Lee J. Cobb (Willy), Mildred Dunnock (Linda), Cameron Mitchell (Happy), Arthur Kennedy (Biff), Don Keefer (Bernard), Howard Smith (Charley), Thomas Chalmers (Uncle Ben) and Alan Hewitt (Howard). The play's most recent New York revival had been in 1975 with George C. Scott (who also directed), Teresa Wright, and Harvey Keitel and James Farentino as Happy and Biff respectively. It was from the mid-seventies that Miller started to enjoy many revivals of his work, and also became more prolific. He was no longer the man whom James Thurber once cruelly called, during Miller's fallow period, a 'playwrote'.

Joining with Robert Whitehead, Roger L. Stevens and Miller as co-producer under his own Punch Productions banner, the star agreed to a minimum salary of $735 a week, after which he would receive a percentage of the gross receipts when and if the show went into the black. The bulk of the finance came from CBS, who would be allowed to make it into a film. 'We couldn't raise the money for the play because we couldn't afford to promise an extended run, given all our other commitments,' Dustin explained.

The Texas-born, British-based Michael Rudman was asked to direct the play, because Dustin had seen and applauded Rudman's splendid revival of *Salesman* with Warren Mitchell at the National Theatre in London a few years before. After nearly two decades in which he belonged to specific theatre companies, the 45-year-old Rudman had decided to go freelance in 1982, and was happy to take the production on.

'When Dustin approached me about directing the play, someone who's very shrewd told me, "Don't make too many jokes; let Dustin make the jokes." So I didn't and it was wonderful,' said Rudman, who is himself known to monopolise jokes during rehearsals. 'He was a pleasure to work with. I've directed more than seventy plays, and I've seen all kinds of bad behaviour. There are at least ten ways of being difficult – being late, being drunk, not learning your lines, trying to fuck everybody – none of these he did. Theatre is a real place. It sorts out everybody sooner or later. There are no tricks you can pull, like in film.'

Then came the task of selecting the cast. Around five hundred actors were auditioned for the thirteen roles. Dustin had the most outrageous ideas. For the role of Willy's larcenous brother, Ben, Dustin wanted to invite Watergate burglar G. Gordon Liddy for a reading. More sensibly, the part went to an old acting friend, Louis Zorich. Red Holzman, the retired basketball coach, was brought in to test for the part of Charley, Willy's successful neighbour. 'Is that what you meant that Charley was like?' Dustin asked Arthur Miller, who sat watching the procession of candidates with a melancholy air. Miller had written: 'Charley is a large man, slow of speech, laconic, immovable.' Dustin had first wanted Gene Hackman, but his old friend had film commitments. (The part finally went to David Huddlestone, a bona fide actor.) Dustin then had a brainwave/storm: he would ask John McEnroe to read for the part of Biff. Fortunately, he was dissuaded from asking the tennis champion.

As a multitude of young women – including a former wife of Norman Mailer – read for the part of the floozie in the hotel room with whom the salesman has a little fling, Robert Whitehead began to put pressure on Dustin to start making decisions because the casting sessions had been going on all through the summer of 1983. But Dustin ploughed on regardless, looking for the right person for the right role.

'Dustin has the motion-picture enthusiasm to cast the elevator man because he might impart a sense of reality to the part,' Whitehead commented. Finally, a strong cast was assembled around Dustin, headed by the experienced Kate Reid as Linda Loman. There was only one part missing, that of the son Biff.

Robert Duvall suggested they look at John Malkovich, whom he had seen in *True West* at the Cherry Lane Theater, off-Broadway. When Malkovich read for them, Dustin and Miller immediately agreed they had found their Biff.

Thirty-year-old Malkovich was based in Chicago and had been Biff in an acclaimed production of the Steppenwolf Theater. But, hesitating about committing himself to a long run, Malkovich signed instead for

Places in the Heart, a movie to be directed by Robert Benton in Texas, in which he was fifth billed. Before deciding to postpone production until the actor was available on his own terms, Dustin came up with a weird alternative. He decided that Robert De Niro would be the perfect Biff.

'You want me to be your son on stage?' said the 40-year-old De Niro in disbelief when Dustin called him. Somehow Dustin convinced De Niro to come down to the audition room. After watching Dustin go through his paces as Willy, De Niro said non-committally, 'Well, I see you're wearing the vest and so on.' Dustin commented: 'It was like a fighter coming to watch another fighter and saying, "I see you're using a left hook and so on."'

Meanwhile, John Malkovich in Texas signalled that he would only be available in December, months after the scheduled start of rehearsals. Dustin and Co. correctly felt he was worth waiting for.

For Willy Loman, Dustin mustered every bit of Harry Hoffman he could. In his late seventies and living in La Costa, California, Harry had married one of Lillian's nurses, thus providing Dustin with a stepmother some years his junior. Harry had struggled through the thirties and forties, constantly searching for elusive success, his disillusionment being very much like Willy's. He had a tough exterior, but would often have to fight back tears when offered a small gift by one of his sons.

When Malkovich was out in Texas, he was sent a cassette of Dustin talking about *Salesman*. Harry Hoffman also spoke on the tape, and at one stage, he yelled at Dustin, 'Biff is bullshit!'

When Lee J. Cobb, who was overweight and a smoker, played Willy, he found his voice giving out and had to be replaced after four months in the part, because he was unable to stand up to the pressures the role imposed. Dustin determined to be in tip-top condition, especially as he had lost nearly 14lb to get Willy to look worn and shrunken so that the 1940s suits would hang from his frame. He was on a strict diet, eating only a salad during the day. 'I eat something yellow everyday: canteloupe, carrots,' he proclaimed, although he only ate the white of the eggs 'to assure a longer life'. He gave up smoking, drank only one cup of coffee daily and refused alcohol – except for a few beers. He also kept up his regular jogging, and pedalled his exercise bike, which accompanied him on the tour.

Once the show had opened, Dustin would sometimes arrive at the theatre feeling particularly weak, and he would take vitamin B12 shots. After years of making movies, he continued to wake up at 5 a.m. but he would stay in bed and read for a while, then go back to sleep until nine or ten o'clock. For three hours in the afternoon, he would hardly speak, as well as taking naps. 'It's just like being a boxer. Boxers always take naps before a fight.'

For all the talk about the actor's ego, he had an insatiable appetite for 'notes', for criticism from those he trusted, not only from the director and playwright, but also from the other actors, especially Malkovich and Stephen Lang who played his sons, even exchanging notes during the interval. 'He is as relentless a performer as I've ever encountered,' Malkovich testified. 'He will never give up on a single moment in the play until he thinks it's perfect, and I don't think he ever will think it's perfect. A lot of stars cast mediocre people around them and put them in dim light, but he wants everybody around him to be very good.' At one point, in the middle of one performance, Dustin actually grabbed Malkovich by the arm and quite literally drew him into the light.

After out-of-town tryouts in Chicago and Washington, DC, the play opened on Broadway at the Broadhurst Theater on 29 March 1984 for a limited season of 97 performances. Because of the huge advance sales and the booming business, the Shubert organisation opened a second box office for the show at the Majestic Theater. On Dustin's dressing-room door had been placed the name of Dave Singleman, the man, in the play, who had 'died the death of a salesman'. 'And Old Dave. . . he'd go up to his room, y' understand, put on his green velvet slippers – I'll never forget – and pick up his phone and call the buyers, and, without ever leaving his room, at the age of eighty-four, he made his living. And when I saw that, I realised that selling was the greatest career a man could want.'

Andy Warhol, in his diary, described a visit backstage: 'Dustin was really up up up, he was camping and screaming, "Andy Warhol is here! Andy Warhol is here!" And he came over and told us a story bout seeing a girl at Sotheby's who is exactly like the first girl he ever fucked, and he invited her to the show and then on that exact same night, the first girl he ever fucked that she looked exactly like came to see the play. And he took the two of them to dinner and they got talking and one said she didn't have a place to stay and the other said she could stay with her and they went off into the sunset together. They still looked alike, he said. When I saw his hair and everything shaved off, I don't know why he does the play in so much make-up when he could just do it straight. And he told me that one day he saw me on the street and we talked it was the day he'd broken up with his first wife, which I didn't know then, and he remembered every word of our conversation because it was such a traumatic day for him.'

Dustin's Willy Loman is a sad, irritable, irritating, shrivelled and stooped little man with a gruff, Yiddish-intonated voice. He is also shrivelled up inside, unable to express his warmer emotions, holding his arms back from the embrace of his son and shutting up his long-suffering wife. Yet

Dustin gains sympathy without seeking it, justifying Miller's aim to prove that the little man (thankfully, Willy Loman is no emblematic Everyman) can be a fit subject for tragedy. The key speech of the play is Linda's plea to her sons (and the audience): 'I don't say he's a great man. Willy Loman never made a lot of money; his name was never in the paper; he's not the finest character that ever lived. But he's a human being, and a terrible thing is happening to him. So attention must be paid. He's not to be allowed to fall into his grave like an old dog. *Attention, attention* must be finally paid to such a person.'

In a sense, without taking anything away from Dustin, it is almost impossible to fail in such a brilliantly written role. However, the crucial dramatic point, the discovery by Biff of the woman in Willy's hotel room, is too flimsy and contrived a situation to hinge the entire relationship between father and son, change Biff's life forever and make him a failure. Dustin's 'shrimp' portrayal has the disadvantage of being less likely a figure for his son to hero worship than a 'walrus' in the Lee J. Cobb mould.

'Cobb had a marvellous voice and looked great but he would always lean on his equipment to get him through narrow spaces. Dustin can't,' Miller opined. '[Dustin] has that kind of feisty quickness that I always associated with Willy, changing directions like a sailboat in the middle of a lake with the wind blowing in all directions. He's a cocky little guy over-whelmed by the size of the world and trying to climb up to the top of the mountain.'

Most critics warmed to the performances and the production, which won a Tony for 'outstanding reproduction of a play'. Frank Rich in *The New York Times* perhaps made the best comment of all, obviously unaware of how the dirty-minded English would read it. He wrote: 'I was overwhelmed by the tragic smallness of Dustin Hoffman's Willy.'

When it came to making the film for the CBS TV special, Dustin and Miller sought a movie director to transfer the play on to the screen. The previous film attempt in 1951, directed by Laslo Benedek, tried to find a filmic solution to the stage conception with photographer Franz Planer pioneering a photographic technique using light alone to show past and present in the same shot. It starred Fredric March and Kevin McCarthy, supported by three of the original cast – Mildred Dunnock, Cameron Mitchell and Howard Smith. It was not to Miller's liking. 'The basic reason it failed as a motion picture,' he wrote '– aside from the gross insensitivity permeating its film production – was that the dramatic tension of Willy's memories was destroyed by transferring him, literally, to the locales he had only imagined in the play. . . It did not solve, nor really attempt to find, a resolution for the problem of keeping the past constantly alive.' Determined that previous misinterpretation should not be repeated, Miller was on hand throughout the 23-day shoot, and neither he nor Dustin accepted salaries for it, although they retained a percentage should it make substantial profits.

Ironically, Volker Schlöndorff, who was employed as director, was engaged originally on the mistaken assumption that he was someone else. 'I got a call from Dustin asking to meet me. We'd never met and I was puzzled, though obviously pleased by the request. We talked a lot about *Mephisto* and then he asked me to direct the film version of *Death of a Salesman*. I was flattered but couldn't figure out why they needed someone given that the play was already there and well-oiled by over two hundred packed performances on Broadway. He told me to see the play a few times and then decide. I realised there was a lot that could still be done, namely taking the whole thing into a studio and placing the camera in the middle. I thought we could film inside the play, not at the play, so to speak, as long as the camera was able to roam three hundred and sixty degrees around itself and follow the action just as it unfolded on stage. Then it suddenly dawned on me. Dustin had asked me to direct because he had mistaken me for István Szabó and that was why we spent so much time talking about *Mephisto*!'

The 46-year-old, German-born Schlöndorff had made such films as *The Tin Drum* (1979) – the Foreign Film Oscar-winner in the year of *Kramer vs Kramer* – *The German Sisters* (1981) and *Swann in Love* (1983). Leaving aside the inability to tell two foreign names apart, even those as different from each other as Schlöndorff and Szabó, the reason the producers had thought of the director of *Mephisto*, whatever his name, was that the 1981 Best Foreign Film Oscar-winner about an actor did contain a number of well-filmed scenes from stage plays.

The shooting schedule was only 23 days and the tension was kept as close as possible to that experienced during stage performances. There were few breaks and very long hours, followed by late night rushes. In the rehearsals for the play as well as during production of the film, Dustin reached the point at which he would have done anything to get the hell out. 'It happens every time. All you need is one bad day of rushes and suddenly you realise that there is something really wrong, either because you're not emotionally connected with the play or because you realise you've been bullshitting yourself and you just don't get on with the character any more. I never "marry" a part for money. It's important for me also to know from the start how the character is actually going to come out.'

Although Schlöndorff was not allowed much initiative by the producers and star – after all, the cast (excepting Charles Durning, replacing David Huddlestone as Charley) and the interpretation had been fairly set by the Rudman Broadway production – he managed to make *Salesman* into a film of a play rather than a filmed play, while respecting its stage origins. The camera moves around the Loman house and the yard, allowing plenty of space without any need for opening out, except for Willy seen at the wheel of his car behind the opening credits and one street scene, which stick out disconcertingly. The use of Alex North's original music written for the very first production, and used again on Broadway in 1984, seemed unnecessarily to underline much of the drama on film.

'I think each generation has to do it again. It's not a question of aesthetics. It's that the times are changing. We hear the lines differently. For me, it's no longer a play on the American Dream, because none of us believes in the American Dream any more,' explained Schlöndorff. 'We're all incredibly cynical about it. The neurosis or psychosis is of the whole family; it's not just Willy who is a failure, who didn't make it and who is a victim of the American Dream. This part of the American family and the way it builds to insanity still exists.'

The whole cast was first rate, particularly the always electrifying John Malkovich, but the *raison d'être* of the film had to be the preservation of Dustin's performance for posterity. In a way, it was more impressive than on stage, more nuanced, more realistic. With more accurate make-up and close-ups, one can see the grey hair slicked back and thinning, the ageing blotches on the skin, and the silver on his teeth which flashes each time he gives his nervous smile. To play Willy, Dustin required special make-up – two layers of a latex ageing solution, powders and gelatins to make the pores, liver spots, blood vessels, and shadows around the eyes look realistic. Dustin seemed literally to have grown into the part. Like the ghost in *Hamlet*, Willy Loman speaks through the image of his own father.

27

Camel Droppings

Don't people realise that you can't make a movie with two big stars for under $35 million today? And that's without Morocco.

ISHTAR WAS BORN one Sunday afternoon in 1985 in Warren Beatty's house in the Hollywood Hills. Beatty had assembled a group of people to read the script by his old friend Elaine May, who had written *Heaven Can Wait* with him and who was set to direct the new picture. Among the gathering were Herb Gardner, unremembered for *Who Is Harry Kellerman . . . ?*, but whose successful *I'm Not Rappaport* had just opened on Broadway; Peter Feibleman, a writer and executor of Lillian Hellman's estate; David MacLeod, a cousin of Beatty's and the associate producer of *Heaven Can Wait* and *Reds*; Marlo Thomas, a longtime friend of May's; Charles Grodin, the actor and May protégé, and Dustin. May passed out scripts, assigned parts and the reading began. The consensus of the cosy group of intimates was that the very funny script would make a very funny movie.

Those in authority at Columbia, owned by the Coca-Cola Company, were of the same opinion, and *Ishtar* (originally called *Blind Camel*) was given the go-ahead. Incidentally, the studio was not aware that there would be a credit for Pepsi-Cola at the end of the picture. (Dustin explained that having Coke in the film would look as if they were 'kissing ass'. It seemed more like '*kicking* ass', because they could have used 7–Up instead.)

The picture was scheduled to be filmed in Morocco, but it took some time before the cameras could start to roll. There had been endless discussions as to whether it was too close to the Middle East for the safety of the American stars. Ronald Reagan, in his inimitable gung-ho manner, had just ordered the bombing of Libya, and Americans were scared to travel anywhere that year. (Sylvester 'Rambo' Stallone cancelled a trip to the Cannes Festival in case some discerning terrorist took a pot shot at him.) There were also financial problems at the initial stage. Columbia was unhappy about the proposed budget of $30 million for what was, after all, only a light comedy in the style of the Crosby–Hope–Lamour 'Road' pictures. It would need to make $70 million to show a reasonable profit.

They agreed to a budget of around $25 million (it ended up costing $43 million), with Beatty and Dustin required to put up the rest of the cash themselves. They would still be getting the tidy sum of $6 million each.

Other qualms voiced around the Columbia offices at the time were that Dustin gave the impression that his heart was not really in the venture, and that putting two of the biggest egotists in Hollywood together might prove destructive and expensive. It might have been as well to have included Elaine May's ego in this equation.

The crew had left for Morocco in September 1985 to find suitable locations and to hold auditions for camels. Elaine May had stated that she wanted big dunes in the movie, so her production designer, associate producer and other key people went looking for big dunes. It was not just a matter of finding the dunes, however: they had to find them alongside a luxury hotel so that the director and stars and crew would not have to trek for hours each day across the desert to shoot the movie. After several weeks, Paul Sylbert, the production designer, found some big dunes to his liking in the south Moroccan Sahara – with two comfortable hotels nearby. No, it was not a mirage.

However, when Elaine May arrived in Morocco she took one look at the dunes and said that people's idea of a desert was endless and flat (as the movie would turn out to be) and she wanted a flat desert. 'You want to shoot on a *flat* desert? But we've got dunes here. You wanted dunes,' Sylbert told her. 'No, I think I want a flat desert.' It took a team of workers ten days to scrape away the dunes. And that was only the beginning of her profligacy. But the omens had been there previously for all to see.

A Broadway play Elaine May wrote in 1962, *A Matter of Position*, closed in Philadelphia because she refused to make changes. She went over budget on her first movie, *A New Leaf*, in 1969 and finally tried to remove her name when Paramount took it away from her. Because of rows with Otto Preminger, she refused the screenwriting credit on *Such Good Friends* (1971), preferring to use the nom-de-plume of Esther Dale, the name of a movie actress who died in 1961.

Elaine May's reputation is demonstrated by a story told to reporter David Blum about the shooting of her third movie, *Mikey and Nicky* (1976), a *film noir* written for her friends John Cassavetes and Peter Falk. It was around 3 a.m. on an LA street, where a scene between Cassavetes and Falk was being shot. The film was largely based on improvisation and the camera would often roll for hours as the two men talked to each other. By now, however, the two of them had wandered off the set. Yet the cameras kept rolling. After a while, during which the camera was shooting a scene with nobody in it, the operator called 'Cut!' and turned off the camera. May, who had been sitting quietly behind him, suddenly jumped up from her seat. 'Why did you turn the camera off?' she yelled. '*You* don't say "Cut!" I say "Cut!" *I'm* the director, and only the director says "Cut!"' The movie, which was already way over budget, then took her two years to edit, and May had a running battle, in the Hoffman manner, with Paramount over control of the picture. Unfortunately, the film, which suppressed what was then considered her greatest forte – humour – bombed. Frank Rich in *The New York Post* called it 'an impenetrable, ugly and almost unendurable mess'.

Nevertheless, *A New Leaf* and her later *The Heartbreak Kid* (1972), with a script by Neil Simon, are two of the most cruelly funny American comedies since the thirties. The horrendous females in these movies are played by the director and her daughter, Jeannie Berlin, respectively. (Elaine May was born Elaine Berlin in Philadelphia in 1932.) And those who saw the cabaret double-act *An Evening with Mike Nichols and Elaine May* in the early sixties, can still quote witty lines from it.

After the fiasco of *Mikey and Nicky*, she co-wrote with Beatty his first directorial venture, the feeble football fantasy, *Heaven Can Wait* (1978), unaccountably nominated for nine Oscars, among which was the screenplay. (It got only one – Best Art Direction.) Then, with her helpful contribution to *Tootsie*, she was back in good odour in Hollywood, at least as a writer.

On *Ishtar*, the cast and crew began to get an inkling as to why she had not directed a movie since *Mikey and Nicky* almost a decade before. Her propensity for multiple takes continued to a ridiculous degree. Dustin and Beatty would do a take and she would say, 'Fine, let's do it again.' They would repeat it over and over again. She hardly ever gave them any instructions; all she wanted was more takes. 'Let's do it again,' became her theme song.

Someone who was on the set at the time said later, 'Elaine May is a woman of many words, but the word "cut" is not among them. I think if Elaine could have her way, she'd still be shooting that movie.' She was what Irving Thalberg once called Erich von Stroheim, a 'footage fetishist'.

In the film, Beatty and Dustin were supposed to be bad song writers. The intentionally terrible songs (variously by Paul Williams, May, Beatty and Hoffman) have lyrics like, 'There's a wardrobe of love in my eyes, Come back and see if there's anything your size.' But the songs had to be just good enough not to seem consciously bad, as did their performances. And the more May shot them singing, the more it became apparent the two stars simply needed more time to rehearse. Already way behind schedule, the production halted for several days to give them a chance to practise. While the two of them ran through their numbers, everyone continued to be paid. Costs were mounting and there was no end in sight.

Throughout all this Dustin retained his sense of humour, and he spent most of his time between takes telling jokes to the extras. He was as charming and pleasant to everyone as could be. He memorised the names of extras and always offered a kind word. Perhaps he was reflecting the ineffectual character he was playing, or perhaps he did not feel as involved as he usually does, or perhaps he knew it would be a stinker so he was philosophic about it all. 'He was exactly the opposite to what we'd been led to expect,' said a colleague of Beatty's. 'He was a good person, a friend to everyone.' Dustin was a friend, most particularly, to Beatty, whom he had not known well before. They almost instantly became comrades in adversity, and were seen together around town in bars and restaurants. 'He has this reputation with women, but I have never met anyone who blushes as much as Warren. He is puritanical, shy, the opposite of his public image,' avowed Dustin. 'I love this guy.' They claimed still to be friends long after shooting. People do cling together during a disaster – after all, the British did during the Blitz.

Beatty, a few months older than Dustin, had been in the movies since Elia Kazan cast him opposite Natalie Wood in *Splendor in the Grass* in 1961, six years before Dustin appeared on screen. A millionaire many times over, he is, according to his older sister, Shirley MacLaine, 'very much into money'. He also was very much into women, and had had affairs with Joan Collins ('Warren was sexually insatiable . . . three, four times a day, every day was not unusual for him. He was also able to accept phone calls at the same time . . .'), Natalie Wood, Susan Strasberg, Leslie Caron (he was cited in her divorce from Peter Hall), Julie Christie, Diane Keaton, singer-actress Michelle Phillips and 31-year-old Isabelle Adjani, his inamorata of the time, and the leading female in the cast of *Ishtar*.

It was Dustin who gave Beatty the idea of finally getting married. He told the notorious playboy, 'Look at me. The greatest happiness I have ever found has been being married and having children. Do you want to go on like you have until you're ninety and wind up with the girls laughing at you?' The actress Mamie Van Doren once said, 'Warren is the type of man who will end up dying in his own arms.' Soon after returning from Morocco, Beatty indeed announced his engagement, though not to Adjani, but to Joyce Hyser, ex-girlfriend of Bruce Springsteen. And then, as the world knows, someone else came along.

On 2 November 1986, David Puttnam joined Columbia as Chairman and Chief Executive Officer, replacing Guy McElwaine, who had been partly responsible for agreeing to finance *Ishtar*. Now head of Columbia, Puttnam found himself again in contact, however distant, with his nemesis from *Agatha* in a project he had not instigated. Meanwhile, both Beatty and Dustin felt they should have been consulted about Puttnam's appointment.

The year before, Puttnam had been asked to consider Dustin for the role of the American journalist Sidney Schanberg in *The Killing Fields*, but he commented that, 'I think it's fair to say that Dustin Hoffman would be as unprepared to work with me as I assuredly am to work with him.' Besides, Puttnam correctly did not see the film as the star vehicle which it certainly would have been had Dustin and his writers come in on it. As it was, the less starry Sam Waterston did a fine job.

A month before Puttnam took up his post at Columbia, some friends of his and Dustin's decided it would be a good idea for them to get together socially and try to seek common ground on which they could work. Dustin had signed a five-picture deal with Columbia, and it seemed the judicious thing to do, as Dustin was reported to have been furious at Puttnam's appointment. Accordingly, they met in October at the Russian Tea Room, but the chemistry did not work, and it was not long before the two men clashed. They began to shout at each other across the table, the heated argument ending with Dustin marching theatrically out of the restaurant leaving Puttnam and the other diners staring incredulously after him.

Just as problematic was Puttnam's relationship with Warren Beatty. In 1981, Puttnam's *Chariots of Fire* was the rival film with Beatty's *Reds* for the most Academy Awards. The Best Picture went to the British film, and Beatty won the Best Director Oscar. In fact, *Chariots* ended up with four awards, one more than *Reds*.

According to Beatty, Puttnam had said things about *Reds* that he termed 'unacceptable chickenshit', and he had felt resentment for Puttnam ever since. They had, in fact, never spoken.

'I don't want to deal with him,' said Beatty. 'He's going to torpedo my picture, and he'll do everything possible to kill *Ishtar*.' When Puttnam expressed his concern as costs on the movie began to escalate, Beatty's response was, 'Who gives a shit what Puttnam thinks? I certainly don't. Just tell the asshole to keep paying the bills.'

Ishtar's release was delayed some months until May 1987, fuelling more rumours that it would be the biggest Hollywood catastrophe since *Heaven's Gate*, something *Tootsie* had also been predicted to become. This time, however, the rumours were justified, and the film lived up to everyone's worst expectations. Clive Hirschhorn in *The Columbia Story* called it 'the cinema equivalent of the Chernobyl disaster . . . so laboured, inept and unfunny that even seeing, on this occasion, was not believing.' *Films and Filming* thought that, 'Hoffman and Beatty are really not good enough to be bad without becoming boring . . . It is not that it's the worst comedy ever made. It isn't. It's just not a very funny film. Nor very pretty to look at. Nor very charming. In fact it is sadly devoid of style almost everywhere you look, except for the unsinkable Charles Grodin . . . His performance is what Hoffman and Beatty's should have been and aren't.' Pauline Kael thought that, 'Just when you think Hoffman is going to skip away with the movie, he appears to decide that he wants to be a sweet simp, too. The little muscleman confesses that his show of confidence was a fraud, and he begins to blubber. Hoffman, who can be funny when he's mean and vain and self-centred, is at his worst when he wants you to like him for his weakness and his innocence. These two major stars with a combined age of 99 are both playing ten-year-olds.' (Their ages are conveniently obscured in close-ups of their passports.)

But *Time* magazine's usually reliable Richard Schickel thought: 'Hoffman has a role nicely suited to the comic whine of his neuroses . . . [the movie is] reasonably genial and diverting. At a cost of $10 million or $15 million, it might have made the studio happy.'

The picture relates how Rogers and Clark, an untalented couple of New York singer/songwriter nerds, modelling themselves on Simon and Garfunkel, are booked by their long-suffering agent (Jack Weston) to perform in a nightclub in Marrakesh, the only gig they can get. No sooner are they through customs than they become involved in a tug of war between the evil Emir, the CIA, Russian agents and the local guerilla freedom fighters represented by a girl (Isabelle Adjani) whom both men initially and separately mistake for an Arab boy. (The exquisite Adjani is unforgivably covered from head to toe in black Arab male attire for most of the film.) She recruits Rogers (Beatty) to her left-wing cause, while Clark (Hoffman) becomes an unwitting accomplice to a CIA agent (Charles Grodin). All these various political factions are after a lost map, which prophesies that the raising of the poor and the humbling of the mighty will coincide with the arrival of two strangers. After surviving many adventures and misunderstandings, including the purchasing of a blind camel, they land a record contract.

'Telling the truth can be dangerous business,' goes one of the horrendously untuneful songs that Beatty and Dustin perform. The dangerous truth is that the film is as maladroit and as unfunny as the songs – which were, astonishingly, put out by Capitol Records! There are few oases of laughter in this heavy comedy, which seems as though the blind camel had in fact directed it.

One of the few ideas in the film, which the makers must have thought terribly funny at the time, was the casting of handsome lover-boy Beatty as a 'nebbish', useless with women (playing against his on- and off-screen reputation as an insatiable Don Juan); and Dustin, not exactly renowned as a screen Casanova, as a man nicknamed 'The Hawk', irresistible to the opposite sex.

To emphasise the difference, Dustin dresses flashily – Hawaiian shirts, gold medallion around his neck, a headband and sunglasses – while Beatty wears square clothes and woolly hats, and cannot pronounce 'schmuck' even though he is one. He tells Dustin, 'You got that kinda face. Kinda mean-looking but with character. The way you walk you can only do that with a small body. Ever hear of a big sports car? I mean, if I looked like you . . .'

The sloppiness of the film can be seen in the moment when, in order to demonstrate how dim Beatty is, he says as they come across a group of gun-runners in the desert, 'Maybe it's a mirage.' Dustin, the wised-up one, sighs in dismay, 'How can it be a mirage when both of us see it?' The joke is meaningless because, unlike a hallucination, a mirage can of course be seen by more than one person.

During the duo's performance in a nightclub, the audience, instead of laughing, booing and enjoying themselves as audiences would do at a lousy act, sit with their mouths agape in horror like the Broadway audiences during the 'Springtime for Hitler' production number in *The Producers*. The reaction rings untrue in both cases. In Mel Brooks's film, the show is obviously a parody and a vaudeville, which only the most unsophisticated member of the audience could fail to recognise. As for Rogers and Clark – like those in the inane *Gong Show* – the act is too self-consciously bad to shock anyone.

May's direction moves too slowly for comedy (though perhaps the movie might have had a little more style if only one person had had the final cut, rather than the director and the two stars), and she fails to make the more spectacular scenes either exciting or eye-catching. Middle East politics are trivialised without the compensation of wit or satire. In a sense, May and company behave as naively as Americans are supposed to abroad. An example of their naivety is shown by an end title: 'The Producers wish to gratefully acknowledge the kindness and cooperation of His Majesty Hassan II, King of Morocco.' In the film there is a portrayal of a dictatorial Emir, not dissimilar from the kind of ruler Hassan is. And Dustin didn't want to 'ass-lick' the Coca-Cola company!

Neither star really earns his six million smackers. All Beatty has to do is play a Stan Laurel-type sap, while Dustin can do little with a zero character except for one set piece when he pretends to be able to speak various Arab dialects. Gene Wilder, whose manner Dustin seems to be imitating, would have made a little more of the flimsy material.

The name Ishtar belongs to the Babylonian goddess of love and war (the name frequently invoked in the Fall of Babylon sections in D. W. Griffiths's 1916 *Intolerance*), but here it is a fictional Arab country. If the film had been called *El Ishtar*, it would have been a perfect anagram for Real Shit. As it was, the title already seemed close enough, and the critics and the public readily consigned the picture to the dung-heap.

28

'A Pain in the Ass!'

This is the only art form when you aren't allowed to make a mistake and then go back and get it right, because it's too costly, without someone complaining about you.

ALTHOUGH THE DISASTROUS *Ishtar* was released in 1987, Dustin's collaboration on it had ended many months before. He had not played a major creative role in a movie since *Tootsie*, six years earlier, excluding the TV filmed version of *Death of a Salesman*. To stay alive as a Hollywood star, it was time he resurfaced in a hit.

It is always fascinating to contemplate films that were never actually made. Projects such as Garbo in the title role of *The Picture of Dorian Gray* are often far more exciting than those that got onto celluloid. Hardly in the same category, but interesting nevertheless, were the projects that were announced at various times between Dustin's pictures. The reasons for the aborting of many of them could be put down to a clash of interests, 'creative differences', a wilting of enthusiasm once the ideas were exposed to the light, or Dustin's 'little green knot'. ('There's a little green knot in me. Once the little green knot starts I know something's not right.')

A 'property' is what a movie is called in Hollywood, and after *Ishtar* Dustin began to look over a number of them to find which he would feel most comfortable in, to test the safety of the foundations and the solidity of·the structure, and to see if it had a good prospect.

Dustin was ready to star in *The Yellow Jersey*, based on the 1973 novel by Ralph Hurne, to be directed by Michael Cimino (still associated with the *Heaven's Gate* flop rather than *The Deer Hunter* hit), set against the background of the Tour de France. Cimino had begun working on the movie in 1975, travelling with the Tour de France of that year. 'These things take time,' he said. Actually, the producer Carl Foreman, who owned the rights, had delayed matters, and it was only Foreman's death in July 1984 that got Cimino moving on it again. The story tells of a 38-year-old British cyclist, retired to coaching, who is lured back to competing to help his protégé win the world's most famous cycle race. The protégé falters but by a wonderful coincidence the veteran takes the lead when the first four finishers of a daily stage are disqualified for drug use. So keen was

Dustin on the idea of giving a dramatic performance while tearing along the highways on a bicycle, that he followed the 1984 Tour de France, and spoke of getting a cycle coach. Of course, he might not have reckoned on having to shave his legs again, as he had to in *Tootsie*. Curiously, for someone as keen on sports as Dustin, he has never made a movie with a sporting theme, unlike most of his male contemporaries.

The script was to have been written by Colin Welland, presumably because of his sporting screenplay for *Chariots of Fire* six years before. Welland, who knew Dustin from *Straw Dogs*, went over to France with Dustin and Cimino. 'I cannot say I'm impressed by the book,' commented Welland, 'but we won't know what we have until I finish the first draft.' But a first draft was as far as the aborted movie ever got.

Then there was talk of Dustin's having a role in *Not a Penny More, Not a Penny Less*, a six-hour adaptation of a Jeffrey Archer novel for the BBC (later broadcast in 1990). Another possibility was Dustin as Dmitri Shostakovich in Tony Palmer's *Testimony*, based on the Russian composer's memoirs. Palmer said, 'Hoffman approached me and told me he would make his decision after he had read the script.' Dustin wisely declined. Ben Kingsley eventually played the role in the interminable 1987 film.

Dustin had optioned *Random Hearts*, a novel based on the 1982 Air Florida disaster in Washington, DC; he would do a biopic of Harry S. Truman; he would appear in *Diamonds*, for United Artists; he would star in *1968* for director Taylor Hackford; he was to direct and star in a picture later called *Dead Poets Society* for Touchstone. (The latter was finally made without him, with Peter Weir directing Robin Williams in the role of the inspirational teacher.)

Dustin then had a meeting with French director Louis Malle and playwright-screenwriter John *'Atlantic City'* Guare about a movie entitled *Moon Over Miami* (not a remake of the Betty Grable musical), the story of a great con man in the Boesky mould. Malle and Guare had envisaged the lead as an irredeemable bastard, but Dustin insisted he be made more sympathetic. Malle claimed he disliked working with big stars with big ideas. There came another parting of the ways.

Director-screenwriter Alan Shapiro next accused Dustin of killing his screenplay *Stonybrook*. 'When Dustin gets involved,' said Shapiro, 'it puts inordinate heat on a project. He's impulsive, doesn't think ahead. He could have been more responsible, more aware of the impact he had. It was a nightmare. I wish in retrospect he'd never gotten involved with it.'

Dustin denied that *Stonybrook* collapsed because he suddenly lost interest. 'They portray me like I take a bite out of a juicy apple here, a chunk out of a pear there – it's so hard to find fresh ideas, good scripts. Once you do, there's nothing that can tear you away. It's like glue.'

Walter Mirisch, who held the option on *La Brava*, an Elmore Leonard novel about a secret service agent involved in blackmail, wanted Dustin to play the lead. The 52-year-old Leonard, who had had a number of films made from his novels, some of them scripted by himself, was a highly respected bestselling thriller writer. For the next seven months, Leonard flew back and forth between Detroit and New York, meeting Dustin, Murray Schisgal, and a succession of directors, among them Volker Schlöndorff, Martin Scorsese and Hal Ashby. 'But nothing happened,' said Leonard. 'One day, we're all sitting around in a meeting at the Sherry Netherland, and Hoffman gets up, says, "I forgot, I have to take my little girl to the movies," and leaves. Next day he comes in, says, "Wasn't yesterday a nice day? Whadja all do? Go to the park?" *Go to the park!* I travelled six hundred miles to meet with him. I coulda gone out in my own back-yard!. . . Ultimately, Hoffman's people set up *La Brava* at Cannon Films. But he didn't care for the advertising campaign – "Welcome to the Cannon family", or something, so he pulled out. But the meetings were fun. He's an entertaining guy.'

Dustin claimed Mirisch set up the deal with Cannon 'without telling anybody. I didn't back out – I flew. I was frightened of Cannon. They could do anything, and would.' The Israeli cousins, Menachem Golan and Yoram Globus, jumped the gun and made the unforgivable error of running full-page colour adverts for *La Brava* in the trade press in which they used a photo of Dustin without his permission.

Another picture which never got beyond the talking stage but contributed to Dustin's reputation for vacillation was called *My New Partner*, derived from the popular French movie *Les Ripoux* (entitled *Le Cop* in the USA), which starred Philippe Noiret as a veteran plain-clothes policeman who educates his priggish new young partner, Thierry Lhermitte, in his corrupt ways. Claude Zidi's amiable comedy-drama seemed ripe for transposition from Paris to New York for a movie combining an older star with a younger one. At one time Sean Penn was mentioned as a possible co-star for Dustin. Twentieth Century-Fox were willing to put up the money. The producer Lawrence Gordon, director Martin Brest, Dustin, the inevitable Murray Schisgal and screenwriter Larry Gross, who was one of the writers on *48 Hours*, the cops 'n' robbers buddy-buddy movie that introduced Eddie Murphy to the screen, met every day for about five months without even emerging with a script outline. 'Brest and Hoffman were equal in their insane ambivalence about taking the next step – committing to a script, getting the project going. Each of them alone is enough to postpone a million projects,' remarked Gross.

Gordon remembers that Marty Brest 'wimped out' after weeks working on the script, eight to ten hours a day, when Dustin suddenly turned to him and said, 'Let's go in January.' The director said, 'Well, uh, uh, I'm not ready.' Brest walked out ostensibly because he would not work for the new production head at Fox, Leonard Goldberg, who had fired him from United Artists' *War Games*.

At the same time, Mike Nichols suggested that Nora Ephron, Carl Bernstein's ex-wife, write *The Ditto List*, based on a novel by Steven Greenleaf in which Dustin would play a lawyer. Needless to say, the movie never happened. This was the third time Ephron and Dustin had avoided doing a picture together. (She and Bernstein had of course attempted to foist their script of *All the President's Men* on Robert Redford, and Dustin had been asked to play Bernstein again in *Heartburn*, about Ephron's divorce from the *Washington Post* journalist.)

They spent most of the preliminary time on *The Ditto List* saying unflattering things about each other. '*Ditto List* is about two people who fall in love *after* they get divorced,' Dustin commented. 'Nora couldn't relate to that. "People kill each other in divorce," she said. She was really upset. I said, "I'm not the guy you were married to, Nora; I just played him."' Ephron attacked Dustin to a friend by comparing him to the producer Ray Stark, with whom she had had a bad experience. Dustin heard about this remark and confronted her. 'How dare you say I'm like Ray Stark.' 'I didn't say you were *like* Ray Stark. I said working for you makes me *miss* Ray Stark,' she retorted.

Since the litigations against First Artists and the strident sounds of altercation that emanated from the sets of *Tootsie*, Dustin had become notorious as a 'difficult' person to work with. In other words the relatively straightforward 'pain in the ass', dating back to his off-Broadway days, grew into a legend. 'Well, you bet I'm a pain in the ass. Yes, I am very difficult.'

'But people have said terrible things about me. And they're all lies. Disgusting, terrible lies. People have said I was on cocaine, that I had been in mental hospitals, that I was erratic, insane. Now the first question anyone ever asks me is, "Are you on coke?" I had to fight them. It's a question of standards. Now when I'm called a perfectionist, I feel I'm cursed. It's like you're on the operating table, and they say, "You're gonna love this surgeon – he's a nice guy but he's not a perfectionist." Well, gee, can I have the perfectionist? I find as I get older that the key to compromising myself less is to give up the habit of caring what others think – of wanting everybody to love me. It's part of what makes you become an actor, yet it's a killer.'

'He would have four or five people on a string at one time, telling them that he probably planned to make their films,' explained Dustin's ex-business manager Jarvis Astaire. 'He can be totally relentless about wasting a year of a man's time, but after that year he drops them. He'd never say, "Give that guy $20,000 for his trouble," or anything like that. He just decides that he won't do it. It's not as though he breaks his word. He does not give his word in the first place. He just doesn't give people a thought.'

Because of Dustin's reputation for going through screenwriters like toilet paper, he was considered anti-writer. 'I'm not anti-writer, I'm *pro*-writer,' he claimed. 'They should be on the set. They should be at the looping. They should be a partner of the director. But what if the script is not working? Do you shelve the project? I know David Puttnam once came out and said you should stick to one writer, but that's ludicrous. It's purely a political statement, purely made to get every writer to love him.'

Back came Puttnam. 'It's not a political statement. It's my track record. There's enormous pressure on executives to be seen to be moving ahead. If a project appears to have slowed down, the easiest thing is to change the writer. It's a quick fix. You've made a decision, and then the perception is that the project is not in trouble. It's two different philosophies; mine works for me.'

According to screenwriter Larry Gross, 'Dustin will never say, "My character wouldn't do that." In fact, he's constantly ahead of you about the terrible things his character would do. "You show me why my character should fuck a sheep, I'll do it." He courts dislikeability, knowing that if he can get the audience back – and he's confident he can – he'll take them on an incredible ride. For all the difficulty, it was eminently worth it, and I would go through it again. Dustin puts out too much to make you feel ripped off.'

Bill Murray commented that: 'People get pretty tired making a movie, but Dustin's got the juice. Well, he's not Dustin Hoffman, because he's Joe Schmo. He does every single take differently. I don't know how the hell they cut the movie [*Tootsie*]. He virtually made seven films! He's always looking for material to push him to the limit.'

'If someone is saying to me, "That's fine, don't worry about it", well for me, "fine" ain't good enough,' Dustin explained. 'That's the personality I've been dealt, and the people I like to work with tend to be that way, too. You go to sleep and you wake up and that's all you're thinking about. I envy people who can just look at a sunset. I wonder how you can shoot it.'

'When he asked me to do *Death of a Salesman*,' recalled John Malkovich, 'everyone told me not to do it, because he was such a horrible man, so dreadful to work with. I found that charming. It intrigued me. I never had the least trouble with him. He is incredibly competitive, but in the best way. When I was doing *Burn This* in New York, Dustin comes backstage looking sour. I say, "What's your problem?" He says, "Why do we have to assume we have a problem?" "Because you're sitting there like a fuckin' mope." "Do you get laughs every night?" "No, Dustin, just tonight." "Is it always this crowded?" "No, Dustin, just tonight. No one ever laughs, no on ever comes. Do you feel better?" "Yes, but you don't have to be so snotty about it!" If he thinks you're doing better than he is, he'll make fun of you and torture you, but what he really wants is to be better.'

Between all the non-productive chatter, backbiting and recriminations, Dustin found some time to front and narrate a four-part TV series for Channel 13 called *Strokes of Genius* on the abstract expressionists Jackson Pollock, Willem de Kooning, Franz Kline and the sculptor David Smith, a subject on which he was especially passionate. 'I love what he feels about women,' Dustin said of de Koonig: 'The fear, anger and childlike joy.' He was also the co-narrator (with Ossie Davis) of a performance of Proko-fiev's *Peter and the Wolf* in Central Park.

Meanwhile, Dustin continued to have an interest in *My New Partner*, and hired Vince Patrick to work on the script. (Patrick would later write the screenplay of *Family Business* from his novel.) The notion of working with a new young star was part of the story's attraction. It was to happen soon, but not quite in the way he'd planned.

29

Uh, Oh!

I'm convinced that we're all a little bit autistic, just like we're all a bit crazy.

BILL WAS A mentally retarded man who cleaned at a restaurant in Minneapolis. He struck up a friendship with musician and social worker Barry Morrow, whose wife worked as a waitress at the restaurant. Morrow wrote a newspaper article about Bill, which was the basis for the television film, *Bill* (1981), in which Mickey Rooney played the title role. Morrow then wrote the follow-up teleplay *Bill: On His Own*.

In the spring of 1986, Morrow had an idea for a film (subsequently called *Rain Man*) about two brothers, one of whom was mentally retarded. He made his suggestion to producer Roger Birnbaum, then president of the Guber-Peters production company. Birnbaum set the project up at United Artists and in September 1986 Morrow turned in his first draft. It was sent to Dustin by his agent with the hope that he would play the part of the normal brother, because the script originally saw the brothers as both middle-aged. But Dustin was fascinated by the retarded character, the smaller role.

United Artists thought this was fine, and suggested offering Jack Nicholson the fast-talking con-man brother. That sounded good to Dustin, who had never worked with Nicholson before. The news of the Hoffman–Nicholson pairing began to get around, naturally reaching Mike Nichols's ears, because Nichols's name invariably came up as director each time Dustin embarked on a new film. Someone was always imagining a billboard reading: '*The Graduate* team of Dustin Hoffman and Mike Nichols together again', forgetting that for the bulk of movie-goers in the eighties, *The Graduate*, if they had even heard of it, was just another old movie. As for 'Dustin Hoffman and Jack Nicholson together for the first time', which would have followed *Ishtar*, Nichols offered Dustin this caveat: 'Be careful of putting two middle-aged guys together on the screen again.'

So the notion of a much younger brother was floated around. Dustin originally suggested Bill Murray, but Michael Ovitz, president of Creative Artists, the biggest agency in Hollywood, brought up Tom Cruise's name. The 40-year-old Ovitz virtually invented 'the package' which allows studios to abdicate responsibility for stitching together the various elements in any given movie. Packages do not always succeed: for example, *Legal Eagles* (1986), starring an all–CAA cast of Robert Redford, Debra Winger and Daryl Hannah, made a fortune in commissions for CAA but lost Universal $30 million.

Dustin thought the idea of Cruise was 'a kind of brainstorm. Who else would have thought of that? Ovitz is known as a packager, and there are people gonna say, "Ah, he just put them together because he's packaging."' There were other cynics who went around saying that Cruise was merely Dustin's insurance policy in case the wider, younger audiences did not want to come to see him.

Dustin had been introduced to Cruise in a restaurant two years previously at the time of *Death of a Salesman* on Broadway, and had offered the young star tickets for the play. After the show, Cruise came backstage, and the two men wound up sitting in the dressing-room for about three hours. Dustin felt 'there was something between us. He was like family. He was treating me like I was his big brother before we ever read the script. That was what was taking place in the movie because in the movie he doesn't know he has an older brother.'

'We talked backstage. I felt like he was a good friend,' Cruise remembered, echoing Dustin. 'There was something there between us, something familial almost. So to play his brother, that was just exceptional as far as I was concerned.'

After the backstage meeting, Dustin went home to Lisa and said, 'I just met this guy Tom Cruise and there's something weird. It's as if we had some kind of connection. It was a very funny feeling. There was something very emotional between us as if we were brothers. We shared personal things. He started to tell me about his background and his family life and I told him about mine and we had almost parallel lives growing up as children. Neither of us had a nice childhood. Like we had come out of the same house.'

Jenna, then sixteen years old, who had overheard her father, screeched, 'You met Tom Cruise! Gee, I wish I'd been there!' Apparently, she had seen *Legend* about half a dozen times, the film in which Cruise played a woodsprite. Dustin, who had never seen any of Cruise's movies, went to see *Risky Business* and a few others out of curiosity. The experience did not deter him from wanting Cruise as a co-star.

Not only did Tom Cruise feel an empathy with Dustin, but the story of *Rain Man* struck a personal chord with him as well. His parents got divorced when he was twelve years old, and he did not speak to his father again until just before he died of cancer in 1984. Like Dustin, Tom went to over a dozen different schools, so he was always the new kid on the block, always the outsider, always getting into fights. In addition, he is dyslexic, which might have been at the root of many of his early problems. As a seven-year-old he was adept at impersonations of John Wayne, Donald Duck and Woody Woodpecker, and had a little acting experience beyond school productions of *Guys and Dolls* and *Godspell*. Yet it had taken him less than five years, from his brief screen debut in Franco Zeffirelli's emetic teen sex movie *Endless Love* in 1981, to reach a position in which he could ask for more than $2.5 million a picture.

By the time he was set to co-star as Dustin's highly unlikely sibling, the five-foot-nine-inch, 25-year-old, dark-haired, brown-eyed Tom Cruise was the top young gun among the new Hollywood heartthrobs of the tee-nage set. He first came to the public's attention in 1981 in *Taps* as an uptight military cadet. There followed Coppola's *The Outsiders*, but *Risky Business* in 1983 was the breakthrough, especially in one sequence in which he sexily flounced around in a pair of white briefs and socks, playing an imaginary rock guitar. The gung-ho *Top Gun* in 1984 grossed more than $435 million, then came two further hits, the empty *Cocktail*, which pro-ved there were enough people out there who would see him in anything, and Martin Scorsese's disappointing *The Color of Money* which paired him with Paul Newman, good practice for working closely with another much older actor.

The cocktail of Dustin and Cruise was ready to be mixed. The only thing that was required now was a screenplay. Director Martin Brest, Barry Morrow and Roger Birnbaum met Dustin and his scribe, Murray Schisgal, for breakfast at the Sand Castle in Malibu. Thirty-four-year-old Brest, with whom Dustin had almost made *My New Partner*, had shot his first feature, the low-budget *Hot Tomorrows*, in 1979, and was now hot from *Beverly Hills Cop* (1984).

'The meeting lasted three hours,' Morrow recalled to the writer Peter Biskind. 'Midway through, Dustin seemed to relax and began regaling us with his own tales of working in a mental institution. Suddenly, he took over, stood up, and started doing these characters from his past. Every eye in the restaurant was on him. I was thrilled. All I could see were bright lights for *Rain Man*. On the way out to the parking lot, Dustin said he would do the picture. He said, "At the end of my career, I'm going to be remembered for two roles – Ratzo Rizzo and Rain Man." He wanted to start immediately. He didn't want this to be one of those pictures that got all screwed up.'

The project did, however, nearly get screwed up. It took about a year and a half of toing and froing of writers and directors before it went into production, which was now becoming par for the course on a Hoffman movie.

Morrow was the first to leave *Rain Man*. 'I was resistant to changing the Charlie Babbitt role to a younger person. Nobody questioned Tom Cruise's box-office appeal, but I wasn't sure it would be believable that these guys would be brothers. That damaged my relationship to the project.'

In mid-January 1987, Brest brought in Ron Bass, who had just completed Francis Coppola's *Gardens of Stone*. But Bass immediately came down with chickenpox, forcing discussions on the script to be held with him over the phone. Then Bass told them he could only give them three weeks, because his wife would divorce him if he didn't take a vacation. When they finally did get the first draft of the script, with five weeks to go before shooting, a general disappointment with it was expressed.

So Richard Price, who had written *The Color of Money*, was approached to take over the baton. At first, he did not want the job, because his wife had just had a baby and he wanted to be with them as much as possible. But a big fat baby needs a big fat cheque, and Price had his price.

After he had produced over thirty pages, both Brest and Dustin felt he was going off in the wrong direction. No sooner had they lost their third writer, than the director, Martin Brest, decided to up and leave. 'It's hard for me to commit to something knowing that I'm going to be spitting blood for the next year and three quarters,' he said. 'Making a movie is so painful that it's much easier just not to do it.' Nevertheless, he went straight off to make *Midnight Run*, asking Dustin to go with him and play what was to be the Robert De Niro role. But Dustin decided to stick with *Rain Man*. On departing, Brest made a farewell crack about Dustin being 'a microsurgeon', implying the actor took too much time over too little, which annoyed Dustin no end. Brest had also objected to the fact that Cruise would be on screen for fifteen minutes before Dustin appeared. 'My God, Tom's the biggest star in the world; he can hold a movie for two reels!' Dustin exclaimed.

In the meantime, Ovitz called Steven Spielberg, who was in Spain shooting *Empire of the Sun*. Spielberg got interested, came back to LA and met Michael Bortman (*The Good Mother*), the fourth writer on the movie. But Spielberg decided that he would like to go back to the script of Ron Bass, who had got over his chickenpox, had a vacation and was available again. Bass then wrote a draft that pleased Dustin, as well as Murray Schisgal, the oracle whom Dustin always consulted. Spielberg was then shown it, but he was so busy cutting *Empire of the Sun* that he found it difficult to focus on the new screenplay. He then announced, unadventurously, that he wanted to make his third Indiana Jones film first. UA wasn't prepared to wait. Exit Steven Spielberg.

Spielberg later regretted not having done it. 'I was hungry to work with Dustin. Dustin was an icon before I ever got into the business.' He felt he could have said to George Lucas, his friend and producer, 'Get someone else for the *Indiana Jones*.' In fact, Spielberg worked almost six months on *Rain Man*. However, given his unpopularity with the Oscar givers, he was convinced that if his name had been on *Rain Man*, even if it had turned out the same, shot by shot, it would not have won any Academy Awards.

Enter Sydney Pollack, the man who had found making *Tootsie* the 'worst experience of his life'. Obviously, he was not ready to jump at the chance of making another picture with Dustin and needed quite a lot of persuasion. Dustin remonstrated with him for having Oscaritis: 'You get an Oscar, then everything's gotta be a masterpiece after that. It kinda paralysed you.' Pollack had not made a movie since *Out of Africa* won a collection of Oscars in 1985. Using the sort of pressure that got Pollack to play the agent in *Tootsie*, Dustin forced the director to give in to his blandishments, suppress all his doubts and take up the *Rain Man* gauntlet, which was now getting a little grubby. A mixture of the Hoffman persistence, charm and power usually manages to snare the prey.

Unfortunately, from Dustin's point of view, Pollack wanted his own favourite writers, Kurt Luedtke (*Out of Africa* and *Absence of Malice*) and David Rayfiel (*Three Days of the Condor*), brought in. Dustin submitted reluctantly, and Pollack and Co. worked on the script for about a month.

While they were slaving away, Dustin ran into Barry Levinson at the Cirque du Soleil on the Santa Monica Pier. Levinson, fresh from *Good Morning Vietnam*, had come in briefly on the script of *Tootsie*, and had offered Dustin one of the two leads in *Tin Men*, which 'I had turned down like a jerk'. They had liked each other, so Dustin confided in him. 'I'm having a lot of trouble with this *Rain Man* thing. I'm just hanging on by my fingernails.'

Dustin then outlined the story with the Ron Bass structure to Levinson, who enthused about what he had heard. 'So, what's the problem?' he asked. Dustin explained that Pollack and his writers were departing from it. He asked Levinson to do him a favour and take some of the pressure off him by calling up Pollack, who was a friend, and advise him to stop wrestling with a new script but to go back to the Bass one. So Levinson called Pollack and told him how good the movie could be if he stuck to the script that Dustin had recounted to him. Pollack said he would give it some thought. After Levinson had hung up, his wife, who had overheard her husband's passionate advocacy of the film, said, 'This is *your* kind of movie. Barry, do it.' 'I know, but Sydney's doing it,' he replied regretfully.

Actually, a short time after Levinson's call, Pollack started to have doubts about his involvement in *Rain Man*. He had not really wanted to do it in the first place, and was never comfortable with the road-movie aspect of the picture.

'Speaking to Levinson made me feel better about being brutal about my own feelings,' Pollack explained. 'I knew it would get made. But it was not something I could get to work for me personally, which is what I try to do with all my movies. There are a lot of movies that turned out to be terrific hits but probably wouldn't have been hits if I had done them. So I called Dustin, and he understood my problem. He was wonderful!'

As it turned out, Dustin was wonderful because he was relieved that Pollack had opted to leave of his own free will before he was fired, and also because he had decided that Levinson would be the best director for the movie.

Forty-five-year-old Barry Levinson was born and brought up in Baltimore, where he set his first (and probably best) movie, the semi-autobiographical *Diner*. Previously, he had made his living writing for TV comedians Marty Feldman, Tim Conway and Carol Burnett, and was co-writer on a couple of Mel Brooks pictures, *Silent Movie* and *High Anxiety* – in the latter he played the bellhop who stabs Brooks in the shower with a rolled-up newspaper. Fairly sharp character comedy seemed to be his forte. His one venture into drama had been the puerile baseball fantasy vehicle for Robert Redford, *The Natural*.

The disability of the older brother had now changed from an unspecified form of mental retardation to autism. This disability, the name of which was coined in 1943, is thought to come about when part of the brain is damaged before birth. An autistic person is unable to interact with other people, to show affection and receive affection, and to make eye contact. This immutability of autistic people was an apparent stumbling block to the previous three directors, Brest, Spielberg and Pollack, who wanted the character to develop. But medical opinion was that autistic withdrawal was irreversible. Levinson told Dustin, 'Let's not be gun-shy and say, well, I don't know if an audience really wants to deal with an autistic person. Let's go for that.'

'Barry was the first director who wasn't apprehensive about what I was telling him. All the other directors, to different degrees, would say, "Am I hearing you right? You don't want to make eye contact with anyone in the movie? And another thing. You don't talk voluntarily?" The other directors would say, "So how can we have scenes?" They didn't know I was getting a lot of stuff off the people I was meeting and was moved – without eye contact. Tom and I were besides ourselves because we were the only ones who had done the research and we kept saying there is something terribly moving about these people. They said, "You can't make a film about autism. No one knows what it is. No one's interested in that. What is it going to be? A film for science class in school?"'

'I accepted the fact that in order to be authentic, Raymond [the Hoffman character] couldn't have the dramatic arc that actors always look for in roles,' explained Levinson. 'And instead of a full-scale painting, I would have to do a pen-and-ink drawing – a poem, a haiku. I realised that Raymond is going to be Raymond; Raymond doesn't change. Somebody who's autistic doesn't suddenly become another person. He is who he is.' This is not in fact entirely borne out by the film, which mistakenly attempts to show some evolution in Raymond.

Dustin's research had become massive. Following leads provided by Gail Mutrux, the film's associate producer, he consulted experts on autism at the Institute for Child Behavior Research in San Diego, the UCLA Neuropsychiatric Institute, and on the East Coast.

'I think I met thirty or forty autistic people during the research for the film. Some autistics have extraordinary gifts that are mind-boggling. Some can calculate faster than a computer. Everything about the character that I'm playing has been taken from factual people. It's all an actual compilation of case-histories put into one person.' Actually, an infinitesimal minority of autistics are savants of the sort played by Dustin, which might have given a distorted view to the public about the nature of autism in general. (An autistic savant, while still incapable of normal relationships, is highly developed mentally in some areas.)

Barry Morrow introduced Dustin to a retarded man named Kim P., who was able to perform extraordinary mental feats. 'Dustin amazed me with his obsession with watching Kim. He would subtly mimic his characteristics. I would watch his hands move as Kim's hands moved. His eyes never left him the whole afternoon. He had a way of directly relating to him that others who weren't comfortable talking to a retarded person didn't. This meeting changed Kim's life. It was like Babe Ruth visiting an orphanage. When the production was finished, Dustin sent him a director's chair autographed by him and the cast.'

Dustin and Cruise got to know two brothers, not dissimilar from the two brothers in the film. Dustin had trouble with the walk and the autistic one fell in step right behind him.

'We hung out with them. Went bowling and had lunch. That was the most helpful,' said Cruise. 'I also remember we were in a hotel when we were meeting all the autistics' families early on. Dustin and I started laughing at something one of the autistics had said or done. We looked at each other and tried to hold it back, and we didn't want them thinking we were laughing at this person. But there's just something so charming and funny about what they were saying and doing. Afterwards the mother came over and said, "Listen, that's one of the beauties of these people. It's okay to laugh. It's part of the joy of knowing these people." We all know people with disabilities. We know that humour is a part of it. The families wanted to be assured that we'd include that in the film.'

As rehearsals approached, Dustin began to feel the full weight of his research. 'The challenge then became to do what I always try to do, which is to bring it home and not try to do a character that is not myself. . . I'd gone into analysis years ago, and someone told me that Freud said the problem with us is that what we feel about ourselves is based upon what we think others feel about us. We spend a lifetime trying to get to say, Fuck 'em. The question never hits autistics: what do you think of me? Am I boring this person? It doesn't exist.'

In rehearsals, Cruise would also improvise as Raymond, and Dustin improvised as Cruise's character. 'I had a lot of trouble as I always do, and Cruise and I constantly traded parts in the trailer. "I don't know how to do this," I'll say. "You play my part, and I'll play your part." There was a lot of give and take.'

'I remember we were rehearsing about the second week,' said Cruise. 'It just got a little frustrating. . . But once we hit our stride, it became effortless, totally effortless. I couldn't wait to get up in the morning and I didn't want to finish at the end of the day. . . I'd heard things people said about Dustin, but I didn't anticipate problems. I mean, he's an actor's actor. He's so bright, so brilliant.'

Dustin continued with the mutual admiration. 'We're both very compulsive and monk-like. When we're shooting, we both like to work out, keep a strict diet, not go out at night. He gets up early, he goes home early, he studies, he works out again at night, he doesn't drink, he doesn't smoke, and he always wants to rehearse. And he writes his dialogue over and over in his own handwriting – as if they're your own words, until you feel you are the writer – which is how I memorised *Death of a Salesman* . . . Also, for the first time I was working with someone who was going through what I did twenty years ago – that first flush of stardom following *The Graduate*. So we were linked into each other – which allowed us to be rough with each other. There's an emotionality between us that's very difficult to act – that permitted moments to happen between us.'

'In the beginning Dustin was fighting to hold the character,' Levinson recalled. 'Acting is relating to someone else, but this character does not look or listen – before you know it, you're out of the scene. But at some point it all clicked.' The point was reached during rehearsals for the scene in which Raymond realises he is not wearing any underwear and refuses to let up about it ('I'm definitely not wearing my underwear . . . I get my boxer shorts at K Mart, Cincinnati'). Cruise and Dustin were encouraged to improvise by Levinson, and the two actors expanded the dialogue as if it were a comedy routine. 'Dustin loosened up after that and really started to nail the character.'

The moment Dustin knew he had really broken through came when he, ordinarily 'a very tactile person', felt 'little shocks when I was touched' by co-workers between takes. 'It disturbed where I was. It was like what Temple Grandon, author of *Autobiography of an Autistic*, told me: contrary to belief, autistics don't want to be held and touched. They shrink from physical contact because it's too powerful an experience; they get little jolts.' (This, too, is belied in the latter part of the film, when Raymond submits himself to dancing closely with both his brother and his brother's girlfriend.)

One of the less elevated moments came in the scene in the phone booth when Raymond farts. 'That came accidentally from rehearsals,' Dustin explained unashamedly to the press. 'I just farted. I like to fart sometimes when I'm amongst my men friends. I make no bones about it. I cut a beauty. You could hear Barry Levinson cracking up and scribbling it down into the script.'

All the rehearsals and script changes were going well, but pressure began to be put on them for the screenplay to be ready before the writers' strike in May 1988, and, if they had not got started within the week, the whole project, already two years old, would have had to be abandoned. So the picture was shot while the screenplay was still being worked on as they went along. 'We needed to work quickly, and mainly on locations,' said Levinson. 'We were improvising all the time. This is something I've always done since *Diner*. I like the danger.'

The film took the cast and crew to Cincinnati, Oklahoma City, Las Vegas, Kentucky and Indiana. For the car in which the two leads travel across the country, Levinson chose a '49 Buick Roadmaster convertible. 'There's something very classic about it, and not many American cars of this era qualify as a classic,' he explained. Since only eight thousand were originally produced, the transportation department were hard put to it to find three which were up to the rigours of the film.

Shooting was concluded in a little less than three months, two days under the sixty-day schedule and $2.5 million under the approximately

$24 million budget. The combined salaries of the two stars were around $9 million. *Rain Man* was ready to be released in time for Christmas 1988.

The finished screenplay concerned Charlie Babbitt, a smooth-talking young car-salesman who takes off for Palm Strings with his girlfriend/ assistant Susanna (Valeria Golino), only to be recalled to be told that his father has died in Cincinnati. He is shocked to hear that he has been bequeathed only his father's prized rose bushes and the 1949 Buick, while $3 million has gone to an unnamed beneficiary. He tracks the latter down to the Wallbrook home for the mentally handicapped; one of the patients recognises the Buick and Charlie hears in disbelief that Raymond, an autistic savant, is his brother, institutionalised soon after the death of their mother when Charlie was two. Determined to get the money for himself, Charlie gets his brother to come back to LA with him, but Raymond refuses to fly, because he knows all the accident statistics. Neither will he take major highways or travel in the rain. On the four-day trip, Charlie discovers that Raymond is Rain Man, the friend who used to comfort him when he was a baby, and whom he subsequently supposed was imaginary. At Las Vegas, Charlie puts Raymond's amazing skill with numbers to work on a game. Later he fights for the custody of Raymond, having learned to feel love for him. 'It's not about the money any more,' he says, but reluctantly has to give his brother up when the court decides that Raymond must be returned to Wallbrook.

As was to be expected from Levinson's past films, the humour is the most successful element in a movie that never becomes po-faced or preachy about its subject. It was a great advance on previous American pictures that dealt with mental disability. Twenty years earlier, a tendentious and mawkish piece called *Charly*, in which a retarded man gets a new brain, won Cliff Robertson, in the title role, a Best Actor Oscar. (As Dustin was to find out, playing a mental deficient usually goes down well with the Academy panel.)

A lot of humour is extracted from the character of Raymond, who, literally, has no sense of humour, and never smiles, except near the end when he recognises a joke, one of the spurious moments that indicate that there has been some sort of a breakthrough. 'Charlie Babbit made a joke,' he says. In fact, the famous Abbott and Costello routine of 'Who's on first', which Raymond retells endlessly, he takes as a riddle and not humorously, so that Cruise says at one point, 'You're the comedy team of Abbott and Abbott.' Actually the two of them are reminiscent of another comedy team for most of the way – Cruise is Dean Martin to Hoffman's idiot Jerry Lewis.

Curiously, *Rain Man* can be lumped together with two other road movies released in the same year – Martin Brest's *Midnight Run* (the overland journey across America taken by Robert De Niro and Charles Grodin takes place because of the De Niro character's refusal to fly) and *Planes, Trains and Automobiles* with Steve Martin and John Candy in the Cruise and Hoffman roles respectively. In all three cases, the scriptwriters had to find some excuse for people not travelling by air in order to give the ill-assorted duos time to get to know each other.

It is a pity, though, that such an interesting and off-the-beaten-track subject should have been fashioned into merely a reasonably entertaining Hollywood-caper-cum-odd-couple road movie, padded out with endless hackneyed shots of the Buick moving through the American landscape with rock music on the soundtrack. Just as Raymond hardly develops as a character and lives by rituals, so the film is restricted inside conventional modes.

Nevertheless, the movie works expertly within these limitations for most of the time, until the rather glib and sentimental last twenty minutes; from the moment of the corny revelation in the bathroom that Raymond is Rain Man, and from when the money-hungry yuppie, who only saw his brother as a meal ticket, suddenly becomes a warm, loving, protective human being. It must be acknowledged, however, that, although some scenes are beyond Cruise's dramatic capabilities, he manages quite well to negotiate the sudden change.

There is a change also in Raymond from then on. He becomes less emptily loquacious and more affectionate when he dances with Charlie and then with Susanna in the elevator, even allowing her a kiss. He also seems to want a date with a girl who tried to pick him up in Las Vegas because she thinks he has money. (The possibility that Raymond might have sexual desires is not explored.) Despite the six credited experts on autism on the film, it is difficult to believe that the character actually understands the concept of gambling, so that the use of Raymond's phenomenal abilities to win at Las Vegas seems a rather cheap plot device. And the question that Charlie asks throughout the film, 'Why didn't anyone tell me I had a brother?', is never satisfactorily answered.

In the custody hearing scene, in which Charlie makes an appeal to the psychologist (the grey-haired, bespectacled and uncredited Barry Levinson, reluctantly taking over from J. T. Walsh at the last moment), Raymond is not aware of what is going on, yet he suddenly puts his head on his brother's shoulder, not from any character motivation but because the film demands an emotional gesture at the climax even if it is at odds with anything that went before. The sentimentality undermines the thoroughness of the characterisation.

The film actually has a happy ending despite the separation. It is only a temporary sadness for Charlie. He will get on with his life much more easily without having to run around looking after Raymond all the time, and Raymond will be much happier back in the ritualistic life of the institute without having his routine disrupted.

Although the movie is virtually a two-hander, the Italian actress Valeria Golino provides a sensitive counterbalance between the brothers for a while. (Lisa Hoffman's grandmother, Blanche Salter, and little Jake Hoffman, spinning around on a stool, are also seen for a brief second sitting at the pancake counter.)

Dustin's year-long research into the behaviour of autistic people shows in every detail of his touching and funny performance as Raymond. Dustin with institutionalised haircut holds his head aslant, plays with his ring, rocks backwards and forwards, hops from one foot to another, holds one hand over his ear when frightened, and stares unblinking ahead of him, avoiding eye contact. He has a peculiar, lop-sided little-boy walk that sometimes makes him seem like a clockwork doll as he repeats catch-phrases such as 'Uh oh!' and 'I dunno know'. It's a role which has similarities with and is just as memorable as Peter Sellers's blank Chauncey Gardner in *Being There*. It is no coincidence that Dustin was a great admirer of this performance: 'I don't think I've ever seen any actor stretch the way Peter Sellers stretches in that movie, one of the best things I've ever seen an actor do.'

When it came to publicising *Rain Man*, Cruise insisted that the only TV appearances he made were in the company of Dustin and never alone. Dustin joked about how Cruise got all the attention when the two of them were in public together.

Pauline Kael sprayed most of her venom on the younger of the stars. 'Cruise as a slimeball is just a sugarpuss in Italian tailoring. He doesn't even use his body in an expressive way. His performance here consists of not smiling too much – so as not to distract his fans from watching Hoffman. (This could be called "restraint".) Cruise is an actor in the same sense that Robert Taylor was an actor. He's patented: his knowing that a camera is on him produces nothing but fraudulence.' It is to be hoped that Cruise's dyslexia has protected him from reviews of this kind all the way to the bank. It would take him a little over a year to prove he was not just a pretty face with his performance in *Born on the Fourth of July*, for which he was Oscar-nominated.

Kael and a few other critics notwithstanding, *Rain Man* was presented with the prestigious Golden Bear for Best Film at the Berlin Film Festival, where a tearful Dustin received an honorary award for 'contribution to cinema'. At the Academy Awards Ceremony in April 1989, *Rain Man* received Best Picture, Best Direction, Best Actor, and Best Original Screenplay (Ronald Bass and Barry Morrow). In addition it went on to make a fortune, as well as making sure that no one who saw the movie would ever again confuse the word autistic with artistic.

30

Dustbone Meets Shakespeare

I don't know anything about Shakespeare. I follow my nose, which is a long journey.

OVER HIS LONG acting career, Dustin's contact with the Bard of Avon had been limited to his playing Brutus in the Tent Scene (Act IV, Scene III) from *Julius Caesar* at the Pasadena Playhouse. In order to prepare for it, he got a recording of the play and learnt both his part and that of Cassius. Otherwise, there is only Dustin quoting from *King Lear* ('Oh, God, let me not be mad') in *Who Is Harry Kellerman . . . ?*, adding, 'Shakespeare's a winner, man. Those sonnets!'

After *Tootsie*, Dustin had an itch to return to the stage, an itch temporarily satisfied by *Death of a Salesman* in 1984. Never one to shirk a challenge, he thought he might tackle Shakespeare. 'I didn't want to die and go to actor-heaven or actor-hell and have some guy come up to me and say, "You were a star and you didn't do Shakespeare?"'

But instead of practising on the lower slopes, he went straight towards the Everest of *Hamlet*. He got as far as learning the first three acts, memorising all the parts. He had the original text on the left-hand page with a contemporary English version on the facing page. 'It's the only way we Americans can get into it . . . Hamlet is a loser. He's thirty-two and he's still in college. His step-father wants to know what Hamlet is going to do with his life. Why is he hanging out with actors?'

For Dustin, Hamlet would be just another in the long line of losers he had played – Ratso, Dega, Lenny, Max Dembo, Willy Loman and Raymond.

When he heard that Peter Hall was forming his own company, the daring thought crossed his mind that here would be a chance for him to bring his Hamlet to the stage. After fifteen years as Director of the National Theatre, from 1973 to 1988, Hall had taken the plunge into independence by staging Tennessee Williams's *Orpheus Descending* at the Haymarket, with Vanessa Redgrave in the lead. As soon as the success of the play was assured and seemed Broadway-bound, Hall was open to all suggestions for his second production.

Before Dustin contacted Hall direct, he took the precaution of ringing

London-based director Michael Rudman from Los Angeles. 'I wanted to know if Peter Hall would be prepared to talk to me. I was surprised when Rudman said he would.' He therefore called Peter Hall about making his Shakespearean debut as Hamlet. Hall was blunt. 'You're too old for it, for a start,' he said. Then Hall suggested Shylock, another loser. 'It's a wonderfully economic part for someone going into Shakespeare for the first time,' Hall said. Something else, however, had dictated Hall's choice of the role for Dustin. 'It's a role for a great Jewish actor who can use his Jewishness in the play.'

Hall had been thinking of doing either *Twelfth Night* or *Measure for Measure*, but he changed his ideas when the possibility of Dustin's doing Shylock came up.

Dustin went away and read *The Merchant of Venice* and discovered that Shylock was not even the title role! No matter, he had not taken the title role in *Midnight Cowboy, Papillon* or *Agatha*, either. 'Because of my ignorance of Shakespeare I didn't know until I read it that the play is a time-bomb, very controversial. I called Peter Hall and said this is a very anti-Semitic play. He explained it could be done in that way but if you look at the text it isn't. Shylock lives in the ghetto, he is spat upon, he is excluded from the business community, he is not allowed to know about fleets and ships, yet if he went into the church and became a Christian he'd be in. Then they steal his daughter. Christ, it's incredible! He is certainly a member of the powerless class, like women. The play is not just about anti-Semitism but about colour, feminism, the issues that concern us now. It's not a complicated part. It's about a man stopped from doing what he wants to do, which is to be a businessman. It's about frustration, too.'

The goy director and the Jewish actor met for two days in California. 'I wanted him to know what he was letting himself in for so we discussed text and approach,' said Hall. 'There is a tune to Shakespeare, there is a shape to Shakespeare, you have to breathe in certain places, you have to ride on the rhythm like a water skier or a roller skater, and if you surrender yourself to it until it supports you, it makes it very easy, and if you fight it and split it up and breathe in all sorts of odd places and try to make it real, it gets up and strangles you. I wanted Dustin to know that, to know what it was. Because if he didn't feel comfortable it would have all ended in tears.'

When they had agreed to do it and the contracts were signed – Dustin accepted £2000 a week – Hall went back to LA to do some coaching on the speaking of the verse at Dustin's home. 'Until then I didn't know what I was talking about. I didn't understand all that shit about iambic pentameters. Then when I understood it, I wasn't sure if I could do it. I can't think of anything I've done which I've found more stimulating. Learning the verse is like doing scales on the piano. You don't do Shakespeare unless you can play the instrument. His interest is to keep that line as smooth and as light and tripping and as whole as possible. It's exactly like jazz. If you have that sense of rhythm of where the end of the line is and where it goes to the next, and yet you inflect it naturally, you get a cross rhythm. It's like a great jazz musician who plays just off the beat but at a crucial moment just catches it again.'

Dustin had already learned all his lines and grown a greying beard when he arrived in London in April 1989 with his wife Lisa and a brood of children: Jacob (eight), Rebecca (six), Max (five) and eighteen-month-old Alexandra, the newest addition to the Hoffman clan. The family was later swelled by the arrival of Karina (twenty-two) and Jennifer (nineteen). They all settled into the four-bedroomed semi in Victoria Road, Kensington, that Dustin had bought in 1986 for £725,000, most of which came out of his $4 million for *Ishtar*.

As the only American in a company of English actors, he was an outsider, like Shylock in Venice, and exhibited a certain initial shyness. Billing was strictly in alphabetical order and he refused to be interviewed or photographed without other members of the cast. He wanted to be considered just another member of the company, and did not want to be treated as a star. He was also insistent that Geraldine James as Portia take the final bow.

'As an American coming in to do Shakespeare for the first time I could easily have been a puppet with a million strings on me. I was never aware of strings. I never felt Sir Peter had a preconception of what he wanted me to fill. What we start doing is learning the lines and getting the metre right. Then you start looking at the character, as you would in Clifford Odets, Arthur Miller or Tennessee Williams. I find this exciting.'

'If someone is that big and famous the most interesting story is that he's difficult to work with,' commented Hall. 'One had read that sort of thing. I didn't find him ever difficult to work with, ever less than open and trusting and wanting to work dangerously. And most of all he was wonderful with the rest of the company. He provoked them to greater heights. They were all like tennis players. A great actor certainly takes direction. He exhausts the director. Takes everything he can out of him.

'There's one thing that fascinated me in rehearsal with him. Most actors cook slowly and they don't have it all in rehearsal. They build it up. Perhaps they take three or four weeks to get a point. But he goes from nothing straight up to total creation. Again that's the film actor. It's tremendously

inventive. Since he rehearses like that, I've seen few actors get more tired
at rehearsal because actually he performs for six or seven hours. Flat out.
Trying this, trying that. Not, as many actors do, saying, "When I get to
the performance I'll probably do it something like this." That makes it
much more exciting to direct him. It makes it much more exciting for his
fellow actors, because the electricity they're getting off him is terribly
stimulating. But it's very, very taxing for him. He's a very wise theatre
rat. I'm sure if he does a bigger Shakespeare part he'll have learned how to
tread not perhaps a little more cautiously but more sparingly to himself.
But that was fascinating. It made the rehearsals very incandescent.'

Rehearsals with Dustin did go on at inordinate length. Sometimes some
of the cast would feel that he was nitpicking, but it was more often than
not stimulating. He would not do anything until it felt right. Knowing of
his legendary obsessive striving for perfection and the living of his parts,
some members of the company would not have been surprised to hear of
his going around London in his 'Jewish gabardine' and demanding pounds
of flesh from Christian passers-by. One the whole, however, there was a
lot of good humour, wisecracking and occasional horseplay during
rehearsals. Dustin's conversation is more liberally sprinkled with expletives and comes in more impassioned surges than is usual with English
actors. He also regaled them from his fund of dirty Jewish jokes.

What obsessed Dustin more than anything else seemed to be the iambic
pentameter of the verse, something he continually referred to in conversation. 'The idea is to be on stage and the audience should not be aware that
you're doing pentameter. That you're adhering to the ends of lines. That it
seems odd and yet they don't know. I'd drill it every day at nine-thirty. I'd
work for an hour and a half.

'Sometimes when you turn the TV on you see a close-up of a guy looking very relaxed and talking casually and suddenly his hand comes up and
the camera pulls back and you see he has shorts on and the camera keeps
pulling back and you see that he's on the side of a rock mountain. In the
middle of nowhere. He's seemingly very relaxed but one false move and
that's it. And I feel that rehearsals felt that way for me, when your body is
relaxed and yet very alert because there was no time to lose. Every day in
rehearsal I knew that the clock was ticking. Five weeks – I knew there'd be
an audience there.'

In fact, audiences had to wait a little longer than five weeks. Dustin got a
call from the USA to inform him that his father had taken a turn for the
worse after a stroke and was in a coma. Dustin therefore decided that his
father should take precedence over the notion of 'the show must go on',
and flew back to California to be with Harry. The play's out-of-town run,

which had been booked in at the Theatre Royal, Bath, before the West End opening, had to be cancelled and the many pre-booked customers had their money refunded. Harry recovered enough to be able to watch Dustin winning his Best Actor Oscar for *Rain Man* on a rented TV in the hospital. 'This one's just for you, Dad,' said Dustin, brandishing the statuette.

On Sunday, 30 April, Dustin took time off to be interviewed by a raucously-laughing Simon Callow at the National Film Theatre. Dustin, in jeans and sneakers and clutching a mysterious briefcase, was at his most relaxed, moving from telling a lengthy John Wayne joke with accurate mimicry, to heights of rhetorical fancy such as saying that when rehearsals go well, 'There's no death, there's no pain, you're never going to die, you're just in this timeless thing, it's the jazz of life', to readings of three poems by e. e. cummings, in the poet's own tempo. In the audience were Peter Hall and most of *The Merchant* cast, as well as Lisa and Jake. At one stage, Hoffman Jr asked a question, and Dustin dared him to come up on stage and ask it, which he did. What he asked was, 'What would you rather do, drama or comedy, or sort of in between?' 'I don't think there's any difference. It's like life. If I'm doing drama I try to find what's comic in it, if it's a comedy I try to find out what's serious in it.'

Dustin was so carried away by the enjoyment of entertaining the enthusiastic audience that he was reluctant to leave the stage, although crowds were gathering outside for the next film. ('Is it a Pacino movie?') Like a child being told he had to go to bed, he begged to be allowed just a few more minutes. It was then that he drew the book of cummings's poems from his briefcase. The last poem he read seemed to have the most significance for him. As the small figure stood on the stage with the book in his hand, it was not difficult to imagine the days when he stood in front of a class reading – self-conscious about his nose, acne and height.

> i am a little church (no great cathedral)
> far from the splendor and squalor of hurrying cities
> i do not worry if briefer days grow briefest
> i am not sorry when sun and rain make april
>
> winter by spring, i lift my diminutive spire to
> merciful Him Whose only now is forever;
> standing erect in the deathless truth of His presence
> (welcoming humbly His light and proudly His darkness)

As opening night approached, Dustin felt a greater trepidation than ever before. 'I didn't quite know what it was going to be like. All I knew was that I would learn something. I'd fail probably but I'd learn something. Why not? You get to a certain point in your life and the ultimate freedom is not to be concerned with whether you fail or succeed but you've done something new and learned.' He knew that he was putting himself on the line. During a film of some of the rehearsals, broadcast on *The South Bank Show* on 24 September 1989, the night after *The Merchant* closed, Dustin suddenly turned to the camera and said in close-up, 'This is tough shit, this is really tough shit, I shouldn't have taken this fuckin' job, I should be back in the fuckin' States.'

Nerves apart, he continued to be open and generous with the company right down to the most junior member. One day he wanted to send out for a steak sandwich (a steakwich). When he was told that it was not as easy as in the USA, he went to the phone and twenty minutes later a boy arrived with steak sandwiches for everyone. He also used to bring in boxes of fruit from time to time because he felt the cast looked rather pasty. After the first preview he supplied everybody with a bottle of champagne, and on the first night, there were presents from him to the cast. He had gone to the wardrobe and got everyone's measurements in order to have towelling robes made up with their initials sewn on.

There was an air of expectancy about Dustin Hoffman's Shakespearean debut in England at the opening on Thursday, 1 June 1989. There were those in the audience who had already decided that it was a mistake to bring over a Hollywood film star to play Shylock, and that it was sheer *chutzpah* on the part of Dustin to accept it. When there is such good water to drink on this side of the stream, why bring water over from the other side? Yet, though there might be better Shylocks, Dustin had the magic tinsel of the screen clinging to him. Because of his name, *The Merchant of Venice* had the biggest advance booking for a straight play in the history of the West End. Even if he got bad reviews, people would still flock to see him.

The celebrity-packed first-night audience gave the production and Dustin a hearty welcome. Afterwards, he announced that, 'It was the greatest moment in my life as an actor when Dame Peggy Ashcroft and Sir John Mills, idols from my youth, came backstage to congratulate me.' No matter that Dame Peggy could not have been an idol of Dustin's youth when most of her work was done on the London stage, and she only made very rare film appearances, none of them in the idol-making class, but dressing-room talk is notoriously insincere. Dame Peggy simply declared, 'It was perfection. It's thrilling that he should make his debut in Shakespeare in this country.' Paul and Linda McCartney posed with

Dustin and Lisa in the dressing room. Peter Hall declared that the first night was, 'The best we have done, despite the missing of an odd line or two,' and of Dustin, 'I've never known such a nice person.'

It was up to the critics to speak the truth. The first reviews that came out might have dissipated the warm glow somewhat. The *Guardian* called it 'A modest, low-key, small-scale Shylock' which lacked 'the tragic dimension'. *The Times* found 'All the clamouring hype and slavering expectations are a poor preparation for the modest Shylock who arrived on the Phoenix Theatre stage.' The *Standard* pronounced that, 'If Prince Charles had been appearing as Hamlet in the West End, he could hardly have received more pre-production attention than Dustin Hoffman . . . As a victim of this hysterical hype, Hoffman was on a hiding to nothing. If he was good, he could never be as good as the great Shylocks of Olivier, Redgrave, or Wolfit; and if he was average or bad, he would be dismissed as an American film star from whom nothing more was expected . . . Hoffman's performance is sound and well-spoken, but it is never fierce enough to make Shylock an interesting monster nor despised enough to make him an oppressed victim.'

The Sunday papers brought better news, the most positive being Michael Radcliffe in his piece in the *Observer* headed 'Dustin Come to Judgement': 'To come straight to the point, Dustin Hoffman takes to the London stage in *The Merchant of Venice* with a Shylock of striking physicality, unsentimental pride and sardonic power . . . The hands are remarkable. They are his advocates and his defenders, sweeping aside compromise, shaping an argument, clawing a threat of revenge out of thin air . . . The voice is guttural and dark . . . He breaks up the verse with idiosyncratic confidence . . . The brilliant smile is concealingly humorous and, once, even benign . . . Hoffman's unselfish performance justifies the Peter Hall Company's decision not to promote him as a star outside the ensemble. If only the ensemble were worthy of him . . . This is British acting by the book beside American acting at its most scrupulous and unpredictable.'

On the whole, it was a rich performance in a rich production. In fact, it was difficult to separate the two. It was, like most of the best theatrical evenings, a brilliant ensemble work. Shylock can sometimes unbalance the play which is, after all, a comedy. For once, the awkward dichotomy between the Venice and Belmont scenes disappeared, bringing it much closer to the cruelly comic and magical tone of *Twelfth Night*, with Shylock as Malvolio. Dustin and Hall knew there was no need to play for pathos, as so many Shylocks do. The pathos is in the text and situation. Neither was there a need to stress the evils of anti-Semitism, as so many other productions do. No post–Auschwitz audience can fail to bring their own views on the subject to the play. No concessions were made to audiences that contained a larger share of star-gazers than is usual for Shakespeare productions in London.

Dustin succeeded where so many other Shylocks have failed in striking the perfect balance between the tragic and the humorous. By bringing out the comical elements in the part, he did not diminish the tragic, and he made the Jew not into a grotesque comic villain, a symbol of repression or a dramatic stereotype, but into a real human being. One thing Dustin/Shylock had to endure every evening was having his face spat into so often that *Variety* suggested the play could have been subtitled 'Great Expectorations'. Each liquid and verbal insult was greeted by Dustin with a submissive fixed grin.

Although it is by no means necessary for a Jew to play Shylock, it certainly helps. There is something in the guts or *kishkas* of the role that only a Jew can bring to it. Of Laurence Olivier's Shylock, a critic noted that, 'He isn't a Jew, but an actor with a Jewish director [Jonathan Miller] up his sleeve.' Alec Guinness as Shylock, great actor though he is, was not very semitic – or what a Yiddisher momma would call *yokse nakhes*. The intonation and the vocal quality are intrinsic even to the most assimilated Jew. As Shylock, Dustin used a slight Jewish–American accent, and the quality of his voice was an important basis of his characterisation.

During the four months of the run, in the warmest English summer for many a year, queues formed around the corner on Charing Cross Road, with ticket touts clinging to them like leeches every night. Because Shylock spends more time offstage than on, Dustin occupied himself by reading and living up to his reputation as a flirt, cuddling the girls in the cast and orchestra, and often enjoying massaging their feet. Invariably, however, Lisa was backstage standing in the wings with a bottle of mineral water ready for her husband as he made his exits. Also, after every performance, Dustin's dressing room was packed with celebrities – Robert De Niro, Jack Nicholson, Barbra Steisand, Sean Connery and Jack Lemmon could all be seen crowding in to congratulate him.

After the performance of 6 June, despite always being meticulous with his diet, Dustin went down with a severe stomach complaint. He thought he might have picked it up from his kids, who were going to school. He spent a terrible night of throwing up, and Thelma Holt, the executive producer of the company, sent her doctor along to his house the next morning. The doctor, finding Dustin with a high temperature and still vomiting, advised him to take to his bed. However, Dustin insisted that he would play that evening. Thelma was firm. 'I'm sorry, but we won't let you into the theatre. We don't want you.' 'You're the Jewish mother I never had,' Dustin replied with a wan smile, and resigned himself to missing a performance.

Meanwhile, Brian Poyser, who played the small role of Balthasar and was Dustin's understudy, was enjoying a lunch and a pleasant stroll in Holland Park with a friend before arriving at the theatre as usual at around 6 p.m. There, the company manager, Roger Richardson, was tearing out what little hair he had left in anguish. He had been trying to reach Brian all day to tell him he was to play Shylock. After the initial shock, Poyser had little time to think about it. Inevitably, when the theatre manager announced to the audience that Dustin was not able to perform that night, a huge groan, enough to shake the chandeliers, went up. Most of the people who had queued for tickets or bought them from touts for more than double the price had done so to see Dustin, for them the *raison d'être* of the production, and were not particularly interested in Shakespeare *per se*. Over half the audience left and had their money refunded. Pity those who had to try and track down the touts. Those that remained were obviously more interested in the play and production than the star who was Shylock.

Although ill in bed, Dustin, who knew exactly the times of Shylock's exits and entrances, phoned the theatre three times during the performance to speak to Poyser – after the first scene, at the interval and after the Trial scene. Each time, he asked his understudy, 'How is it going? Did you get a laugh at that moment? Did they like it?' and so on. He was ringing to reassure himself that his absence had not caused a disaster, because he suffered an element of guilt about letting the company and audiences down. (The calls may not have been so reassuring for Poyser.)

On the last call, he asked Poyser if there was something he could steal from him. Poyser replied, 'You don't steal from me, I steal from you.' 'You're full of shit!', replied Dustin. When the final curtain came down, he had Lisa hold the phone to his ear to hear what the applause was like.

Against doctor's orders, Dustin was back for the next day's performance. That evening, Poyser found a bottle of champagne in his dressing-room: 'In appreciation – Dustin'.

Although Dustin avoided interviews and spent most of his free time with his family during the run, he was no shrinking violet when it came to certain causes taken up by the British acting establishment. He became involved in a campaign to save the remains of the Elizabethan Rose Theatre on Bankside, where it was said Shakespeare had acted and where it was probable that *Henry VI, Part I* was first performed. He was among prominent figures from the theatre world, including Lord Olivier (shortly before his death), Dame Peggy Ashcroft, Dame Judi Dench, Ian McKellen and Vanessa Redgrave, who stood on the site that was about to be buried by the building of a skyscraper.

On Thursday, 7 September, a gala production of *The Merchant* was held before a celebrity audience in aid of the reconstruction fund for the Globe Theatre on Bankside. It raised about £250,000, which was added to the £3 million already raised towards the £15 million target. The audience, paying upwards of £100 a ticket, included Prince Edward, Michael Caine, Bob Hoskins, and Sam Wanamaker, the Globe's driving force. After the play, four hundred and fifty guests had dinner at the Savoy's Lancaster Room, taken there by five specially commissioned London buses. Dustin did another star turn by attempting to sort out the seating arrangements at the hotel, where problems meant that dinner started twenty minutes late.

After the final performance of *The Merchant of Venice* on Saturday, 24 September, Dustin held a ritual shaving-off of his beard. He then trotted down Shaftesbury Avenue like the Pied Piper, followed by a growing band of admirers, until he reached a Greek taverna off Tottenham Court Road. He ran upstairs and started showering his fans with red roses. A passing motorist, who was distracted by the scene, smashed into the back of another car.

The adventure in England was over. He would now go home, rest, and then prepare to play Shylock on Broadway, taking with him Leigh Lawson (Antonio), Nathaniel Parker (Bassanio) and Geraldine James (Portia) from the London cast. Because of Equity restrictions, some of the others had to be left behind and nine Americans were added. Dustin was the perfect host. As backstage conditions in Broadway theatres are often appalling, he made sure that members of the company were as comfortable as possible, seeing that they were provided with hot water and heating.

The Merchant of Venice opened on 19 December 1989 for a limited run of twelve weeks at the West 46th Street Theater, where there was already a box-office advance of more than $20 million, a proof of how film-star status can swell American theatre audiences, even for Shakespeare. It had to be extended another few weeks because of 'public demand'.

The critics were not completely sold. Frank Rich in *The New York Times* said, 'Contrary to Broadway gospel, Dustin Hoffman does not have star billing in the new *Merchant of Venice*. That honour is reserved instead for the Peter Hall Company – or, to put a finer point on it, for Peter Hall. Once you've seen the production, in many ways an unexpected one, you'll understand that Mr [sic] Hall isn't being pretentious and that Mr Hoffman hasn't suddenly been struck by false modesty. This really is the director's *Merchant* – at times Shakespeare's too – and Mr Hoffman plays a supporting role. It's the modern practice that Shylock dominates any version of the *Merchant*, whatever the interpretation, despite the fact that he appears in five of the twenty scenes. Mr Hoffman's Shylock – meticulous, restlessly intelligent, emotionally and physically lightweight – does not. His performance is a character actor's polished gem rather than a tragedian's stab at the jugular . . . Mr Hoffman looks unprepared to take the dangerous leap or risk an audience's revulsion or condemnation.'

Howard Kissel of the *New York Daily News* wrote: 'Dustin Hoffman has cleaned up his quirky Shylock somewhat since London, but it's still undeniable that if he were an unknown actor auditioning for the role, he wouldn't get it . . . but he does less obnoxious grinning than he did in London.'

However, *Variety* thought that Dustin was 'Outstanding as an ironic, maligned Shylock . . . [He] plays Shylock as a humorous, soft-spoken, reasonable businessman who only turns nasty when the full fury of the Christian majority's hate is unleashed on him . . . Hoffman's not a physically imposing actor, but he has a great authority on stage, and his underplaying is very effective. He's apparently done a lot of work in the vocal woodshed, since his voice is deeper and more penetrating than in the past . . . Quality British Shakespeare with an American star is a recipe for big ducats at the b.o. and this *Merchant* would clean up as long as Hoffman cared to stay with it.'

Again, even more than in London, Dustin received a multitude of visitors backstage – there were so many that he had to take a special reception room in the theatre. Dustin, Geraldine James and Sir Peter Hall were nominated for Tony Awards on 3 June 1990, although they all came away empty-handed. The fulfilling experience determined Dustin to return to the stage in the near future, and to tackle Shakespeare again.

31

Mongrels, Mumbles and Munificence

*An actor must work. There's no deeper depression for an actor than waking up
in the morning with no one to perform to.*

SOME MONTHS BEFORE he had even thought of putting on Shylock's Jewish gabardine and *yamulka*, and while he was still spouting
chunks of *Hamlet* to anybody who would listen, Dustin was sniffing
around a few film projects. In the summer of 1988, Cinecom Pictures had a
contract for Lasse Hallström, the Swedish director, to make his first
American picture. Dustin, who adored Hallström's *My Life as a Dog*
('Why can't I be in a movie like that?') was set to star in the film, to be
called *Once Around*, due to start shooting in February 1989. Because he was
still busy filming *Rain Man*, Dustin requested a delay, putting it off until
late August 1989, but when *The Merchant of Venice* came up, he dropped
out of the movie altogether, too late to get the film back on track.

Meanwhile, Dustin had decided to work for the first time with veteran
director Sidney Lumet, who had just completed the old-fashionedly
liberal *Running on Empty*. This project was *Family Business*, New York
story based on a novel by Vincent Patrick, with whom Dustin had wanted
to do *My New Partner*. So instead of playing a cop, Dustin settled, for the
fifth time in his film career, for portraying someone on the wrong side of
the law. (The other four were *Midnight Cowboy*, *Papillon*, *Lenny* and
Straight Time.)

Aside from the wish to associate with Lumet, there was the prospect of
co-starring with two stars from generations on either side of his own, the
now increasingly respected 58-year-old Sean Connery, and 27-year-old
Matthew Broderick, Tom Cruise's contemporary.

Ever since his early days in live television, Lumet believed in a lengthy
rehearsal period followed by a speedy shooting schedule. If Dustin was
going to do any soul-searching and research on this one, he had to do it
during the three weeks of rehearsal in a large hall on New York's Lower
East Side, before filming began on 14 November 1988.

'In a sense, you've killed the first three weeks with most movies because
it usually takes that long before people start letting others into their lives,'
Dustin commented. 'At the start of any film there is a kind of barrier

separating the actors. The way Sidney works, you're at a place when you start shooting that you wouldn't be in most pictures until you were halfway through them.'

The 64-year-old Lumet had been part of the first generation of TV directors who made it in the movies. Seven of his first nine movies, shot in black-and-white, were marked by heightened naturalism and theatricality, the first and best being *Twelve Angry Men* (1957). He had directed Dustin's idol, Marlon Brando, in *The Fugitive Kind* (1959); *View from the Bridge* (1961), based on the play in which Dustin made his acting debut at college; and Dustin's lookalike, Al Pacino, in *Serpico* (1973) and *Dog Day Afternoon* (1975). Lumet had already directed Connery in four films, one of them, *The Anderson Tapes*, a heist movie that begs comparison with *Family Business*, unflattering to the latter. In general, Lumet is more in his element among the cops, crooks and corruption of the city streets than with overblown woolly fables like *The Pawnbroker* (1965), *Network* (1976), *Equus* (1977) and *The Wiz* (1978). No so here. Although Lumet is one of the few directors of real stature that Dustin has worked with, he did not provide him with a movie of comparable weight.

Despite being mostly filmed on location in New York, the city in *Family Business* is not used very imaginatively, apart from the opening sequence in which the camera moves from the conventional Manhattan skyline to the tattier Bronx. Some of the scenes were shot in the 2nd Avenue Deli in the East Village, where the waiters remembered Dustin from when *Death of a Salesman* was playing at the Broadhurst Theater and they used to send food up to the cast.

The first person we see in the film is Dustin, complaining about the cab fares to the Bronx where he is visiting his Jewish wife's parents at a Passover dinner. It takes some time to realise with growing disbelief that Dustin plays the son of Connery (exactly seven years Dustin's senior) and the father of Broderick. It is explained thus: Scottish Connery, with Red Indian blood, married a Sicilian, who gave birth to Dustin who married a Jew, who gave birth to Broderick. The fact that an Irish wake is held for Connery in the end should surprise nobody. If Lumet's and Patrick's aim was to represent the New York melting pot in one family, then it is a cackhanded idea, because it is as unintentionally risible to cast the three vastly contrasting stars as grandfather, father and son as it was intentionally amusing to co-star Arnold Schwarzenegger and Danny De Vito as the eponymous *Twins*. 'He would have been at least five feet taller if he'd had more Scottish genes,' says Connery of his 'son'.

The curious casting would not have mattered greatly, despite the central importance of genes to the plot, if the movie were not as much of a mishmash as the fictional family. Broadly, the story concerns the McMullen clan, patriarch Jessie (Connery), whose vocation is crime, his son Vito (Hoffman) raised to be a thief but now in the meat business, and *his* son Adam (Broderick), an MIT graduate who hopes to follow in his grandfather's felonious footsteps. Their women (Rosana DeSoto, Janet Carroll and Victoria Jackson) are merely peripheral.

Connery, a loveable rogue, who has spent a good deal of his time in prison, is seen as someone to be emulated. The Scottish-accented star turned down the film at first because he thought, quite rightly, that Lumet should have got someone like Burt Lancaster, who would have been much more in the mould of the character. Nevertheless, Connery generates some charm, as does Broderick as his grandson. But charm has obviously skipped a generation when we consider Dustin's Vito, this time overdoing his familiar little moues. He is a petty thug who beats up one of his badly-paid employees for stealing some meat; it is an essentially unsympathetic role, but not a very challenging one. It was bound to disappoint because Dustin has always created high expectations in audiences over the years.

Dustin's nose seems longer than usual, he keeps blowing it for no reason at all, and his face without make-up has never looked so lined. It is sobering to observe that the days when the adjective 'boyish' was used to describe him are now firmly over, no matter what he plays. He has finally entered the category of middle-aged actor, admittedly long after most other actors of his age. But as Dustin (as Michael Dorsey in *Tootsie*) says, 'I'm a character actor – age has no effect on me.'

Family Business never settles for one thing or another, moving jerkily from comedy to drama, farce to tragedy, melodrama to thriller. It is best as the last, although it takes over an hour before there is any action. The heist in which the three generations are involved provides an indication of what the film might have been. Connery and Hoffman flee the scene of the crime while Broderick is caught like a rabbit in the headlights of the police car. An interesting denouement seems in prospect as the moral dilemma revolving around whether the two older men should admit guilt in order to free the youngest is posed. Unfortunately, it resolves itself in a pretty feeble and overly sentimental manner with Connery's death. The threat of life imprisonment does not alter the rather dubious philosophy that the family that steals together stays together. Dustin as Vito claims that the caper was 'the most fun we've had since we were kids'.

'You turned out to be a piece of garbage,' Broderick yells at his father near the end, a dangerous line that a nasty critic could easily have paraphrased. Despite the impressive superstar line-up, American audiences stayed away. It grossed only $12 million in its two months' release – a figure not much higher than the combined fees of its three stars.

Most of the reviews were unflattering, although *Variety* considered it 'one of the year's better films' – and this was written in December 1989! The critic went on: 'Director Sidney Lumet has crafted a film with real pathos mercifully bereft of the shameless sentimentality that's run rampant this season, while writer Vincent Patrick injects enough bawdy humour to create a delightful mixed bag spiced with almost European sensibility . . . Hoffman has worked his own quiet magic following his Oscar for *Rain Man* with another deft performance that's less flashy but calls for greater inner strength.'

After *Family Business* had opened to complete indifference in the USA, and while Dustin was limbering up to take on Shylock, his erstwhile co-star from *Ishtar* was gathering a starry cast for his loudly hyped *Dick Tracy* (referred to in the business as Warren Beatty's Dick). Chester Gould's original comic-strip, on which the film was based, began life in 1931, and had already been made into four Saturday afternoon serials, four shoestring RKO feature films (with Morgan Conway and Ralph Byrd as the jut-jawed detective, in two each) and, on TV, both a live-action and an animated cartoon series.

Among the directors considered along the way, from when the film option was bought in 1974, were Martin Scorsese, Roman Polanski, Brian De Palma, Walter Hill, Richard Benjamin and John Landis, while Harrison Ford, Clint Eastwood and James Caan were all keen to play the title role. (Caan ended up with two minutes in it.) But Warren Beatty won out to produce, direct and star, with a budget of around $20 million, and another $10 million for marketing and post-production.

The part of Breathless Mahoney was especially written for Madonna, Beatty's girlfriend at the time; Al Pacino played the leading heavy, Big Boy Caprice, and Beatty managed to talk James Caan, Charles Durning, Mandy Patinkin, Paul Dorvino, Dick Van Dyke and others into doing cameos and spending hours in make-up. At one stage there was a suggestion that they try and get Ronald Reagan to play Pruneface (without make-up?). However, they gave R. G. Armstrong a vaguely Reaganite look in the role. And with Al Pacino in the cast, how could Dustin refuse? Beatty knew he had to work fast before the actor left for England for the run of *The Merchant of Venice*, and, a few days before he was due in London, Dustin was sitting in the make-up chair for three hours at a time, being transformed for the part of Mumbles, with a blonde wig, thick false eyebrows and a prosthetic twisted mouth and bulging lips that would make his lines barely audible. It was back to the agonies of *Little Big Man* and *Tootsie* – but he was much younger then.

'Next time Warren calls, say "no",' he muttered to himself as he submitted to the make-up experts. Because Mumble's diction makes him incomprehensible, Dustin was able to say anything he wanted against Beatty and get away with it. While waiting for the lighting and cameras, he could pace around the stylised sets in his purple suit and hat, mumbling Shylock's iambic pentameters. As Beatty only had Dustin for three days, he shot without rest, so by the time Dustin left for England there was a full hour of Mumbles on film, about five minutes of which found its way into the entertaining, visually striking but ultimately mindless movie.

Al Pacino, looking like Robert De Niro as Richard III, steals the picture, and the rest of the cast, including Madonna, injects some life into the two-dimensional comic-book characters. However, Warren Beatty miscast himself in the title role. He is far too bland and soft to convince as a hero in the Dick Tracy mould. And although he wears no prosthetic mask (unlike most of the cast), it looks nonetheless as if ageing lines have been drawn over his still handsome face.

It was said that Dustin's cameo was based on Robert Evans, though only intimates of the movie mogul would have got the joke. His few appearances are fairly funny, playing on the single gag of being a stool-pigeon whose ratting on his friends to the police cannot be understood. When Tracy gives him the third degree, he repeats Raymond Babbitt's phrase, 'I dunno know, I dunno know', in a garbled manner before blurting out something like, 'Beep, beep,' which completely baffles the stenographer. This, when played back slowly on a tape recorder, reveals that he was saying 'Big Boy did it.' Unfortunately, the comic idea is ruined by the tame twist (like his mouth) that shows he is in fact able to be more lucid should he so wish.

In May 1990, before the release of *Dick Tracy*, a tanned Dustin appeared as one of the many stars on a Time Warner TV Special celebrating Earth Day – ninety minutes of anti-pollution propaganda, rather like those wartime documentaries in which famous people warned the populace about 'careless talk' and food hoarding. On the whole, the show, though over-long, was informative and done with a light touch. In his sketch with Robin Williams, Dustin represented the unconcerned, selfish individual, while Williams played 'Everyman'. Dustin advises Williams not to worry about oil slicks ('If all the fish in the world died, you could always eat imitation crab meat. It's delicious,'), the hole in the ozone layer ('Have you never heard of sunscreen?'), the cutting down of the rain forests ('They were so big you'd get lost in them,'), the melting of the polar caps ('If you want snow you go to Maine,'), or the pollution of the atmosphere ('You keep your windows closed or you go to the Mall'). It was a pity, though, that Dustin presented a face that had plainly been exposed to the harmful rays of the sun, thus going against one of the programme's messages. Or was it in keeping with the reactionary character he was playing?

Because of Dustin's well-known championship of 'good causes', he is continually being asked to lend his name to charities and campaigns, some of which he is pleased to associate himself with. In 1983, he helped Nazi-hunter Simon Wiesenthal by sending letters to public figures and the press to boost recruitment at the secret centre where Wiesenthal works. Dustin also provided the commentary for *Common Threads*, on Oscar-winning documentary about AIDS; and in April 1990, he was one of the sponsors (others included Paul Newman, Harold Pinter and Sir Peter Hall) of Symposium 90, a five-day conference on Soviet history held at East Grinstead, Sussex, and organised by Vanessa Redgrave.

Over the years, there have been a number of instances of Hoffman the Munificent. An example has been his generous contribution to Camp Good Times in California, for children with cancer. He first got involved in it when Lisa's cousin told him of her dream to build a camp where her eleven-year-old son David, who had leukaemia, could go without being the victim of ridicule because of his physical disability. 'These kids are so upbeat,' Dustin says of the children there, 'it really knocks me out. They have this wonderful optimistic outlook of "live the day and whatever happens will happen".'

In March 1990, a terminally ill student who needed a bone marrow donor received Dustin's support. He made a five-figure donation to the cause of twenty-year-old Allison Atlas, who was told she had between three and six months to live unless a marrow transplant checked her leukaemia. Dustin refused to say how much money he gave, but his publicist confirmed it was more than £62,500. He asked his showbusiness friends to help, and offered to pay for a holiday for the donor who matched Miss Atlas. Unfortunately, the chances of finding a donor were about one in twenty thousand and, before a match could be found, Allison died.

A man with cerebral palsy, who claimed to be Arthur Miller's nephew, and told Dustin that he had always wanted to act, appeared as one of Dustin's acting students in *Tootsie*. Dustin wanted to send him to acting school, but was told by teachers it would be fruitless. But he did put a salesgirl he met in a Madison Avenue dress shop through acting school, and did the same for Carl Olsen, a construction superintendent who renovated the Hoffman's apartment. A girl with bad teeth won a beauty pageant after Dustin had arranged to have them fixed. And Dr Amy Rosenman, the obstetrician who had delivered Lisa's first child against all the odds, was offered a trip to Hawaii – if she lost 30 lb.

'I don't like just to write a cheque to charity. It's so much better to see the impact. I see people with bad teeth or bad skin, and I walk away feeling bad because I couldn't find a way to help them without hurting their feelings. It's something they can't control.'

Apart from Dustin's genuine altruism, finely balancing his egotism, there is a compulsion to have as much control as possible over his own destiny and that of others. That is why he has often regretted that he never became the doctor his parents once encouraged him to be. Then he really would have been in control of life and death. The process has fascinated him to such a degree that a doctor friend has allowed him into the operating theatre to photograph operations. If, unlike George Burns, he would not get the chance to play God in a film, he could still do his utmost to play Him in life.

32

Dusty Meets His Maker

We had to find something new to worship, so we replaced God with the orgasm.

'I'M SORRY, GOD, that I once called you a mother-fucker. I felt so bitter after my mother died. Of course, you couldn't be, could you? But you might be pleased to hear that, since my marriage to Lisa, I have rediscovered you and my ethnic roots. I used to have so much guilt about my lack of Jewish faith that I'd block out all the holidays. Lisa encouraged me to become more observant of Judaism and pass it on to the children. I want to learn Hebrew now, and I would love to be bar-mitzvahed. I regret I never was. I've been reading a vast amount of books about the people you chose. What a responsibility! Irving Howe's *World of Our Fathers*, Elie Wiesel's *A Jew Today, Asimov's Guide to the Bible*, books on the prophets and the Torah, so I know a little more of what you are about.

'I used to feel that if the devil came and offered me a dramatic masterpiece in exchange for the rest of my life, I would instantly sign a contract with him. Now I wouldn't sign quite so quickly – that's the difference. Only kidding. But I still can't control the demons inside me. Now I'm fifty-two, I crave something positive to calm them down. I'd like myself better if I didn't have my demons, but they're part of my internal furniture, and they always come back. I've prayed to you all my life, even when I didn't believe you existed. But I can't shake off the feeling that your protective wing isn't exactly over me and mine.

'My greatest fear is that my home will catch on fire and my children will be caught in it. I'm pretty sure I'd go in and save them, but it would be from the head, not the heart. The whole time I'd be doing it, I'd be saying, "Isn't there some way we could all get out of this? Maybe the kid could lose a leg or something." The babies were at the door to greet us the other night. "Hi, Mommy, hi, Daddy." It was one of those beautiful images that almost made me cry. After they want to bed, Lisa said, "Will you ever forget the way they looked?" and I said, "No." But much as I loved it, it frightened me. It's really prolonged happiness I'm suspicious of. As soon as things are really good, I always have the feeling the rug is about to be pulled out from under me. On a beautiful day in California, there's always a thin layer of smog. With me, there's always a thin layer of fear. It's the old too-good-to-be-true business that never leaves me. A big wave of happiness surges over me, like a shaft of light from heaven, and I hear a voice behind it saying, "Are you sure there isn't an earthquake coming?"

'Life can be so great and yet everything is sad because it's going to be over. It hit me in the shower the other night, watching my young child rock from one foot to the other, going "ul-ul-ul-ul". It was so great to watch, but under the best of circumstances everything is still dying. That's why religion is so important. That's why I pray to you more now.

'My life was like a jump-cut. Before I knew it, I was suddenly married, successful beyond my wildest dreams, and I had a town house. But the same person was still on the couch. Perhaps I'd like to have as an epitaph on my gravestone: "He plummeted to stardom". One of the main things about being successful is that I stopped being afraid of dying. I was always obsessed with death, obsessed with things ending, my career being finished. Now I'm not so much. I couldn't understand why that was for a long time, and finally I realised it's because, when you're a movie star, you're already dead. You're embalmed.

'I've often thought that I missed out, that I got hoodwinked by this movie stardom because I was beginning to build a reputation for myself on stage. But then I determined to take as much care as I could in the films I would make. But producers never understand that. All they want is to get it together, get the people that package it, boom-boom, get it on the floor and start shooting. Yet you read about Ingmar Bergman walking up and down his island with Sven Nykvist, talking about the feeling and lighting of a film for three months. Of course, you might not approve of his God-less universe, but that's besides the point. Everybody else does this in art – painters, writers. That's the wonderful thing about art, the daydreaming aspect of it, the sharing of it. That's why you do it! Because you have a feeling for what you add to it. You know what I mean, being a bit of a producer yourself, as well as that great director in the sky. Maybe that's why I've never really trusted you.

'Just because I strive for perfection, I'm accused of being "difficult". I've had fifteen film directors and there are probably four of them whom I had a tough time with. I'd like to say, though, that it was some of their best work. If they don't see something you see, then you're "difficult"; and worse than that, if they're satisfied before you are, then they really hate you. As I once sang in a film whose title I prefer to forget: "Telling the truth can be a dangerous business". The plight of the actor, even if he's a star, is the plight of the women's movement. They're saying the same thing to us. Get into bed, give me a good time, then give me something to eat, go get the laundry, be a good girl and behave yourself and let us men get on with what counts. That's how they treat actors. Actors, in a sense, have always been designed to play the so-called passive feminine role. That's always displeased me.

'I suppose sex freed me from the responsibility to live life; I allowed myself to get lost in a moment of ecstasy. Somehow, when I work, it gets easier because I can truly lose myself and work with people I love. My real fear is to reach that point in my life when there is no turning back and suddenly you know you've blown it. You know, I really blew it!

'I believe in life *before* death, but I also believe in life *after* death. I guess I'm very susceptible to mystery and I have to believe that after you die you really do go on. But I want to decide when it's a good day to die. But the emotional knowledge of death tells me I can't. I start to clock things more, to delineate more between what's really important and what isn't. The fuller my life gets, the less wasted time and energy I spend arguing and fighting.

'You nearly got me a few times, didn't you, God? You threw fire, bombs and electric shocks at me, but I survived. You tried to take my wife and baby. But they came through. I know you're going to catch me one day, but I'm going to be moving awful fast until you do. So now I want to have my dance before it's over.'

FILMOGRAPHY

THE TIGER MAKES OUT
USA 1967. Elan for Columbia. *Director*: Arthur Hiller. *Producer*: George
Justin. *Screenplay*: Murray Schisgal (from his play). *Director of Photography*:
Arthur J. Ornitz. *Music*: Milton (Shorty) Rogers. *Cast*: Eli Wallach (Ben),
Anne Jackson (Gloria), Bob Dishy (Jerry), David Burns (Mr Ratner),
Charles Nelson Reilly (Registrar), Ruth White (Mrs Kelly), Roland Wood
(Mr Kelly), Dustin Hoffman (Hap). 94 mins.

**MADIGAN'S MILLIONS (EL MILLION DE MADIGAN/UN DOLL-
ARO PER 7 VIGLIACCHI)**
Spanish/Italian 1967. Westside International for Trans America Films.
Director: Stanley Prager. *Producer*: Sidney Pink. *Screenplay*: Jim Henaghan,
J. L. Bayonas. *Director of Photography*: Manolo Rojas. *Music*: G. Gregory
Segura. *Cast*: Dustin Hoffman (Jason Fister), Cesar Romero (Mike Madi-
gan), Elsa Martinelli (Vicky Shaw), Gustavo Rojo (Lt Arco), Fernando
Hilbeck (Burke), Franco Fabrizzi (Condon). 76 mins.

THE GRADUATE
USA 1967. Embassy. *Director*: Mike Nichols. *Producer*: Lawrence Turman.
Screenplay: Calder Willingham, Buck Henry (based on the novel by Charles
Webb). *Director of Photography*: Robert Surtees. *Production Design*: Richard
Sylbert. *Music*: Paul Simon. *Costume*: Patricia Zipprodt. *Make-up*: Harry
Maret. *Cast*: Anne Bancroft (Mrs Robinson) Dustin Hoffman (Benjamin
Braddock), Katharine Ross (Elaine Robinson), William Daniels (Mr
Braddock), Murray Hamilton (Mr Robinson), Elizabeth Wilson (Mrs
Braddock), Brian Avery (Carl Smith), Walter Brooke (Mr Maguire),
Norman Fell (Mr McCleery), Buck Henry (room clerk). 105 mins.

MIDNIGHT COWBOY
USA 1969. United Artists. *Director*: John Schlesinger. *Producer*: Jerome
Hellman. *Screenplay*: Waldo Salt (based on the novel by James Leo Her-
lihy). *Director of Photography*: Adam Holender. *Production Design*: John
Robert Lloyd. *Music*: John Barry. *Cast*: John Voight (Joe Buck), Dustin

Hoffman (Ratso Rizzo), Sylvia Miles (Cass) Brenda Vaccaro (Shirley), John McGiver (Mr O'Daniel), Barnard Hughes (Towny), Ruth White (Sally Buck), Jennifer Salt. 113 mins.

JOHN AND MARY
USA 1969. Debrod for Twentieth Century-Fox. *Direction*: Peter Yates. *Producer*: Ben Kadish. *Screenplay*: John Mortimer (based on the novel by Mervyn Jones). *Director of Photography*: Gayne Rescher. *Production Design*: John Robert Lloyd. *Cast*: Dustin Hoffman (John), Mia Farrow (Mary), Michael Tolan (James), Sunny Griffin (Ruth), Tyne Daly (Hilary), Stanley Beck (Ernest). 92 mins.

LITTLE BIG MAN
USA 1970. Stockbridge/Hiller/Cinema Center for Twentieth Century-Fox. *Director*: Arthur Penn. *Producer*: Stuart Millar. *Screenplay*: Calder Willingham (from the novel by Thomas Berger). *Director of Photography*: Harry Stradling. *Production Design*: Dean Tavoularis. *Music*: John Hammond. *Costumes*: Dorothy Jenkins. *Make-up* (for Dustin Hoffman): Dick Smith. *Cast*: Dustin Hoffman (Jack Crabb), Martin Balsam (Alardyce T. Meriweather), Faye Dunaway (Mrs Pendrake), Chief Dan George (Old Lodge Skins), Richard Mulligan (General George Custer), Jeff Corey (Wild Bill Hickok), Amy Eccles (Sunshine), Kelly Jean Peters (Olga), Carole Androsky (Caroline), Robert Little Star (Little Horse). 147 mins.

WHO IS HARRY KELLERMAN AND WHY IS HE SAYING THOSE TERRIBLE THINGS ABOUT ME?
USA 1971. Cinema Center. *Director*: Ulu Grosbard. *Producers*: Grosbard, Herb Gardner. *Screenplay*: Gardner. *Director of Photography*: Victor Kemper. *Production Design*: Harry Horner. *Music*: Shel Silverstein. *Cast*: Dustin Hoffman (Georgie Soloway), Barbara Harris (Allison), Jack Warden (Dr Moses), David Burns (Leon), Gabriel Dell (Sid), Dom DeLuise (Irwin) Rose Gregorio (Gloria). 108 mins.

STRAW DOGS
UK 1971. Talent Associates/Amerbroco. *Director*: Sam Peckinpah. *Producer*: Daniel Melnick. *Screenplay*: David Zelag Goodman, Peckinpah, Hoffman (based on the novel *The Siege of Trencher's Farm* by Gordon M. Williams). *Director of Photography*: John Coquillon. *Music*: Jerry Fielding. *Cast*: Dustin Hoffman (David Sumner), Susan George (Amy), David Warner (Henry Niles), Peter Vaughan (Tom Hedden), T. P. McKenna (Major Scott), Colin Welland (Revd Hood). 118 mins.

ALFREDO ALFREDO
Italy/USA 1971. Rizzoli/Francoriz RPA. *Director*: Pietro Germi. *Screenplay*: Leo Benvenuti, Tullio Pinelli, Piero De Bernardi. *Director of Photography*: Aiace Parolin. *Music*: Carlo Rustichelli. *Cast*: Dustin Hoffman (Alfredo), Carla Gravina (Carolina), Stefania Sandrelli (Mariarosa), Clara Colosimo (Carolina's mother), Daniele Patella (Carolina's father), Saro Urzi (Mariarosa's father), Danika La Loggia (Mariarosa's mother). 98 mins.

PAPILLON
USA 1973. Papillon Partnership/Corona/General Production Company. *Director*: Franklin Schaffner. *Producers*: Robert Dorfmann, Schaffner. *Executive Producer*: Ted Richmond. *Screenplay*: Dalton Trumbo, Lorenzo Semple Jr (from the novel by Henri Charrière). *Director of Photography*: Fred Koenekamp. *Production Design*: Anthony Masters. *Music*: Jerry Goldsmith. *Costumes*: Anthony Powell. *Make-up*: Charles Schram. *Cast*: Steve McQueen (Papillon), Dustin Hoffman (Dega), Don Gordon (Julot), Anthony Zerbe (leper colony chief), George Coulouris (Dr Chatal), Woodrow Parfrey (Clusiot), Victor Jory (Indian chief). 150 mins.

LENNY
USA 1974. United Artists. *Director*: Bob Fosse. *Producer*: Marvin Worth. *Screenplay*: Julian Barry (from his play). *Director of Photography*: Bruce Surtees. *Production Design*: Joel Schiller. *Music*: Ralph Burns. *Cast*: Dustin Hoffman (Lenny Bruce), Valerie Perrine (Honey Harlow), Jan Miner (Sally), Stanley Beck (Artie Silver), Gary Morton (Sherman Hart). 111 mins.

ALL THE PRESIDENT'S MEN
USA 1976. Wildwood Enterprise Production for Warner Bros. *Director*: Alan J. Pakula. *Producer*: Walter Coblenz. *Executive Producers*: Robert Redford, Pakula. *Screenplay*: William Goldman (based on the book by Carl Bernstein and Bob Woodward). *Director of Photography*: Gordon Willis. *Production Design*: George Jenkins. *Music*: Nicholas C. Washington. *Cast*: Dustin Hoffman (Carl Bernstein), Robert Redford (Bob Woodward), Jack Warden (Harry Rosenfeld), Martin Balsam (Howard Simon), Hal Holbrook (Deep Throat), Jason Robards Jr (Ben Bradlee), Jane Alexander (bookkeeper), Robert Walden (Donald Segretti). 138 mins.

MARATHON MAN
USA 1976. Paramount. *Director*: John Schlesinger. *Producers*: Robert Evans, Sidney Beckerman. *Screenplay*: William Goldman (from his

novel). *Director of Photography*: Conrad Hall. *Production Design*: Richard MacDonald. *Music*: Michael Small. *Cast*: Dustin Hoffman (Babe), Laurence Olivier (Szell), Roy Scheider (Doc), Marthe Keller (Elsa), William Devane (Janeway), Fritz Weaver (Prof. Biesenthal). 126 mins.

STRAIGHT TIME
USA 1978. First Artists/SweetWall for Warner Bros. *Director*: Ulu Grosbard. *Producers*: Stanley Beck, Tim Zinnemann. *Screenplay*: Alvin Sargent, Edward Bunker, Jeffrey Boam (based on the novel *No Beast So Fierce* by Bunker). *Director of Photography*: Owen Roizman. *Production Design*: Stephen Grimes. *Music*: David Shire. *Costumes*: Bernie Pollack. *Cast*: Dustin Hoffman (Max Dembo), Theresa Russell (Jenny Mercer), Harry Dean Stanton (Jerry Schue), Gary Busey (Willy Darin), M. Emmet Walsh (Earl Frank), Sandy Barron (Manny), Kathy Bates (Selma Darin). 114 mins.

AGATHA
UK/USA 1979. First Artists/SweetWall/Casablanca. *Director*: Michael Apted. *Producers*: Jarvis Astaire, Gavrik Losey. *Screenplay*: Kathleen Tynan, Arthur Hopcraft. *Story*: Tynan. *Director of Photography*: Vittorio Storaro. *Production Design*: Shirley Russell. *Music*: Johnny Mandel. *Cast*: Vanessa Redgrave (Agatha Christie), Dustin Hoffman (Wally Stanton), Timothy Dalton (Archie Christie), Helen Morse (Evelyn), Timothy West (Kenward), Tony Britten (William Collins), Alan Badel (Lord Brackenbury), Celia Gregory (Nancy Neele). 105 mins.

KRAMER VS KRAMER
USA 1979. Columbia. *Director*: Robert Benton. *Producer*: Stanley R. Jaffe. *Screenplay*: Benton (from the novel by Avery Corman). *Director of Photography*: Nestor Almendros. *Production Design*: Paul Sylbert. *Music*: Antonio Vivaldi, Henry Purcell. *Cast*: Dustin Hoffman (Ted Kramer), Meryl Streep (Joanna Kramer), Justin Henry (Billy Kramer), Jane Alexander (Margaret Phelps), Howard Duff (John Shaunessy), Jobeth Williams (Phyllis Bernard). 105 mins.

TOOTSIE
USA 1982. A Mirage/Punch Production for Columbia. *Director*: Sydney Pollack. *Producers*: Pollack, Dick Richards. *Executive Producer*: Charles Evans. *Screenplay*: Larry Gelbart, Murray Schisgal. *Story*: Don McGuire, Gelbart. *Director of Photography*: Owen Roizman. *Production Design*: Peter Larkin. *Music*: Dave Grusin. *Costumes*: Ruth Morley. *Make-up (for

Dustin Hoffman): Dorothy Pearl, George Masters. *Cast*: Dustin Hoffman (Michael Dorsey/Dorothy Michaels), Jessica Lange (Julie), Teri Garr (Sandy), Dabney Coleman (Ron), Charles Durning (Les), Bill Murray (Jeff), Sydney Pollack (George Fields), George Gaynes (John Van Horn), Geena Davis (April). 100 mins.

DEATH OF A SALESMAN
USA 1985. A Roxbury-Punch Production for CBS. *Director*: Volker Schlöndorff. *Producer*: Robert F. Colesberry. *Screenplay*: Arthur Miller. *Director of Photography*: Michael Ballhaus. *Production Design*: Tony Walton. *Music*: Alex North. *Costumes*: Ruth Morley. *Make-up*: Bob Laden. *Cast*: Dustin Hoffman (Willy Loman), Kate Reid (Linda Loman), John Malkovich (Biff), Stephen Lang (Happy), Charles Durning (Charley), David S. Chandler (Bernard), Louis Zorich (Uncle Ben), Jon Polito (Howard), Kathy Rossetter (woman in Boston). 133 mins.

ISHTAR
USA 1987. Columbia-Delphi V Productions. *Director*: Elaine May. *Producer*: Warren Beatty. *Screenplay*: Elaine May. *Director of Photography*: Vittorio Storaro. *Production Design*: Paul Sylbert. *Music*: Dave Grusin. *Costumes*: Anthony Powell. *Make-up*: Bob Jiras, Alan Boyle. *Cast*: Dustin Hoffman (Chuck Clarke), Isabelle Adjani (Sirra Assei), Warren Beatty (Lyle Rogers), Charles Grodin (Jim Harrison), Jack Weston (Marty Freed), Tess Harper (Willa), Carol Kane (Carol), Aharon Ipale (Emir Yousef), Fuad Hageb (Abdul). 107 mins.

RAIN MAN
USA 1988. A Guber-Peters Company Production for United Artists. *Director*: Barry Levinson. *Producer*: Mark Johnson. *Executive Producer*: Peter Guber, Jon Peters. *Screenplay*: Ronald Bass, Barry Morrow. *Story*: Morrow. *Director of Photography*: John Seale. *Production Design*: Ida Random. *Music*: Hans Zimmer. *Costumes*: Bernie Pollack. *Make-up*: Rick Sharp, Ed Butterworth. *Cast*: Dustin Hoffman (Raymond Babbitt), Tom Cruise (Charlie Babbitt), Valeria Golino (Susanna), Jerry Molen (Dr Bruner), Jack Murdock (John Mooney), Michael D. Roberts (Vern), Ralph Seymour (Lenny), Barry Levinson (psychiatrist). 133 mins.

FAMILY BUSINESS
USA 1989. Tri-Star Pictures. *Director*: Sidney Lumet. *Producer*: Lawrence Gordon. *Executive Producers*: Jennifer Ogden, Burtt Harris. *Screenplay*: Vincent Patrick (based on his novel). *Director of Photography*: Andrzej

Bartkowiak. *Production Design*: Philip Rosenberg. *Music*: Cy Coleman. *Costumes*: Ann Roth. *Make-up*: Joseph Cranzano. *Cast*: Sean Connery (Jessie), Dustin Hoffman (Vito), Matthew Broderick (Adam), Rosana DeSoto (Elaine), Janet Carroll (Margie), Victoria Jackson (Christine). 115 mins.

DICK TRACY
USA 1990. Touchstone Pictures. *Director*: Warren Beatty. *Producer*: Beatty. *Executive Producers*: Barrie M. Osborne, Art Linson, Floyd Mutrux. *Screenplay*: Jim Cash, Jack Epps Jr. *Director of Photography*: Vittorio Storaro. *Production Design*: Richard Sylbert. *Music*: Danny Elfman (songs Stephen Sondheim). *Costumes*: Milena Canonero. *Make-up*: John Caglione Jr., Doug Drexler. *Cast*: Warren Beatty (Dick Tracy), Charlie Korsmo (Kid), James Caan (Spuds Spaldoni), Glenne Headly (Tess Trueheart), Madonna (Breathless Mahoney), Al Pacino (Big Boy Caprice), Dustin Hoffman (Mumbles), William Forsythe (Flattop), Charles Durning (Chief Brandon), Mandy Patinkin (88 Keys), Paul Sorvino (Lips Manlis), R. G. Armstrong (Pruneface), Dick Van Dyke (DA Fletcher). 103 mins.

BILLY BATHGATE
USA 1991. Touchstone Pictures. *Director*: Robert Benton. *Producers*: Benton, Arlene Donovan. *Screenplay*: Tom Stoppard, Robert Benton. *Cast*: Dustin Hoffman (Dutch Schultz), Bruce Willis, Nicole Kidman, Loren Dean (Billy Bathgate).

INDEX

Abbott, Bud 13, 233
Abbott, George 40
Absence of Malice 189, 228
Academy Awards (Oscars) 54, 62, 69–70, 74, 79–80, 100, 105, 117, 121, 131, 135–7, 144–5, 151, 162, 169, 179–80, 189, 200, 208, 212, 214, 228, 233, 235–6, 241, 251, 253
Ace in the Hole 143
A Christmas Carol 14
A Clockwork Orange 114
A Cook for Mr General 378
A Country Scandal 39
Actors Studio, 4, 21, 24, 26, 29, 31, 39, 124, 128
Adjani, Isabelle 213, 215, 263
Adventures in the Screen Trade 122, 149
Agan, Patrick 110
Agatha 49, 117, 157, 160–70, 173–4, 201, 214, 238, 262
Ages of Man, The 33
A Hard Day's Night 48
A Hatful of Rain 124
A Jew Today 255
A Kind of Loving 74
Albee, Edward 54, 62
Albertson, Jack 42
Alda, Alan 47
Aldrich, Robert 99
Aldwych Theatre 47
Alexander, Jane 36, 141, 143, 176–8, 180, 261–2
Alfredo Alfredo 60, 116–19, 123, 125, 261
Algren, Nelson 51
Alice 193
Alice Doesn't Live Here Any More 137
Alice's Restaurant 67, 95
A Lion in Winter 84
All About Eve 145
Allen, Cathy 78
Allen, Fred 10
Allen, Steve 128
Allen, Woody 94, 105, 124, 132, 136, 171, 175
All Over Town 137–40, 175, 193
All Quiet on the Western Front 145
All That Jazz 127, 135, 145
All That Money Can Buy 145
All the King's Men 145
All the President's Men 8, 31, 36, 140–5, 151–2, 166, 176, 193, 221, 261
Almendros, Nestor 262
A Man Escaped 125

A Matter of Position 211
Amerbroco 260
American International Pictures (AIP) 51, 79
American Place Theater 46
American School of Ballet 52
An Actor Prepares 24
Anderson Tapes, The 249
And Justice for All 180
Andrews, Julie 192
Androsky, Carole 260
A New Leaf 211–12
An Evening with Mike Nichols and Elaine May 212
Annie Hall 94
Ann-Margret 194
An Officer and a Gentleman 201
Anouilh, Jean 64
Anspach, Susan 40
ANTA 45
Antonioni, Michelangelo 116
Any Wednesday 35
Apache 99
Apocalypse Now 180
Apple Tree, The 47, 56
April Fools, The 75
Apted, Michael 160–1, 164–6, 169, 201, 262
Arceri, Gene 56
Archer, Jeffrey and Mary 1, 219
Arden, John 45, 49
Arkin, Alan 48, 51, 58
Armstrong, R. G. 251, 264
Arrabal, Fernando 39
Arrick, Larry 46
Arthur, Jean 10
Ash, Dan 51
Ashby, Hal 146, 155, 189, 220
Ashcroft, Dame Peggy 1, 242, 246
Asimov's Guide to the Bible 255
A Simple Kind of Love Story 50
Astaire, Jarvis 49, 160, 165, 167, 170, 222, 260
A Streetcar Named Desire 193
Atlantic City 219
Atlas, Allison 253
Attenborough, Richard 200
A Thousand Clowns 103
Autobiography of an Autistic 232
Avery, Brian 55, 259
A View from the Bridge 23, 40–1, 78, 202
A Warm December 121

Bach, Richard 168
Bad Company 173
Badel, Alan 262
Bailey, Jim 201
Baker, Carroll 133
Ball, Lucille 82, 131
Ballhaus, Michael 263
Balsam, Martin 141, 260–1
Bananas 124
Bancroft, Anne 38, 56, 58, 61, 67, 69, 259
Barbash, Fred 142
Barefoot in the Park 54, 140
Barnes, Clive 87
Barron, Sandy 262
Barry, John 259
Barry, Julian 127, 261
Barrymore, Lionel 192
Barthlemess, Richard 66
Bartkowiak, Andrzej 263–4
Baryshnikov, Mikhail 190
Basehart, Richard 116
Basement, The 50
Bass, Ron 227–8, 236, 263
Bates, Alan 74
Bates, Kathy 262
Baxter, Warner 62
Beatles, The 48, 91
Beatty, Warren 62, 67, 69, 70, 92, 210–16, 251–2, 263–4
Beck, Stanley 70, 90, 260–2
Beckerman, Sidney 147, 261
Beckett, Samuel 39–40
Beery, Wallace 6, 176
Behan, Brendan 39
Being There 180, 235
Belack, Doris 193
Bell, Arthur 195
Bellini, Carl 96
Belmondo, Jean-Paul 121
Benedik, Laslo 207
Benjamin, Richard 73, 251
Benny, Jack 192
Benton, Robert 121, 173–7, 179–80, 205, 262
Benvenuti, Leo 261
Bergen, Candice 157
Berger, Thomas 95, 260
Bergman, Ingmar 106, 153, 256
Berle, Milton (Uncle Mitty) 13, 16
Berlin, Jeannie 212
Berlin Film Festival 235
Bernhardt, Melvin 47
Bernstein, Carl 31, 140–2, 144, 146, 201, 221, 261
Bertolucci, Bernardo 23, 90
Best Man, The 54, 121
Best Plays of the Year 7, 38
Beverly Hills Cop 226
Big Soft Nellie 47
Big Street, The 81
Bill 224
Bill: On His Own 224
Billy Bathgate 179, 264

Billy Liar 74
Biograph Studios 86–7
Birnbaum, Roger 224, 226
Biskind, Peter 226
Bisset, Jacqueline 197
Black, J. Anderson (Gordon M. Williams, q.v.)
Blackmer, Sidney 24
Black Stallion, The 180
Blade Runner 201
Blake, Robert 41
Blanc, Mel 81
Blazing Saddles 99
Blind Camel (*Ishtar*, q.v.)
Blossom Time 53
Bluebeard 96
Blum, David 211
Boam, Jeffrey 154, 262
Bobby Deerfield 151, 189
Boesky, Ivan 219
Bogarde, Dirk 116
Bogart, Humphrey 4, 123
Bond, James 51, 162
Bonnie and Clyde 62, 66, 70, 95, 121, 173
Boone, Pat 21
Boorman, John 197
Booth Theater 50, 139
Born on the Fourth of July 235
Bortman, Michael 227
Boudin, Kathy 101–2
Bound for Glory 155
Boyle, Alan 263
Bradlee, Ben 141–2, 144
Brando, Marlon 4–5, 21, 29, 33, 76, 90, 128, 148, 201, 249
Brasselle, Keefe 133
Brecht, Bertolt 39, 131
Bresson, Robert 125
Brest, Martin 220–1, 225, 227, 229, 234
Brice, Fanny 20
Brinks Job, The 146
Britten, Tony 262
Broderick, Matthew, 3, 248–50, 264
Broken Arrow, The 99
Brooke, Paul 165
Brooke, Walter 259
Brooks, Mel 55, 58, 191, 215, 229
Brooks Atkinson Theater 87, 127
Brother Sun and Sister Moon 101
Brown, Barney 24–5
Brown, Pat 69
Bruce, Honey 128–9, 133, 135
Bruce, Kitty 128, 134–5
Bruce, Lenny 30, 44, 127–30, 132–5, 137, 140, 146
Brynner, Yul 21, 75
Büchner, Georg 24
Bufman, Zev 84, 87, 202
Bullitt 85–7
Bunker, Edward 153–4, 262
Burbank Studios 141–2
Burge, Stuart 45
Burnett, Carol 229

Burns, David 103, 259–60
Burns, George 254
Burns, Ralph 261
Burn This 222
Burstyn, Ellen 137
Burton, Richard 54
Busey, Gary 159, 262
Butch Cassidy and the Sundance Kid 80, 95, 141, 145
Butterworth, Ed 263
Buzzi, Ruth 23
Bye, Bye, Birdie 53
Byrd, Ralph 251
Byrne, Anne (Hoffman's first wife) 52–3, 64, 69, 71–3, 78, 93–4, 97, 101–2, 106–8, 110, 116, 123, 126, 138, 156–7, 170–1, 182–3
Byron, Lord 65

CAA 225
Caan, James 28, 251, 264
Caglione, Jr, John 264
Cagney, James 154
Cagney and Lacey 91
Caine, Michael 246
Cahill, Tim 132
Calder, Ritchie (Lord Ritchie-Calder) 162
Callow, Simon 241
Camp Good Times 253
Canby, Vincent 82, 39, 125, 159, 198
Candid Camera 32
Candy, John 234
Can Heironymus Merkin Ever Forget Mercy Humppe and Find True Happiness? 105
Cannon Films 220
Canonero, Milena 264
Cantor, Eddie 67, 133
Capitol Records 215
Capra, Frank 8, 10–11
Car 54, Where Are You? 51
Carney, Art 13, 136
Caron, Leslie 1, 213
Carradine, David 153
Carradine, Keith 147
Carroll, Janet 250, 264
Casablanca (production company) 262
Cash, Jim 264
Cassavetes, John 211
Cazale, John 179
CBS 203, 207, 263
Chagall, Marc 87
Chalmers, Thomas 203
Champ, The 181
Chandler, David S. 263
Chandler, Jeff 96
Chandler, Raymond 173
Chaney, Lon 98
Chaplin, Charles 40, 120–1, 167, 181
Chapman, Lonnie 29, 31
Chariots of Fire 214, 219
Charles, Ray 29, 104
Charlie's Angels 175
Charley's Aunt 192, 199

Charly 233
Charrière, Henri 121–2, 261
Chase, Chevy 188
Chase, The 95
Chastity Belt, The 189
Cheers 90
Chekhov, Anton 24, 39
Chicago 131
Childe Harold 65
Children at Their Games 35
China Syndrome, The 180
Chinatown 136, 146, 201
Chomsky, Noam 105
Chopin, Frédéric 16
Christie, Agatha 160, 162–3, 165, 168, 262
Christie, Julie 74, 160, 213
CIA 140, 215
Cicero 108
Cimarron Strip 77
Cimino, Michael 218–19
Cincinnati Kid, The 123
Cinecom Pictures 248
Cinema Center Films 95, 103, 106, 260
Circle-In-The-Square 47, 61
City of Glass 19–20
Clark, Jim 164
Clayburgh, Jill 133
Clift, Montgomery 4
Close Encounters of the Third Kind 191
Clutinger, Judi 21
Coal Miner's Daughter 169
Cobb, Lee J. 10, 41, 203, 205, 207
Coblenz 261
Coburn, James 22
Cochran, Steve 116
Cocktail 226
Cocktail Party, The 39
Cocteau, Jean 198
Cohn, Harry 10–11
Coleman, Cy 264
Coleman, Dabney 191, 263
Colesberry, Robert F. 263
Collins, Joan 1, 213
Colman, Ronald 8
Color of Money, The 226–7
Colosimo, Ciara 261
Columbia Pictures 8, 10–11, 50, 173, 175, 181, 184, 188–90, 210–11, 213–14, 259, 262–3
Columbia Story, The 215
Come Blow Your Horn 51
Coming Home 189
Common Threads 253
Connection, The 27
Connery, Sean 92, 244, 248–50, 264
Connolly, Billy 1
Conway, Morgan 251
Conway, Tim 229
Cool Hand Luke 70
Cook, Fielder 37
Cook, Peter 45
Cooper, Gary 8, 21, 71, 113
Coppola, Francis 226–7

Coquillon, John 260
Corey, Jeff 260
Corliss, Richard 66
Corman, Avery 173, 262
Corona 261
Costello, Lou 13, 192, 233
Costello, Mariclare 50
Coulouris, George 261
Count of Monte Cristo, The 118
Country Girl, The 79
Courtenay, Tom 74
Craig, Michael 116
Cranzano, Joseph 264
Crawley, Tony 176
Crawford, Broderick 116
Crawford, Joan 4, 133
Creative Artists 224
Crist, Judith 93, 151
Cromwell, Richard 66
Crosby, Bing 210
Crowther, Bosley 65
Cruise, Tom 3, 224–7, 230–5, 263
Cukor, George 11
cummings, e. e. 241
Curtin, Valerie 190
Curtis, Tony 25, 106, 189, 193

Dailey, Irene 42
Dale, Esther 211
Dalessandro, Joe 83
Daley, Mayor 102
Dalio, Marcel 125
Dalton, Timothy 162, 169, 262
Daly, Tyne 91, 290
Daniels, William 55, 103, 259
Danton's Death 24
Darling 74
Darling, Joan 30–1
Darrow, Clarence 24
Daves, Delmer 99
David, Thayer 96
Davis, Bette 98
Davis, Geena 263
Davis, Miles 128, 133
Davis, Ossie 223
Day, Doris 56
Day for Night 156
Dead End 36
Dead End Kids 26, 36
Dead Poets Society 219
Dean, James 4–5, 19, 21, 29, 97
De Antonio, Emile 102
Death of a Salesman 7, 12, 39, 41, 79, 97, 137, 202–3, 218, 222, 225, 231, 237, 249, 263
De Bernardi, Piero 261
Debrod 260
Deer Hunter, The 175, 218
Defenders, The 41
de Kooning, Willem 223
Delicate Delinquent, The 187
Dell, Gabriel 260
Delphi V Productions 263

DeLuise, Dom 260
De Mille, Cecil B. 8
Demsky, Issur Danielovitch (Kirk Douglas, q.v.)
Dench, Dame Judi 246
De Niro, Robert 5, 148, 205, 227, 234, 244, 252
Denner, Charles, 201
Dennis, Sandy 35
De Palma, Brian 251
Derek, Bo 194
Dern, Bruce 29, 189
De Sica, Vittorio 55
DeSoto, Rosana 250, 264
Devane, William 262
Devil Doll, The 249
De Vito, Danny 249
Dexter, John 45
Diamonds 219
Diary of a Superfluous Man 46
Dickens, Charles 14
Dick Tracy 127, 161, 251–2, 264
Diner 229, 232
Dirty Hands 39
Dishy, Bob 259
Disneyland 26
Ditto List, The 221
Divorce Italian Style 117
Dixon, MacIntyre 57
Doctorow, E. L. 179
Dog Day Afternoon 249
Dohrn, Bernardine 102
Dorfmann, Robert 121, 123, 261
Door, William 82
Dorvino, Paul 251
Douglas, Kirk 4, 25
Douglas, Melvyn 180
Douglas, Michael 198
Dressler, Marie 6
Drexler, Doug 264
Dreyfuss, Richard 5, 55, 95, 174, 181, 191
Driver, Donald 87
Duff, Howard 262
Dukakis, Olympia 92
Dumb Waiter, The 39
Dunaway, Faye 96, 99, 133, 260
Duncan, Isadora 30
Dunn, James 36
Dunne, Irene 10
Dunnock, Mildred 41, 203, 207
Durante, Jimmy 13–14
Durning, Charles 190, 209
Dutchman 84
Duvall, Robert 8, 27–8, 32–3, 35, 37, 40, 140, 146, 154, 180, 204–9
Duvall, Shelley 197
Dylan, Bob 104

East Harlem Boys' Club 39
Eastwood, Clint 251
Eccles, Amy 96, 260
Edward, HRH Prince 246
Edwards, Blake 201–2
Eh? 47, 49, 51, 56–8, 61, 76, 139

Ehrlichman, John 140
8½ 55
Elan 259
Elcar, Dana 47
Electric Horseman, The 190
Electric Kook-Aid Acid Test, The 91
Elfman, Danny 264
Eliot, T. S. 33, 39
El Testamento de Madigan (*Madigan's Millions*, q.v.)
Embassy Pictures 55
Emmy Awards 131, 175
Empire of the Sun 227
End as a Man 55
End Game 39
Endless Love 226
End of the World in Our Usual Bed in a Night Full of Rain, The 157
Enigma Productions of London 166
Entertainer, The 147
Ephron, Nora 141, 201, 221
Epps, Jr, Jack 264
Equity Library Theater 36
Equus 249
Evans, Charles 187–8, 262
Evans, Robert 147, 187–8, 252, 261

Fabrizzi, Franco 259
Factory 82–3
Fairbanks, Douglas 120–1, 167
Falk, Peter 146, 197, 211
Falk, Shera 197
Family Business 60, 82, 223, 248–50, 263–4
Farentino, James 203
Far from the Madding Crowd 74
Farmer, Frances 190
Farnum, Dustin 8
Farrell, Charles 66
Farrow, Mia 84, 88–9, 90–2, 260
Fearless Frank 51, 77, 79
Feibleman, Peter 210
Feldman, Marty 229
Feldman, Phil 166–7
Fell, Norman 55, 259
Fellini, Federico 55, 82, 87, 116
Ferrer, José 195
Fielding, Jerry 260
Fields, W. C. 133
Finney, Albert 136
Fiorello 53
First Artists Productions 120, 146, 153–5, 157–8, 161–2, 164–9, 174, 221, 262
First Monday in October 177
Fitzgerald, F. Scott 65, 73
Flame and the Arrow, The 75
Flaming Frontier, The 8
Flesh 83
Flight from Ashiya 75
Flim Flam Man, The 55, 76
Flynn, Errol 141
Fonda, Henry 82, 159, 177
Fonda, Jane 201

Ford, Harrison 201, 251
Foreman, Carl 218
Forman, Milos 122
Forsythe, William 264
48 Hours 220
41st Street Theater 36
42nd Street 62
Fosse, Bob 127, 129–31, 133–5, 153, 155, 261
Fox 10
Fowler, Gene 13
Fragments 50
Frances 190, 200
Frank, Robert 27
Frankenstein 98
Frankfurt Ballet 53
Franks, Chloe 108
Frank's Great Adventure see *Fearless Frank*
Freedland, Michael 165
Frei, Nicky 1
Fremont-Smith, Eliot 49
Friday, the Rabbi Slept Here 146
Front Page, The 143
Fugitive Kind, The 249
Fuller, Sam 99
Funny Girl 81

Gabin, Jean 125
Gable, Barra 182
Gabler, Carl 47
Games 55
Gandhi 200
Garbo, Greta 192, 218
Gardens of Stone 227
Gardner, Herb 103, 105, 210, 260
Garfunkel, Art 67, 215
Garland, Robert 190
Garr, Teri 190, 200, 263
Gassner, John 7
Gay Liberation Front 68
Gaynes, George 191, 263
Gazzara, Ben 124
Geeson, Judy 109
Gelbart, Larry 189–90, 262
Gelber, Jack 27
General Production Company 261
Genet, Jean 125
Gentil, Giorgio 51
George, Chief Dan 96, 100, 260
George, Susan 109–13, 260
Gere, Richard 3
German Sisters, The 208
Germi, Pietro 116–17, 119, 261
Gershwin, George and Ira 181
Getaway, The 121, 123
Gethers, Steven 37–8
Getting Straight 67
Ghostbusters 191
Ghostley, Alice 55
Giannini, Giancarlo 157
Giant 97
Gibson, William 38
Gielgud, Sir John 33

Gilbert, Lewis 33
Gilroy, Frank D. 42, 44, 103
Ginsberg, Allen 27
Give a Girl a Break 131
Glass Menagerie, The 19–20
Gleason, Jackie 13
Gleason, Ralph 134
Globe Theatre 245–6
Globus, Yoram 220
Glory Boys, The 201
Godard, Jean-Luc 91–2
Godfather, The 128
Godfather II 136
Godspell 226
Godunov, Alexander 197
Golan, Menachem 220
Gold, Lillian (Hoffman's mother) *see* Hoffman, Lillian
Gold, Ted 101–2
Goldberg, Leonard 221
Golden Boy 11
Golden Girls 86
Goldman, William 80, 122, 141, 144, 146, 149, 261
Gold Rush, The 120
Goldsmith, Jerry 261
Goldwyn, Samuel 10, 13, 157, 168
Golino, Valeria 233, 263
Gong Show 216
Goodbye Girl, The 193
Goodman, David Zelag 108, 260
Good Morning, America 178
Good Morning Vietnam 228
Good Mother, The 227
Gorcey, Leo 26, 36, 128
Gordon, Don 261
Gordon, Lawrence 220–1, 263
Gorgeous George 146
Gorky, Maxim 27
Gorky Park 201
Gorman, Cliff 127
Gottlieb, Dr Louis 134
Gottsegen, Lee 201
Gottsegen, Lisa (Hoffman's second wife) *see* Hoffman, Lisa
Gould, Chester 251
Gould, Elliott 28, 106, 188, 197
Gould, Joie 109–10
Grable, Betty 219
Graduate, The 5, 27, 47, 49, 54–74, 78, 82, 93–5, 118, 133, 145, 157, 168, 184, 224, 231, 259
Graham, Katherine 142
Graham, Sheilah 65
Grandon, Temple 232
Granger, Farley 116, 159
Grant, Cary 10, 71, 192
Gravina, Carla 118, 261
Great Brink's Robbery, The 146
Great Waldo Pepper, The 122, 141
Green Berets 79
Greenleaf, Steven 221
Greenwich Village 193

Greer, Germaine 192
Gregorio, Rose 40, 86, 260
Gregory, Celia 168, 262
Griffin, Sunny 92, 260
Griffith, D. W. 88, 120–1, 167, 217
Grimes, Stephen 262
Grodin, Charles 210, 215, 234, 263
Grosbard, Ulu 40, 42, 55, 63, 78, 86, 103, 105, 146, 155–6, 158, 202, 260, 262
Gross, Larry 220–2
Grusin, Dave 262–3
Guare, John 219
Guber, Peter 263
Guber-Peters Company 224, 263
Guess Who's Coming to Dinner? 70
Guinness, Sir Alec 180–1, 244
Gummer, Don 179
Gunsmoke 77
Guthrie, Woody 155
Guys and Dolls 226

Hackett, Buddy 188
Hackford, Taylor 201, 219
Hackman, Gene 22–3, 25, 27–8, 32, 35, 37, 41, 50, 55, 62, 137, 140, 154, 204
Hageb, Fuad 263
Hair 137
Hall, Conrad 262
Hall, Jennifer 1
Hall, Sir Peter 1, 47, 237–9, 241, 243, 246–7, 253
Hallström, Lasse 248
Hamilton, George 188
Hamilton, Murray 62, 259
Hamlet 237–8, 243, 248
Hammond, John 260
Hampton, Christopher 165
Hannah, Daryl 225
Hardy, Andy 76
Harlow, Jean 133
Harper, Tessa 263
Harris, Barbara 104–5, 260
Harris, Burtt 263
Harris, Julie 74
Harris, Richard 116
Harron, Robert 66
Harry and Tonto 136
Harry, Noon and Night 41
Hart, Sherman 129
Harvey, Anthony 84
Haskell, Molly 198
Hassan II of Morocco, King 215
Hawks, Howard 11
Headly, Glenne 264
Heartbreak Kid, The 212
Heartburn 201, 221
Heaven Can Wait 210, 212
Heaven's Gate 190, 214, 218
Hellman, Jerome 76, 259
Hellman, Lillian 210
Henaghan, Jim 259
Henry, Buck 55, 259
Henry, Cliff 178, 180

Henry, Justin 176–8, 180–1, 262
Henry, Michele 176, 180
Henry, Victor 49
Henry VI, Part I 246
Hepburn, Katharine 70, 192
Hercules 55
Herlihy, James Leo 74, 259
Hesse, Hermann 129
Heston, Charlton 121
Hewitt, Alan 203
High Anxiety 229
High Noon 113
Hill, George Roy 122
Hill, Walter 251
Hillbeck, Fernando 259
Hiller, Arthur 50, 58, 175, 259–60
Hirschhorn, Clive 128, 215
Hitler, Adolf 195
Hoffman, Alexandra (Hoffman's daughter) 239
Hoffman, Dustin
  beginning of acting career 19–25
  burns to hands 43–6
  childhood and family background 6–18
  early days in New York 25–34
  emergency operation to save baby 185–6
  escapes bomb attack on house 101–3
  filming in Cornwall 108–15
  filming in Harrogate 163–6
  filming in Morocco 210–14
  first child born 107
  first lead on Broadway 84–7
  first major film 54–63
  first professional acting job 36
  in London 1, 106, 239–46
  marriage to Anne Byrne 93–4
  marriage to Lisa Gottsegen 185
  marriage break-up 156–7, 161
  mother's illness and death 184–6
  nominated for Oscar 69, 200
  off-Broadway 47–53
  psychoanalysis 73–4
  Royal Command Performance 106
  schooldays 13–19
  screen debut 35–42
  sued for divorce 170–2
  youth 19–25
Hoffman, Harry (Hoffman's father) 6–15, 20, 34, 44, 60, 70, 90, 136, 180, 183–4, 205, 209, 240
Hoffman, Jacob (Hoffman's son) 186, 197, 235, 239, 241
Hoffman, Jennifer Celia (Jenna) (Hoffman's daughter) 107, 156, 166, 172–3, 175–6, 180, 195, 225, 239
Hoffman, Karina (Hoffman's stepdaughter) 52, 64, 69, 73, 97, 101, 103, 106, 156, 166, 172–3, 180, 239
Hoffman, Lillian (Hoffman's mother) 7–15, 20, 34, 44, 60, 70, 136, 159, 180, 183–7, 205
Hoffman, Lisa (Gottsegen) (Hoffman's second wife) 184–5, 195, 197, 225, 235, 239, 241, 243, 245
Hoffman, Max (Hoffman's son) 239

Hoffman, Rebecca (Hoffman's daughter) 201, 239
Hoffman, Ronald (Hoffman's brother) 6–9, 19–20, 27, 140, 184, 187
Hoffman, Abbie 66
Holbrook, Hal 261
Holden, William 21
Holender, Adam 259
Holiday 11
Holliday, Polly 192
Hollywood 4, 10, 21, 25–6, 37, 39, 61, 64, 66, 89, 95, 120–2, 137, 141–2, 146, 162, 167, 192, 214
Holm, John Cecil 40
Holocaust 175
Holt, Thelma 244–5
Holzer, Adela 137
Holzman, Red 204
Honeymooners, The 13, 136
Hopcraft, Arthur 162, 165, 262
Hope, Bob 70, 99, 135–6, 192, 210
Horner, Harry 260
Hoskins, Bob 246
Hot Rock, The 141
Hot Tomorrows 226
Hour of the Gun 77
Howe, Irving 255
Huddlestone, David, 204, 209
Hudson, Rock 21, 25, 65, 96–7
Hughes, Barnard 78, 138, 260
Hughes, Howard 168
Hughes, John 178
Hunchback of Notre Dame, The 148
Hunter, Tab 25
Hurne, Ralph 218
Hurt, William 201
Hyser, Joyce 213

Ibsen, Henrik 22
I Could Go On Singing 54
Ihnat, Steve 21–3
I'm Not Rappaport 210
Indiana Jones films 228
Inherit the Wind 24, 202
International Violet 82
In the Heat of the Night 70
In the Jungle of the Cities 39
Intolerance 217
Ionesco, Eugene 33
Ipale, Aharon 263
Ishtar 11, 67, 74, 190, 210–18, 224, 239, 251, 263
Italiano, Anna Maria Louisa (Anne Bancroft, q.v.)
It Happened One Night 10
It's All True 157
I Was a Male War Bride 192

Jackson, Anne 50–1, 259
Jackson, Glenda 84
Jackson, Kate 175
Jackson, Victoria 250, 264
Jaffe, Stanley R. 173–6, 180, 262

James, Geraldine 239, 246–7
Jane Eyre 13
Jaws 176
Jaws 2 176
Jenkins, Dorothy 260
Jenkins, George 261
Jewison, Norman 123
Jimmy Shine 74, 84, 86–8
Jiras, Bob 263
John and Mary 12, 18, 70, 82, 84–6, 88–93, 106, 260
Johnny Concho 187
Johnson, Mark 263
Jonathan Livingstone Seagull 168
Jones, Carolyn 22
Jones, Indiana 228
Jones, Mervyn 84, 89, 260
Jory, Victor 261
Journey of the Fifth Horse, The 46, 50, 56
Julia 162, 175
Julie 155
Julius Caesar 33, 237
Justin, George 259

Kadish, Ben 84, 260
Kael, Pauline 66, 93, 105, 114, 119, 125, 134, 145, 151, 159, 169, 215, 235
Kane, Carol 263
Karloff, Boris 98
Kaufman, Bob 187–8
Kaufman, Phil 51, 77
Kauffmann, Stanley 46, 59
Kazan, Elia 24, 77, 103, 156, 203, 213
Keach, Stacy 98
Keaton, Buster 49, 56–7, 181
Keaton, Diane 171, 213
Keefer, Don 203
Keeler, Ruby 62
Keitel, Harvey 203
Keller, Marthe 149, 151, 262
Kelly, Grace 79, 113
Kelly's Eye 47
Kemelman, Harry 146
Kemper, Victor 260
Kennedy, Arthur 203
Kennedy, George 70
Kennedy, John F. 70, 76, 186
Kenton, Stan 19
Kerr, Walter 49, 51
Kesey, Ken 32
Kerouac, Jack 27
Kibbee, Guy 181
Kid, The 181
Killing Fields, The 214
King, Billie Jean 179
King, Revd Martin Luther 69, 135
King Kong 190
King Lear 237
Kingsley, Ben 200, 219
Kingsley, Sidney 36
Kissel, Howard 247
Kiss Me Kate 131

Kline, Franz 223
Koenekamp, Fred 261
Korda, Alexander 168
Korsmo, Charlie 264
Kostinoff, Vladimir 28
Kramer, Stanley 106
Kramer vs Kramer 3, 11, 36, 42, 49, 93–4, 137, 171–82, 184–5, 198, 208, 262
Kubrick, Stanley 55
Kugell, Joan (Joan Darling, q.v.)
Kurosawa, Akira 113

La Brava 220
Laden, Bob 263
Laguardia, Robert 56
La Loggia, Danika 261
Lamour, Dorothy 210
Lancaster, Burt 4, 75, 96, 116, 250
Landis, John 251
Lang, Stephen 206, 263
Lange, Jessica 135, 190–1, 196, 200, 263
Lansing, Sherry 175
Lark, The 64
Larkin, Peter 262
La Rue, Danny 201
Lasky, Jesse 10
Lasky, Zane 139
Last Emperor, The 23
Last Tango in Paris 90
Last Tycoon, The 73
Late Show, The 173
Laughton, Charles, 148
Laurel, Stan 192, 215
Lawson, Leigh 246
Leach, Will 36
Léaud, Jean-Pierre 91, 156
Le Cop 220
Lee, Peggy 22
Left-Handed Gun, The 95, 99
Legal Eagles 225
Legend 225
Lehar, Franz 163
Lehman, Ernest 54
Lemmon, Jack 65, 75, 180, 193, 244
Lenny 12, 37, 70, 127–37, 248, 261
Lenny Bruce Performance, The 128
Leonard, Elmore 220
Lerner, Irving 17
Les Grands Ballets Canadiens 52
Leslie, Alfred 27
Les Ripoux 220
Levine, Joseph E. 40, 55, 58–9, 137
Levinson, Barry 190, 228–34, 263
Lewis, Jerry 21, 132, 187, 233
Lhermitte, Thierry 220
Liddy, G. Gordon 204
Lilith 62
Lincoln Center 64
Linson, Art 264
Literary History of the United States, The 27
Little, Cleavon 86, 91, 139
Little Big Man 8, 49, 55, 95–100, 105, 252, 260

Little Lord Fauntleroy 120, 192
Little Star, Robert 96, 260
Livings, Henry 47–9, 139
Living Theatre, The 27
Liza with a Z 131
Lloyd, Harold 60
Lloyd, John Robert 86, 259–60
Lombard, Carole 133
Lookin' to Get Out 189
Losey, Gavrik 262
Lou Grant 144
Love at First Bite 188
Love Story 106
Lowe, Rob 3
Lu, Lisa 23
Lubitsch, Ernst 195
Lucas, George 228
Luedtke, Kurt 228
Lumet, Sidney 103, 248–9, 251, 263
Luv 48, 50, 54
Lynley, Carol 133

McCarthy, Sen. Eugene 69, 92, 150
McCarthy, Kevin 207
McCarthy, Mary Abigail 69
McCartney, Paul and Linda 1, 242
McClanahan, Rue 86
McCorkindale, Simon 110
MacDonald, Richard 262
McEnroe, John 204
McElwaine, Guy 213
McGinn, Walter 44
McGiver, John 37, 78, 81, 260
McGovern, George 140
MacGraw, Ali 123, 187
McGuire, Don 187–8
McKellen, Ian 246
McKenna, T. P. 110, 112, 260
McLaglen, Victor 6
MacLaine, Shirley 213
MacLeod, David 210
McQueen, Steve 22, 86–7, 92, 120–6, 261
Macy, Bill 36
Mad Dog Call 35
Madigan's Millions 51, 79, 116, 259
Madonna 251–2, 264
Magnificent Ambersons, The 157, 168
Maharishi Mahesh Yogi 88
Mailer, Norman 204
Major Dundee 111
Making Love 175
Malden, Karl 4
Malle, Louis 219
Malkovich, John 79, 204–6, 209, 222, 263
Mamoulian, Rouben 11
Mandel, Johnny 262
Manhattan 171, 175
Mann, Theodore 47
Man with the Golden Arm, The 51
Man Who Loved Women, The 201
Mao, Madame 202
Marathon Man 17, 146–53, 187, 261–2

March, Fredric 207
Marcus, Frank 87
Maret, Harry 259
Marjorie Morningstar 22
Marowitz, Charles 50
Marr, Sally 128, 135
Marrero, Tony 194
Martin, Dean 233
Martin, Dewy 22
Martin, Steve 234
Martin, Strother 110
Martinelli, Elsa 51, 259
M*A*S*H 189
Masters, Anthony 261
Masters, George 194, 263
Matchmaker, The 28
Matinee Theater (NBC) 23
'Maude' 36
May, Elaine 54–5, 168, 190, 210–12, 215, 263
Mayer, Louis B. 10
Meade, Taylor 82
Measure for Measure 238
Meisner, Sanford 28
Melnick, Daniel 109, 260
Mephisto 208
Merchant of Venice, The 1–2, 38, 117, 238–48, 251
Merry Widow, The 153
Method school of acting 4, 27, 29, 31, 95, 144, 147
MGM 10, 95, 103, 120
Midnight Cowboy 37, 51, 60, 74–84, 93, 106, 124, 147, 160–1, 238, 248, 259–60
Midnight Run 227, 234
Mikey and Nicky 168, 190, 211–12
Miles, Sylvia 78–9, 81, 260
Millar, Stuart 260
Miller, Ann 2, 186
Miller, Arthur 7, 9, 23, 40–1, 202–4, 207–8, 239, 253, 263
Miller, Jonathan 244
Miller, Stuart 96
Mills, Sir John and Lady Mary 1, 242
Miner, Jan 37, 261
Minnelli, Liza 135
Miracle Worker, The 56, 95
Mirage 262
Mirisch, Walter 220
Mississippi Burning 23
Mitchell, Cameron 203, 207
Mitchell, Warren 203
Mitchum, Robert 4
Molen, Jerry 263
Molnar, Ferenc 87
Monroe, Marilyn 202
Montalban, Ricardo 96
Moon Over Miami 219
Moore, Dudley 95
Morath, Ingeborg 202
Moreau, Jeanne 56
Morley, Ruth 262–3
Morrison, George 35, 41
Morrissey, Paul 82

Morrow, Barry 224, 226–7, 230, 236, 263
Morse, Helen 160, 162, 262
Morse, Richard 28
Morse, Robert 28, 36–7
Mortimer, John 84–5, 89, 91, 260
Morton, Gary 129, 132, 261
Mostel, Zero 33–4, 58
Moulin Rouge 195
Mozart, W. A. 89
Mr Buddwing 55
Mr Deeds Goes to Town 10
Mr Smith Goes to Washington 8, 11, 170
Mulligan, Richard 96, 260
Muni, Paul 97
Murder on the Orient Express 136
Murdock, Jack 263
Murphy, Eddie 220
Murphy, Michael 171
Murray, Bill 190–1, 196, 222, 224, 263
Muscle Beach 17
Music Box Theater 35
Mutiny on the Bounty 147
Mutrux, Gail 230
Mutrux, Floyd 264
My Life as a Dog 248
My New Partner 220, 223, 226, 248
My Sister Eileen 131

Nagrin, Daniel 30
Naish, J. Carrol 96
Naked City 36
Namath, Joe 28
National General Pictures 120
Natural, The 229
NBC 23
Neighborhood Playhouse 28, 124
Neil, Fred 82
Network 249
New Jersey Ballet 53
Newman, David 121
Newman, Paul 4–5, 21, 34, 69–70, 95, 106, 120,
    141, 154–5, 226, 253
New York City Ballet 71
Next Stop 193
Nicholas and Alexandra 121
Nichols, Mike 47–8, 54–8, 60–2, 66–8, 70, 76,
    140, 155, 201, 212, 221, 224, 259
Nicholson, Jack 136, 152, 190, 201, 224, 244
Night of the Living Dead 194
Nil Carborundum 47
Nilsson, Harry 106
1968 219
Nixon, Chris 166
Nixon, Richard M. 140, 143–4
No Beast So Fierce 154, 262
Noiret, Philippe 220
North, Alex 209, 263
Not a Penny More, Not a Penny Less 219
Not with My Wife You Don't 189
nouvelle vague 56, 91
Nutcracker 157
Nykvist, Sven 256

Obie Awards 46, 49
Odets, Clifford 239
Ogden, Jennifer 263
*Oh Dad, Poor Dad, Mamma's Hung You in the
    Closet and I'm Feelin' So Sad* 105
Oh God! 189
Old Jew, The 50
Olivier, Lord (Laurence) 147, 149–51, 243–4,
    246, 262
Olsen, Carl 253
Once Around 248
Ondine 82
O'Neal, Tatum 198
One Flew Over the Cuckoo's Nest 32
Only Angels Have Wings 11
On My Way to the Crusades I Met a Girl Who . . .
    189
On the Road 27
On the Waterfront 76
Open Space Theatre 50
Ornitz, Arthur J. 259
Orpheus Descending 237
Osborne, Barrie M. 264
Oscars *see* Academy Awards
Oughton, Diana 101–2
Our Gang 41
Our Man Flint 22
Out of Africa 228
Out of It 77
Outsiders, The 226
Ovitz, Michael 224–5, 227

Pacino, Al 5, 95, 113, 127–8, 136, 146, 151, 174,
    180, 241, 249, 251–2, 264
Page, Geraldine 29
Paget, Debra 96
Pakula, Alan 142–4, 155, 261
Palmer, Tony 219
Papas, Irene 78
Papillon 121–3, 128, 161, 171, 238, 248, 261
Papillon Partnership 261
Parallax View, The 143
Paramount 10, 101, 168, 187, 211–12, 261
Parfrey, Woodrow 261
Parker, Charlie 128
Parker, Nathaniel 246
Parolin, Aiace 261
Parsons, Estelle 70
Pasadena Playhouse College of Theater and Arts
    21, 23–4, 36, 78, 237
Patella, Daniele 261
Paths of Glory 55
Patinkin, Mandy 251, 264
Patrick, Vincent 223, 248–9, 251, 263
Patton 100, 121, 136
Pawnbroker, The 249
Payton-Wright, Pamela 83,138
Pearl, Dorothy 263
Peck, Gregory 4
Peckinpah, Sam 108–11, 113–15, 121, 153, 166,
    260
Peer Gynt 22

Penn, Arthur 38, 95, 99, 260
Penn, Sean 220
Pennsylvania Ballet 52
Perkins, Anthony 4
Perrine, Valerie 129–30, 132, 136, 197, 261
Peschowsky, Michael Igor (Mike Nichols, q.v.)
Peter and the Wolf 223
Peters, John 263
Peters, Kelly Jean 260
Peters, Laurie 17
Phillips, Michelle 213
Picnic on the Battlefield 39
Picker, David V. 74, 79, 135, 146
Pickford, Mary 120–1, 167, 192
Picture of Dorian Gray, The 218
Pinelli, Tullio 261
Pink, Sidney 259
Pinter, Harold 39, 253
Pippin 131
Places in the Heart 205
Planer, Franz 207
Planes, Trains and Automobiles 234
Planet of the Apes, The 121
Platonov 39
Playhouse in the Park 47
Pocket Theater 41
Point, The 106
Poitier, Sidney 106, 120–1, 154
Polanski, Roman 251
Polito, John 263
Pollack, Bernie 262–3
Pollack, Sydney 77, 147, 189–91, 193, 196–7,
    199, 228–9, 262–3
Pollock, Jackson 223
Pope, Alexander 70
Porter, Cole 33
Portnoy's Complaint 73
Postman, The 50
Postman Always Rings Twice, The 190
Potter, Dennis 104
Powell, Anthony 261, 263
Poyser, Brian 245
Prager, Stanley 51, 259
Preminger, Otto 211
Presley, Elvis 21
Pressman, David 37–8
Previn, André 89
Previn, Dory 89
Price, Richard 227
Producers, The 55, 58, 215
Prokofiev, Serge 223
Pulitzer Prize 42
Pull My Daisy 27
Pumpkin Eater, The 56
Punch Productions 201, 203, 262–3
Purcell, Henry 181, 262
Puttnam, David 160–1, 164–5, 213–14, 222

Quare Fellow, The 39
Queen Christina 192
Queen Elizabeth the Queen Mother 106
Quigley, Jane (Jane Alexander, q.v.)

Quinn, Anthony 116

Rachel and the Stranger 75
Radcliffe, Michael 243
Rafelson, Bob 190
Raft, George 51, 154
Raging Bull 148
Rain Man 13, 23, 32, 74, 76, 124, 224–36, 241,
    248, 251, 263
Random, Ida 263
Random Hearts 219
Raphael, Frederic 74
Ray, Charles 66
Rayfiel, David 228
Reagan, Ronald 67, 210, 251
Rebel Without a Cause 5
Record, Don 22
Redford, Robert 57, 69, 92, 122, 140–3, 145,
    152, 189, 191, 221, 225, 229, 261
Redgrave, Sir Michael 243
Redgrave, Vanessa 160, 162, 164–7, 169, 237,
    246, 253, 262
Reds 201, 214
Reeve, Christopher 197
Reeves, Paula 163
Reeves, Steve 55
Reid, Kate 204, 263
Reilly, Charles Nelson 259
Rescher, Gayne 260
Resnik, Muriel 35
Reverberations 50
Rexroth, Kenneth 27
Reynolds, Burt 201
Rhinoceros 33
Ribman, Ronald 41,46
Rich, Frank 145, 207, 212, 246
Richards, Dick 188, 262
Richardson, Jack 95
Richardson, Roger 245
Richmond, Ted 261
Risky Business 225–6
Rizzoli/Francoriz RPA 261
RKO 10, 157, 251
Robards Jr, Jason 103, 141, 144, 151, 166, 261
Robbins, Terry 101–2
Roberts, Michael D. 263
Roberts, Cliff 233
Rogers, Milton ('Shorty') 259
Roizman, Owen 155, 262
Rojas, Manolo 259
Rojo, Gustavo 259
Romero, Cesar 51, 71, 259
Romero, George 194
Room, The 39
Rooney, Mickey 2, 180, 224
Roosevelt, Eleanor 34
Roosevelt, Franklin D. 10
Rosemary's Baby 84, 89
Rosenberg, Philip 264
Rosenberg, Stuart 75
Rosenman, Dr Amy 186, 254
Ross, Katharine 55, 57, 69, 259

Rossen, Robert 62, 103
Rossetter, Kathy 263
Roth, Ann 264
Roth, Philip 73
Rowland, Richard A. 120
Roxbury 263
Royale 42, 44
Royal Hunt of the Sun, The 45
Royal Shakespeare Company 47
Rudman, Michael 203, 209, 238
Run of the Arrow 99
Running on Empty 248
Russell, Ken 168
Russell, Shirley 168, 262
Russell, Theresa 158, 262
Russians Are Coming, The 58
Rustichelli, Carlo 117, 261

Saint, Eva Marie 77
Salt, Jennifer 78, 260
Salt, Waldo 75, 80, 259
Salter, Blanche 184, 235
Sandrelli, Stefania 117, 261
Sarah Lawrence College 36
Sargent, Alvin 155, 262
Saroyan, William 87
Sarris, Andrew 66, 76
Sarrazin, Michael 77
Sartre, Jean-Paul 39
Saturday Night Live 191
Say, Darling 28
Saye, Nora 119
Schaffner, Franklin J. 121–2, 124–5, 261
Schanberg, Sidney 214
Scheider, Roy 147, 174, 178, 262
Schenck, Joseph M. 168
Schickel, Richard 198, 215
Schiller, Joel 261
Schisgal, Murray 48, 50, 54, 84–7, 137, 139, 155,
  161–2, 165, 179, 188, 190, 195–6, 220, 225,
  227, 259
Schisgal, Renee 195
Schlesinger, John 74–6, 80, 82, 84, 146–50, 155,
  259, 261
Schlöndorff, Volker 208, 220, 263
Schlote, Winfried 52
Schneider, Maria 90
Schnozzola 13
Schram, Charles 261
Schroeder, Ricky 181
Schwartz, Bernard (Tony Curtis, q.v.)
Schwarzenegger, Arnold 249
Scorsese, Martin 220, 226, 251
Scott, George C. 100, 136, 203
Scott, Ridley 201
Seale, John 263
Second City troupe 55
Seduction of Joe Tynan, The 175
Segal, George 57, 141, 188
Segura, G. Gregory 259
Sellers, Peter 97, 118, 180, 235
Selznick, David O. 10, 168

Semple Jr, Lorenzo 122, 261
Sergeant Musgrave's Dance 45, 49
Serpe, Robert 146
Serpent's Egg, The 153
Serpico 128, 249
Seymour, Ralph 263
Shaffer, Peter 44
Shakespeare, William 237–47
Shapiro, Alan 219
Sharp, Rick 263
Shaw, Irwin 35
Shearer, Lloyd 65
Sheehan, David 135
Sheen, Martin 42
Shenandoah 55
Sheridan Square Playhouse 40
Shire, David 262
Shopworn Angel 75, 80
Shorr, Lia 157
Shostakovich, Dmitri 219
Shubert Theater and organisation 139, 206
Siege of Trencher's Farm, The (*Straw Dogs*, q.v.)
Silent Movie 229
Silverstein, Shel 260
Silvis, Donahue 78
Simon, John 87, 99, 114, 133, 151
Simon, Neil 51, 54, 140, 212
Simon, Paul 67, 215, 259
Sinatra, Frank 3, 21, 88, 136, 187
Singing Nun, The 55
16 Candles 178
Slaughterhouse Five 129
Small, Michael 262
Smith, David 223
Smith, Dick 98, 260
Smith, Howard 203, 207
Some Like It Hot 193, 199
Sometimes a Great Notion 155
Sondheim, Stephen 264
Son of Paleface 99
Sophie's Choice 200
Sordi, Alberto 118
Sorvino, Paul 264
Sound of Music, The 77, 109
South Bank Show, The 242
Speedy 60
Spiegel, Sam 30
Spielberg, Steven 227–9
Splendor in the Grass 213
Springer, John 195
Springsteen, Bruce 213
Squaw Man, The 8
Squeeze, The 169
Stage Door 193
Stallone, Sylvester 3, 210
Stamp, Terence 116
Stand Up and Cheer 10
Stanislavsky, Konstantin 4, 24, 29
Stanton, Harry Dean 159, 262
Stapleton, Maureen 119
Stardust 169
Stardust Memories 132

Stark, Ray 221
Steiger, Rod 4, 21, 70, 133
Stein, Gertrude 36
Steinbeck, John 10
Steinberg, Saul 176
Steve Allen Show 128
Stevens, Andrew 175
Stevens, Roger L. 203
Stewart, James 8, 21, 80, 170
Stockbridge 260
Stonybrook 219
Stop It, Whoever You Are 47
Storaro, Vittorio 168, 262–4
Stradling, Harry 260
Straight Time 70, 82, 154–9, 161, 174, 181, 189, 199, 248, 262
Strange One see *End as a Man*
Strasberg, Lee 24, 29–30, 55, 191
Strasberg, Susan 213
Strawberry Statement, The 67
Straw Dogs 17, 48, 108–17, 150, 153, 219, 260
Streep, Meryl 137–8, 170, 175, 178–80, 198, 200–1, 262
Streisand, Barbara 71, 81, 120, 143, 153, 197, 244
Strick, Joseph 17
Stripper, The 121
Strokes of Genius 223
Stulberg, Gordon C. 106
Subject Was Roses, The 42–3, 103
Such Good Friends 211
Sugar Babies 2–3
Sullavan, Margaret 80
Superman 173
Surtees, Bruce 133, 261
Surtees, Robert 69, 259
Sutton, Willie 146
Svenson, Bo 141
Swann in Love 208
Sweet Charity 131
Sweet Prince of Delancy Street 36
Sweet Ride, The 77
SweetWall Productions 161, 166, 262
Sylbert, Paul 211, 262–3
Sylbert, Richard 61, 259, 264
Sylvia Scarlett 192
Symposium 90 253
Szabó, István 208
Szyogt, Alex 39

Talent Associates 260
Tamiris, Helen 30
Taps 226
Taras Bulba 75
Tate, Sharon 102
Tavoularis, Dean 260
Taylor, Elizabeth 54, 97
Taylor, Robert 235
Temple, Shirley 181
Testimony 219
Thalberg, Irving 212
That Summer, That Fall 78
Theater-de-Lys 45

Theatre Company of Boston 39
They Live by Night 159
They Shoot Horses, Don't They? 77, 189
Thief of Baghdad, The 120
Thomas, Marlo 210
Thomas Crown Affair, The 123
Thomson, David 82, 93, 114, 133, 145, 159
Three Days of the Condor 189, 228
Three Men on a Horse 40
Thurber, James 203
Tiger, The 50
Tiger Makes Out, The 49, 58, 61, 259
Tiger Town 178
Till Divorce Do You Part (Alfredo Alfredo, q.v.)
Time Bends 41
Tin Drum, The 208
Tin Men 228
To Be or Not to Be 195
To Kill a Mockingbird 35
Tolan, Michael 92, 260
Tony Awards 46, 127, 131, 137, 207, 247
Tootsie 7, 11, 20, 39, 46, 94, 98, 147, 181, 186–201, 212, 214, 218–19, 221–2, 228, 237, 250–1 253, 262–3
Top Gun 226
Touch, The 106, 153
Touchstone Pictures 264
Towne, Robert 146
Tracy, Spencer 70
Trans America Films 259
Travers, Bill 37
Travers, Henry 181
Travolta, John 3
Triple Echo 168
Tri-Star Pictures 263
Troublemaker, The 55
True Grit 79
True West 204
Truffaut, François 156, 173, 201
Truman, Harry S. 219
Trumbo, Christopher 122
Trumbo, Dalton 122, 261
Turgenev, Ivan 46
Turman, Lawrence 54–6, 58, 61, 63, 259
Turner, Tina 198
Twelfth Night 238, 243
Twelve Angry Men 249
Twentieth Century-Fox 84, 88, 220, 260
Twenty-Seven Wagons Full of Cotton 137
Twins 249
Two for the Seesaw 38
Two Jakes, The 201
Two Women 55
Tynan, Kathleen, 160, 162, 262
Typists, The 50

Ultra Violet 82
Un Dollaro per 7 Vigliacchi see *Madigan's Millions*
United Artists (UA) 74, 79, 120, 127, 146, 167, 190, 219, 221, 224–5, 228, 259, 261, 263
Universal Studios 77
University of Chicago 55

Up the Sandbox 121
Urzi, Saro 261

Vaccaro, Brenda 78, 260
Van Doren, Mamie 213
Van Dyke, Dick 251, 264
Vaughan, Peter 108, 110, 112, 260
Victor/Victoria 192
Vidal, Gore 54
View from the Bridge 249
Visconti, Luchino 116
Viva 82
Vivaldi, Antonio 181, 262
Voight, Jon 28, 40, 51, 77–9, 81–2, 126, 174, 189, 195, 259
Vonnegut, Kurt 96, 129
von Stroheim, Erich 212

Waiting for Godot 40, 51
Walden, Robert 144, 261
Wallace, George 69
Wallach, Eli 4, 21, 50, 259
Walsh, M. Emmet 158, 262
Walsh, J. T. 234
Walton, Tony 263
Wanamaker, Sam 246
Warden, Jack 104, 141, 260–1
War Games 221
Warhol, Andy 82, 145, 197, 206
War Hunt 191
War Lord, The 121
Warner, brothers 10
Warner Bros (studio) 10, 22, 36, 54, 141–2, 144, 161, 165, 187, 261–2
Warner, David 47–8, 108, 110, 112, 260
Washington, Nicholas C. 261
Waste Land, The 33
Watergate affair 140, 142–3, 204
Waterston, Sam 47, 214
Way Down East 120
Wayne, John 4, 21, 69, 79, 226, 241
Way We Were, The 189, 191
Weathermen/Weather People, the 101–3
Weaver, Fritz 262
Webb, Charles 54, 59–60, 68–9, 259
Webb, Eva ('Fred') 68–9
Weekend 91
Weill, Kurt 131
Weir, Peter 219
Welland, Colin 110, 112, 219, 260
Welles, Orson 157
Wenders, Wim 82
Wertmuller, Lina 157, 171
West, Timothy 262
Weston, Jack 215, 263
Westside International 259
What's Up Doc? 121, 173
Where Were You When the Lights Went Out? 42
Where the Money Was 146
White, Ruth 78, 259–60
Whitehead, Robert 203–4

Who Is Harry Kellerman and Why Is He Saying Those Terrible Things About Me? 74, 103–6, 155, 210, 237, 260
Who's Afraid of Virginia Woolf? 54, 57, 62, 171
Why Would I Lie? 171
Wiesel, Elie 255
Wiesenthal, Simon 253
Wild Bunch, The 111, 166
Wilde, Cornel 16
Wilder, Billy 193, 199
Wilder, Gene 217
Wildwood Enterprise Production 261
Wilkerson, Cathy 101–2
Wilkerson, James P. 101
Williams, Gordon M. 108, 110, 260
Williams, Jobeth 175, 262
Williams, Paul 212
Williams, Robin 181, 219, 252
Williams, Tennessee 19, 137, 237, 239
Willingham, Calder 55, 95, 259–60
Willis, Gordon 261
Will Success Spoil Rock Hunter? 104
Wilson, Elizabeth 47, 55, 61, 259
Winger, Debra 197, 225
Winters, Roland 37
Wise, Robert 103
Witness, The 122
Wiz, The 249
Wizard of Oz, The 3
Wolfe, Tom 91
Wolfit, Donald 243
Wood, Natalie 213
Wood, Robin 99, 114
Wood, Roland 259
Woodward, Bob 140–2, 144, 261
Woodward, Joanne 4, 69, 106
World According to Garp, The 181
World of Our Fathers 255
Worth, Marvin 127, 135–6, 261
Would I Lie to You? 187
Wright, Teresa 203

Yale School of Drama 137
Yates, Peter 84–5, 88–9, 91–3, 260
Yellow Jersey, The 218
Yes Is for a Very Young Man 36
Ying Ruocheng 202
Young, Robert 26
Young Doctors, The 54
Young Frankenstein 191
You Only Live Once 159

Zabriskie Point 67
Zeffirelli, Franco 101, 181, 226
Zerbe, Anthony 261
Zidi, Claude 220
Zimmer, Hans 263
Zinnemann, Tim 262
Zinnemann, Fred 113
Zipprodt, Patricia 4
Zorich, Louis 204, 263
Zorro, the Gay Blade 188
Zuckerman, Buck Henry (Buck Henry, q.v.)